CREATING DATABASE WEB APPLICATIONS WITH PHP AND ASP

JEANINE MEYER

CHARLES RIVER MEDIA, INC.

Hingham, Massachusetts

Associate Acquisitions Editor: James Walsh
Production: Publishers' Design and Production Services
Cover Design: The Printed Image

CHARLES RIVER MEDIA, INC.
10 Downer Avenue
Hingham, Massachusetts 02043
781-740-0400
781-740-8816 (FAX)
info@charlesriver.com
www.charlesriver.com

This book is printed on acid-free paper.

Jeanine Meyer. *Creating Database Web Applications with PHP and ASP.*
ISBN: 1-58450-264-9

Library of Congress Cataloging-in-Publication Data

Meyer, Jeanine.
    Creating database Web applications with PHP and ASP / Jeanine Meyer.
        p. cm.
    ISBN 1-58450-264-9
    1. Web databases.   2. PHP (Computer program language)   3. Active
server pages.   4. Application software—Development.   I. Title.
    QA76.9.W43M49 2003
    005.75'8—dc21
                    2003007395

Printed in the United States of America
03 7 6 5 4 3 2   First Edition

CREATING DATABASE WEB APPLICATIONS WITH PHP AND ASP

To my father

Joseph Louis Minkin

1913–2002

CONTENTS

ACKNOWLEDGMENTS

Many people helped in the creation and production of this book (but are not responsible for any errors): Michael Conry built and maintained the server for the first and subsequent offerings of the course; Gretchen Culp worked on her fish of the Hudson River project, which stimulated us to work harder; Anne Kellerman read and gave suggestions on the text; Connie Knapp taught me how to teach databases; Stephanie Lee has been an excellent student and teaching assistant in multiple courses; Amit Mangal was the official reviewer and provided many helpful suggestions; Aviva Meyer kept me from devolving and helped in many ways; Esther Minkin fed me oatmeal on very cold days and serenaded me by playing the piano; Marge Oztunali gave technical advice and support; Alexander Pinnock rescued me when my hard drive crashed; and Jenifer Niles, Jim Walsh, Bryan Davidson, and others at Charles River Media provided the highest level of support and guidance for this author. Thanks to all my students and colleagues at Purchase College/SUNY.

PREFACE

This book covers the design and development of Web applications involving server-side programming for computational tasks, or, more importantly, access to databases and files on the server computer. Two sets of tools are featured: the open-source middleware system called PHP and the database management system MySQL, and the Microsoft Corporation middleware product ASP (standing for active server pages, *not* application service provider) with JavaScript as the scripting language and the Microsoft Office Suite database management system (DBMS) Access. Both PHP and ASP produce HTML that is displayed on the client computer. The Structured Query Language (SQL) is used in both systems for interaction with the databases.

The book was written with the idea that readers would attempt to recreate the coding examples. To run these examples, you need access to a server computer to which you are allowed to upload and run middleware programs, or you need to turn your own computer into a server. Appendix A, "Running ASP and PHP Scripts on Your Own Computer," provides instructions on installing server software (including MySQL and PHP) on a computer running Windows XP Professional. It is beyond the scope of this book to cover how to operate a server computer, although some hints are provided as to how things are done at our institution where we run PHP, ASP, MySQL, and Access on a server running Windows NT and Apache. Similarly, the book does make note of issues you will need to clarify with the people we call your server administration. The capability to upload and run PHP or ASP files and access databases is not included automatically in typical Internet service provider (ISP) contracts. You might need a special contract to support Web hosting services.

The book also features the use of diagramming techniques for the design and documentation of applications. These include entity-relationship diagrams, process diagrams, and storyboards. The reader is encouraged to spend time on this part of the material and not just jump to the coding sections. Tools exist for creating these diagrams in various software engineering packages. However, you can sketch the diagrams by hand or use the drawing facilities in a word processor such as Microsoft Word.

The book's coverage of SQL, regular expressions, and the stand-alone use of MySQL and Access has applicability outside of the use of these technologies and products on the Web.

The assumption in the text is that you will be creating the databases "from scratch." In the real world, a database for your application probably exists and is in use in a non-Web implementation. Development will involve creating a small database for the initial testing. The final deployment of the Web application might involve a batch operation in which an existing database is converted for use on the Web. It is important to know how to define and create a database and how to modify the database when necessary.

Additional Notes to Teachers

Most of the material in this book is the topic of a one-semester course at Purchase College called *Creating Databases for Web Applications*. The prerequisite for the course is a course in HTML and JavaScript. Students are encouraged to have an additional course in programming. The workload includes homework assignments on regular expressions and the diagramming techniques, presentations by student teams on the shopping cart and quiz show applications, and a project involving a database, which the students define for themselves. The project can be done by teams or individuals. The students are both undergraduates and students with degrees, many working professionals. The student responses to the offerings of the course have been positive, although students do say that the work is challenging. The format of the midterm and final is open books and open notes.

The students have the exclusive use of a server just for this course, and student technical assistants maintain the server. Although Appendix B, "About the CD-ROM," contains instructions for installing the server software on local computers, we recommend the use of a remote server with students using a program such as ws-ftp. This serves to reinforce the notion that the code is executed on the server. It also avoids the complexities of the installation process.

1

INTRODUCTION

Thehe purpose of this chapter is to provide an introduction to the subject matter of the book, with samples of the code and the diagrams you will read about and produce.

BACKGROUND

The Web is a significant technological, economic, and cultural phenomenon. For relatively little cost and modest efforts, people can disseminate (publish) text, images, and multimedia to anyone with a computer with a connection to the Web. Furthermore, these computer connections are becoming increasingly widespread and powerful. The initial and still most common Web offerings were and are basically information. They are "read-only" for the viewer, termed the *visitor*, to the site. After review of the basics, this book explains how to build complex Web applications that incorporate reading and writing to databases and files. Examples of these types of applications are e-commerce sites and sites that gather information for research.

The Web is constructed using complex and still evolving software, hardware, and communication technologies. Products from different companies and organizations work together not perfectly, but fairly successfully based on published technical standards. In this text, we focus on what is termed *middleware*; namely, software products that bridge between ordinary Web pages to be interpreted and displayed on the visitor's computer (called the *client*) and operating systems and database systems resident on the server computer (your computer or, more typically, your organization's computer, which you have established as a node on the Web). We do not cover all the products that provide these functions. However, we have chosen to present two distinct sets:

- **PHP Hypertext Preprocessor (PHP)**, formerly named Personal Home Page, and database management system MySQL
- **Active Server Pages (ASP)** with JavaScript as the scripting language and database management system Microsoft Access

The PHP and ASP systems, the latter used with JavaScript, are examples of middleware. MySQL and Access are examples of database management systems operating on the server computer.

The first set is open source. *Open source* refers to a worldwide movement in which software is made available as source code so that anyone can examine the internal workings and make suggestions for changes. Open-source software is also available for free, although many people and organizations find it easier to purchase it together with installation, maintenance, and other services. The second choice constitutes an example of proprietary software. The vendor for ASP and Access is the Microsoft Corporation. Proprietary software is generally sold only in its executable (also called *compiled*) form and the original source code is not revealed.

By including two choices, we can describe points of commonality and points of difference. This is mainly to prepare you to learn yet another product or sets of products as technology evolves. PHP, which comes with its own language, and JavaScript, which we will use with ASP, are referred to in this context as *server-side* scripting languages. JavaScript also is a *client-side* scripting language, and you'll learn about its use with HTML files in Chapter 3, "HTML Forms and Client-Side JavaScript."

It should be noted that multi-user computer applications existed before the Web, and Web applications involving server-side resources existed before PHP or ASP came into existence. PHP and ASP offer ease of use for the developer and improved robustness and security for the owner of the server. If you have not used the older products, do not expect to appreciate fully these claims, although we do provide some reasons. Just as there were applications before these middleware products came into existence, new products are coming into use every day. Hopefully, what you gain from using this book will help you evaluate and master the new products.

Building a complex Web application is not just programming code. It involves analysis of the technical environment, consultation with the many groups of people to be involved in the project, and extensive planning. Entire courses and numerous books exist on systems analysis, systems design, usability, and other information technology and business topics. In this book, we introduce you to the planning and documenting aspects through methods of diagramming the information content of a database (entity-relationship diagram), the processes of an application (data flow diagram), and the flow of control of the scripts (storyboard).

CONCEPTUAL EXPLANATION

In this section, we give an overview of the concepts that will be explained and demonstrated in more detail in the rest of the book. Before proceeding, keep in mind that you, the reader of this text, are assumed to be the designer, creator, programmer, and writer of all the files involved. This includes any HTML documents and PHP and ASP files. (You are also assumed to be the database designer.)

Middleware: PHP and ASP

The PHP and ASP files are called *scripts*, and we will use that term and the term *files*. Scripts refer to files in languages that are stored more or less as you write them and translated into action when they are used. This "just-in-time" translation process often is called *interpretation*. In contrast, files in programming languages such as C++ and Java are translated into machine code in a distinct step in the development process. That translation process is called *compilation*.

You, the creator/programmer/script writer, have placed your files on a computer that is connected to the Internet. This computer is called "the server." The basic actions of the Web begin with a person sitting at a computer connected to what is called the *Internet*, invoking a program called a *browser*. Examples of browsers include:

- All versions of Netscape
- All versions of Microsoft Internet Explorer
- All versions of Opera
- Programs embedded in the product furnished by some Internet Service Providers (ISPs) such as AOL

This person, whom you might view as a member of your target audience, a customer, a client in the normal English meaning of the word, a friend, family member, and so forth, together with the computer is referred to as "the client." The person enters an address into the location field of the browser. This address consists of a server name, a path, and a filename; for example, *http://newmedia.purchase.edu/~Jeanine/index.html*. The technical name for an address is Uniform Resource Locator (URL). The first part of the URL indicates the computer holding the file: newmedia.purchase.edu. It is the server. The browser responds to the person entering in a URL by sending a request for the particular file to the server computer (Figure 1.1).

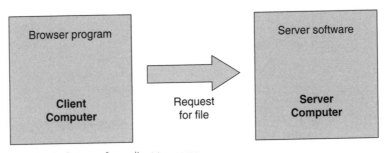

FIGURE 1.1   Request from client to server.

This computer, running one of several possible server programs, receives this request and responds by sending the requested file to the client. The browser, upon receiving the HTML file, might determine that other files are referenced in the original file. Typically, these include image files. This means that the browser might submit more requests.

The process is more complex than just described. For example, the browser might determine that there is no need to send a request for a file, since the file is already on the client computer in an area called the *cache*. The path for the request might consist of many steps to get from client to server. The original HTML file might make references to files of various types; for example, a swf file holding a Macromedia Flash movie. In such a situation, the browser might use something called a *plug-in* or *helper application* to display the movie. If the browser cannot find an appropriate plug-in, it will display a window giving the person the option to save the file to the client computer. The browser's next task (actually, it is done concurrently with making the additional requests) is to display the original HTML file and the referenced files as governed by the HTML standard. The HTML file can contain scripting code, typically in JavaScript, or, less commonly, VBScript. In this context, these are called *client-side scripting*. The execution of the script is performed by the browser on the client computer. The next chapter provides explanation and examples of basic HTML, and the following chapter discusses HTML forms and JavaScript. We mention only two possibilities here. You might include in your HTML file a hyperlink; that is, a text or image that when clicked by the client causes this entire process to begin again with a request from the browser for the specified address. Alternatively, you might include a form in which the person can enter information, including making choices from drop-down menus or clicking on check boxes. The HTML for the form indicates an address for handling the form.

Now, let us assume that you need to do something more complicated, such as produce an HTML file that is customized using data stored on the server computer in a database. One example could be that the person at the client computer is a potential customer who has chosen a category of products through making a selection in a form. For this situation, you will learn how to write PHP and ASP scripts to construct a customized Web page with information on products in the chosen category. The server program, upon receiving a request for a PHP or ASP script, does not simply send the file to the client. Instead, using programs installed on the server, these scripts are interpreted; that is, executed or run. In the situation described here, the PHP or an ASP script will access (no pun intended) a database and obtain information on products in the chosen category. The code (your code) uses that information to construct an HTML file. The server sends this customized HTML file to the client.

To develop an application using middleware, you will need to either have access to a server with programs such as Apache or Windows IIS, or make your own desktop computer into a server, using software such as Personal Web Server. To put it another way, an ordinary browser cannot interpret ASP or PHP files.

Systems Analysis and Design

Before jumping right into the technical considerations for building your application, you should stop and plan what the application is to do. Book examples and exercises typically do not require extensive analysis and design. However, to provide you with preparation for this very important step in systems development, we do devote a chapter on techniques and concepts useful for planning. Process modeling, also known as data flow diagramming, requires you, the developer, to identify the agents, processes, and data stores for your application. The requirement to identify agents means that you do not fall back on calling everyone connected with your project "users." In the example we described, one agent is the customer or potential customer who has asked to view a set of products. The term *data store* applies to any collection of information for the project. A data store could be a (computer) database, but it could also be a file or information on a clipboard. Once you have defined the functionality of the application, and you make the decision to use middleware, you can use storyboarding to plan and document what scripts you will write and how they are connected. Storyboards are used for movies, animation, and other multimedia projects.

Databases

In computing, the term *database* refers to data organized in a specific fashion. Databases hold what are called *tables*; tables are made up of *records*, and *records* hold fields. An example of a database table would be a company catalog. (Figure 1.2 shows a special type of diagram, called an *entity-relationship diagram*, representing this database.) Each record in the catalog table holds information on a specific product. That information consists of a set of fields. Sample fields would be product identification number, product name, product category, product base cost, and the name of an image file that shows the product. The product identification number is called the *primary key*. It is possible for the database to hold the actual image file itself, but we will try this other approach, which is more common. Each record is called a *row* of the table, and fields are often called *columns*. Each record or row holds the same fields—different values for the fields, but the same fields. To make this example database more interesting, we will specify that it has a second table, called the *category* table. The records in the category table correspond to categories. Each category record has a category name, a category description, and a current discount rate to be applied to any product in this category. The value of a product category field in a product record in the catalog table would be the name of one of the categories. The product category field is called a *foreign key* since it essentially points to a record in another, a foreign, table. Several products might have the same product cat-

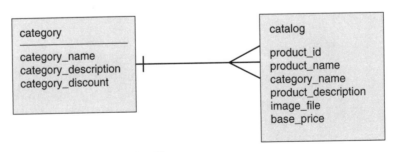

FIGURE 1.2 Entity relationship diagram.

egory field, meaning that they are in the same category. This connection represented by the field in one table referring to records in another table is called a *relationship*.

The design of a database, deciding what the tables should be, and what fields go in what records, is a complex task in its own right. Generally, more than one application makes use of a database. This makes it more challenging, but also more worthwhile to be careful in the design. In a later chapter, we will describe methods to improve the chances that a database design will serve the organization well over time. System developers often use diagrams for the design and documentation of databases. Products exist just for design and documentation. In this book, we will describe a technique called *entity-relationship modeling*. An ER model or ER diagram (ERD) shows the tables, the fields making up the records in each table, and the relationships between the tables. The symbols for the relationships also indicate the nature of the relationship, how many records in one table are related to how many records in another table.

There are other ways to organize data, but when the term *database* is used, it refers to data organized into tables, with tables holding records and records holding fields. The nice thing (where nice is too mild a word to express how wonderful and rare this situation is) is that there are many competing products that support databases, and though these products do have differences and compete based on these differences, they have much in common. For example, they all support the table, record, field model, and they all support a language for creating, querying, and modifying databases called Structured Query Language (SQL). For example, the following SQL statement will cause what is called a recordset to be created that holds the product names and base costs of all the products whose category is "chairs."

```
SELECT product_name, base_price FROM catalog
WHERE category_name='chairs'
```

Ignore the capitalization and the punctuation for now. This is a stand-alone SQL statement. We will show later how to issue such a statement from a PHP or ASP script. We give more examples of SQL later. The term for these products is *database management system* or DBMS. MySQL is a DBMS, as is Microsoft Access. Note: Access was not designed to be a multi-use DBMS for Web applications. However, it will work for our examples. We chose to use it because the Microsoft Office suite probably is already available to you. The proprietary "industrial-strength" DBMSs, such as SQL Server and DBII, tend to be expensive and require more effort to install. Since the basic mechanism of SQL is essentially the same for all database products, you will be able to apply what you learn here to other situations. The DBMS is a program running on the server that handles the SQL statements for reading and writing to databases.

Before presenting an overview of PHP and ASP scripts, we will describe what *objects* are in computing. Objects refer to information and procedures packaged together. Many different computing languages implement some form of objects. Both PHP and ASP use the methodology of objects, although in PHP, simple, built-in functions provide many of the facilities. In contrast, one can say that ASP is a set of objects. To use ASP, you need to use a scripting language, and we have chosen to use JavaScript, the same language that is most commonly used for client-side scripting. It also resembles, but is not identical to, the language of PHP.

The basic designs of PHP and ASP/JavaScript files are quite similar. Both files are text files and contain a mixture of HTML and PHP or ASP/JavaScript coding. The PHP or ASP sections are set off with delimiter symbols. The standard delimiters are <?php or <? and ?> for PHP, and <% and %> for ASP. Since we choose to use JavaScript for ASP, the first line of our ASP scripts should be:

```
<%@ Language="JavaScript"%>
```

to indicate the scripting designation. You might go "in and out" of PHP or ASP when writing your scripts. For example, you might start an HTML tag outside of PHP, start PHP and write code to generate attribute values, and then end PHP and use straight HTML to close the tag.

When the server interprets the file, the HTML is output directly to the HTML document being created "on-the-fly" to be passed to the client computer. The non-HTML parts resemble other programming languages with assignment statements, expressions, procedure calls, and invocations of functions, object methods, and calls on object properties. To create the customized HTML page based on data from a database involves several steps. One of the steps uses expressions and assignment statements to create a character string that is the SQL command. This string becomes a parameter to a function or method that passes the command to the DBMS. Other functions or methods are used to take information from the result of the SQL statement and combine it with text and tags to create the HTML document sent to the client.

The workings of PHP and ASP/JavaScript are best described through examples, which we give in the next section, and in the rest of the book.

EXAMPLES

ON THE CD

In this section, we show some examples of diagrams and code fragments. The samples shown here are simple php and asp code. The CD-ROM contains the code in the folder named chapter1code.

Entity-Relation, Process, and Storyboard Diagrams

The term *entity* is a fancy name for *thing*. Entities might be concrete things that exist in a business or organization, such as customers and products, or they might be abstract or ephemeral, such as an order number-product number pair that represents part of a customer's order. Any single entity is represented by certain information, and the items of information are called *attributes, proper-ties,* or *fields,* depending on the context. The technical term *relationship* has the regular, "English" meaning. The two-table database described in the preceding section is represented by the ERD shown in Figure 1.2.

Notice that we have made up names for all the fields that are now legal names with no internal blanks as opposed to descriptions. The line connecting the two boxes represents the relationship between the two tables. The markings indicate that each product—that is, each record in the catalog table—refers to ex-actly one category record. Put another way, a category can have many products. More than one product can be in a category. It, however, does not guarantee that each category has at least one product.

A slightly more complex database is shown in Figure 1.3. This database supports a quiz show application using three tables.

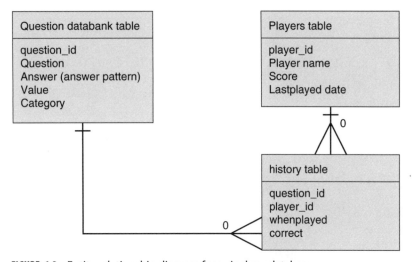

FIGURE 1.3   Entity relationship diagram for quiz show database.

The history table keeps records of the play of the game, with information on which player answered which question when and with what result. The history table serves as what is commonly called a "join table" to relate the question and the player entities. There is a one-to-many relationship between the question table and the history table and the player table and the history table. There can be none, one, or many entries in the history table for each question. Similarly, there can be none, one, or many entries in the history table for each player.

The process diagram in Figure 1.4 for the quiz show application reveals how the application is to function.

Notice that there are two agents; that is, two types of users. Players play the game, with that process making use of three distinct data stores. These data stores correspond to the tables of the database, but that implementation detail is not critical in the process diagram. Editors input, delete, and modify questions.

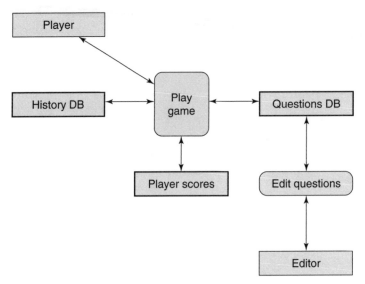

FIGURE 1.4 Process diagram for quiz show application.

The book will show you the inner workings of the quiz show application in PHP and ASP versions, and another application, a slightly more elaborate online store. Figure 1.5 shows a storyboard indicating the distinct files (scripts) we designed and wrote for the quiz show. You will learn about this application in Chapter 15, "Quiz Show." For now, just look at the diagram as an example of representing an application made up of multiple files. The arrows represent one script calling another. One type of call is for handling a form, and another type is as the target of a hyperlink. Form handling is represented by thick arrows, and links by thin arrows. With this information, this diagram shows many things. First, there are eight scripts. One script, called opendbq, is an include/required file. This special file type will be explained later. The diagram also indicates the relationship among the files. For example, the diagram indicates that the choose category script invokes the ask question script to handle a form. The ask question script has a link back to the choose category script. The choose category script also has links from check answer and clear tables. There are links in both directions between the choose category script and the show scores script.

Code Examples

We now look at simple code examples of PHP and ASP script.
An example of PHP coding:

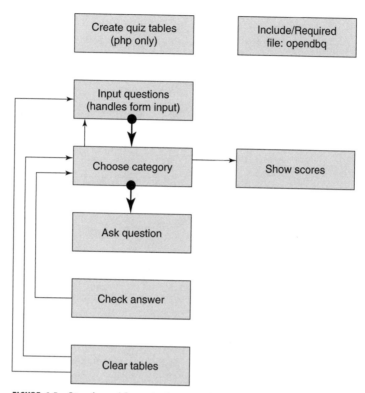

FIGURE 1.5 Storyboard for quiz show application.

```
<html>
<head><title>first PHP </title></head>
<body>
<?php
$today=  Date('d-m-Y');
$now = Date('g:i');
print ("Hello World!<BR> Today is $today");
print ("<br>The time is $now");
?>
</body>
</html>
```

The standard HTML boilerplate (we provide a review of HTML in the next chapter) is given in the PHP file as regular HTML. The <?php starts the PHP section. You can omit the PHP if the file has extension *.php*. The four lines within the delimiters do the following tasks:

1. Invoke the built-in Date function with the parameter specifying the format for the date. All variables in PHP start with the dollar sign.
2. Invoke the built-in Data function (again) with a different parameter to get the time.

3. Invoke the print function to output the string that is the argument of the function call to the HTML document. The PHP interpreter will use the value of the variable $today.
4. Invoke the `print` function again. In this case, the PHP interpreter will use the value of the variable $now.

The following ASP script produces a similar (although not identical) HTML document:

```
<%@ Language="JavaScript" %>
<html>
<head> <title>Hello World, Active Server Pages!
</title>
</head>
<body>
<%
var now = Date();
Response.Write(
  "Hello World!<BR> The date and time now is " + now);
%>
</body>
</html>
```

One of the ASP objects is the `Response` object. It has a method named `Write`. Thus, `Response.Write` is the ASP equivalent of PHP's `print`. Variables in the ASP/JavaScript system can start with any alphabetic character. However, this is one reason why we cannot use the PHP trick of embedding variables within strings. The plus sign is the string concatenation system in JavaScript.

It is possible to write an even simpler "Hello, World" program. These programs do something on the server, namely calling the date functions, and it is doing something on the server that characterizes middleware.

REFLECTION

As mentioned, complex Web applications existed before the invention and use of middleware software such as ASP and PHP. The feature of writing a mixture of pure HTML and either PHP or ASP with the chosen scripting language is what makes these newer technologies an improvement over the older way to program middleware. The older methods, making use of a standard called *common gateway interface* (CGI), had no resemblance to HTML. However, readers be warned that PHP and ASP/JavaScript syntax (punctuation) can be tricky. This arises because pieces of the PHP or ASP/JavaScript might be subject to interpretation in three different places: on the server, by the PHP or ASP program; by the operating system or the DBMS; or by the browser on the client. Be patient and give yourself time.

EXERCISES, QUESTIONS, AND PROJECTS

1. Define and describe the following terms: client, server, browser, middleware, database, database management system, entity, relationship, entity-relationship modeling, and process modeling.

2. Define and describe the following terms: HTML, Internet Explorer, Netscape, CGI, ASP, PHP, JavaScript, SQL, Access, MySQL. Your knowledge of most of these will increase as you read the rest of the book. For each term, is it the name of a product of a company, and, if so, which company? Does the term refer to a standard? Which terms refer to open source projects?

3. Go online using any browser and visit several different Web sites. Use the View command (or click the right mouse button and choose View Page Source). Describe what you see.

4. Go to an e-commerce site (you can stop before you spend any money). Make choices by clicking on links and filling out forms. Observe the Web address showing up in the address area of the toolbar. What are the filenames and what are the extensions? In some, not all cases, you will see the input data you have entered into forms as part of the address. More on this in later chapters.

5. Do a search, using Google or another search engine, on some or all of the topics: PHP, ASP, JavaScript, HTML, Open Source, MySQL, and Access. Visit some of the sites. Who or what organization supports the site? Be on the lookout for sites from product vendors, sites set up for developers to help each other out, sites from schools, and so forth.

2

BASIC HTML

The purpose of this chapter is to introduce you to the Hypertext Markup Language (HTML), the standard for Web pages.

BACKGROUND

HTML was devised as a method of representing complex documents, namely documents containing text; images; other media, such as sound, including types of media not invented at the time of the original specification of the language; and hyperlinks, that is, specifications of links from one document to another. Furthermore, the goal of the method was to provide a way to display such documents on any computer so that people—at that time, mainly scientists—could share information even though some might be using one type of computer with one operating system and others totally different computer hardware and/or different operating systems software. Tim Berners-Lee at CERN, the European Organization for Nuclear Research, and others (including Cailliau, Andreesen, and Bina) are credited with inventing HTML and the other technologies that support what is called the World Wide Web. The definition of HTML and other, related technologies, are maintained by an organization called the World Wide Web Consortium (W3C).

The following factors:

- Support for mixed media and hyperlink
- Design allowing a systematic way for the system to grow with new media types
- Independence to any particular hardware/software platform

made the invention of the Web and HTML a tremendous achievement. However, technologies evolve, both in response to invention and demand. The original HTML did not specify the exact format for display. This would have been very difficult and maybe not even possible given that the intent was to provide for presentation of the documents on screens of vastly different sizes on computers with different capabilities. Instead, the designers included features to specify a more general, logical level of formatting.

Another perceived deficit of the original HTML is the main subject of this book. The design of HTML and the communication standards that support the Web do not provide facilities for customizing the documents based on information in databases or files. Moreover, the way operations work between the server computer and the client computer is that the server sends the files requested by the client and does not save information on the request. This is not quite true, since log files can be kept, but the Web is designed to be what is called "stateless," and information on requests is not readily available. This would mean that collecting data for research or e-commerce would be impossible. To address this need, people developed and are still developing new standards and new products. After this chapter on basic HTML and the next chapter on forms and client-side scripting, you will learn about middleware, technologies to bridge the gap between Web pages and databases and other resources on the server.

CONCEPTUAL EXPLANATION

HTML files consist of ordinary text with the addition of what are called *tags*. Tags, which represent the "markup" of the text, are special codes surrounded by pointy brackets. Most of the tags come in pairs and specify what is to be done with what is in between the starting and the ending tag. For example, an HTML document begins with <html> and ends with </html>. All pairs of tags have that same form: the ending tag has a slash followed by the name of the starting tag. Some tags just have one constant value, such as "html"; others contain what are called *attributes*, extra information contained in the starting tag, which we will show later. A browser is a program that "knows how" to interpret HTML and use the standardized communication protocols of the Internet to request documents from other computers connected to the Web. The most common browsers are the different versions of Microsoft Internet Explorer, Netscape, and Opera. Table 2.1 lists the most basic tags.

TABLE 2.1   Basic HTML Tags

TAG(S)	WHAT A BROWSER DOES
<h1> … </h1>	Makes the text in between big and, possibly, bold as appropriate for a header. The exact appearance is up to the browser
<h2> … </h2>	Makes the text prominent in some way, but less than for an h1
<i> … </i>	Makes the text italic
<b> … </b>	Makes the text bold
<img src="bird.gif">	Sends a request for a file called bird.gif and displays the image. Here, src is an example of an attribute with value "bird.gif". The two main file formats for image files for the Web are gif and jpg
<img src="bird.gif" height="100" width="50">	Sends a request for a file called bird.gif and displays the image with size 50 by 100 pixels (even if that distorts the original image). This tag has three attributes
<p> … </p>	Displays the in-between material as a distinct paragraph. The exact spacing is up to the browser

(continues)

TABLE 2.1   Basic HTML Tags *(continued)*

TAG(S)	WHAT A BROWSER DOES
` `	Produces a line break.
`<a href="nextpage.html">` `Continue </a>`	This is the coding for a hyperlink. The in-between text, Continue, in this example, is displayed, with the common default format being in blue and underlined. If the person at the computer uses the mouse to click on Continue (also called the *hypertext*), the browser will put in a request for the file nextpage.html at the same folder as the current document and then interpret and display nextpage.html

`<table>`
`<tr>`
`<td> … </td>`
`<td> … </td>`
`</tr>`
`<tr> … </tr>`
`</table>`
	These are tags associated with tables. Tables contain rows, which contain table data (a way to remember the term *td*). Tables are useful for general layout and for displaying information in rows and columns

The line break `<br>` and the paragraph `<p>` and `</p>` tags are easy to omit, both in writing regular HTML and in PHP and ASP code to produce HTML. The browsers generally ignore what is referred to as *white space*. Therefore, if you want the text to "go to" a new line, you must include explicitly a tag to force that to happen. Similarly, white space along a line, such as this will be ignored. A special character, written as ` ` will force a space.

The table tags often are used to lay out text and images on the screen, not just for things like tables of numbers. Later, you will work on examples in which each record from a database will generate a row of a table, including images, buttons, and hyperlinks.

HTML has other tags! You can learn about them by using the View Source option in the browsers and by looking at references. You also can investigate Cascading Style Sheets (CSS), an addition to HTML for more elaborate formatting. The tags described here are the basics that you will use in your PHP and ASP scripting.

Another description of the process is the following: You, the person using the client computer, invoke a browser such as the latest version of Netscape. You enter in a location on the Web in the form of a URL. The browser sends a request for that particular file to the server computer, the computer described by the URL. As part of the process of interpreting the file, the browser might request other files, such as all the image files mentioned in the src attribute of img tags. If the document had any hyperlinks, coded using `<a>` tags, then if and when you click on one, the process repeats. However, this time, the browser sends a request for the particular file indicated by the `href` attribute of the `<a>` tag.

An important feature of how browsers work is, to put it in anthropomorphic terms, they do not complain. That is, if your HTML file has errors, such as incorrectly formatted tags, missing ending tags, improper nesting or misspelling of filenames, the browser will display something and give no indication of the existence or the location of errors. You will need to check out the display to see if it is what you intended. This is different from working in programming languages such as C++ or Java when minor syntactic errors in notation prevent you from proceeding beyond compilation, many errors are detected during runtime, and special functions are provided for debugging, getting the errors out of your application. If you have had such experiences, you will come to miss them when working with HTML. Read on for suggestions on how to "debug" HTML.

EXAMPLES

ON THE CD

In this section, we show some examples of simple HTML, HTML with links and images, an example to demonstrate debugging, and HTML tables. The projects demonstrated here are basic HTML. The CD-ROM contains the code for the projects in the folder named chapter2code.

Simple HTML

The following is an example of the simplest possible HTML document. Notice that it contains a head section and a body section. The head section can contain other tags.

```
<html>
<head><title>Simple html file </title>
</head>
<body>
something
</body>
</html>
```

Start any text editor. Notepad is the one that comes with any Windows operating system. Do not use Microsoft Word and do not use any special HTML editors until you have a firm grasp of how tags work. Type in these lines of text. You can (and should) change what is between the <title> and </title> tags and what is in between the <body> and </body> tags to make it your own example. Please be aware that spacing and line breaks are ignored. Suppose you type the following:

```
My first HTML File
The quick brown fox jumped over the lazy dog's back.
```

A browser may display

```
My first HTML file The quick brown fox jumped over the lazy dog's
back.
```

Save the file with the name test1 and the extension html. To do this in Notepad, you must click on All Files so that the file does *not* have the extension txt.

Now invoke a browser. Click on File (see Figure 2.1) and then Open (Open File in Netscape) and browse to the file you just created.

FIGURE 2.1   Browser File pull-down menu.

You should see something resembling Figure 2.2. (We show here the original example.)

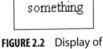

FIGURE 2.2   Display of simple HTML file.

HTML with Formatting and a Hyperlink

Here is another example to try and then modify to make sure you understand the role of the tags:

```
<html>
<head>
<title>Second example </title>
```

```
</head>
<body text="red">
<h1>A Red page </h1>
<p>This is a Web page showing examples of
 the basic formatting tags <br> that you could use.
 </p>
<p>You do need to remember: <i>Less is more </i>
when it comes to formatting. </p>
<h6>This may be too small to read. </h6>
<center>You may choose to <br> <b> center </b>
your text.
</center>
<a href="test1.html">Back to the first example.
</a>
</body>
</html>
```

ON THE CD

Save this file as test2.html and open it in a browser as before. You should see something resembling Figure 2.3. Please note that all figures are in full color on the CD-ROM.

A Red page

This is a Web page showing examples of the basic formatting tags
that you could use.

You do need to remember: *Less is more* when it comes to formatting.

This may be too small to read.

You may choose to
center your text.

Back to the first example.

FIGURE 2.3 HTML example.

The text attribute in the body tag changes the text color to red. The default color is black. The text is centered on the screen; the screen capture shown here is of the upper-left corner of the screen. Notice also the small text produced by the h6 tags.

You also can specify a different color for the link text under the different situations indicated in Table 2.2.

TABLE 2.2   Attributes for Link in Body Tag

ATTRIBUTE NAME	SITUATION
`link`	Original link text
`vlink`	Link text after link has been taken: the visited link
`alink`	Link text when the mouse button is down: the active link

Before going on to another example, do the following experiment in the browser: change the size of the window. The browser changes the layout to fit the new window. Figure 2.4 shows the window, which has been narrowed.

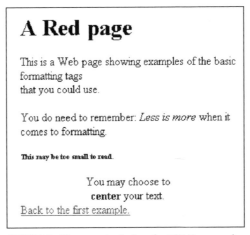

FIGURE 2.4   Narrowed window for HTML example.

HTML with Images

To demonstrate the display of images, you need to have an image file! You can *acquire* (acquire is the technical term) an image file by creating one in a program such as Photoshop or Paintshop Pro or downloading one from a Web site. You do the latter by clicking on the right mouse button and following the instructions to Save picture as…. or Save image as…. You will be given a chance to name the image. The image type is indicated by its extension; generally.gif or .jpg. You cannot change the type of image. What you can do is use one of these programs to save it in a different format. Our example will use an image file named heart.gif. Create the following file, using the name of the image file you have acquired.

```
<html>
<head><title>File with images </title>
```

```
</head>
<body>
<center>
<h3>A page with images </h3>
<img src="heart.gif">
</center>
This is actually a page with the same image used
several times.  Here is a tiny one:
<img src="heart.gif" width="50">
and here is another one:
<img src="heart.gif" width="50" height="100">.
Its aspect ratio (proportions) has been changed.
<br>
<a
href="http://newmedia.purchase.edu/~Jeanine/origami">
<img src="heart.gif"></a>
</body>
</html>
```

The hyperlink differs from the previous one in two ways. The writing between the <a> and the </a> tags is an image tag and not plain text. This coding makes the image the link. This is referred to as an *icon*. Often, small versions of images are links to larger versions. In this case, the small image is called a *thumbnail*. You can use text, an image, or both as the displayed link. The value of the href attribute is more complex than the one used in test2.htm, although the first one actually requires more explanation. When the browser comes upon a value for the href attribute that is a simple filename, it "assumes" that the file is located in the same place as the HTML document being displayed. In contrast, when the browser "sees" an href value starting with http://, then it "knows" to go to that location on the Web. There is one more item to note here. The href value is not complete because it appears to refer to a folder without a filename, namely the folder origami. When this happens, the server looks for a default file in the folder specified. A file named "index.html" or "index.htm" can serve as this default file. This is the file returned to the client.

Save this file as test3.html and invoke it from a browser. You should see something like Figure 2.5. We have resized the window.

Notice the border around the last heart on the screen. This indicates that this is a hyperlink. If you click on it, the browser will take you to the page specified by the href attribute, assuming you are connected to the Web. If you have a connection that requires you to tie up your telephone line, you might consider doing your development work without being connected. The local file references will all work, and you can move the cursor with the mouse over a link and then look at the lower toolbar to see what the href value is. This allows you to check the hyperlink destination without actually clicking on the link.

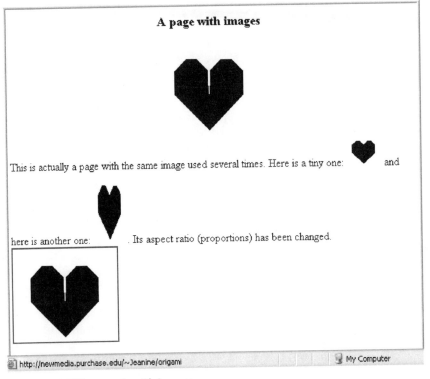

FIGURE 2.5 HTML example with images.

Debugging

To demonstrate what happens if you make mistakes, try the following altered version of the previous HTML file:

```
<html>
<head><title>File with images </title>
</head>
<body>
<center>
<h3>A page with images </h3>
<img src="heart.gif">

This is actually a page with the same image used
several times.  Here is a tiny one:
<img src="hart.gif" width="50">
and here is another one:
<img src="heart.gif" width="5" height="100">.
Its aspect ratio (proportions) has been changed.
<br>
<a
```

```
href="http://newmedia.purchase.edu/~Jeanine/origami">
<img src="heart.gif"></a>
</body>
</html>
```

Internet Explorer produces the display shown in Figure 2.6.

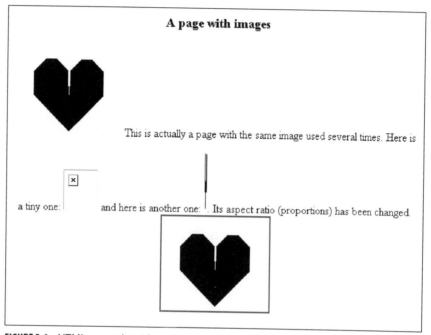

FIGURE 2.6   HTML example with mistakes.

Examine the screen shot shown in Figure 2.6 and the HTML source to see if you can determine what needs to be fixed before reading on.

There seems to be three problems: an image is missing, one of the hearts is very skinny, and the text and images appear to be laid out strangely on the screen. Missing images arise from bad filenames or image files that are actually missing. Therefore, you need to determine that it is the second image and check the filename in the second img tag. The third image is the skinny one. Check out the width and height attributes. The layout is the subtlest problem. It arises from a fairly common error. Try to match up all the paired tags. The layout problem happened because centering is turned on and never turned off.

Table Tags

The last two examples use the table tags. The first example is a table of data.

```
<html>
<head><title>Pretty Dull Data </title>
</head>
<body>
<center>
<h3>Numbers</h3>
<table border="4">
<tr>
<td>2</td><td>4</td><td>8</td>
</tr>
<tr>
<td>3</td><td>9</td><td>27</td>
</tr>
</table>
</body>
</html>
```

This produces the screen shot shown in Figure 2.7.

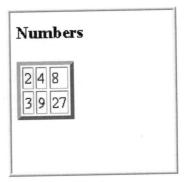

FIGURE 2.7   Table of numbers.

If the border attribute is omitted, as you will see in the following example, there is no border. The value for the border attribute can be a number or other designations. The value 4 produces this three-dimensional effect.

Another use for table tags is to control the layout. The following HTML with table tags will position images and accompanying text.

```
<html>
<head><title>Layout using tables </title>
</head>
<body>
<h3>Models</h3>
<table>
<tr>
<td>Traditional crane</td>
<td><img src="crane.gif"></td>
```

```
</tr>
<tr>
<td>Broken heart</td><td>
<img src="heart.gif"></td>
</tr>
<tr>
<td>Business card frog</td><td>
<img src="frog.gif"></td>
</tr>
</table>
</body>
</html>
```

This example demonstrates nesting of HTML tags similar to the example showing how to make an image into a link. In that example, the img tag was between the <a> and the </a> tags. Here, image tags are between the <td> and the </td> tags. Another way of expressing this is that the <img> tags are the contents of the td elements. The layout using tables produces the display shown in Figure 2.8. The screen shot shows the internal contents of the window. The browser used was Internet Explorer.

FIGURE 2.8   Names and images formatted using a table.

Practice using these tags, combining and mixing what you learned from each example. Although it might make you uncomfortable, make some intentional mistakes to see what is produced. For example, leave out some of the starting and ending tags for tables. This will exercise your debugging skills for later.

REFLECTION

At this point, you might be tempted to say that you cannot learn these tags and can get along without using them by using one of the special HTML editors. The editors can help you, but these too require learning. They often throw in extra tags and inappropriate references for images and other files, making it difficult to move your project to a new computer. The biggest reason to learn the tags is that you will need to know HTML to write the PHP and ASP scripts to produce HTML. It really is not that difficult. Tags begin and end; you need to remember the opening and closing pointy brackets. You need to write attribute values, such as image filenames, and use quotation marks around them. You need to pay attention to opening and closing of tag pairs. If you fail to include a `</a>` tag, for example, the rest of the document will be a link.

A problem in writing HTML that you might be wondering about if you have done any programming of languages such as C++ and Java is that no program catches what to you are obvious errors. Neither the text editor nor the browser catches an error, such as not including a closing tag or mistyping the tag for a level-one header as the letter h followed by the lowercase l. Instead, the browser always displays something. You need to look at the display and confirm that it is what you intended. If there are problems, you need to examine the source file to see what the error is. The browser is forgiving of errors. It also ignores things like improperly nesting tags:

```
<b><i>Italic and bold </b> </i>
```

You can also mix upper- and lower-case for the tags: `<BODY>` or `<body>` or `<boDy>`.

As we have indicated, the HTML system does not specify exact display. This can be unfortunate in cases when you really need to specify formatting. Technologies, products, and standards exist now to address some of the formatting issues. These include cascading style sheets (CSS), eXtensible Markup Language (XML), and eXtensible Stylesheet Transform (XSL). We mention these acronyms to give you terms for reference and will not address them in this book.

The HTML language is constantly evolving. One emerging standard is called XHTML, or extensible HTML. It requires us to be more careful about properly nesting the tags, using lowercase for HTML tags, and using quotation marks around all attribute values. We tried to do that in this text, but you might see examples elsewhere that do not follow these rules. Another rule of XHTML is that the so-called singleton tags, such as for line break and images, must contain a closing slash:

```
<br />
<img src="heart.gif" />
```

We do not follow that rule here because some of the older browsers actually complain. However, you might see this usage elsewhere.

There are more attributes for these tags and there are more tags. However, what you have learned so far provides substantial functionality. You can learn more tags by examining the HTML source code for existing pages. You see the source by using the View command on the browser toolbar and clicking on View Page Source, or by clicking the right mouse button and clicking on View Page Source. You can also use the Web to find online tutorials or references.

The next chapter will review client-side scripting using JavaScript and the HTML for forms.

EXERCISES, QUESTIONS, AND PROJECTS

1. Define and describe the following terms: browser, tag, attribute, and source code.
2. What do each of the following tags do (indicate also whether the tag is used as the start of a pair and if the tag needs attributes): html, head, title, body, h1, b, i, img, a, table, tr, td?
3. How do you do the following tasks?
   a. Make text bold.
   b. Make text italic.
   c. Cause a line break.
   d. Indicate a paragraph.
   e. Insert an image of a file named frog.gif.
   f. Insert an image and specify its dimensions to be 60 pixels by 80 pixels.
   g. Insert a table of three rows and two columns.
   h. Create a hyperlink to go to one of your favorite Web sites.
   i. Create a hyperlink to go another HTML file you will create in the same folder.
   j. Create a hyperlink in which an image is the link.
4. Go on the Web and use a search engine to find online sources for HTML tags. Look up how to do these particular tasks: ordered list, font size, and frames.
5. Go on the Web and use the View Source command in the browser to examine the HTML source for sites. Try to find simple (non-database or XML driven sites).

HTML FORMS AND CLIENT-SIDE JAVASCRIPT

The purpose of this chapter is to continue with HTML, focusing on forms, and to introduce client-side scripting, using JavaScript. Most of the rest of the text is concerned with server-side scripting. JavaScript will be shown in use with ASP; the PHP system has its own scripting language.

Background

The HTML tags introduced in the last chapter provide you ways to present information to your audience that does not change. The next steps are to learn how to gather information from the audience viewing your Web pages and how to use a scripting language, JavaScript, to make the pages dynamic. We will describe these two topics separately and then together.

In this chapter, we will show you how to design Web pages that go beyond showing information using HTML forms and client-side JavaScript. Much of what you learn and use for client-side scripting will apply to server-side scripting and programming in general.

Conceptual Explanation

This section includes examples of client-side JavaScript programming, including handling forms and events.

Basic Programming Constructs

As noted in Chapter 1, "Introduction," scripts refer to files in languages that are stored more or less as you write them, and translated into action when they are used. This is in contrast to the procedure used in "full" programming languages in which source files are transformed in a process called *compilation* into a format for execution. Having established that, JavaScript still has many features in common with "full" programming languages, including variables, functions, expressions, statements, and event handling.

Variables are the computer science term for associating names with values. The values might vary—hence the name. The type of value might be a string of characters representing something such as a name, or a number representing the number of items someone wants to purchase.

Function is the term used in JavaScript for giving a name to a set of statements. When you use the name, the whole set of statements is executed. It is like defining a "shorthand" way of specifying a long process. The function can be used as if it were part of the basic language. Other programming languages use the term *function* in a more restrictive way, and the terms *procedure*, *method*, and *subroutine* are also commonplace. You will be using functions that are part of JavaScript, functions that are methods associated with objects (using the Document Object Model to be described), and functions you define. A function can have as part of its definition the specification of an argument or a set of arguments. These are values that will be used by the function.

Expressions are combinations of variables, operators such as +, and invocations of functions or methods. The JavaScript language is made up of a certain set of allowable statements. An example is an assignment statement, in which a variable is assigned the value of an expression.

```
cost = num_of_items * price;
```

The asterisk (*) is the operator designating multiplication. Its use for multiplication is common to many computer languages. The plus sign (+) is for addition of numbers and also for concatenation of strings. The minus sign (–) is for subtraction, and the slash (/) is for division.

Assuming that `num_of_items` and `price` are each variables set earlier to be numeric values such as 5 and 1.25, respectively, the interpretation of this statement is: Determine the current value of `num_of_items` and multiply it by the current value of `price`. Take the result and assign it to be the current value of the variable `cost`. The thing doing these operations of determining values, multiplying, and assigning is the JavaScript program.

Statements are ended with semicolons. JavaScript (and other computer languages) does not use periods because periods are used as decimal points in numbers. Periods (dots) also are used to indicate the properties or the methods (procedures) associated with objects. Objects encapsulate data, formally called *attributes* or *properties*, and operations or procedures, formally called *methods*. The definition of ASP, which you will study in this book, consists of the definition of several objects.

Events refer to situations that the underlying system can recognize. If the person at the client computer uses the mouse to click on a button, that is an event, and you, the programmer, can specify how the event is to be handled; that is, what you want to happen. Similarly, submitting a form is an event.

Forms

The HTML discussed in this chapter is somewhat more intricate than the previous chapter. There are tags within tags. You will need to distinguish between the attributes within the pointy brackets of the tag and the HTML between the starting tag and the ending tag; for example, the <form> and the </form>.

HTML has a set of tags that provide ways to gather information. The <form> tag has attributes that specify how the form information is to be processed. Two examples of a form tag are:

```
<form name="order" action="takeorder.php">
```

```
<form name="order" action=""
  onSubmit="calculatebill(this);">
```

In both cases, the form is named `"order"`. For the first example, the input from the form will be sent to a file named `takeorder.php`. This script is called the *handler* of the form. How the PHP file accesses the form data is the subject of a later chapter. In the second example, a function is called named `calculatebill`. The argument `this` has a special meaning, referring to the object, the form itself. The input of the form is not sent to another file for action as indicated by the action attribute being set to an empty string. This example will be expanded later in the book.

Form tags come in pairs. Within the `<form>` and `</form>` tags, you can place any HTML (text and/or tags) and several specific tags that specify the type of input and output. By output, we mean displaying information generated by the program for the person to see. The input tags have attributes in common, such as name, used for referring to the input contents, and value, used to specify a default value. Table 3.1 shows the basic tags for forms.

TABLE 3.1   Basic Tags and Attributes for HTML Forms

EXAMPLE	PURPOSE
`<input type="text" name="lname" >`	Text input and output
`<input type="hidden" name="pw">`	Hidden: text input in which asterisks (*) hide what the person types from someone peeking at the screen
`<input type="submit" value="SEND">`	Submit button
`<input type="reset" value="CLEAR">`	Reset button
`<select name="drink">` `<option value="coffee">Coffee` `<option value="cocoa">Hot Cocoa` `<option value="chai">Chai` `</select>  `	Drop -down menu

`<input type="radio" name="sizef"`
`value="sm">Tall <input type="radio"`
`name="sizef" value="med">Grand`
`<input type="radio" name="sizef"`
`value="big"> Super`
	Radio buttons (the name attribute defines a set in which only one in the set is allowed to be selected)

Document Object Model and Client-Side Scripting

These tags will be shown in use in the *Examples* section. As the first step in demonstrating JavaScript, we introduce the Document Object Model (DOM). The DOM defines how any scripting language must refer to the HTML document, and is relevant to client-side scripting only. The DOM uses object syntax. The following is an example of use of the DOM:

```
order.lname.value
```

This could refer to the `value` entered by the customer to the input named `lname` of the form named `order`. Another use of the DOM is to dynamically add something to the HTML document. You will do this using the `write` method of the `document` object. A simple example of this is:

```
document.write("<h1>Welcome</h1>");
```

In this example, `document` is an object, a very special one, in fact, and `write` is one of its methods. A method is a type of function or a procedure. The `write` method uses its argument, the information in the parentheses, and does something with it. This should not be confused with `Response.Write`, shown in Chapter 1 in an example of a server-side script using ASP with JavaScript.

A more interesting example is:

```
document.write("Today is " + Date());
```

The proper way to describe how this statement is interpreted is to begin inside the parentheses and work out. The "`Today is`" is a string (character string). Notice that the very last character is a blank. The plus sign is not addition of numbers, because there are no numbers here. Instead, it is the concatenation of strings. The `Date()` is an invocation of a built-in JavaScript function. It has an empty argument. The `Date()` function returns the current date and time in a special format. However, because the context here is concatenating strings, JavaScript turns the returned Date into a string. This result is what is written out to the HTML document.

More examples of use of the DOM and other functions come later.

The previous assignment statement is one type of JavaScript statement. The use of `document.write` is another type, namely a function or method invocation. JavaScript also provides a way to do something only if a certain condition is true. This is known as an `if` statement. The `if` statement uses curly brackets to set off what is done if the condition is true. Uses of `if` follow in the *Examples* section.

It is not strictly necessary to do what is called *declaring variables*, but we will try to follow the discipline of doing so. A declaration lets the JavaScript program "know" ahead of time the name of a variable. A variable is declared with the statement such as:

```
var cost;
```

The `var` statement can also include an assignment statement. This is often called *initialization* because it sets the initial value of the variable.

```
var total =0;
```

In programming, you often need to do something repeatedly. This is called *looping* in computing. JavaScript has the `for` compound statement for this purpose. It is a compound statement because it generally contains multiple statements. An example of a for loop would start out like this:

```
for (i=0; i<n; i++) { one or more statements }
```

This statement uses a variable named i and starts with i set to zero. If i is less than n, the statements between the curly brackets are executed. These statements might or might not make reference (use) the variable i. Next, the variable i is incremented by 1 and again compared to the value of the variable n. If i is less than n, the statements are executed again, with i now set to 1. This goes on until i is *not* less than n. You do not have to use the names given here. The increment or change does not have to be "adding 1," which is what the ++ does. Similarly, the halting condition can be whatever makes sense for your situation. Looping, also called *iteration*, is a powerful tool.

The less than symbol (<) is one of several comparison operators. To make the test be: is i less than or equal to n, you use <=. You can figure out what > and >= mean. To test for equality, you use two equal signs put together: ==. The reason for this is that a single equal sign indicates assignment.

In your HTML files, you will put examples of individual JavaScript statements, and also define your own functions. Beginners tend to resist defining their own functions. Hopefully, the examples in the book will help you in your own work. Terms for running a function are *invoking* or *executing* or *calling*.

You can place the definition of functions anywhere inside a tag, but the standard place for client-side scripts is within <script> and </script> tags in the head section. You will use curly brackets to set off the function definitions. It is often the case that you have nesting of sections set off by curly brackets. Errors such as leaving off a closing bracket or putting one in the wrong place are commonplace and annoying. However, you can find and correct them by drawing lines from each opening bracket to the one that closes its section.

Some examples of JavaScript put in special delimiters to set off scripting. This prevents the older browsers that did not have the facility to interpret JavaScript from displaying the code. We show examples both with and without these delimiters.

A function can have an argument—that is, information to be used on a particular invocation of the function—more than one argument, or no arguments. Different types are shown here. If a function called movein is to use the string "bird.gif", the call would be:

```
movein("bird.gif");
```

You define a function and you write a JavaScript statement that invokes the function. If the function does not have any arguments, the requirements of JavaScript are that you still use parentheses. Therefore, if you have defined a function called change, with no arguments, the call is:

```
change();
```

Client-Side Events

The critical events discussed in this chapter include the submission of a form, moving the cursor over a certain area on the screen, moving the cursor out from a certain area, and clicking on the mouse. You define how these events are to be handled—that is, what the response is to be for these events—by assigning a quoted string containing the appropriate JavaScript code to certain variable names. These names are onSubmit, onMouseOver, onMouseOut, and onClick. Typically, the JavaScript code is a call to a JavaScript function you write. This is to make the code easier to read and to change.

You must specify timed events in a slightly different way in JavaScript. You will use strings of code that can be function calls, but there is not an analog to onMouseOver. To establish that a certain thing is to happen at a set interval of time, you invoke a function called setInterval. The first argument to the function is a string representing the JavaScript code. The second argument is the time interval, in milliseconds. Therefore, to specify that the function change is to be invoked every 800 milliseconds (somewhat less than every second), you write:

```
tid=setInterval('change()',800);
```

A variable, such as the tid indicated here, can be viewed as the name of this timing event. To stop responding to a particular timed event, you write:

```
window.clearInterval(tid);
```

This means: For this window, stop checking for the timing event indicated by the value of   tid.

At this point, you might be asking yourself, "how do I know when to define a function or a variable or an event?" The answer is first, that you learn by experience; and second, there is no one answer. Programming or scripting is like writing an essay or a story; it does not follow a set procedure.

EXAMPLES

ON THE CD

This section contains examples of forms and JavaScript. The projects explained here include handling form input, changing an image when the mouse moves over it and a slide show. The CD-ROM contains the code for the projects in the folder named chapter3code.

Forms

The handling of form input by server-side scripts using PHP and ASP is the focus of much of this book. However, to start the explanation of forms, we begin with what could be dismissed as a "write-only" program. It accepts data, but does not do anything with it except demonstrate how forms are displayed.

```
<html>
<head><title>Form data </title>
</head>
<body>
<h1>Student Information </h1>
<hr>
<form action="test.html" method="get">
First Name <input type=text name='fname'>
Last Name <input type=text name='lname'><br>
Choose one <input type='radio' name='category'
value='newmedia'> New Media
<input type='radio' name='category' value='math'>
Math/Computer science
<input type='radio' name='category' value='LAS'>
Other LAS
<input type='radio' name='category'
value='arts'> Conservatories
<input type='radio' name='category' value='CE'>
Continuing education
<br><input type=submit value="SEND">
</form>
<body>
</html>
```

The <hr> tag (hr stands for horizontal rule) creates the line across the screen.

Create this in your text editor and save it as test.html. When you open it in a browser, it should look like Figure 3.1.

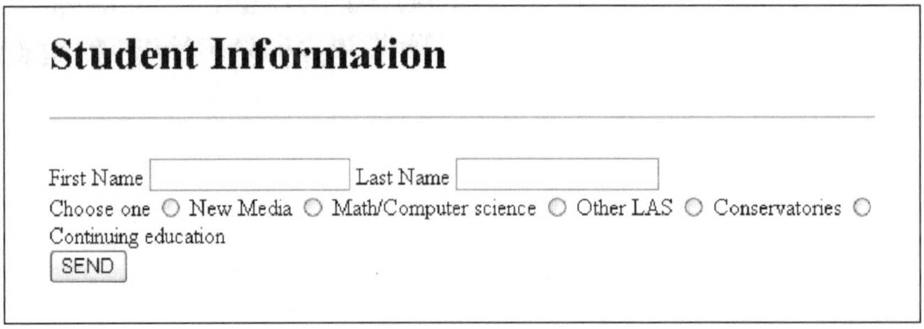

FIGURE 3.1   Sample form.

You can fill out the form. Notice how you can only choose one of the "Choose one" categories. This is because they are specified as radio inputs with the same name. Click on the SEND button. You will see something like what appears in the location field in Figure 3.2.

Address	file:///F:/Documents%20and%20Settings/Jeanine/My%20Documents/test.html?fname=Jeanine&lname=Meyer&category=newmedia

FIGURE 3.2   Entity relationship diagram.

We say "something like" because presumably you used another name. The text starting with test.html shows how the browser handles form submission. The form input field names and the values typed in are added to the name of the file specified by the action attribute. This is called the *query string* and is made up of the filename, followed by a question mark, and then field name and values separated by equal signs and strung together using ampersands. We have made the action file the same as the file holding the form just to make it a file that we know exists. In later chapters in this text, you will see some examples in which one file both presents the form and handles the form input, and other cases in which a different file is specified to handle the form.

The next example is more complex, but actually does something! The client-side script takes the input, performs calculations, and displays the results on the page. The following notes provide an outline for the coding. You will find it useful to prepare similar notes for your own work.

Head section containing a definition for a function named addup.

The function addup extracts the form data, does a calculation, and then does a further calculation to make sure the answer is formatted as dollars and cents. The result is displayed back in the form.

Body section containing a form. The form is used for input and output.

This example uses a plan for pricing that might or might not be what is done at the coffee shop you visit. There are three types of drinks. A base price is associated with each type and a size factor with each size. The cost of a drink is the base price times the size factor. This coffee shop also applies a tax rate of a fixed 8%.

Table 3.2 shows the code in the first column and an explanation in the second. Keep in mind that explaining code or script often poses "chicken and the egg" type problems. Be patient with the book and with yourself.

TABLE 3.2   HTML/JavaScript Calculation Example

`<html> <head><title> Calculation</title>`	Normal HTML.
`<script language="JavaScript">`	Sets off the script. Indicates the language. An alternative is VBScript
`function addup(f) {`	A function definition. The mate of the curly bracket is below at #. The argument has the name f. It will be the name of the form
`var total; var taxrate = .08 ; var drinkbase; var opts;`	Declaration of variables. The value of tax rate is set to .08
`opts=f.drink;`	This will be the set of options within the drink tag

(continues)

TABLE 3.2   HTML/JavaScript Calculation Example *(continued)*

`drinkbase = f.drink[opts.selectedIndex]` `.value;`	The `opts.selectedIndex` will hold the number (position) of whatever the person filling out the form has selected. Using this value as an index (square brackets) to f.drink indicates the option. Using "dot value" then extracts the value
`var sizefactor; var i; var totals;` `var dp;`	More declarations
`for (i=0;i<f.sizef.length;i++) {`	`for` statement to go through all the possibilities for sizes
`if (f.sizef[i].checked) {`	Check if this was the size checked
`    sizefactor = f.sizef[i].value;`	If so, set `sizefactor` equal to the corresponding value
`  } }`	Ends the `if`. Ends the `for` loop
`total = sizefactor * drinkbase;`	Multiply the `sizefactor` by the drinkbase
`total = total*(1 + taxrate);`	Add in taxes
`f.label.value="Total with tax";`	Output a description of what the answer is
`f.totalf.value=total;`	Output the total (but this could change)
`totals = f.totalf.value + "00";`	Make sure it is dollars and cents by adding the string "00"
`dp = totals.indexOf(".");`	Determine if there was a decimal point
`if (dp<0) {`	If there wasn't a decimal point, the indexOf method for strings will return −1 if it couldn't find a decimal point
`f.totalf.value = "$" +` `f.totalf.value+".00";`	Format the output value with a dollar sign and trailing zeros, and place in the totalf position in the form
`return false;`	This return false stops the browser from taking the action for the form
`}`	Ends the `if` clause
`else {`	Otherwise (if the condition isn't true), do the `else` clause
`totals = "$" + totals.substr(0,dp+3);`	Add the number of zeros that you need
`f.totalf.value = totals;`	Put in the totalf position
`return false;`	Return false as before
`}`	Ends the `else` clause
`}`	Ends the function definition

TABLE 3.2   *(continued)*

`</script> </head>`	Ends the script tag and the head tag
`<body> <h2> Coffee shop </h2> <p>`	Normal HTML
`<form name="orderf" onsubmit="return addup(this);">`	Form tag. Indicates a name. Indicates that when the submit event happens, call the `addup` function using this form as the argument. Return whatever it returns
`<select name="drink">`	Select tag. It has the name "drink"
`<option value="2.50">Coffee`	The options will be the base prices for the three options for drinks
`<option value="2.25">Hot Cocoa`	See above
`<option value="1.00">Chai`	See above
`</select>  `	End the select. HTML line break
`<input type="radio" name="sizef" value="1">Tall`	First of three radio input tags. Grouped by the common name. The value is the size factor
`<input type="radio" name="sizef" value="1.5">Grand`	Second of this group of radio buttons
`<input type="radio" name="sizef" value="2"> Super`	Third of this group of radio buttons
`<input type=submit value="Order">  `	Forms the submit button. The label is "Order"
` <input type="text" name="label" value="">`	The is an input tag, but it will be used to show the customer something, namely the phrase "Total with Tax"
`<input type=text name="totalf" value="">`	Another input tag used for output. It will have the calculated, formatted total
`</form> </body></html>`	HTML closing tags

The DOM is in heavy use in this example, defining how to read from and write to the form. The select and option tags, which implement the menu, require you (your code) to get the index of what was selected and then use that number to get the actual value.

```
f.drink[opts.selectedIndex].value
```

You interpret this by reading from the inside out: the `opts` is the name of the select tag. The programmer of this example chose that name; there is nothing special about it. The property `selectedIndex` is from the DOM. This returns the index (you can think of it as a position). A selection of coffee would yield a zero; hot cocoa, a one; and chai, a two. Indexing starts from zero, and not one, in JavaScript. Coding `f.drink` (the `drink` tag in the form f) followed by square brackets containing a number, will produce that option tag. The last operation is to extract the `value` attribute of that option tag. All the option tag values, as indicated previously, have been set to be used directly in the calculation.

This HTML file produces the screen shown in Figure 3.3.

FIGURE 3.3   Form to be filled out.

Once you have this (or something like it—do put in different names for the drinks and the sizes to test and strengthen your understanding), select a drink from the pull-down menu, click on a size, and then click on the Order button. Notice that filling out this form does assume that the customer is familiar with filling out these types of forms. What do you see? Figure 3.4 shows a possible result.

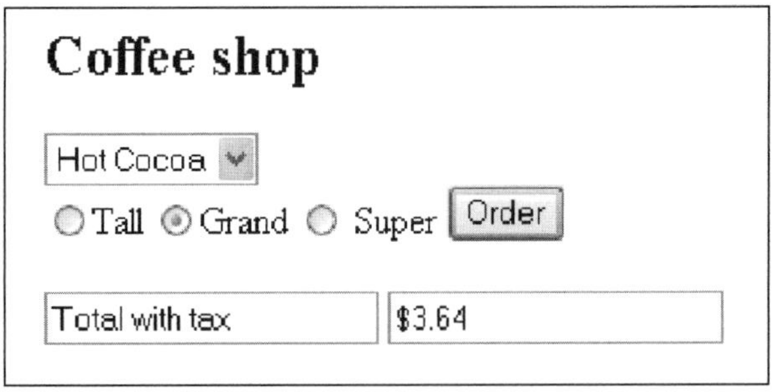

FIGURE 3.4   Filled-out form.

Client-Side Debugging

To prepare you for debugging your own scripts, what if you made the mistake of writing the `for` statement as:

```
for (i=0;i<=f.sizef.length;i++) {
```

This is understandable: the reason it is wrong is because the indexing of arrays starts with zero and ends with one less than the length of the array. The effect of this mistake is that nothing happens, except clearing the form. The dot disappears from whichever radio button you selected. The browser "knows" that there is a problem, but does not tell you what it is. You need to examine your code. In Netscape, you have a feature that might help. You can type:

```
javascript:
```

in the location field where you generally type in a URL. Netscape will display a JavaScript Console window (see Figure 3.5).

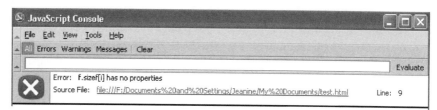

FIGURE 3.5   Error message in JavaScript console. Web browser ©2003 Netscape.

Internet Explorer does not have this feature.

If you count the line numbers in the html source, you will see `f.size[i]`. The message is telling you that `f.sizef[i]` does not exist. This is a hint—it certainly is not a direct message—that you need to check out the value of the variable `i`. Hopefully, this will cause you to examine the `for` statement and realize that the limiting condition on the loop was an error. Alternatively, you could insert a statement such as:

```
alert("The value of i is: "+i);
```

right after the opening curly bracket. In this situation, you will see screens resembling Figure 3.6 when the browser displays an alert window for `i` equal to zero, 1, 2, and 3. You will need to click OK to continue each time.

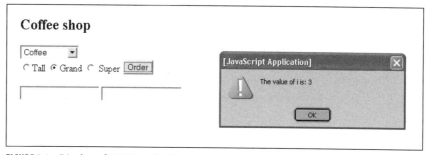

FIGURE 3.6   Display of HTML with Alert box.

When you see the 3, you need to figure out that this was the problem: the variable i should not have been greater than 2. Alert statements are one of the few tools you have for debugging HTML and JavaScript.

The system detected a problem situation at one place; the problem actually occurred at another place. You will need to cope with such situations.

The previous example demonstrated one type of bug. It was troublesome because the system did not indicate much more than that there was a problem. What if you made a mistake in the values you inserted for the tax rate or the prices of the types of drinks? The answer is that this might be a problem for the coffee shop and the customers, but it is not a problem to the browser. This is sometimes referred to as a *logical bug* and not a syntactic or programming problem. You need to detect and find these by yourself. One approach is to prepare what is elegantly called a *test suite* of input conditions, with the corresponding correct output recorded to be compared with what the system produces. It is also a good tactic to have someone else help debug your work.

Mouse Rollover to Swap Images

The next example might be the most frequently used JavaScript application: swapping images when the mouse goes over and out from the image. The coding makes use of a JavaScript function defined in the head section and small pieces of JavaScript in the <a> tags. The example also shows event handling. The event in the previous example was the submission of a form. The events here relate to the mouse. The outline for the script is as follows:

Head section containing
definition of a function called movein. *Its argument will be the name of the image to be moved into a set image tag. This means that the same function can be used for moving in either image.*

Body section containing
an a tag. The attributes of the <a> tag specify event handling. The content of the a tag is an image tag. The image tag has a name.

Here is the code shown and explained in Table 3.3.

This example follows the practice of using comments to set off the contents of the script tags. This is less necessary then it once was, because most browsers now recognize the <script> tags.

To implement this example, you need two image files. Figure 3.7 shows what the book example looks like when first opened in the browser.

TABLE 3.3   HTML/JavaScript for Mouse Rollover Image Swap

`<html>`	HTML tag
`<head>`	Head tag
`<title> Rollover test </title>`	Title tag
`<script language="JavaScript">`	Starting script tag
`<!-`	Comment (used to shield the code from older browsers)
`function movein(image)`	Start of function named movein. Its argument will be the name of an image file
`{`	Start of function body
`window.document.picture1.src=image;`	Make picture1 display image
`}`	End of function body
`// End ->`	Ending comments
`</script>`	Closing script tag
`</head>`	Closing head
`<body>`	Start of body
This is the start of the page.	Normal text
`<a href=""`	Start of an a tag. The href attribute is empty
`onMouseOver="movein(frog.gif');"`	Specifies the handling of the mouse over event to be calling the function movein with argument the frog file
`onClick="return false;"`	Specifies the handling of the click event to be return false. This means that the browser won't do anything. (Otherwise, it would refresh the screen and restore the original image)
`onMouseOut="movein('bird.gif');"`	Specifies the handling of the mouse out event—moving the cursor out from the a tag—to be calling the function movein with argument the bird file
`>`	Ends the a (starting a) tag
`<img src="bird.gif" name="picture1" height="100" >`	The contents of the a tag, what is between the a tag and the /a tag, is an image tag. It has a name attribute of "picture1." It also has src and height attributes
`</a>`	The /a tag
`</body>`	End of body
`</html>`	End of HTML

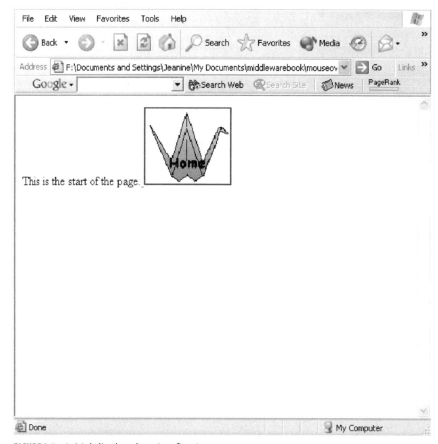

FIGURE 3.7 Initial display showing first image.

When a visitor moves the mouse over the image of the bird, the screen becomes what is shown in Figure 3.8.

Slide Show

The last JavaScript example is a slide show. The project makes use of JavaScript functions that set up timed events, setInterval and clearInterval. The example also uses an *array*. An array is a list of items; in this case, a list of names of image files. Actually, you were introduced to arrays in the coffee shop example. The select element held an array of options. Arrays have their own set of properties. One property used here is the length of the array. Particular elements of an array are referenced using square brackets. The outline for this project is shown followed by Table 3.5 showing the HTML and JavaScript.

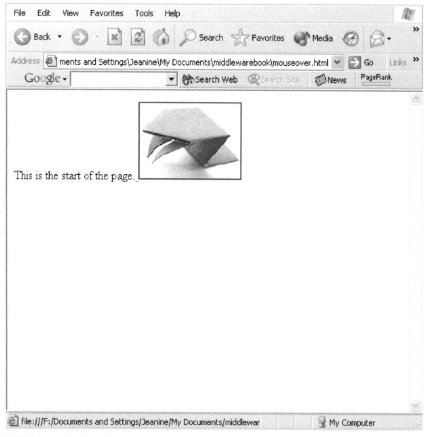

FIGURE 3.8   Display of second image.

Head section containing

An array of filenames

Definition of the change function, for changing the image

Definition of the startss function that starts the timing event process that implements the slide show

Definition of the stopss function that stops the timing event

Body section containing

An a tag, contents, and closing a tag that implements the button to start the slideshow

An a tag, contents, and closing a tag, that implements the button to stop the slideshow

An image tag, distinct from anything else

TABLE 3.5   HTML/JavaScript for Slide Show

`<html>`	Start html
`<head><title>Slide show </title>`	Head and title
`<script LANGUAGE="JavaScript">`	Script tag
`<!—`	Comment to set off script
`slides = new Array(`	Defines slides as an array, using the term "new." The array contains three elements:
`'bird.gif',`	A string holding the name of an image
`'frog.gif',`	Another image filename
`'heart.gif'`	Another image filename
`);`	Closes the array definition
`var sn = 0;`	A variable declaration and initialization
`var ns = slides.length;`	A variable declaration and initialization: ns will hold the number of items in the array
`var tid;`	A variable to hold the timing event number
`function change() {`	Start of the definition of the change function. It has *no* arguments
`document.pic1.src = slides[sn];`	The value of sn is assumed to hold the number for the next image. The slides array holds the names of all the image files. The sn one is now made the value of the src attribute. This effectively changes the image shown
`if (ns<= ++sn) {`	The variable sn is incremented (by the ++ operator *before* the variable). This is done compared to ns. If the new value of sn turns out to be greater than or equal to ns, then the if clause is executed
`  sn = 0;`	sn is put back to zero
`  }`	Close the if clause
`}`	Close the function
`function startss() {`	Start of startss function definition. It has no arguments
`tid=setInterval('change()',800);`	The timing event is established. The function change() will be called every 800 milliseconds. The number identifying this event is stored in the variable tid
`}`	End the startss function
`function stopss() {`	Start of stopss function. No arguments
`window.clearInterval(tid);`	Stop the timing event, using tid
`}`	End the function

TABLE 3.5   (*continued*)

`//-></script>`	End the comment and the script
`</head>`	End the head section
`<body>`	Start the body section
` `	Line break
`<a href="javascript:startss()">`	The a tag has as the value of the attribute href some JavaScript code. The code is `startss()`. This means that when the viewer clicks this hyperlink, this code gets invoked
`Start show </a>    `	The contents of the hyperlink (the words *Start show*, the /a tag and then two spaces. This special coding for blanks is required to space out the two hyperlinks
`<a href="javascript:stopss()" >Stop Show </a> `	Another a tag, contents and closing a tag. The href in the a tag indicates a call to `stopss()`
`<img src='bird.gif' name='pic1' id='pic1'>`	An image tag. Notice that it has a name and an id
`</body>`	End body
`</html>`	End html

Figure 3.9 shows the starting display for this example.

Figure 3.10 shows a display after the slide show has been stopped, with a different image.

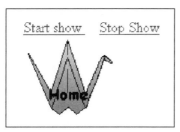

FIGURE 3.9   Starting display of HTML slide show.

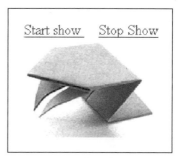

FIGURE 3.10   Display of slide show with a different image.

The event that occurs every 800 milliseconds is handled by calling the change function. Its tasks are to increment the variable sn (done using the ++ prefix operator) and then use sn to move to the next image. The critical part of the incrementing is to know when to start over. Recall that the indexing starts at zero. This means that the last element has index one less than the number of elements in the array. The ns variable in the example here will have the value 3. Therefore, when sn gets bumped up to 3, the code resets it to zero. The constant 3 does not occur in the code. The length property of the array named slides returns the correct value.

Make a slide show with four images. All you need to do is squeeze in a line before the parentheses ending the array definition.

Preventing Errors

When writing HTML and JavaScript applications such as these, it is good practice to review your work by doing the following:

- Check that opening tags are matched with closing tags.
- Check that opening braces (curly brackets) are matched with closing braces, opening pointy brackets are matched with closing pointy brackets, and opening parentheses with closing parentheses.
- Check that you have quotation marks around attribute values and character strings, and make sure you have not omitted the closing quotation marks. Use single quotes within larger strings delimited by double quotes.
- Check that spelling agrees between the setting of a variable and its name in an expression, or the definition of a form input element and its use in JavaScript.
- Check references to filenames for spelling. This is more difficult than the prior check because it involves something outside the HTML file.
- Check the starting and stopping values in any looping (e.g., for statement).

Errors will still occur, but these are the most common sources of problems. A general strategy is to proceed slowly. Try to build on what you know by taking a script that works and making changes to it to turn it into a script that does a new task. Test the changes one at a time.

REFLECTION

As you already might know, the different browsers developed distinct interpretations and enhancements for the DOM, negating the claimed purpose of defining consistent ways to access the HTML document. However, the standards organization for the Web, the World Wide Web Consortium (W3C), is working on this problem. There will still be the problem of coping with older browsers, but the new ones probably will be more consistent.

Although your projects will be more complex once you start doing PHP and ASP/JavaScript, there will be help with debugging. The PHP and ASP systems on the server produce error messages.

The examples described in this chapter require information such as the coffee shop prices and the names of image files to be kept in the HTML file. The disadvantages of this approach are that this information is visible and, if it were to grow in size, would become burdensome to manage. This leads to the need for a way to produce HTML pages using information stored on the server, and that, in turn, leads to a need for the "middleware," server-side software technologies that are the subject of the rest of this book.

EXERCISES, QUESTIONS, AND PROJECTS

1. Define and describe the following terms: *variable, function, expression, event,* and *form.*
2. What do each of the following tags do (indicate also if the tag is used as part of a pair and any relevant attributes): form, input, select, and option?
3. How do you do the following tasks?
   a. Specify the handler of a form to be the program handles.php.
   b. Specify a place in a form for the customer to write his or her name.
   c. Specify a set of choices for the customer, allowing only one choice.
   d. Specify a pull-down menu of choices.
   e. Create a button that starts something—say, a call to a function doit()—every three seconds.
   f. Define a JavaScript function that gets called with a number (just the first line of the function definition).
   g. Specify that something—say, a call to a function changeit()—happens when the mouse is moved over an image.
   h. Specify that something—say, a call to a function undoit()—happens when the mouse is moved out from over an image.
   i. Within a JavaScript function, write the first line of a loop that will occur four times.
4. Construct your own shop, with a different set of products and a different display. For example, you can combine the coffee shop and the mouse rollover examples to produce an online menu in which the radio buttons are pictures of the products and rollover produces price information.
5. Go online and research the current state of the DOM.

SERVER-SIDE BASICS

The purpose of this chapter is to introduce the basic mechanics of ASP/JavaScript and PHP. This is server-side scripting in contrast to the client-side scripting discussed in the previous chapter.

BACKGROUND

Server-side programming, also called *middleware,* was developed to satisfy the need for processing on the server computer. The common gateway interface (CGI) can be used for this purpose. You, the developer, write a program that uses the CGI rules to access information such as form data and generate a new HTML document to be sent to the client. The Perl language is a frequent choice for these programs, which is the reason why you would read about "cgi/perl" programs. The new generation of server-side programming supplies this same function with an approach that eases the programming task. Since the main output of a server-side program is to produce HTML, each of these newer products is designed to be HTML interspersed with the coding logic. The first of the new middleware products, ColdFusion®, now a product of the Macromedia Company, uses the approach of defining its own tags to specify logic. The tags fit in well with the HTML tags. This book will not cover ColdFusion, but the knowledge you gain from working with ASP and PHP should help you understand the ColdFusion examples. The ASP and PHP approach is to use scripting languages with built-in functions (in ASP, these functions are constructed as object methods). The middleware scripting is interspersed with regular HTML. The PHP `print` and the ASP `Response.Write` can be used to generate HTML. This HTML along with the HTML written directly in the file is what is sent to the browser computer.

CONCEPTUAL EXPLANATION

The server computer recognizes ASP and PHP files from the extension to the filename. When a request from the client for a file named *something.asp* or *something.php* arrives at the server, the action is not simply to send that file over the network to the client, but to open and examine the file and process it. These files consist of a mixture of "straight" HTML and ASP or PHP code.

Delimiters for ASP and PHP

Delimiter symbols set off the ASP or PHP portions of the file. In the case of ASP, the first delimiter tag specifies JavaScript as the language, assuming you choose to use JavaScript, which is what will be done in this text. The default language for ASP is VBScript. An ASP file would resemble the following:

```
<%@ language="JavaScript"%>
<html>  Other HTML
```

```
<%
 JavaScript code with ASP
%>
</html>
```

You can go in to and out of ASP/JavaScript as many times as you want. A PHP file would take the following form:

```
<html>  Other HTML
<?php
    PHP
?>
</html>
```

(You can also use ASP style delimiters with PHP, but we will stick to the question marks to prevent confusion in the examples.)

Obtaining Form Data and Outputting HTML

The tasks of a server-side file, also commonly referred to as a *script*, are to access resources on the server and use the information to construct a customized HTML document to return to the client computer. One category of resources available on the server encompasses databases and files. The following chapters will cover databases; in this chapter, we stick to basic ASP/JavaScript and PHP. To generalize, to do ASP or PHP, you need to know how to use the appropriate programming language to perform the logic, and you need to know how to access and change resources.

When doing ASP, your code will include invocation of the methods of a small set of objects. The terms *method* and *object* both have specialized meanings in computing. Objects are encapsulations of data and procedures. The data is referred to as *properties* or *attributes,* and the procedures are called *methods.* For example, to obtain the value of a form input field called "first_name" when the form was submitted using the get method, you write:

```
Request.QueryString("first_name")
```

The way to describe this using the language of objects is: QueryString is itself a collection of data within the object Request. The individual items within the query string are referenced using the name of the input tag in the original form.

Assume the person filling out the form entered the name "Aviva" and clicked the Submit button. This data is included as part of the query string. To display a formatted greeting, you would code:

```
Response.Write("<h1>Hello, "+
Request.QueryString("first_name")+"</h1> <br>");
```

Reading and interpreting from the inside out, the `Request.QueryString` (`"first_name"`) yields the string "Aviva". It is concatenated with other strings in front and in back, to produce: "`<h1>Hello, Aviva</h1> <br>`". The Response object has a method named `Write`. This is the method (in the regular English meaning of the word *method*) to write out text to the HTML document to send to the client computer. The `Write` method of the Response object takes one argument, a string.

In the small fragment of ASP/JavaScript, the `Response.Write` and the `Request.QueryString` (`"first_name"`) are ASP. The part that is JavaScript is the plus sign for the concatenation operator and the semicolon for ending the statement.

Most ASP/JavaScript scripts make use of variables. You, the programmer, set up a variable to hold a value. The following code fragment sets up and initializes a variable named `first_name` to be whatever was entered into the form. That variable is then used to output the customized HTML page:

```
var first_name = Request.QueryString("first_name");
Response.Write("<ht>Hello, "+first_name+"</h1><br>");
```

The variable name could be anything you choose. We did not have to make it the same name as the name of the form input tag. However, having said that, you do need to be consistent. Once you choose a name, you need to stick to it when making references to the variable. The system will not understand something you might think of as simply a shorthand. For this reason, make the names something meaningful.

The PHP system includes the programming logic and built-in procedures and variables for accessing the resources on the server computer. For example, to output something to the HTML document to be sent to the client, you use either the function `print` or the function `echo`. The PHP language has many similarities to JavaScript, but there are differences. One of the most obvious differences with ASP is that variable names start with dollar signs. This requirement enables what can be called a special trick concerning character strings to be demonstrated later in the chapter. Another difference is that the operator for concatenation of string is a period and not a plus sign.

The people who install the PHP system on the server computer have choices to make concerning many of the built-in procedures. One choice concerns the way to access the form input values. The so-called long form is similar to ASP. However, a common choice is to allow a short form. When this choice is in place, the form input values are referenced by a dollar sign followed by the name of the tag. The PHP version of the example with the form input of a first name is:

```
print("<h1>Hello, $first_name</h1><br>");
```

With the short form in place on the server, PHP treats variable names, form input using the get method, form input using the put method, and, to be covered in a later chapter, cookies all in the same straightforward way: a dollar sign followed by the name. It is not a big conceptual difference, but this feature along with the ability to embed these names within strings does tend to make the PHP scripts shorter than the ASP/JavaScript (or ASP/VBScript) scripts.

The PHP language does support concatenation. If you do need to concatenate two strings together, the PHP operator is a period.

ASP/JavaScript and PHP Programming

The ASP/JavaScript and PHP do have many technical features in common. JavaScript used "on the server" is essentially the same language as on the client, and PHP provides many of the features, often using very similar syntax. For example, each supports array variables. Remember: arrays are sets of data, indexed by numbers starting with zero. Both ASP/JavaScript and PHP provide features for checking a condition and executing code only if a condition is true. The basic feature for checking conditions is the if statement. It has the structure:

```
if (condition) {
    Some code
}
```

The condition could be a comparison: is the price greater than 10? If the condition is true, then the code, denoted as "Some code" here, is executed. If the condition is not true, then execution continues after the closing bracket. Another form of the if statement is:

```
if (condition) {
    code for true case
}
else {
    code for false case
}
```

This performs in the expected way. The condition is evaluated. If that evaluation returns a true value, then the code of the true case is executed; otherwise, the code for the false case. The general syntax for PHP and ASP/JavaScript are the same. A brief aside: VBScript, the other language used with ASP, has a very similar feature. The terms are:

```
If (condition) then
 Code for the true case
Else
 Code for the false case
End If
```

Both ASP/JavaScript and PHP have features for looping. Both have ways to bring in the material in other files. These and other features will be shown in the examples here and in the rest of the text.

Include File Facility

One important feature of both ASP and PHP is the ability to bring in other files. Dividing a problem into smaller problems is a well-established programming technique. In the simple quiz show application to be shown in the *Examples* section, you can put the question and answers in one file and make the files with the logic much more manageable. The PHP command for this is:

```
include("statecapitals.php");
```

If this line of code is executed, then the file called *statecapitals.php* is brought into the script. Alternatively, you can use:

```
require("statecapitals.php");
```

If you use this function, the *statecapitals.php* file will be brought in whether or not that line of code is reached.

The ASP version of this is:

```
<!- #include file="statecapitals.asp"  ->
```

This expression is placed typically as the second line in the file, under the statement indicating the language choice. The include file is always brought into the script.

You can use any file extensions that you want for this. However, using PHP and ASP means that these files will not be shown by the browser if a player tries to look at the file; that is, the answers.

Random and Other Math Functions

Many computer applications, most notably games and quizzes, require the making of choices in an apparently random manner. For example, if you want to be quizzed on the states, you do not want to always start with Alabama. Among other things, you will probably never stay around to get asked about Wyoming. Most computer languages provide what are called *pseudo-random functions*. The "pseudo" is because the system uses a well-defined procedure to arrive at a result. There is no little man inside the computer flipping coins. For PHP, the function to be used in this chapter is:

```
$choice=rand(0, 49);
```

This statement assigns to the variable `$choice` the results of a call to the built-in function `rand`. When the built-in function is called with two arguments, it returns an integer (whole number) value from 0 to 49.

The ASP counterpart to this is:

```
choice=Math.floor(Math.random()*50);
```

The function `Math.random()` returns a fraction greater or equal to zero and less than one. If you multiply such a value by 50, you get a number greater or equal to zero and less than 50 (but possibly greater than 49). The next step indicated in the expression is to take the floor of this value. The floor is the biggest whole number that is not more than its argument. The effect of this expression is to produce a whole number from zero to 49, exactly what we want.

The steps represented by this expression are shown in Table 4.1.

TABLE 4.1   Steps in Expression Calculating Choice

EXPRESSION	RESULT
`Math.random()`	Value from zero to [just] less than one
`*50`	Value from zero to [just] less than 50
`Math.floor`	Whole number value from zero to 49

EXAMPLES

This section starts with simple examples of ASP and PHP. It is important for you to try them because it will determine that you have workable arrangements with your server. Keep in mind that ASP and PHP scripts must run on a server computer. You will upload the examples to the server using a program such as ws-ftp, or you will run them on your own computer after establishing your computer as a server using Personal Web Server or Windows IIS or another facility. The remaining examples are the ASP and PHP implementations of a quiz program on the states and the capitals. The example demonstrates use of form input, multiple scripts, and several programming features. You will find the code for the simple examples and the two state capital applications on the CD-ROM in the folder named chapter4code.

ON THE CD

Beginning ASP and PHP Scripts

Write the following and save it as *test.asp*.

```
<%@ language="JavaScript"%>
<html><head><title>First ASP </title>
</head>
<body>
<%
```

```
Response.Write ("This was done on the server");
%>
</body>
</html>
```

Upload this to your server and open it. You should see the display produced by the following HTML file:

```
<html>
<head><title>First ASP </title>
</head>
<body>
This was done on the server
</body>
</html>
```

Similarly, write the following and save it as *test.php*.

```
<html>
<head><title>First PHP </title>
</head>
<body>
<?php
print("This was done on the server");
</html>
?>
```

If you have taken any computing course and feel obliged to do a *Hello, world* program, feel free to do one or both as an exercise. For PHP, there actually is a standard first program and it is the following:

```
<html>
<head><title>First PHP </title>
</head>
<body>
<?php
phpinfo();
</html>
?>
```

The function `phpinfo()` is an example of a built-in function; it is part of the PHP language. The opening and closing parentheses with nothing in between indicate that it is a function without arguments. No information is passed to the function. This particular function will display on the client computer a very lengthy list of information about the server. Try it; type it up; save it as *phptest.php*; upload it to your server; and then open it using a browser. You will see an extensive display of information on the settings of your server.

States and Capitals Quiz

The next set of examples (one in PHP and one in ASP) will implement a quiz/drill on U.S. states and their capitals. This requires information to be kept on the server; namely, the 50 pairs of state name and capital name. For these examples, the information will not be in a database but in a file on the server. The application is implemented using three files: one file presents one form to the player (the person at the client computer) giving a choice of how to ask the question and then presents the question, also using a form. The second file checks the answer. A third file holds the state/capital information.

Both the PHP and the ASP implementations of the quiz use a trick common to middleware projects. Files (scripts) both present forms and handle form input. You write program logic to detect which of the situations it is by checking on form input. The plan is to have one script present the question choice and then the question and another check the result. If the player gets it wrong, the program presents two options: get a new turn, or try again with the same question.

Now, at this point, there is a semantic issue on how to phrase the question giving the player a choice in the asking of the question. The first form is for the player to choose between being told a state (e.g., New York) and being asked for its capital (Albany), or being told a capital (Albany) and being asked to come up with its state (New York). Rather than presenting this very long message, this example produces the screen shown in Figure 4.1.

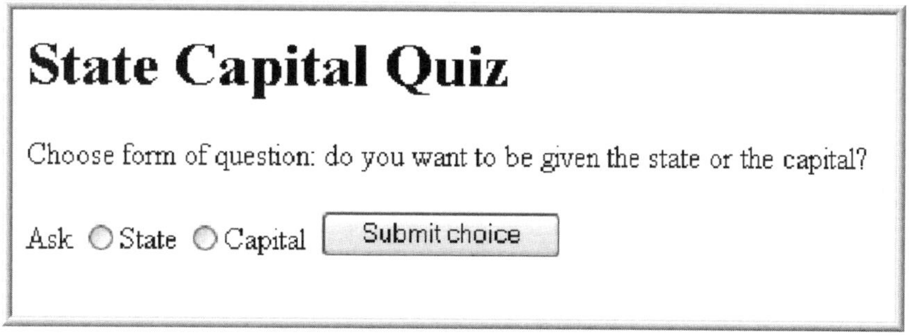

State Capital Quiz

Choose form of question: do you want to be given the state or the capital?

Ask ◯ State ◯ Capital [Submit choice]

FIGURE 4.1   Initial screen for state capital quiz.

If the player clicks the radio button to the left of State and then clicks the Submit choice button, the next screen will resemble Figure 4.2.

The reasoning here is that the state is what gets named and the player must supply the capital. Good people might claim that being "asked the state" should mean the opposite: being told the capital and being asked to come up with the state.

Let's show the rest of the screens before turning to the code. Memphis is a city in Tennessee, although not the capital. Programming games (and other

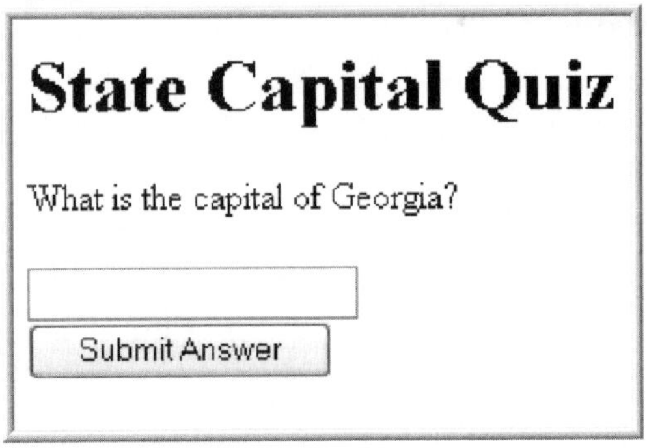

FIGURE 4.2   Asking for the capital.

applications) require you to try all types of input, including incorrect answers. Figure 4.3 shows the player entering an incorrect answer.

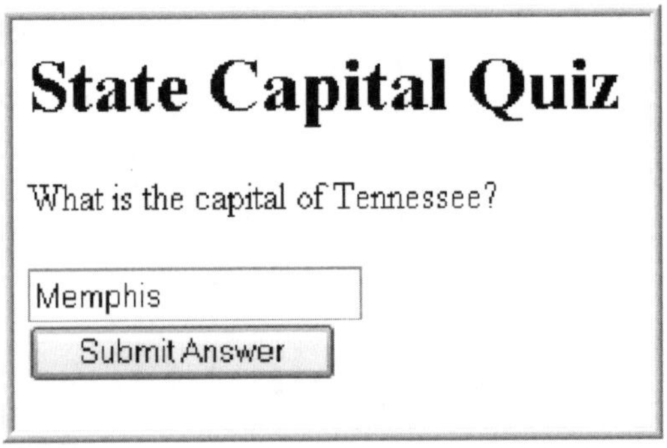

FIGURE 4.3   Player enters an incorrect answer.

After clicking the Submit Answer button, the person who entered Memphis would see the screen in Figure 4.4.

The player has a choice of giving up on this state and getting the very first screen again with the choice of type of question, or trying again. Let us say the player chooses to try again and with the correct answer. The resulting screen is shown in Figure 4.5.

This sequence does *not* test all the possibilities. For one thing, the choice of being asked a capital first was not shown. When you prepare this and any other project, you need to try all possibilities and all combinations (sequences) of possibilities. However, it is time to look at the scripts.

Here is the outline for the *miniquizask* script.

HTML including head section, start of body, and a header
Get into PHP or ASP
Make the choice of state/capital using a facility that produces random results

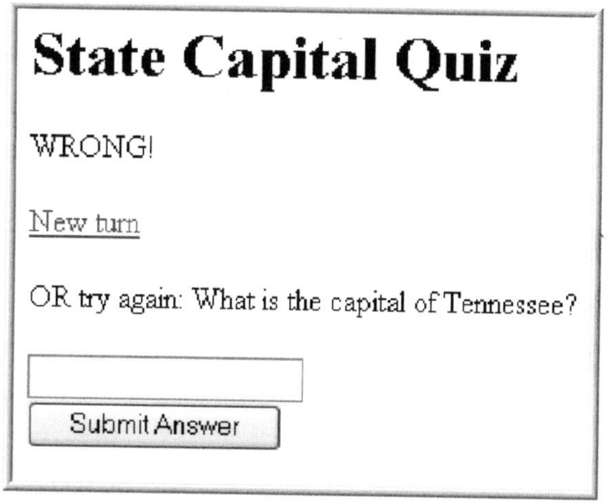

FIGURE 4.4   System responds to incorrect answer.

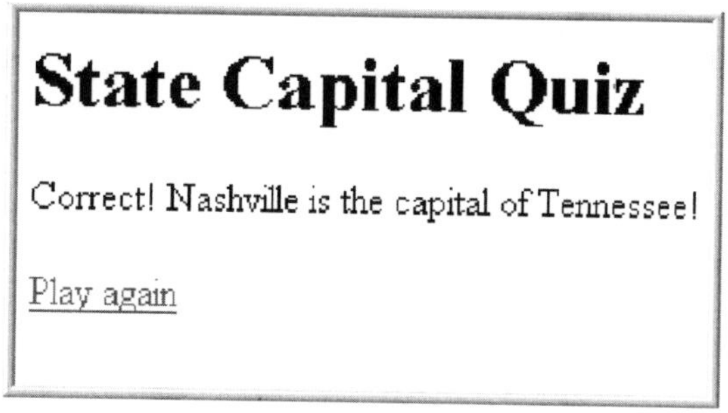

FIGURE 4.5   System responds to correct answer.

Determine if the player has been shown the choice form
If this is the case, then determine if the choice was state or capital
    If state, present that question (display that form)
    If capital, present that question (display that form)
If the player has not been shown the choice form yet, display it
Get out of PHP or ASP and produce the rest of the HTML

States and Capitals Quiz in PHP

Having determined the general approach, now is the time to get into the nitty-gritty code, starting with the PHP version. Remember that the PHP script outputs HTML using the print function. To produce a line break in the HTML file, the print function outputs the special symbol \n. Keep in mind that this is only for the HTML file. To get the browser to display a line break on the screen, the PHP file needs to include a `<br>` or a `<p>` either in the HTML that occurs outside the delimiters for the PHP or inside the string arguments of a `print` function.

```
<html>
<head><title>Mini-quiz: ask</title>
</head>
<body>
<h1>State Capital Quiz </h1><p>
<?php
if (@$saywhich){
  include("statecapitals.php");
  $choice=rand(0, 49);
  if ($which=='state') {
  $state = $states[$choice];
  print("What is the capital of $state?<br>");
  print("<form action='miniquizcheck.php' ");
  print("method='get'>\n");
  print("<input type='text' name='capital'><br>\n");
  print("<input type='hidden' name='which' ");
  print("value=$which>\n");
  print("<input type='hidden' name='choice' ");
  print("value=$choice>\n");
  print("<input type='submit' value='Submit Answer'>");
  print("</form>\n");
 }
 else   {
  $capital = $capitals[$choice];
  print("$capital is the capital of which state?<br>");
  print("<form action='miniquizcheck.php'");
  print(" method='get'>\n");
  print("<input type='text' name='state'><br>\n");
  print("<input type='hidden' name='which'");
  print("value=$which>\n");
  print("<input type='hidden' name='choice' ");
  print("value=$choice>\n");
  print("<input type='submit' value='Submit Answer'>");
  print("</form>\n");
  }
 }
 else {
    print("Choose form of question: ");
    print("do you want to be given the state ");
    print("or the capital?<br>");
    print("<form action='miniquizask.php' ");
    print("method='get'>\n");
    print("Ask <input type='radio' name='which' ");
    print("value='state'>State");
```

```
    print(" <input type='radio' name='which' ");
    print("value='capital'>Capital\n");
    print("<input type='hidden' name='saywhich' ");
    print("value='true'>\n");
    print("<input type='submit' ");
    print("value='Submit choice'>");
    print("</form>");
  }
  ?>
  </body>
  </html>
```

Look at the overall structure of the code (trying not to get caught up ini-tially in the details). You will see that it does follow the outline. There is an outer if/else statement, and within the first clause of the if statement, there is another if/else statement. Notice also that the script goes in to and out of PHP. You have some flexibility in how often you choose to do this. For exam-ple, in the preceding code example, starting with the else, you could write:

```
else {
?>
Choose form of question: do you want to be given the
state or the capital?<br>
<form action='miniquizask.php' method='get'>
Ask <input type='radio' name='which'
value='state'>State
<input type='radio' name='which'
value='capital'>Capital
<input type='hidden' name='saywhich' value='true'>
<input type='submit' value='Submit choice'>
</form>
<?
}
?>
</body>
</html>
```

In all the clauses, there are several print statements, outputting HTML to the client computer. The arguments of the print statements include <form …> and <input …> tags. There is a mixture of HTML and PHP variables. Single quotes are used within strings that are defined using double quotes. The form presenting the choice of question has this script as the handler by citing it as the value of the action attribute. The forms that actually ask a question specify *miniquizcheck.php* as the action attribute.

The condition tested by the outermost if statement is intended to ask: should the player be shown the form for indicating choice of question, or has this been shown and the program needs to interpret and act on the result? The construction in PHP is:

```
if (@$saywhich)
```

The @ symbol tells the PHP interpreter to not complain if the $saywhich variable does not exist because, indeed, it might not exist. That is exactly what you want to test for in this situation. In other situations, a variable or form input value not existing would be an error and you want the system to let you know. If $saywhich does not exist, essentially if it has not been set, then the condition is false. The else clause is what is executed, and the initial form offering the choice about the question is displayed. Notice that 'saywhich' is a hidden input tag and its value is set to true. Hidden input tags are ways to carry information from one script to another or one script to itself. If the $saywhich variable exists and has been set to true, the first clause of the if statement gets executed.

At this point, you might be asking, where are the states and the capitals? That information is in a separate file called statecapitals.php. The start of that file is:

```
<?php
$states =  Array();
$capitals= Array();
$states[]='Alabama';$capitals[]='Montgomery';
$states[]='Alaska'; $capitals[]='Juneau';
$states[]='Arizona';$capitals[]='Phoenix';
   ...
```

The delimiter <?php is necessary to specify that this script is PHP code. This is not strictly logical, but omitting it makes the entire file be displayed in the HTML document. The next two lines set up two array variables, one called $states and the other $capitals. The following statements come in pairs, and each statement in a pair adds an element to the appropriate array. The fact that they are in pairs means that the Ith element of $states corresponds to the Ith element of $capitals. Arrays are indexed starting with zero and ending with one less than the number of elements. Therefore, the $choice variable, which is set to something between zero and 49, can be used to point to a state and a capital that match.

At this point, to understand the code, you need to go back and forth between the forms. The form presenting the choice of question to the player will set $which. When the script is executed subsequently, $saywhich will be true, and the inner if statement checks if $which is equal to "state." If it is, then the "giving the state" form of question is presented. Otherwise, the "giving the capital" form of question is presented. In either case, the $choice variable is passed to the next script in the form of hidden data.

The code here uses the get method so you can see what your scripts are doing. After you get the scripts working, change to the put method. This is preferable for this type of application. For PHP, you simply change the method attribute in all the form tags. The code for reading the form input remains the same. For ASP, you need to do something more. The code to get (excuse the term) any form input acquired with the post method uses the Request.Form method.

Continuing with the example, here is an outline for the checking the result:

HTML start, head, title, body, heading
Start PHP or ASP
> *Using the form input indicated by choice, set up variables to hold the state and capital*
> *If the question asked was 'state', check the answer (held in the capital form input)*
>> *If correct, say so and display a hyperlink back to the first script*
>> *If wrong, say so and display a hyperlink back to the first script and re-ask the question*
> *If not (if the question asked was not 'state', that is, it was 'capital'), check the answer (held in the state form input)*
>> *If correct, say so and display a hyperlink back to the first script*
>> *If wrong, say so and display a hyperlink back to the first script and re-ask the question*
Close up PHP or ASP
Closing HTML material

Here is the code for *miniquizcheck.php*:

```
<html>
<head><title>Mini-quiz: check answers</title>
</head>
<body>
<h1>State Capital Quiz </h1><p>
<?php
include('statecapitals.php');
$correctstate=$states[$choice];
$correctcapital=$capitals[$choice];
if ($which=='state')
   {
    if ($capital == $correctcapital)
     {
      print(
        "Correct! $correctcapital is the capital of ");
      print("$correctstate!");
      print("<p><a href='miniquizask.php'>");
      print("Play again </a>");
     }
```

```php
    else {
      print("WRONG!<p>\n");
      print("<a href='miniquizask.php'>");
      print("New turn </a><p>\n");
      print("OR try again: What is the capital ");
      print("of $correctstate?<br>");
      print("<form action='miniquizcheck.php' ");
      print("method='get'>\n");
      print("<input type='text' name='capital'><br>\n");
      print("<input type='hidden' name='which' ");
      print("value=$which>\n");
      print("<input type='hidden' name='choice'");
      print("value=$choice>\n");
      print("<input type='submit' ");
      print("value='Submit Answer'>");
      print("</form>\n");
      }
  }
  else {
    if ($state == $correctstate)
      {
       print("Correct! The capital of $correctstate ");
       print("is $correctcapital!");
       $saywhich='false';
       print("<p><a href='miniquizask.php'>");
       print("Play again </a>");
      }
    else {
      print("WRONG!<p>\n");
      print("<a href='miniquizask.php'>");
      print("New turn </a><p>\n");
      print("OR try again: ");
      print("$correctcapital is the capital ");
      print("of what state?<br>");
      print("<form action='miniquizcheck.php' ");
      print("method='get'>\n");
      print("<input type='text' name='state'><br>\n");
      print("<input type='hidden' name='which'");
      print(" value=$which>\n");
      print("<input type='hidden' name='choice' ");
      print("value=$choice>\n");
      print("<input type='submit' ");
      print(" value='Submit Answer'>");
      print("</form>\n");
      }
    }
  }
?>
</body>
</html>
```

Again, look at the general form of the code and gradually notice more detail before examining it line-by-line. Notice how the nested if statements correspond to the outline. Notice the print statements with the arguments being strings surrounded by double quotes. The strings are often mixtures of HTML and variables, with the variable names beginning with dollar signs. Notice that the action attributes indicate that the handler is this script again. Notice that the hyperlinks back to the first script are implemented using regular HTML a tags, with the href attribute having the value miniquizask.php.

You can try and make this example work right now. If you do not want to type in all 50 states, type in 5 and in the line $choice = rand(0, 49), change the 49 to 4. Alternatively, a more robust approach is to have the program detect the size of the arrays. The PHP function that does this is sizeOf. Change the assignment statement that produces a random choice to:

```
$choice=rand(0,sizeOf($states)-1);
```

When testing the project, notice the form input that shows up in the browser address window after submitting each form. For example, Figure 4.6 shows the address with the form data after selecting the capital choice of question and Figure 4.7 shows the address with the form data after answering the question.

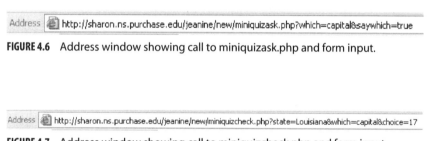

Address   http://sharon.ns.purchase.edu/jeanine/new/miniquizask.php?which=capital&saywhich=true

FIGURE 4.6   Address window showing call to miniquizask.php and form input.

Address   http://sharon.ns.purchase.edu/jeanine/new/miniquizcheck.php?state=Louisiana&which=capital&choice=17

FIGURE 4.7   Address window showing call to miniquizcheck.php and form input.

The form data is displayed because the form tag specified the method as get. Being able to examine the form data in this way will help in the debugging of your code. Once you have the application debugged, you can choose to switch to the put method.

States and Capitals Quiz in ASP

This text will have some examples with PHP explained first and some with ASP explained first. Assume you have the PHP version working. What do you need to change to produce an ASP version? You need to do the following:

- Change the delimiters, including adding `<%@ Language="JavaScript"%>` at the top.
- In all strings, you need to use concatenation wherever there are embedded variables. You can do this and remove the dollar signs from the variable names.
- Remove the dollar signs from any other variable names.
- Explicitly declare (use the `var` statement) variables.
- Explicitly set variables to hold the form input. This is done using `Request.QueryString`(*form input tag name*).
- Use the ASP/JavaScript form of include to get the statecapitals file.
- Change the file references to be the ASP files. This also applies to the statecapitals file.
- Use the JavaScript `Math.floor(Math.random()*50)` expression in place of the PHP one using rand.
- Change print to `Response.Write`.

This might seem like so much that you are better off writing the ASP/JavaScript code from scratch. This determination will be left to the reader. Here is the ASP/JavaScript code for *miniquizask.asp*:

```
<%@ Language="JavaScript"%>
<!- #include file="statecapitals.asp" ->
<html>
<head><title>Mini-quiz: ask</title>
</head>
<body>
<h1>State Capital Quiz</h1><p>
<%
var saywhich=String(Request.QueryString("saywhich"));
if (saywhich !="undefined") {
 choice=Math.floor(Math.random()*50);
 var which = String(Request.QueryString("which"));
 if (which=='state') {
   state = states[choice];
   Response.Write("What is the capital of ");
   Response.Write(state+"?<br>");
   Response.Write("<form action='miniquizcheck.asp' ");
   Response.Write("method='get'>\n");
   Response.Write("<input type='text' ");
   Response.Write("name='capital'><br>\n");
   Response.Write("<input type='hidden' ");
   Response.Write("name='which' ");
   Response.Write("value="+which+">\n");
   Response.Write("<input type='hidden' ");
   Response.Write("name='choice' value="+choice+">\n");
   Response.Write("<input type='submit' ");
   Response.Write("value='Submit Answer'>");
   Response.Write("</form>\n");
```

```
      }
    else
    {
      capital = capitals[choice];
      Response.Write("$capital is the capital of which ");
      Response.Write("state?<br>");
      Response.Write("<form action='miniquizcheck.asp' ");
      Response.Write("method='get'>\n");
      Response.Write("<input type='text' ");
      Response.Write("name='state'><br>\n");
      Response.Write("<input type='hidden' ");
      Response.Write("name='which' value="+which+">\n");
      Response.Write("<input type='hidden' ");
      Response.Write("name='choice' value="+choice+">\n");
      Response.Write("<input type='submit' ");
      Response.Write("value='Submit Answer'>");
      Response.Write("</form>\n");
    }
  }
  else
  {
    Response.Write("Choose form of question: ");
    Response.Write("do you want to be given the ");
    Response.Write("state or the capital?<br>");
    Response.Write("<form action='miniquizask.asp' ");
    Response.Write("method='get'>\n");
    Response.Write("Ask <input type='radio' ");
    Response.Write("name='which' value='state'>State");
    Response.Write(" <input type='radio' ");
    Response.Write("name='which' ");
    Response.Write("value='capital'>Capital\n");
    Response.Write("<input type='hidden' ");
    Response.Write("name='saywhich' value='true'>\n");
    Response.Write("<input type='submit' ");
    Response.Write(" value='Submit choice'>");
    Response.Write("</form>");
  }
%>
</body>
</html>
```

Do the same review of this code as was suggested for the PHP example. Observe the general format. The if statements correspond to what is indicated in the outline. The include statement is at the top.

The form data is extracted using the ASP object method Request.Query String() and then applying the String function. The String function completes the process of getting a value from the form. It does not appear to be required in every case, but it is required here.

The change to making the code robust with respect to the number of states is the following:

```
var num = states.length;
choice=Math.floor(Math.random()*num);
```

You could combine the two (not use the variable num). Note that length is a property of the array states, whereas sizeOf is a function that takes as its argument the name of an array. The *miniquizcheck.asp* code is the following:

```
<%@ Language="JavaScript"%>
<!- #include file="statecapitals.asp" ->
<html>
<head><title>Mini-quiz: check answers</title>
</head>
<body>
<h1>State Capital Quiz </h1><p>
<%
var choice=Request.QueryString("choice");
var correctstate=states[choice];
var correctcapital=capitals[choice];
var which=Request.QueryString("which");
if (which=='state')
  {
   var capital=Request.QueryString("capital");
   if (capital == correctcapital)
     {
      Response.Write("Correct! "+correctcapital);
      Response.Write(" is the capital of ");
      Response.Write(correctstate+"!");
      Response.Write("<p><a href='miniquizask.asp'>");
      Response.Write("Play again </a>");
     }
   else
     {
      Response.Write("WRONG!<p>\n");
      Response.Write("<a href='miniquizask.asp'>");
      Response.Write("New turn </a><p>\n");
      Response.Write("OR try again: ");
      Response.Write("What is the capital of " );
      Response.Write(correctstate+"?<br>");
      Response.Write("<form action='miniquizcheck.asp'");
      Response.Write(" method='get'>\n");
      Response.Write("<input type='text' ");
      Response.Write("name='capital'><br>\n");
      Response.Write("<input type='hidden' ");
      Response.Write(" name='which' value="+which+">\n");
```

```
        Response.Write("<input type='hidden' ");
        Response.Write("name='choice' ");
        Response.Write(" value="+choice+">\n");
        Response.Write("<input type='submit' ");
        Response.Write("value='Submit Answer'>");
        Response.Write("</form>\n");
      }
    }
  else
    {
    var state=Request.QueryString("state");
    if (state == correctstate)
      {
      Response.Write("Correct! ");
      Response.Write("The capital of ");
      Response.Write(correctstate);
      Response.write(" is "+correctcapital+"!");
      saywhich='false';
      Response.Write("<p><a href='miniquizask.asp'>");
      Response.Write("Play again </a>");
      }
    else
      {
      Response.Write("WRONG!<p>\n");
      Response.Write("<a href='miniquizask.asp'>");
      Response.Write("New turn </a><p>\n");
      Response.Write("OR try again: ");
      Response.Write(correctcapital);
      Response.Write(" is the capital of what ");
      Response.Write("state?<br>");
      Response.Write(
          "<form action='miniquizcheck.asp'");
      Response.Write(" method='get'>\n");
      Response.Write("<input type='text'");
      Response.Write(" name='state'><br>\n");
      Response.Write("<input type='hidden' ");
      Response.Write("name='which' value="+which+">\n");
      Response.Write("<input type='hidden' ");
      Response.Write("name='choice' ");
      Response.Write("value="+choice+">\n");
      Response.Write("<input type='submit' ");
      Response.Write(" value='Submit Answer'>");
      Response.Write("</form>\n");
      }
  }
%>
</body>
</html>
```

Again, look the code over and compare to the outline. In this case, it is again the nested ifs, the outermost if referring to the choice of question, and the inner ifs, in both cases, corresponding to right and wrong answers.

The last file to display, which, again, we will do only partially, is *statecapitals. asp*:

```
<%
var states = new Array();
var capitals= new Array();
states[0]='Alabama'; capitals[0]='Montgomery';
states[1]='Alaska'; capitals[1]='Juneau';
states[2]='Arizona'; capitals[2]='Phoenix';
```

Notice that JavaScript forced the slightly more complex syntax: it was necessary to put in the array element numbers explicitly. The PHP syntax allowed saying $states[] = ... to get the next element. In case you, the reader, are feeling sorry for the typist, please be aware that XML and XSLT scripts were used to generate these files. Consequently, the states and capitals were only typed once, and two different XSLT scripts were used to generate the PHP and the ASP files.

The ASP system distinguishes between form data submitted via the query string:

```
Request.Querystring("   ");
```

and form data submitted via the HTTP headers.

```
Request.Form("    ");
```

The query string is what is used by the get method or by forming your own query string in an <a> tag. (This technique will be used in the origami store example.) The HTTP header is used by the put method. However, you can "get away with" just using:

```
... Request("   ");
```

which will work in either case. This is considered somewhat less secure, because a knowledgeable hacker could create a call with its own query string and trick your program. The PHP system also has long forms versus short forms for this same reason. Consider yourself warned.

The most obvious type of error you could have in a project such as the state capital quiz is to make a typo in the spelling of a state or a capital. The system does not help you here, and because of the random feature, it might be a long time before you or a player lets you know. In professional situations, it often is the practice to replace the random element with other code for some of the testing so that all options are taken to be checked.

REFLECTION

The code fragments and the mini-quiz examples begin to show you what is possible with server-side scripting. You also saw scripts that served as their own form handlers. You also could compare an ASP/JavaScript and a PHP project. The script outlines worked for both projects, an example of how design can be independent of implementation details.

Just as the last chapter demonstrated a need to place information on the server, the quiz example, with the data file to be included in each script, should make you see a need for something to handle more complex information. In the next chapter, you will have a break from PHP and ASP coding, to read about database and application design.

EXERCISES, QUESTIONS, AND PROJECTS

1. Define and describe the following terms: *server-side*, *delimiters*, *objects*, *methods*, *collections*, and *arrays*.
2. Go online and find sources for ASP, PHP, and JavaScript. These sources can complement your reading of this text.
3. Describe the role of the following HTML constructs: the action attribute in a form tag, a type of hidden in an input tag, a type of submit in an input tag, a type of reset in an input tag, method equal "get" versus method equal "put" in a form tag.
4. What do the following ASP/JavaScript constructs do (what is the PHP counterpart)? `Request.Querystring`, `Response.Write`, `+` (the plus sign), `<%...%>`.
5. What do the following PHP constructs do (what is the ASP/JavaScript counterpart)? echo, . (period or dot), <?php ... ?>, `print`.
6. Using JavaScript, assuming a variable named cost holds the price of an item, and assuming a variable named `discount` holds either 'yes' or 'no', write the code that resets (use an `assignment` statement) cost to 85% of its current value if the `discount` variable is equal to 'yes'.
7. Write the PHP version of the previous problem (hint: pay attention to the names of the variables).
8. Create your own fact guessing game. You would use the same structure as the state capitals, but insert different paired facts in the two arrays and different prompting messages.
9. Add a third type of question to the state/capital games; specifically, use the shape of each state. You need to locate images representing the shape of the states, without the name of the state or any city. The answer to a shape question would be the state name. You will need to create a third array with element values the names of the image files, *or* you can dynamically construct the names of files using the state name concatenated with ".gif" if indeed the files are all of type .gif. Otherwise, use whatever the file type is. Remember, you can put any HTML within the <form...> and </form> tags.

10. Create a "number facts" game. Use the random feature to select two integers, and ask the player to add or multiply. The handler program will perform this same operation and compare to what the player has entered.
11. Add scoring keeping to the state/capitals or another game. This would be a task for cookies, which will be described later, but you can simulate the function of cookies by passing along as a hidden variable the score.

5

DATABASE BASICS

The purpose of this chapter is to introduce the basic concepts underlying databases, including entity-relationship diagrams, a technique for representing the structure of a database and normalization, and a technique for refining a database design.

BACKGROUND

The term *database* might have a generic meaning as any organized collection of information, but in computing, *database* usually refers to relational databases. This is a very specific way of organizing data; namely, using tables, records and fields, with support for the Structured Query Language, SQL. *Database management systems*, DBMS, is the term for any product that supports this standard way of organizing data. The Microsoft Access product and the open-source MySQL software are each examples of a DBMS.

Database design is part of what is termed *information design* or *modeling*. It takes place before or concurrently with focus on the processes of an application. Process design is the topic for the next chapter. Database design done in the early or analysis phase is also called *logical* design. The actual design is then called *physical* design. During the physical design phase, you must specify the data types and sizes of the fields. You can be somewhat product independent here, but it might make more sense to do this in the context of a specific product.

Database design can be independent of any particular application. Historically, the move to databases as replacements for unstructured files came about when people in organizations realized that many applications made use of the same information. The cost and benefit of the database thus can be amortized over several applications. This point is easier to say than to implement in practice, since it means that different departments in an organization need to work together to design and implement the database.

This chapter is about database concepts. The concepts apply to Access and to MySQL; they are independent of ASP/JavaScript and PHP. In a later chapter, you will read about SQL statements, called *queries*, and, hopefully, compose queries. In subsequent chapters, you will learn how to program the composition of an SQL query in ASP/JavaScript and PHP, and how to pass on these queries to Access and MySQL systems on the server and how to receive information back.

CONCEPTUAL EXPLANATION

A standard database consists of one or more *tables*. Tables hold *records*. Records are made up of *fields*, also called *attributes*. If you visualize a table in terms of rows and columns, the records are the rows and the columns are the fields. To use nontechnical language, each record defines one thing, with each field in the record holding a different attribute of that thing. Each table holds records of a single type, and each record has the same set of attributes. In databases incorporating more than one table, an attribute of records in one table might consist of pointers to records in another table. The technical, all-encompassing term for thing or type is *entity*. An entity can correspond to a physical object or an abstraction with meaning within the organization. The technical term for the situation in which attributes in records in one table refer to records in another table is *relationship*.

Entity Relationship (ER) diagrams are ways to plan and to document databases. The boxes hold information on the fields making up the records in each table. The lines connecting the boxes represent relationships between tables. Marks and numbers on the connecting lines indicate what is called the *cardinalities* of the relationship. These are the minimum and the maximum number of records in the table at one end for each record in the table at the other end. In most cases, the counts are 0, 1, or many.

Normalization is a process by which a systems designer examines and, possibly, modifies a design. You will read later about the requirements for a database design to be in first, second, and third normal form.

EXAMPLES

To make these concepts more understandable, let us go through the thinking process in designing databases for a very simple mail-order business, a slightly more complex one, and a set of college courses. Database design is not automatic and obvious, unlike the impression given in textbooks. It generally is an iterative process.

Simple Mail-Order Business

The business for this example sells a set of products described in a catalog. Since most of the business is repeat business, the organization maintains a list of its customers. Customers order products, one at a time, although a customer can have more than one order in the system. The orders can be in different stages: ordered, backorder, in-transit, arrived but unpaid for, and complete. The stage will be called the *status*. The company wants to keep information on orders around for a long time, perhaps purging them based on the date, so the date is an attribute of an order. The product is shipped to an address the customer has specified, and the bill is handled in a way the customer has specified. In the example, we will not go into the internal details of the shipping or the billing information. These two items of information are part of the customer record. You, the reader, should realize that the description just given for the business could have been different. Billing and/or shipping information should be kept with each order if it is subject to change with each order. Some businesses might not keep a record of customers. The specifications for the particular case help you design the database for that situation.

With the business information in mind, the systems designer decides the following plan. The database will consist of three tables: customers, catalog, and orders. Records in each table will be assigned identification numbers; that is, values that are unique for each record in the table. When you use a DBMS, you typically specify a field as the primary key, the unique identifier for the record. You can let the system assign these values, or you can input them. So-cial security numbers or driver's license identification numbers could be used for primary keys, but that is not the approach chosen here. In some cases, two or more fields jointly represent the primary key, and you will read about an example of that situation later in this section.

The customers table holds a record for each customer. A customer record consists of the following fields:

- Customer identifier
- Customer name
- Customer billing information
- Customer shipping information

The catalog table holds a record for each product. We could have used the name "products" for this table, but since the term *catalog* connotes something that probably exists at the company, we use it instead. A product record holds the following fields:

- Product identifier
- Product name
- Product cost
- Product category
- Product description

The orders table holds information on customer orders. Note that in this system, an order refers to a single product. A customer order consists of the fol-lowing fields:

- Order identifier
- Product identifier for product ordered
- Customer identifier for the customer making this order
- Date
- Quantity
- Status

The long names for the fields are not typical, but are meant to help you, the reader, understand this example. You probably can infer from the names what data type is indicated. The names are short to medium length character strings; the description and the billing information and shipping information probably require more space. The date is a date, and the cost is given in the currency used by the company. The first two tables are independent of each other. The orders table is different. The product identifier in the product or-dered field in the orders table identifies a product. Think of this as a pointer into the catalog table that indicates what product was ordered. Similarly, the customer identifier for the customer making this order indicates the customer by identifier, not by name. The status field in the orders table could be a number, a code, or a description.

The diagram in Figure 5.1 is an entity-relationship diagram for the orders database. The blocks are the entities, and the connecting lines indicate the relationships.

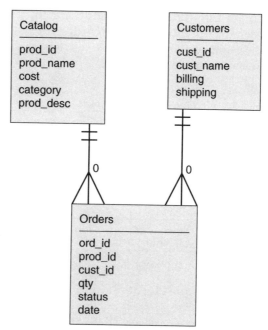

FIGURE 5.1   Entity-relationship diagram for simple orders.

The names here are fairly arbitrary. Notice that the name of the attribute representing the product id in the orders table is the same as the name in the product table. This is not necessary. However, what is necessary for there to be a relationship between two tables is for a field in the records in one table to refer to records in another table using values that correspond to the primary key.

In the simple mail-order company situation, the diagram indicates that there are three tables; the catalog and customers tables have no relationship to each other. However, each of these two tables is related to the orders table. Each order is for one and only one customer, indicated by the two short horizontal lines near the customer table. This says that the minimum is one and the maximum is one. Similarly, each order is for one and only one product in the catalog table. In contrast, each product can be the subject to zero or one or many orders. This is indicated by the crow's foot type of symbol with a zero next to it. The crow's foot indicates many. The same set of symbols is on the line connecting the orders and customers table. How can it be that a customer is responsible for zero orders? The answer is that the business might keep customers in the database even if they never order, or if they did order something at one time and those orders were purged.

Sample Data

To make this example less abstract, Tables 5.1, 5.2, and 5.3 show the fields in three representative tables, capturing the database when there four products, two customers, and five orders. The data is not too realistic, but it should give you an idea of what data in tables can be.

TABLE 5.1   Catalog (Product) Records

PROD_ID	PROD_NAME	COST	CATEGORY	PROD_DESC
1	Bird	2.50	Animal	Flapping bird
2	Crane	3.00	Animal	Traditional crane
3	Box	1.00	Box	Magazine cover box
4	Ornament	2.00	Modular	6-part preliminary bas

TABLE 5.2   Customer Records

CUST_ID	CUST_NAME	BILLING	SHIPPING
1	John Smith	cash	123 Main Street NY, NY 12345
2	Mary Jones	Mastercard XX	10 Elm Street, apt 23 Town, State 11111

TABLE 5.3   Order Records

ORD_ID	PROD_ID	CUST_ID	QTY	DATE	STATUS
1	3	2	5	Sept 23, 2002	Shipped
2	1	2	3	Sept 23, 2002	Backordered
3	2	1	3	Sept 24, 2002	Shipped
4	1	1	4	Sept 24, 2002	Backordered
5	4	2	1	Sept 25, 2002	Shipped

A real database would split up the name into first, last, and middle names, and the address into street number and street, optional apartment, town, state, and zip code. Many Web businesses need provision for addresses out of the United States, so the shipping fields can be quite extensive.

By making use of the information in all three tables, you can derive several facts. For example, Mary Jones has made three orders, two on September 23 and one on September 25. The early orders were for five boxes and three birds; the later order was for one ornament. John Smith has ordered three cranes and four birds on September 24. The crane orders are both on backorder. All other orders, all three of them, have been shipped. The prod_id and the cust_id fields in the orders table are called *foreign keys*. This is because they refer to primary keys in other tables.

At this point, you, the reader, should do the following exercises: make up a new customer, a new product, and two or three new orders. Make one of the new orders refer to one of the original customers and products, and the other new orders refer to the new customer and/or the new product.

Normalization

The example database design for the mail-order company satisfies the conditions shown in Table 5.4.

TABLE 5.4   Normalization Conditions

Each field in each table consists of exactly one value, and that value is dependent on the primary key
Each field in each table is dependent on the whole primary key
Each field in each table is dependent on nothing but the primary key

Any database design satisfying the first condition is said to be in *first* normal form; if it satisfies the first and second condition, it is in *second* normal form, and if it satisfies all three of these conditions in *third* normal form. The critical term in the second condition is the *whole* key. This is significant when a primary key is a concatenated key. An example of this will be described later in the chapter. Databases in third normal form are more robust with respect to changes. To demonstrate this, a more complex situation will be described later.

The design and the tables for the mail-order example demonstrate something fundamental about databases with relationships. If you were to remove records in one table, records in another table might point to nonexistent entries. That is, if you remove a product, then all the orders that make reference to that product have meaningless fields. This means that the application must have procedures for deleting records that check for these situations.

Each of the tables in the mail-order example had as a primary key a number that would be produced by the system. Presumably, the DBMS generates unique numbers for each table. This is a common situation, but it is not the only way to get unique values for primary keys. The data in an application can have its own inherent identifier. For example, social security numbers, driver's license numbers, and passport numbers each exist independent of any computer application. You need to decide what is best for your project.

Physical Database Design

Moving from logical database design to physical database design means that you must plan the implementation. This includes deciding on what aspects of your application are to be computer based and what are to be manual. You need to decide whether you will use databases or files or a combination thereof. You need to specify the nature and size of the fields. Computing systems refer to this as the *datatype*. In this example, all the id fields are whole numbers to be assigned sequentially by the database management system. Most DBMS do have the facility to do this. The qty field is also a whole number, but not one generated automatically. The cost field would be described as currency, or numbers with two decimal points.

Most DBMS systems have a datatype called Date. Unfortunately, ASP/ JavaScript, Access, MySQL, and PHP have different formats for dates, but we will tackle this problem later.

The product name, product description, shipping, address, and customer name fields are each of the datatypes called *character string* or *string* or *text*. You will need to specify how big to make these fields. You need to weigh the costs in storage space of providing too much room with the danger of having a problem situation if someone comes in with a really long name. Do remember, however, that while you might not be able to control the names of your customers or the size of their addresses, you can control the size of product names and product descriptions.

More Complex Mail-Order Business

Suppose the mail-order store allowed customers to order more than one product at a time. Suppose also that the designer decided to put the cost of each product as part of the order. An order would be:

- Order id
- Customer id
- Any number of sets of product id, quantity, and cost
- Date

This definition of an order makes sense, but you can see how it would be awkward for a computer system to handle a situation in which the number of values for fields varies. A formal way of saying this is that the design for the more complex mail-order business does not satisfy the first normalization condition in Table 5.4. Certain fields have multiple values. It also does not satisfy the third condition, since the cost field is dependent on the quantity and the cost kept in the product record of the catalog table.

Normalization is a process. The first step in the process is to handle the multiple fields. This is done in a way typical of computing: divide large problems into smaller ones. In place of the single table for orders, define two tables: one for order information that refers to the whole order, and the order for order information that refers to each product ordered. To make this concrete, you can think of it as orders versus product_on_order or order_line. The two tables will be the following:

Orders
- Order id
- Customer id
- Status
- Date

Product_on_order
- Order id
- Product id
- Quantity
- Cost

The systems designer could choose to add a product_on_order id to the records. However, the two fields order_id and product_id together do uniquely identify the record and so could be the primary key. This is called a *concatenated* or *composite key*. The significance of the second normalization condition now becomes meaningful. If the product_on_order record contained fields such as the product name, then these fields would not be depend on the whole primary key, but just the product id part. If you did put the product names in the product_on_order records, you could have problems. If the name of a product changed, it would be necessary to change all the product_on_orders that mentioned it. The normalization process is to make modifications to make the design in first normal form, and then make modifications to make the design in second normal form.

Continuing with the normalization process, the next step is to consider the third condition in Table 5.4. Are all the fields in each table dependent only on the primary key field of the table? The cost field is suspect. The cost field is dependent on multiplying the quantity of product ordered with the cost per individual item stored back in the catalog table. It may be best to remove it, even though that means the cost for that portion of the order will need to be re-calculated each time. However, if costs are subject to changes and, therefore, considered dependent on orders as opposed to products, it could be appropriate to leave it or take the approach to define yet another table, called bills or invoices.

The underlying principle of database design is to store data in only one place so that you need to change it in only one place. If you have ever had problems dealing with an institution and thought you had settled something, like changing your address, but found that the institution was still using old information, the problem probably arose because of the same data being stored in more than one place.

The ER diagram for the new design is shown in Figure 5.2.

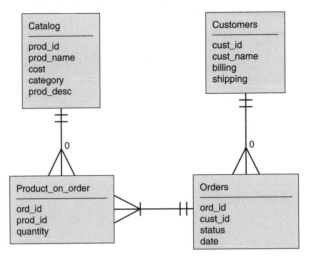

FIGURE 5.2   Entity relationship diagram for multiproduct orders.

The crow's foot symbol on the connecting line from product_on_order to orders indicates that each order has at least one product_on_order and potentially many product_on_order records. Each product_on_order relates to exactly one record in the catalog and exactly one record in the orders. If we had not split the orders information into two tables, then the ER diagram would have indicated what is called a *many-to-many relationship* between orders and the catalog table. Many-to-many relationships are to be changed into one-to-many relationships to ensure a well-defined database.

College Courses

The next example concerns courses at a college. Courses have course numbers, names, and descriptions. Courses might have prerequisites. Courses might be offered in more than one section. A section of a course has a section number, a location, a time, and a teacher. You can put the book down and make a sketch of the ER diagram for this situation.

Figure 5.3 shows a first draft of a design for part of a database for scheduling.

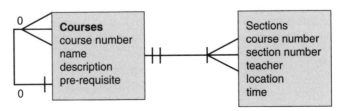

FIGURE 5.3   Entity-relationship diagram for courses.

The diagram indicates that each course has at least one section. This might not be true—some courses are not offered each term. In fact, this design does not indicate the semester offered. Think about why and how this should be changed.

The prerequisite fields define a relationship between the courses table and itself. Each course can have at most one specified prerequisite, in this design. However, courses can be the prerequisite for more than one course.

Tables 5.5 and 5.6 show representative data for a very small offering of courses.

TABLE 5.5   The Courses Table

COURSE NUMBER	NAME	DESCRIPTION	PREREQUISITE
CS101	Computer Basics	Introduction to computer information systems.	None
CS120	Programming Games	Introduction to programming focusing on creating games. Languages are JavaScript and Micromedia Flash ActionScript.	CS101
CS130	Computer Science I	Introduction to programming. Current language is C++.	CS101
MS130	Basic Math	Algebra. Probability.	None

TABLE 5.6   The Sections Table

COURSE NUMBER	SECTION NUMBER	TEACHER	TIME	LOCATION
CS101	01	Irina	MW 09-11	NS3001
CS101	02	Tim	TR 14-16	NS3001
CS120	01	Irina	M 18-22	NS1063
CS120	02	Cathy	TR 09-11	NS1063
CS130	01	Joel	T 18-22	NS1063
MS130	01	Jim	MTRF 10-11	NS2001

The primary key for the courses is the course number. It is assumed that there is some mechanism apart from the computer application for ensuring that these are unique. The course numbers shown are what are sometimes referred to as *coded numbers*. They actually are not numbers, but number and letter combinations with both the letters and the numbers having meaning. The letters indicate department, and the numbers, the level. This fragment does not show any 200 or 300 level courses, but presumably there are some. The primary key for the sections table is a concatenated key: the course number and the section number combined. Some institutions would have some coding in the sections numbers indicating evening or weekend sections. You should know that some database professionals argue against such coding because it carries information that tends not to be verified. This is something to think about when you have the task of analyzing and building an application.

The design decisions indicated previously might not be satisfactory for some situations. What if a course required more than one prerequisite? What if the college administration wanted to define different situations regarding the prerequisites; for example, certain prerequisites could be waived with the permission of the instructor (POI); others could be satisfied by a test? When you have discussions with your client to define the implementation of a computer system, you might find yourself in the middle of the formulation of policy. The issues hinted at here seem to indicate that the design should have another table holding prerequisite conditions. A prerequisite record would point to one course as the one that requires another course, and one course as the required course. The prerequisite record would also have a condition field. Figure 5.4 shows the entity-relationship diagram for the application supporting courses and pre-requisites.

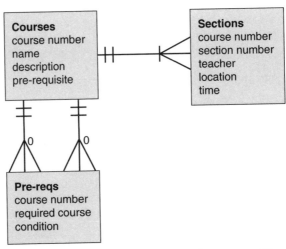

FIGURE 5.4   Entity-relationship diagram for courses with prerequisites.

The diagram in Figure 5.4 indicates that there are two relationships between the pre-reqs table and the course table. This comes about because there are two fields in the pre-reqs table pointing to the course table: one field for the course requiring another course, and the other field for the specification of the required course. If a pre-req record exists, it will have an entry in each of these fields. This is indicated by the two short horizontal lines. The crow's feet and zeros indicate that any course might be present in zero, one, or more pre-reqs records in either the course requiring or the course required position. Table 5.7 shows a sampling of entries for prerequisites.

TABLE 5.7   Prerequisite Table

PRE-REQ ID	COURSE NUMBER	REQUIRED COURSE	CONDITION
1	CS120	CS101	POI
2	CS130	CS101	POI
3	CS130	MA130	POI or test

In this example, the CS120 course has one prerequisite, and the CS130 course has two prerequisites. The courses table would not have the prerequisite field. To determine if a course had any prerequisites, the application would need to search the prerequisite table.

REFLECTION

Database development should be a methodical process involving discussion with your clients, assuming you are the systems analyst and designer. Complex situations will be more difficult than simple ones, and some databases are very complex. It is also true that your client might not have thought about many of the issues that make a difference in the design. The analysis stage is for defining requirements, and the design stage is for generating the plans for building the system.

The concepts you learn by reading this text and the experience you gain by implementing and enhancing the examples will serve you if and when you choose to use other DBMS products, because they all follow the same SQL standards. The reasons to seek out other products (Oracle, SQL Server, DB2, etc.) generally involve issues of scale. The more expensive products generally provide support for managing what are termed *transactions* and handling system outages and recoveries. Transactions are combinations of database operations that need to be considered as a unit in terms of blocking out other access to the database. System outages do happen, and building a robust system means that you need to have procedures for recovery.

Another technology coming into widespread use for storing and handling data is XML, or eXtensible Markup Language. In XML, individuals or groups of people define their own tags. Like HTML, tags have names and attributes and can contain other tags. The nesting is strict: a child tag has to be totally contained in its parent tag. You will need to decide if the content and the functions of your application are suited to the tables and relationships of standard databases, or to the tree-like structure of XML, or both. Independent vendors and the DBMS vendors are offering products that support XML and traditional databases, now called *structured databases*.

EXERCISES, QUESTIONS, AND PROJECTS

1. Start over or add entries to the tables in the preceding examples. As you are doing so, tell yourself what the entries represent.

2. Modify the mail-order example to store shipping information with each order. Shipping information consists of an address and shipping costs.

3. Modify the mail-order example to allow some products to be backordered and some not. This means that both the order and the product_on_order records would contain a status field. It would be appropriate to have an additional field with an expected date for backordered items. This field would sometimes be blank. This does not contradict the goal of having exactly one value for each field; it just means that sometimes the field is not used.

4. Building on the course, section, and prerequisite example, design a database to handle scheduling of courses at a college. You will need tables for courses, sections of courses, prerequisites, and faculty. Consider also that sections are scheduled for rooms or labs or sometimes both. This means that you will probably need a locations table.

5. Design a database for student records. You can build on the scheduling example. You will need tables for student information and student enrollment in a course. This latter table would contain the course grade.

6. Define a database for a library. A library has books, magazines, and other media in stock. More specifically, a library generally has multiple copies of most of its items. This means that your design would involve a table that could be called catalog that holds one record for each title, and another table for all holdings that has one record for each book, CD, and so on. The record for a book would point to the record for its title. The holdings records each indicate that location of the item. A library also has a table for each library cardholder. You need to define how to connect items on loan with the library cardholder who has checked the item out.

7. Define a database for a quiz show. This is in preparation for one of the main examples in later chapters. You will need tables for questions and contestants. In addition, as with the library example, you will need a table, call it history, that indicates what questions were asked by what contestant.

6

ANALYSIS AND DESIGN OF APPLICATIONS

Т   he purpose of this chapter is to introduce the use of process diagrams and
           storyboards. Together with entity-relationship diagrams, described in the
           previous chapter, they constitute modeling tools for the planning and
the documentation of applications.

BACKGROUND

A criticism often made of technical people is that they rush to implement an
application before truly understanding what the requirements are. Furthermore, they are accused of wanting to use technologies independent of whether
or not these technologies serve the function of the application. Whether or not
these accusations are true, it makes sense to understand what an application is
supposed to do in a way that does not involve the implementation. The process
of analyzing the problem is called *systems analysis*. Systems design is when the
decisions are made regarding technologies and products, and when the systems analysts prepare directions for the system builders. The analysis and design stages are characterized by the building of models. Different
methodologies exist for the model making. See the *Reflection* section for a brief
description of object modeling. Along with the various methodologies, many
software products exist for systems analysis and design. This chapter provides
an introduction to a very large topic.

CONCEPTUAL EXPLANATION

Entity-relationship diagrams are used to define the information in a system.
Making such diagrams is called *information modeling*, and was the focus of the
last chapter. In this chapter, the focus is on what happens and at whose insti-
gation. This is called *process modeling*. Since the process diagrams indicate the
flow of data, they are also called *data flow diagrams*.

You can elaborate on process models to use for the design stage. As an alternative, this chapter will explain storyboard diagrams. Storyboard diagrams
specify implementation details, mainly the files (scripts) for the application.
The ER, process, and storyboard diagrams are complementary ways to document your application. This documentation is especially useful when it comes
time to change the application, either to fix a problem or address a new opportunity.

Logical Design

The goal of logical design is to specify the functions of the application. What
does it do? Process diagramming is a tool for doing this.

Process diagrams focuses on three things, the three symbol types in a
process diagram.

- Agents
- Processes
- Data stores

Agents can refer to the people, described by their roles in the business, that invoke particular tasks in the application. An agent can be the system itself. This is appropriate for something like a time-based operation when "the system" initiates action such as sending out bills or purging old records. *Processes* refer to tasks, or, rather, the parts of the application that implement tasks. The term *data store* is intended to be a technology-independent term referring to information required by the application. A data store might turn out to be a table in a database, but it might be more or less complex. It could be a card file on someone's desk, or a set of form letters on someone's computer, or a set of charts mounted on the wall.

Process diagrams make use of distinct symbols for agents, processes, and data stores, with arrows indicating the flow of data. In this text, rectangles that are close to being squares stand for agents, rectangles with rounded corners stand for processes, and long rectangles with a double bar on one side stand for data stores. Arrows will be one- or two-headed.

Developing a process diagram requires you, the systems designer, to think about your users; in particular, to give the users meaningful names. You need to determine what tasks are invoked by what people in what situations. For the simple mail-order business described in the last chapter, we can assume that the following agents use the application involving the database:

- An order-taker enters the information on (new) customers and orders.
- A clerk in the product department adds, edits, and removes the product records in the catalog table.
- A shipping clerk uses the information in the database to pack up the orders and ship them out using the shipping method of choice.
- An agent to be called "the system" because the process it invokes is automated; namely, a process that purges all completed orders over a year old from the system invoked according to a preset time schedule. The process might generate a report on noncompleted orders more than 90 days old over to be handled by a special (manual) process.

Creating a process design is an iterative process in which a process at one level can be expanded to be multiple processes at another level. Consider the process diagram shown in Figure 6.1.

Notice that this diagram is to convey the logic of the application. It is done prior to building the application. As such, it shows one data store called *orders*. As you probably recall from the last chapter, it might turn out that the normalization conditions and the requirements for most database products require the use of two tables. The ship methods data store probably will turn out to refer to a piece of paper posted by the shipping clerks' desks indicating the schedule for

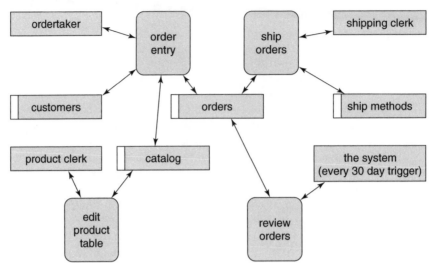

FIGURE 6.1   Process diagram for ordering system.

UPS and FedEx. The ship methods data store is not connected to a process that creates or modifies the data.

The methodology of process diagrams requires that agents are connected to process symbols, and process symbols have connections to data stores. An agent symbol is never connected directly to a data store because the methodology requires that you specify what process does the task. The direction of the arrows indicates reading or writing. Double-headed arrows indicate read and write action. If there is a data store that is never read, but only written, then the system as presented is lacking a function to make the data store meaningful. That might be okay, since all of the system might not be defined, but it is a signal to review what you intended. A data store that is written to but never read is called a *black hole*. A data store that is read, but not written to, is called a *miracle*.

Going over the connections is a way of checking out for yourself, and for the systems owners, if you have specified the functions desired. For example, an order taker invokes the order entry process. This process uses information from the catalog and uses and makes changes in the form of additions to the customer and the order data store. The double-headed arrows concerning the ship order process and the orders data store indicate that this operation does change the orders. This is correct because the act of shipping an order requires the status field to be changed.

Notice that a systems designer could have defined another process: adding or changing the customer data store. The diagram in Figure 6.1 assumes that is part of order entry.

The process diagram gives you a graphical prop for an analysis of the system requirements. You can use it by yourself or as part of a discussion with colleagues.

As indicated previously, another name for process diagrams is *data flow diagrams*. The arrows indicate the flow of information. Some of the information is generated by the process; other information comes from the agents or the data store with little modification from the process. Information flows from agents to processes, which, in turn, store the information "as-is" into data stores or make calculations and store the resulting information into data stores. Going the other way, processes extract information from data stores and present it to agents.

One thing the process/data flow diagram does not do is indicate the flow of goods. Even though this application is intended to support a mail-order business, there is no arrow representing the flow of goods from a warehouse to a customer. This flow of goods can be considered a side effect of the information processing system and not what the diagram is intended to represent.

Physical Design

After the analysis of the application—that is, the gathering of the requirements, and the logical design—the next step is to build the system! This does not mean to jump immediately to coding, but to make implementation decisions and plan. Assuming that you still are the one in charge, you will need to determine how the processes are to be implemented and what technology is to be used for the data stores. You will need to specify the processes at a greater level of detail than the simple functional statement in the process diagrams shown so far. The processes generally turn out to be programs or, using our terminology, scripts holding combinations of HTML, JavaScript, PHP, and ASP. The data stores might turn out to be tables of databases.

In many situations, you will be designing an application that makes use of databases in existence already in the organization. For the cases when the databases do not exist, you will use entity-relationship diagrams to design them. Although some professionals insist on always starting with the ER diagrams for information modeling, and others insist on starting with the process modeling (and still others on object modeling), a balanced approach, fit to the problem, is what is recommended here. You will go back and forth. You will even (gasp!) occasionally find it necessary to go back and change the logical diagrams because of something that occurs to you during programming or testing. You can continue to use process diagrams, expanding the ones you already have made by dividing processes into smaller tasks. Alternatively, you can turn to other techniques such as storyboards.

The last diagramming technique is called *storyboard* and belongs to the building stages and not the analysis and planning stages. A storyboard contains rectangle symbols for files, also called *scripts*, and arrows representing the situations of a file calling a file. An arrow that represents one file invoking another file to handle a form will be a thick arrow. An arrow indicating a hyperlink in one file to another file will be a thin arrow. This format is inspired by the use of storyboards for multimedia applications, which borrowed storyboards from film and animation. However, the different form of arrows is our own. You can use this format or use your own design for your application.

The storyboards for multimedia applications would contain descriptions of any audio, screen shots of video, and clips of graphics. That type of information is not that critical to the applications here. However, you should enhance the simple storyboard techniques shown here to include what is important to you. For example, you might indicate situations when what the person sees at the client computer is the display of a customized HTML file with images specified by filenames from a database.

The diagram in Figure 6.2 is a storyboard for the state capital quiz application described in the previous chapter.

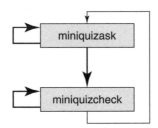

FIGURE 6.2   Storyboard for state capital quiz.

The storyboard visually provides the following facts about this application: there are two scripts. These two scripts contain three forms, indicated by three form action arrows. Each of the two scripts contains directives specifying themselves as the action for forms. The miniquizask script specifies the miniquizcheck script as the form handler for a third form. The miniquizcheck has a link to miniquizask to start the process over again. This visual story "told" by the diagram is a critical benefit of creating storyboards. You will use them before, during, and after the programming stage of your projects. We will return to this example and make an addition in the next section.

EXAMPLES

The act of modeling an application using any methodology is not trivial. Software packages help you produce the symbols, but do not do the task of planning the application. Do not be concerned if you do not immediately know what to write. Whole courses and substantial textbooks are devoted to the systems analysis and systems design process. Techniques include study of the artifacts of any existing system, such as reports and input forms, and structured interviews with the people who will use the system.

State Capital Quiz Logical Design

In the last section, you read about an application involving orders. Let us now apply the same thought process to the state capital quiz, but we will step back before the quiz application was made. Note that this example was called a "mini" quiz because the data for the questions and answers was contained in a file as opposed to a database. The models that will emerge here will not indicate that characteristic.

Who are the potential agents for the mini-quiz?

• The person taking the quiz. An appropriate name for this agent/person is "player."
• The person creating the questions and answers. The name for this agent is more problematical. Let us call him or her the editor for now.

The qualifier "potential" is a hint to you that we are hedging our comments.

What are the data stores for the quiz?

• The set of questions and answers, namely the state and capital pairs.

What are the processes for the mini-quiz?

• Taking the quiz
• Preparing the questions

The process diagram based on this information is shown in Figure 6.3.

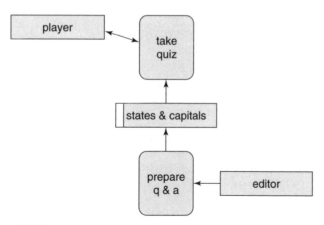

FIGURE 6.3   Process diagram for state capitals quiz.

State Capital Quiz Physical Design

This is the process diagram for the mini-quiz application on state capitals. However, let us now continue by moving from analysis to design. At this point, the systems analyst decides that the preparation and editing of the questions and answers will not be part of the application; that is, not be part of the application after the initial deployment. This does make sense since the set of states is fixed and, if it does change, it tends to be a slow process. The states/capitals data store will be implemented using two parallel arrays, stored in the code. It will be a static data store—no facilities for changes.

Continuing with the "planning out loud" of the implementation, the next step could be to expand the "take quiz" process. It could be appropriate to go straight to defining the scripts and recording those decisions in a storyboard. However, elaborating on the process diagram will reveal aspects of process diagrams that are important to understand.

The first step is to split the take quiz process into three tasks:

- Indicate the choice of question
- Be asked the question
- Answer and have the question checked

Figure 6.4 is a first guess at a new, more detailed process diagram. It has flaws, which will be explained.

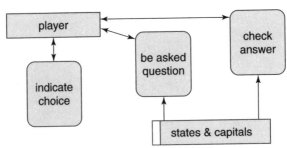

FIGURE 6.4   First draft of process diagram for state capital quiz.

What is missing? The *indicate choice* process actually stores the player's choice (state or capital), and this needs to be stored somewhere. Similarly, the specific question chosen needs to be stored so that the check answer process knows how to check the answer. These are not large amounts of data, but what often is called *state variables*. However, the process diagram methodology is intended to capture this information. An aspect of the application that process diagrams do not convey is the sequence of steps. Another way to say this is that a process diagram does not show time or timing. For completeness sake, Figure 6.5 shows a correct version of the process diagram.

You might ask, "is it necessary to indicate all variables in data stores to make a proper process diagram?" The answer is "no," just the ones that are shared between processes. You might now see that at some point, it might be appropriate to move from the planning stage supported by process diagrams to the implementation design stage supported by storyboards.

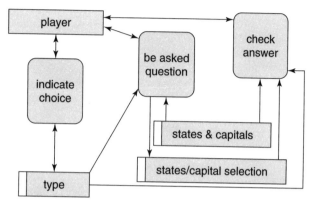

FIGURE 6.5   Process diagram for state capital quiz.

Before continuing with the state capital example, consider the following general ideas. For implementation, you need to decide on the definition of scripts. The process diagram does not make those decisions for you. It might even be appropriate to combine processes into one script. However, a rule-of-thumb in programming is to "divide and conquer." Several smaller programs can be easier to develop and debug than one large program. Note that in contrast to the divide and conquer approach, it is a common practice for a single PHP or ASP script to both display a form and handle the form as specified by the action attribute in the form tag. In the implementation of the state capitals, and the other examples in this text, there will be some "self" handling of forms. The benefit of making one file do both tasks is to put everything in one place and to cut down on the number of files. The disadvantage is that these files are more complex. The examples in this text use a mixture of the two techniques.

Putting everything in one script does not cut down on requests to and responses from the server. The form action specified as the same script still necessitates a call to the server for the PHP or ASP file. The file is interpreted on the server and a new HTML file is sent to the client.

The mini-quiz storyboard given in the previous section reveals the "self" handling of forms. Moreover, the storyboard indicates the sequence of events. It indicates the link from miniquizcheck back to miniquizask. The diagram did not indicate that both the scripts, for either the PHP or ASP implementation, made use of the facility for including files. The fact that the statements setting up the states and capitals array are in separate files does not change the logic of the programming. Putting the array statements in a separate file would probably be a late decision. To make your documentation complete, you can use Figure 6.6 as a model.

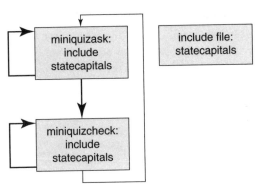

FIGURE 6.6   Storyboard for state capitals quiz, showing included file.

The reason for putting the words *include* and *included* in the diagram is to show how the file is connected to the minequizask and miniquizcheck. When projects contain scripts that have no connection, the storyboard would indicate that by the absence of connecting arrows. If you do build a quiz application with facilities for editing questions, the script or scripts for the editing will not be connected to the scripts for asking and checking questions.

More process diagrams and storyboards will be shown for later examples. Go to the *Exercise* section for practice.

REFLECTION

Complex systems require extensive planning and documentation. It is difficult for authors and teachers to convey this with typical book projects. In addition to the fact that a book project tends to be small, there are two other artificial aspects of book projects.

- The project is more or less defined for you. You do not have to deal with people or understand the history of any organization.
- You are your own systems analyst, systems designer, interface designer, programmer, database designer, database administrator, and so on.

Imagine if these conditions did not hold. You could not jump into programming, but would have to spend time on planning!

If you did do formal systems analysis and design, you probably would make use of computer-aided software engineering software to build and present your ideas. If you were working in a large organization, you would need to master the intricacies of the existing applications. During the design stage, you would need to make one or more "make or buy" (also known as outsource) decisions. In the particular area of Web development, this might mean determining if you should use any Web services; that is, self-contained subsystems for specific functions. No matter what the implementation, you need to know what the application does before you attempt to build it.

An alternative methodology to be used in concert with entity relationship, process, or storyboard diagrams is object modeling. It is appropriate to spend a short amount of time on objects even though it is not the major thrust of this book. Objects are data and procedures packaged together. The procedures are called *methods*. Objects are instances of classes in the way that a variable holding a number can be viewed as an instance of the number data type. The close coupling of data and the procedures using the data has proven to be a useful way of organizing systems.

Many programming languages are "object oriented" or have object-oriented features. There are purists who focus on how certain languages or systems succeed or fail to be object oriented for various reasons. There is possible value in such discussion, but the approach of this textbook is more easy going and practical. Client-side JavaScript uses something called the Document Object Model (DOM) to access and change the HTML document. ASP is a set of objects. This text will show server-side JavaScript making use of the ASP objects. The object-oriented syntax uses periods, such as:

```
Response.Write("<html>");
```

This statement invokes the `Write` method of the ASP `Response` object to send a string to the browser.

Object modeling, as distinct from object programming, is the technique to describe a system using the terminology of objects. The connecting arrows are calls to the methods of objects. Object-oriented systems have a feature called *inheritance*. A class can be defined as a subclass or child of another class. The child class inherits the properties and the methods of the parent class. This can be an efficient way to describe certain situations. For example, you can have an application in which some customers have a special status. These customers are treated the same way as regular customers in many situations, but not in all situations. The inheritance facility allows for a systematic way to reuse the common procedures.

The older way of modeling systems, namely entity-relationship and process diagrams along with the storyboard technique borrowed from multimedia seemed appropriate tools for the Web database applications described in this text.

EXERCISES, QUESTIONS, AND PROJECTS

1. For the library example for which you designed a database in Chapter 5, create a process diagram.
2. For the library example, using the process diagram created in the previous exercise, plan the implementation by producing a storyboard.

3. Create a process diagram for a credit card application. Agents could include sales clerks at establishments who "take" the credit card, clerks at the bank who process your payment, and the system that sends out bills. You might think of more or different agents. Would you, the card owner, be an agent for any process?

4. Create a process diagram for a buy-and-sale, people-to-people operation. How is this different from a store?

5. Create a process diagram for an auction. How is this different from the previous problem?

7

STRUCTURED QUERY LANGUAGE

T he purpose of this chapter is to explain the statements of the Structured Query Language (SQL), the programming language for database interactions.

BACKGROUND

SQL is the standard way for programs to access databases. This includes creating tables, adding records, modifying or deleting records, and reading records. Although there are differences in the implementation of SQL by the different products, those differences are relatively minor. An example is that Access refers to character strings as *TEXT*, and MySQL uses the term *CHAR*.

The PHP and ASP/JavaScript scripts that you write will access the databases by constructing character strings that represent SQL statements. The code will make use of information entered into HTML forms to produce the strings. Each of the two systems, PHP and ASP, provides ways to establish connections to the database management systems (DBMS) software on the server for processing of the SQL statements. After the statements are processed and, in many situations, return information, the PHP and ASP/JavaScript scripts use the information to produce the customized HTML files for the browser on the client computer to display. You will find it useful to distinguish between three areas of computation:

- HTML is interpreted by the browser on the client computer.
- The PHP and the ASP/JavaScript are interpreted by the PHP and ASP interpreters, on the server. Actually, it is possible to separate the ASP case into two: what is pure JavaScript, and what are ASP object methods and properties.
- The SQL statements are interpreted by the DBMS drivers, namely MS Access or MySQL. The DBMS is either on the server or a computer connected to the server.

Thus, your PHP and ASP scripts will contain parts that are to be interpreted right there, so to speak, by the PHP or ASP/JavaScript interpreter, or one of the other two places.

We cover the details of the connections to the database products and the intricacies of preparing the SQL statements in later chapters. This chapter will focus on what you can call "stand-alone" SQL statements—a worthy enough subject in its own right.

CONCEPTUAL EXPLANATION

In the terminology of SQL, everything is a query, even if the query does not ask what to us would be a question. Some queries potentially return a substantial amount of information in the form of what is termed a *recordset*, which is a dynamically constructed table of information. The qualifier "potentially" is used with the term *substantial* because the recordset might be empty. Other queries, such as one to create a table or to insert a record, return true or false indicating success or failure.

Recall that databases are made up of tables; tables are made up of records; and records are made up of fields. In this chapter, you will see examples of the basic SQL statements. There are many statements, with many variations. As is the case with most computer software, you can do useful work even if you do not know every variant of every statement or command.

SQL Statements

SQL has statements for creating databases and then creating the tables within the databases. The `create` statement requires you to specify the name, the datatype, and, optionally, other aspects of each field.

One field can be designated as being the primary key. This means two things to the DBMS—say, Access or MySQL. First, a field designated as a primary key must contain unique values. The system will signal an error and not allow a record to be added to the database if the primary key field has a value already in the database. The second point of significance about a primary key is that the system will create an index for it. This is an internal mechanism to speed access to the record using values for the index field. You can use the `create` statement to designate any field an index field. You do this if and only if your application will involve looking up records using that field a significant amount of time, because building an index costs something in terms of time and storage space.

Fields can be designated as required, meaning that any new record needs to have a value for the field. The definition of a field can include a directive for the DBMS to generate a value by incrementing an internal counter. This is a common setting for a primary field, but is not necessary. Your application might use what could be called a naturally occurring or intrinsic value for a primary key, such as a social security number. Fields that are not required do not have to be set when a new record is inserted into the database table.

SQL also has a command to alter the definition of a table. You can add new fields (called *columns* in some databases), add indexes, change or modify datatypes, and other operations. Use of the `alter` statement does require that you consider carefully what to do about the data already in the table.

The SQL `drop` statement is used to delete an entire table, something that you might decide to do during development. However, it is also something that could happen during normal operations. Some software has provisions for what are called *temporary* tables, and others require you to take care of the creation and deletion of the tables directly. You will see this in the quiz show projects.

Once the database tables are defined, it is time to add data. The SQL command for that is the `insert` statement. One variant of the `insert` statement allows you to specify a set of fields with a set of values. The variant that will be used here sets values for all of the fields defined for the table.

Databases typically are not static. The SQL statement to change the information in a database is update. The update statement allows you to change a field to a value specified using an expression, which could involve the original value of the field. The update statement can apply to this field for all the records or, more commonly, just certain records designated using a condition held in the where clause of the statement.

You can also change a database by deleting records. The SQL delete statement has clauses to specify which records are to be deleted and/or how many are to be deleted.

All the SQL queries mentioned so far perform some change to the database. The only value returned, assuming that SQL is used by a program, is a return code indicating if the operation performed successfully.

Just as databases typically are not static, they are also not intended to be "write only" fields. The SQL select statement is the vehicle for gathering information from the database. The SQL produces what is called a recordset. A recordset is like a table and like an array, but it is best thought of as having its own properties. Recordsets have rows and columns. A pointer indicates what row is the current row of a recordset. You will learn how to manipulate a recordset in subsequent chapters.

You can think of the select statement as being a mini-program all on its own. A select statement allows you to:

- Specify the fields from one or more tables. The use of more than one table is called a *join*, and you can indicate how this join operation is to be done using what is called the on clause or the where clause.
- Specify functions such as the sum, average, min, max, and count for the values of fields for all the records selected or by group.
- Group records by the value of a field using the group by clause. This provides a way to produce summary or aggregated information for specified groups.
- Order the result in regular (ascending) or descending order by one or more fields using order by or order by desc clauses.
- Specify which records using the where clause with one or more conditions. The conditions can involve field values from more than one table.
- Limit the number of records chosen. The limit clause can be used to specify the first N records, or it can be used for something like paging in which you specify a set of records starting at the P position for N more records.
- Designate a condition based on a calculation done after grouping using the having clause. This allows you to limit reports based on conditions calculated in terms of the summary functions.

Joins

Two types of join operations will be described in this text: the *simple* join and the *left* join. The simple join has other names. Explaining joins requires concrete examples; more follow in the *Examples* section of this chapter. Remember the database in Chapter 5, "Database Basics," with catalog, customers, and orders. Table 7.1 holds sample data for the catalog table; namely, product records. Table 7.2 holds data on customers. Table 7.3 holds orders.

TABLE 7.1   Catalog Records

PROD_ID	PROD_NAME	COST	CATEGORY	PROD_DESC
1	Bird	2.50	Animal	Flapping bird
2	Crane	3.00	Animal	Traditional crane
3	Box	1.00	Box	Magazine cover box
4	Ornament	2.00	Modular	Six-part preliminary bas

TABLE 7.2   Customer Records

CUST_ID	CUST_NAME	BILLING	SHIPPING
1	John Smith	cash	123 Main Street NY, NY 12345
2	Mary Jones	Mastercard XX	10 Elm Street, apt 23 Town, State 11111

TABLE 7.3   Orders

ORD_ID	PROD_ID	CUST_ID	QTY	DATE	STATUS
1	3	2	5	Sept 23, 2002	Shipped
2	1	2	3	Sept 23, 2002	Backordered
3	2	1	3	Sept 24, 2002	Shipped
4	1	1	4	Sept 24, 2002	Backordered
5	4	2	1	Sept 25, 2002	Shipped

Suppose you need to examine all the information on all orders by a customer with cust_id equal to 2. You could obtain this information by the following select statement:

```
SELECT * FROM orders WHERE cust_id=2
```

For this situation, you only need to look at the orders table. Before continuing with the explanation of join, please note that the where condition made use of a single equal sign (=) to test for equality. This is in contrast with what you will need to use to test for equality in PHP or JavaScript, where you need to use two equal signs together (==).

However, what if your question actually concerned the orders by Mary Jones, or, more realistically, the orders for each customer? You could perform the first task operation using two queries: one to the customer table to get Mary's cust_id, and the other to make the query against the orders table. To get this information for each customer, you could do multiple pairs of queries. However, the join facility allows you to do everything in one step. The task is to examine the customers table and the orders table together. Moreover, instead of joining every record (row) of the customer table with every record of the orders table, you will join "on" the records having the same value of the cust_id fields. The statement:

```
SELECT * FROM customer JOIN orders
ON customers.cust_id = orders.cust_id
```

produces the temporary set of records shown in Table 7.4.

If you do not want all of this, you can select just some of the fields. You might be especially annoyed by the presence of the cust_id field from the customer table, and then the same value again from the orders table, but this is what is there. The select statement to get the information with just the customer name and the order information is:

```
SELECT customer.cust_id, order_id, prod_id, qty, date,
status FROM customer JOIN orders ON customer.cust_id =
orders.order_id
```

You do not need to use the same name for the customer id field when you design the two tables. If you do, you must use the table name with a dot to "tell" the system which field you wanted in any case when it is ambiguous, even in cases such as this one when it does not matter because those two fields are the same. The table dot construction is called a *qualifier*. The qualifiers are not necessary for the other fields selected, although some professionals feel it is good practice to include them. SQL provides a mechanism for creating a shorthand:

```
SELECT c.cust_id, o.order_id, o.prod_id, o.qty, o.date,
o.status FROM customer as c JOIN orders as o
ON c.cust_id = o.cust_id
```

There is an alternative way to perform this same task of getting the customers' order information. The English explanation of it is subtly different. How about joining together the two tables completely, with all rows of one table paired with all rows of the other, but then selecting only those rows satisfying the condition of equal cust_id fields? The select statement is:

```
SELECT c.cust_id, o.order_id, o.prod_id, o.qty, o.date,
o.status FROM customer as c, orders as o
WHERE c.cust_id = o.cust_id
```

TABLE 7.4 Join of Customer and Orders

CUST_ID	CUST_NAME	BILLING	SHIPPING	ORD_ID	PROD_ID	CUST_ID	QTY	DATE	STATUS
1	John Smith	cash	123 Main Street NY, NY 12345	3	2	1	3	Sept 24, 2002	Shipped
1	John Smith	cash	123 Main Street NY, NY 12345	4	1	1	4	Sept 24, 2002	Backordered
2	Mary Jones	Mastercard XX	10 Elm Street, apt 23 Town, State 11111	1	3	2	5	Sept 23, 2002	Shipped
2	Mary Jones	Mastercard XX	10 Elm Street, apt 23 Town, State 11111	2	1	2	3	Sept 23, 2002	Backordered
2	Mary Jones	Mastercard XX	10 Elm Street, apt 23 Town, State 11111	5	4	2	1	Sept 25, 2002	Shipped

This `select` statement is doing a join, but the `JOIN` term goes away. It is replaced by the comma between the mentions of the table names. The `WHERE` condition does the work of the `ON` condition. You will find yourself coming up with one or the other of these in different situations. As has been stated, at some point in development, review the `select` statements to see if you are using the most efficient form. The MySQL `explain` command is helpful here. Alternatively, some DBMS software provides ways to compile queries to improve performance. This is also called *stored procedures*.

The left join is a feature of the `select` statement to be used to detect the absence of records. Assume one more entry in the customer table: a Sally Bean, with address, billing, and shipping information. The record is shown in Table 7.5.

TABLE 7.5   A New Customer Record

3	Sally Bean	Visa	Hilltop Town, State 22222

Assume no additions to the orders table—Sally has not ordered anything. The SQL statements indicated previously, both the one with the on condition and the one with the where condition, will produce the same results as indicated. This could be what you want. However, if you want the customers who have not ordered anything to be mentioned, you can use the following SQL statement:

```
SELECT customer.cust_id, order_id, prod_id, qty, date, status FROM
customer LEFT JOIN orders ON customer.cust_id = orders.order_id
```

This will produce the result shown in Table 7.6.

Since the table on the right—namely, orders—had no rows with cust_id the same as that of Sally Bean, there is exactly one row joined with Sally's record and the values are null. You can check for these null values and you will see an example of this in the quiz show application covered in Chapter 15, "Quiz Show."

TABLE 7.6   Left Join of Customer and Orders

CUST_ID	CUST_NAME	BILLING	SHIPPING	ORD_ID	PROD_ID	CUST_ID	QTY	DATE	STATUS
1	John Smith	cash	123 Main Street NY, NY 12345	3	2	1	3	Sept 24, 2002	Shipped
1	John Smith	cash	123 Main Street NY, NY 12345	4	1	1	4	Sept 24, 2002	Backordered
2	Mary Jones	Mastercard XX	10 Elm Street, apt 23 Town, State 11111	1	3	2	5	Sept 23, 2002	Shipped
2	Mary Jones	Mastercard XX	10 Elm Street, apt 23 Town, State 11111	2	1	2	3	Sept 23, 2002	Backordered
2	Mary Jones	Mastercard XX	10 Elm Street, apt 23 Town, State 11111	5	4	2	1	Sept 25, 2002	Shipped
3	Sally Bean	Visa	Hilltop Town, State 22222	Null	Null	Null	Null	Null	Null

EXAMPLES

Using a database involves defining the database, modifying the contents, and using the information. This section will show examples of SQL for these tasks.

Defining the Database

How you create databases will depend on your Internet service provider (ISP). In the next chapter, we will suggest methods for Access and for MySQL that do not involve creating the database under program control. However, here is the SQL command:

```
CREATE DATABASE store
```

where create and database are keywords, and store would be replaced by whatever name you choose for your database. The next step is to define the tables for the database. Again, the suggested practice for Access and MySQL will differ. Here is the command for MySQL:

```
CREATE TABLE catalog
(prod_id INT NOT NULL AUTO_INCREMENT PRIMARY KEY,
prod_name CHAR(20),
cost FLOAT(2), category CHAR(20), description CHAR(50))
```

This command creates a table named catalog in the current database. Establishing the current database is part of the connection process. The records in catalog have five fields. Note that the line spacing is to make this clearer and is not necessary.

The first field is named prod_id. Its datatype is an integer (whole number). The command indicates that it cannot be null. The auto_increment directive establishes that this field is to be assigned by MySQL. The last aspect of the prod_id field is that it is set to be the primary key. Telling the DBMS that this is a primary key means that the system builds an index using this field to speed up finding records using the primary key. You can designate other fields as being of type index. The designation of primary key would also put in a mechanism to check that this field contains unique values. However, since this field is also designated as auto_increment, the uniqueness is assured.

The prod_name, category, and description fields are each character strings, indicated here by CHAR. The size limits are different with the prod_name and category limited to 20 characters and the description field allowed 50. It is possible to specify a variable-length field and very large fields, but fixed-length character strings are most appropriate for this particular application.

The cost field is set to be a decimal number with two decimal places.

Field names, like variable names, are up to you, but some general rules apply. In Access, you can use spaces in the field names. However, this requires that you use square brackets in the SQL statements. For this reason, the practice here will be to use underscores and no spaces. Make names long enough to be recognizable but no longer, so that it is neither a strain to write them or a strain to remember what they represent.

In this section, you will see other instances of the `create table` statement. You can try to write these statements for the customers, orders, and ordered_item tables, or the course table that have been discussed. The prior discussion did not indicate the physical details such as the length of character fields, so you are on your own for deciding on these limits.

The `alter` statement can be used to alter the field definitions in a table, even if records have already been inserted. For example, you can add a field of information:

```
ALTER TABLE catalog ADD price FLOAT(2)
```

This particular statement would add a price field in addition to the cost field indicated in the original `create table` statement. Note that the existing records would not have the price field set—see the use of `update` statement later to set these values. New fields are added after the last field unless you add a clause to the alter statement:

```
ALTER TABLE catalog ADD price FLOAT(2) AFTER cost
```

This last `alter` statement positions the price right after the cost field.

The following statement directs the system to create an index for the prod_name field:

```
ALTER TABLE catalog ADD INDEX nameindex (prod_name)
```

This would be an appropriate thing to do if there were many queries against the database using the prod_name field. The use of indexes improves performance.

Modifying the Contents

Let us assume that the database and its table are created. The next step is to put some records into the table. The SQL statement to add a record is INSERT. Here is an example of an insert statement, with made-up values.

```
INSERT INTO catalog VALUES
(0, 'butterfly', 5.95, 12.50,
'animal', 'simple butterfly')
```

This statement inserts one record into the catalog table. The values in the parentheses following the term VALUES are the values for the fields, with the exception of the zero. The order of the values must correspond to the original definition of the table.

Recall that the `prod_id` field is set to be `AUTO_INCREMENT`. MySQL (and Access) will generate the next integer value for the prod_id field. The 5.95 is the cost for chocolate pie, and the 12.50 is the price.

In a program, the typical `insert` statement would use variables in place of the constants: "butterfly," 5.95, 12.50, "animal3," and "simple butterfly." One of the intricacies of producing the query character strings is that you will need to insert the single quotation marks to denote character strings.

Other formats exist for the `insert` statement, some of which allow you to indicate only some of the fields. If there has been a lot of activity changing the definition of the table, it might be prudent to use the following form for insertions:

```
INSERT INTO catalog
(prod_id, prod_name, cost, price,
category, description)
VALUES (0, 'dollar butterfly', 4.50, 9.00,
'money folds', 'dollar version of simple butterfly'
```

The order of the fields is up to you: that is, you need to name the fields to correspond with the order in which you give the values. In this situation, you could omit the prod_id and the system would generate the value.

What if you want to change one or more fields in an existing record or records? The `update` query performs that task. Let us assume that the record with prod_id equal to 5 needs to have the description changed. Yes, this is a fictional situation.

```
UPDATE catalog SET
description='intermediate level  butterfly model'
WHERE prod_id=5
```

A much less artificial use of `update` would be the following:

```
UPDATE catalog SET price=cost*2
```

This sets the price field to be twice the cost field for all products. This would be appropriate if you did indeed add the price field to a table with data already in it. You could then make adjustments, such as the following showing another use of `update`.

```
UPDATE catalog SET price=price*1.07
```

Because no WHERE condition has been specified, this statement changes the price field of each record to 1.07 times the original price. To put it another way, the prices have been increased 7%. Another "wholesale" change would be the following. Let us assume that the catalog has more than 10 records.

```
UPDATE catalog set price=price*1.07 order
by price limit 10
```

This statement orders the records by the price field. It then performs the update operation on the first 10 records (products). This has the effect of raising the prices on the lowest (cheapest) 10 items.

Of course, after adding the price field to the table, you can set the price field of new records by including a value for price in the insert statement.

The SQL statement to delete records from a database is used as follows:

```
DELETE FROM catalog WHERE prod_id=5
```

Another example would be:

```
DELETE FROM catalog WHERE cost<1.00
```

The next statement would remove all records from the table:

```
DELETE FROM catalog
```

Similarly, the following statement removes the table:

```
DROP TABLE catalog
```

As unlikely as it might seem, you might have cause to use the delete statements, especially during the development stages of implementation. However, once the system is up and running, it might be appropriate to limit the chances of making some catastrophic mistake such as deleting all the records. One approach is to make use of the permissions feature of a DBMS product to restrict what privileges users have. In MySQL, the grant statement allows you to set privileges to any or all of the following commands: ALTER, CREATE, DELETE, DROP, INSERT, SELECT, and UPDATE at a table or field level to specific users.

Using the Information

The select statement gathers information from the database, including making calculations involving the fields in one or more tables. The select statement has different clauses and can be quite complex as shown earlier in the explanation of joins. The simplest select query:

```
SELECT * FROM catalog
```

This will return what is called a recordset, a special datatype something like a table. It is made up of all the fields of all the records in the catalog table. You can restrict the fields chosen from the table.

```
SELECT prod_id, prod_name FROM catalog
```

The preceding returns a recordset made up of just the two fields (columns) cited.

You can also return a recordset revealing a calculated value based on the information in the table. There is a set of what are termed *aggregate* or *summary* functions for this purpose:

```
SELECT COUNT(*) FROM catalog
```

The preceding will return the number of records in the catalog table, and the next statement:

```
SELECT SUM(cost) FROM catalog
```

returns the sum of all the cost fields in the records of the catalog table. In each of these last two cases, the recordset contains exactly one row.

The select statement shows its power when you use conditions. You saw two examples in the previous section describing joins. The where clause can be used in statements involving just one table:

```
SELECT prod_name, price FROM catalog WHERE cost>5
```

This produces a list of products with their prices for all products in which the cost is over five dollars. (Note: nothing so far indicates that the currency is dollars as opposed to anything else. The choice of currency will be made apparent if and only if a display is made using dollar signs.) A where condition is made up of the keyword WHERE with a logical expression.

The examples so far have several models in the animal category.

```
SELECT prod_name, description FROM catalog
WHERE category='animal'
```

You can also impose more than one condition and use expressions. The following would return the list of products, by name and description, in the animal category that, allowing for a tax rate of 8%, are over five dollars in price.

```
SELECT prod_name, description FROM catalog
WHERE   category='animal' and (price*1.08)>5
```

The summary functions and the functions in the conditions used so far can be found in most DBMSs. However, all such products have extensive libraries of operators and functions.

What if you wanted to have a list of all categories mentioned in your database?

```
SELECT DISTINCT category FROM catalog
```

The preceding statement will return the set of distinct categories. This is because the distinct term removes any duplicate entries. It can also be used to remove duplicate rows when you are requesting more than one field value. The rows must be duplicates in every field, so, given the presence of primary keys, this would be used when the fields mentioned did not include the primary key field.

The order of the results of a `select` query defaults to be the order of the items in the table. To specify the order, you use the `order by` clause. You have seen the case of ordering by cost. You can order by any field. The order of text fields are in alphabetical order:

```
SELECT prod_id, prod_name FROM catalog
ORDER BY prod_name
```

Assuming the catalog is as given here, the recordset returned by the `select` query would be the following, which we present to you as an ordered list to emphasize the order. The numbers would not be part of the recordset.

1. 1, bird
2. 3, box
3. 2, crane
4. 4, ornament

If you wanted to count how many products you had in each category, you would use the group clause:

```
SELECT category, count(*) FROM catalog
GROUP by category
```

This would return (assuming the original table before any butterflies were added):

1. Animal, 2
2. Box, 1
3. Modular, 1

You can change the default ascending order to descending by placing `DESC` at the end of the statement.

You can calculate more than one summary value for each group. The following will give you the sum of the costs for each group:

```
SELECT category, count(*), sum(cost)
FROM catalog GROUP by category
```

This would produce:

```
1. Animal, 2, 5.50
2. Box, 1, 1
3. Modular, 1, 2
```

Select statements involving multiple tables have been introduced in the previous section. Here are more examples of joins. What if you wanted a list of all customers by name and date of order that ordered models in the animal category? What is the thought process for designing the select statement?

The catalog records contain the category field. That is, only the catalog table indicates anything about animal

The data we want is in the customer table: the cust_name and in the orders table: the date

Consequently, the tables required are the customer, catalog, and orders table.

This is a join of three tables. Let us do this first by where conditions. The start of the query is the following:

```
SELECT c.cust_name, o.date
FROM customer as c, orders as o, catalog as p
WHERE …
```

We interrupt "the thought process" to note that it makes sense to start writing down what will be parts of the query instead of trying to keep it all "in your head."

The where conditions must connect the orders to the customers using the cust_id:
```
c.cust_id = o.cust_id
```

The where conditions must constrain the orders to the products
```
o.prod_id = p.prod_id
```

The where conditions must also constrain the products to be ones with category equal to "animal":
```
p.category = 'animal'
```

The final select statement is:

```
SELECT c.cust_name, o.date FROM customer as c,
orders  as o, catalog as p WHERE c.cust_id = o.cust_id
and o.prod_id = p.prod_id and p.category = 'animal'
```

You can do the following reasonability test on the `select` statement. It involved joining three tables. This would require at least two conditions. The third `where` condition came about by specifying the category to be animal.

Making this reasonability analysis puts us in a good position to create the "on" version for this task. What were "where" conditions become "on" conditions specifying how the tables are to be joined.

```
SELECT c.cust_name, o.date FROM customer as c
JOIN orders as o ON  c.cust_id = o.cust_id
JOIN catalog as p ON o.prod_id = p.prod_id
WHERE p.category = 'animal'
```

This statement will work as is, but it would be neater to use parentheses to set off one join at a time. One possibility is:

```
SELECT c.cust_name, o.date
FROM (customer as c JOIN orders as o
ON  c.cust_id = o.cust_id) JOIN catalog as p
ON o.prod_id = p.prod_id
WHERE p.category = 'animal'
```

You can put a limit on the number of rows returned by the `select` query. The LIMIT clause works in two ways:

```
SELECT prod_name, prod_description FROM catalog LIMIT 2
```

The preceding limits the returned value to no more than two rows. If there are fewer records than the specified number, you will get the actual number of rows there actually are.

A common requirement is to produce a display with a limited number of records at a time. This is called *paging*. If you specify two numbers in the `limit` clause, you get the row indicated by the first number plus however many you indicate by the second number. The following example returns three rows, each containing the product name and the description, with the first row the third (zero indexing) from the database.

```
SELECT prod_name, description FROM catalog LIMIT 2, 3
```

If you are preparing these statements within a program, you will use variables for these two values. You would set the first variable to start at zero, and then increment it by the second value.

As stated previously, you can combine all these features of the `select` statement. For example, consider the statement:

```
SELECT p.prod_name, count(*) FROM catalog as p
JOIN orders as o
ON p.prod_id = o.prod_id
GROUP BY o.prod_id
```

This produces a list of product names with the number of times they were ordered.

```
SELECT p.prod_name, count(o.qty) FROM catalog as p
JOIN orders as o
ON p.prod_id = o.prod_id
GROUP BY o.prod_id
```

This gives a list of product names with the total quantity ordered.

What if you want to group the results, apply a summary function to each group, such as count or sum, and then apply a condition based on that result? That is, what if you want to just list the products that were ordered more than once? You cannot use a `where` condition because that action is done prior to grouping. Instead, SQL provides the `HAVING` clause feature:

```
SELECT p.prod_name, count(*) as pcount
FROM catalog as p
JOIN orders as ON p.prod_id = o.prod_id
GROUP BY o.prod_id HAVING pcount>1
```

You can name the result of a summary function even if you do not use it in a `having` clause.

The previous examples demonstrated joins, using more than one table to extract information from the database. What if you need to use the same table in two different ways? The common example for this situation is a database of airline flights. In the *Exercises*, you will find questions using the course and prerequisite database mentioned in Chapter 5. Consider a database with two tables. One table holds the information on airports:

- airport code: apc
- city
- state
- country

The other table holds flight information:

- flight_code
- from airport code: from_apc
- to airport code: to_apc
- scheduled departure time: depart
- scheduled arrival time: arr

Note that the airport code is what we termed a *naturally occurring value.* Some of the codes such as JFK for JFK in New York City, New York, OAK for Oakland, California, and MIA for Miami, Florida are understandable. However, some, like EWR for Newark, NJ or MSY for New Orleans, LA, must have hidden, historical meaning. However, it would still make sense to use them in a database involving airline flights.

The departure and arrival times would either be stored in the local times or, more likely, Greenwich Mean Time. Dates and times are something that most DBMSs handle in a distinct fashion so you can compare and even do arithmetic. However, the products handle the dates and times in different ways. See the *Exercises* for an assignment.

What if you wanted to obtain a list of cities for the departure and the arrival for each flight? To follow the pattern of previous examples, we need to use the flights table and the airports table. If you think of joining the tables together using a common field, you notice that there is a problem! What is the common field to mention in the ON or WHERE clause? There are two possibilities for joining the tables together. The point is that it is necessary to use the airports table two distinct ways, and this is exactly what is done. The select statement to produce a list of flight codes, departure city, and arrival city is as follows:

```
SELECT flights.flight_code, d.city, a.city
FROM flights, airports as d, airports as a
WHERE flights.from_apc = d.apc AND flights.to_apc=a.apc
```

It is as if there were two tables. This passes the reasonability test: you have three (virtual) tables and you have two conditions connecting them. The join version of this query would be:

```
SELECT flights.flight_code, d.city, a.city
FROM flights
JOIN airports as d ON flights.from_apc = d.apc
JOIN  airports as a ON flights.to_apc=a.apc
```

Now suppose that you want to find out about the numbers of flights. Here is a way to derive the answer. The previous query gave a list of all flights with the departing and arriving cities. Is there a query to sort the list to make all the flights for a common route together? This requires use of the ORDER BY clause with two field names. Consider the following query:

```
SELECT flights.flight_code, d.city, a.city
FROM flights, airports as d, airports as a
WHERE flights.from_apc = d.apc AND
flights.to_apc=a.apc ORDER BY d.city, a.city
```

This produces a list of flights, departing and arriving city ordered by the departing city first and then the arriving city. Therefore, all the flights for a particular route will appear together in the list.

Now, what do you need to do to get the number of flights, not the individual flight information? The answer is the use of the GROUP BY clause and the COUNT aggregate function. You can write a slight variant of the prior query to produce the number:

```
SELECT d.city, a.city, COUNT(*) FROM flights
WHERE flights.from_apc = d.apc AND flights.to_apc=a.apc
ORDER BY d.city, a.city
GROUP BY d.city, a.city
```

Think of the GROUP BY clause as squashing the rows in a group and showing just what the group has in common or summary information. What the elements in the group have in common is what is named by the GROUP BY clause. The following would not make sense. Some systems would produce an error, but others would return an empty recordset.

```
SELECT flights.flight_code, d.city, a.city, COUNT(*)
FROM flights WHERE flights.from_apc = d.apc
AND flights.to_apc=a.apc ORDER BY d.city, a.city
GROUP BY d.city, a.city
```

This is because the flights.flight_code information is not common across the group or derivable as a function of the group.

REFLECTION

SQL is a powerful and extremely concise language. You do not simply sit down and write SQL create statements to define tables in a database. Instead, you use what you learned from Chapter 5, plus your knowledge about the particular problem to design the database. Similarly, if you think of the select statement as being the equivalent of a program, you are more likely to give yourself the time to grasp the meaning of an existing select query or develop the one you need.

There can be more than one way to write a select statement to accomplish a specific task. It might be that one way is more efficient than another. When you need to turn your project into a robust application, you can find tools to analyze the workings of the select statements. MySQL has the explain command that indicates the order of operations for a statement. Such tools also can help in determining if it would be beneficial to define index fields.

A parallel to the notion that SQL statements are little programs is that they perform time-consuming actions. You need to appreciate that a middleware statement involving a select operation might not be as quick as other statements. A corollary to this is that database operations take significant enough amounts of time to perform one of these operations. Why is this something of concern? If you have more than one user reading and writing to the database at the same time, you need to be concerned with interactions between user requests. The basic DBMS makes sure that updates are uninterrupted. However, you might have a set of operations that should be invoked without interruption. Suppose that your code reads and displays information from the database. The person sitting in front of the computer takes his time and then makes a choice. Your code then does a calculation and then updates the database with new values. What if some other person got in there "in between" and made a change? The DBMS products have facilities for locking and unlocking records and, perhaps, defining a set of steps as a transaction. These can include facilities to roll back the database if something should happen in the middle of an operation or a transaction. It is in these areas that the DBMS products differ, and some have more features than others. See Chapter 16, "Scaling Up Your Application," for more on this topic.

In the next chapter, you will read about the specifics of using MySQL and Access on servers, including how to make queries directly against the database. Then, in the following chapters, you will learn how to construct SQL statements and pass them to the DBMS for your database using PHP and ASP functions and methods.

EXERCISES, QUESTIONS, AND PROJECTS

1. Write out the result of joining the orders, customer, and catalog tables. This is the result of:
   ```
   SELECT * FROM orders as o JOIN customer as c ON o.cust_id =
   c.cust_id JOIN catalog as p ON o.prod_id = p.prod_id
   ```
2. Produce a `select` statement that will order the products by price, listing the product name and description.
3. Produce a `select` statement that will list the most expensive (by price) two products.
4. Produce a `select` statement that will list the products by name, cost, price, and percentage markup. Order this list by the percentage markup.
5. Produce a `select` statement that will list the customer name, total the prices of all purchases, and be in order of this total.
6. For the airline flights example, produce the `select` statement that lists all the flights departing from a particular city within a certain time range.
7. Go to the Web to find out how Access or MySQL or other specific DBMS support date and time calculations. In particular, you what to know how to construct a date/time value, add such values, and check if one date/time value is greater than another.
8. For the airline flights example, produce the `select` statement that lists all two-leg flights taking off from a specified airport and arriving at a specified

airport making one stop anywhere in between. You will need the arriving flight of the first leg to be before the departing flight of the second leg. More exactly, you want to constrain the time gap to be not less than a certain amount, say one hour, and not more than a certain amount, say three hours. Consult with a travel agent for typical values. Building on the airline flights example, how would you define a new table that grouped some airports into regions so you could ask questions about flights to and from regions containing one or more airports?

9. Consider the course and prerequisite database described in Chapter 5. You might want to add more courses, with some having one or two prerequisites. Produce the `select` statement that lists all courses that have prerequisites, listing the course name and course id of the course first, and then the course id of the prerequisite course.

10. Building on the previous question, produce the `select` statement that lists the name of the course and the name of the prerequisite. You will need to review the example with flights.

11. Produce the `select` statement that gives a list of courses with the number of prerequisites. You will need to use a left join and a summary function to get the courses to be included that have no prerequisites.

12. Go to the Web and find the list of summary/aggregate functions allowed by Access and by MySQL. Similarly, go online and find the functions provided for expressions.

8

DATABASE MANAGEMENT SYSTEMS: MYSQL AND ACCESS

T he purpose of this chapter is to demonstrate two database management systems (DBMSs): the open-source product MySQL and the Microsoft product Access.

BACKGROUND

A chief purpose of middleware systems such as PHP and ASP is to support interactions with databases. Both PHP and ASP can be used with a variety of different DBMSs. The database products chosen for coverage in this text are the open-source offering MySQL and the Microsoft product Access. Price and availability drove both choices, along with the existence of online information and support. As an open-source offering, MySQL is available for virtually no cost. MS Access is not free, but we make the assumption that most readers and students already have Access as part of the Microsoft Office Suite. Online sources are abundant for both products.

Many academic institutions along with a growing number of commercial organizations chose MySQL because of a strategy of choosing open source. The PHP system has special functions just for MySQL, which we demonstrate in the *Examples* in this text.

The Access system is designed for individual or small group use. If and when you need to design and build a database for high-volume use, with complex transactions, you should consider other products. However, Access has sufficient functionality for you to learn the basics. As mentioned previously, all DBMSs have many features in common, most especially the use of SQL.

This chapter will feature the stand-alone use of MySQL and Access. You will make use of some of this when building your middleware applications, though most of your access (sorry, it is difficult to avoid use of this term) to the databases will be through PHP and ASP scripts to strengthen your knowledge of programming.

CONCEPTUAL EXPLANATION

The choice of DBMS product and how you use it will be partially controlled by your arrangement with your server. You might have total control over the server, or you might contract for services with an Internet service provider (ISP). The DBMS runs on the server machine.

Permissions and Privileges

Permissions and *privileges* are terms concerning the control of access to programs and databases. Think of the ability to limit access as a valuable tool for establishing how the project is to operate. You will read here how you can use MySQL commands to specify rights to use the database. The level of detail is such that you can grant rights to:

- A user by name, identified with a password
- On a specific computer
- For a database, with a specification of
  - which commands (e.g., insert, select)
  - which tables or even fields within tables

Access does not have similar features, but other DBMS products do. However, before explaining the database permissions, please keep in mind that there might be other instances of systems restrictions of concern to your project. You need to distinguish between permissions and restrictions appropriate for the building phase of the project and you as the chief developer, and the operational stage of the project in which you and others will use the system through a browser.

For the building/development phase, you probably have a user ID and password to use a File Transfer Protocol (FTP) program, such as Ws-ftp, to upload your scripts to the server. You might be able to use that ID and password, or you might have another one for telneting to the system. This could be of use for setting up MySQL files. The approach we use at our school is not symmetric between MySQL and Access. For MySQL, we establish for each student a database in which he or she has full privileges. The id and passwords for the database are the same as their FTP ID and password. Students use programs (PHP scripts) to define tables. For Access, the students create the databases on their own computers and upload the database using ws-ftp.

For the operating phase of the project, you will use the commands to set up access from your middleware scripts to the database. The ordinary user of your scripts will not have direct access. You might choose to implement using your own programming a system of controlled access. In that system, you might define a category of more privileged use for yourself, or you might fall back on your other rights, through FTP, for example, or utilities that are available to manage the system.

MySQL and Access

MySQL is an open-source product (see *www.Mysql.com*). To quote from the Web site, "MySQL is available for free under the GNU General Public License (GPL). Commercial licenses are sold to users who prefer not to be restricted by the GPL terms." The reference manual is available at *www.Mysql.com/doc/en/Reference.html*. The authors of the homepage note that the correct pronunciation is "my ess que ell," but you should feel free to use any local pronunciation.

MySQL uses a command-line interface, much like the old DOS personal computers. You can use MySQL directly in the following ways:

- Directly on the server computer
- Through telnet on the server computer
- Use MySQL on your own computer in its remote mode to operate on the server

- Use MySQL on your own computer, using Internet Information Server (IIS) or Personal Web Server (PWS) or their equivalent. At some point, you will need to upload the databases along with the PHP scripts to the server

The screen shots shown in this chapter were based on the last option.

Access is a product of the Microsoft Corporation. The official homepage is *www.microsoft.com/office/access/default.asp*. Access generally is purchased as part of the Microsoft Office suite. In this text, it is assumed that you will do the initial creation of the database in stand-alone mode and then upload the database to the server.

It is possible to use PHP with other types of databases, including Access, and to use ASP with other types of databases, including MySQL.

EXAMPLES

This section shows usage with screen shots of MySQL and Access, each in stand-alone mode. Although you generally will be using the databases through middleware, this material will contribute to your general understanding of databases.

MySQL

Signing on to use MySQL locally requires you to start IIS or its equivalent, and then use the command prompt. Click on the Start button and then the Run option. You will see something resembling the panel shown in Figure 8.1.

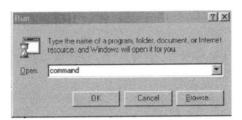

FIGURE 8.1   Windows Run prompt.

If "command" does not appear in the text box, you can type it in or use the downward arrow to scroll over your past uses of the Run window to find command. Click OK. A window much like Figure 8.2 will appear.

This indicates that you are in command mode, in the Desktop folder within the WINDOWS folder. You need to get to the folder for MySQL. For our installation, MySQL is installed in a folder at the topmost level. Therefore, the commands are to back up, so to speak, and then go into the mysql folder. The

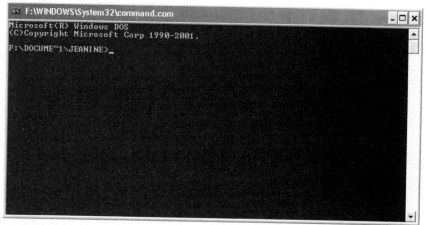

FIGURE 8.2 Command prompt screen.

change directory command is `cd`. To get into the parent folder of the current folder, you type:

```
cd ..
```

Figure 8.3 shows the sequence of commands.

FIGURE 8.3 Sequence of commands to get to the MySql folder.

You need to make one more change of directory command to get into the bin subfolder, indicated in Figure 8.4.

You now start MySQL by entering `mysql` as indicated in Figure 8.5.

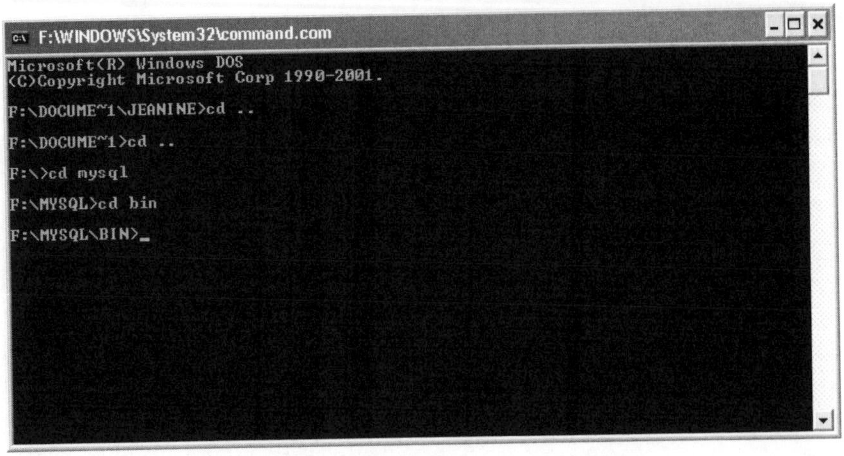

FIGURE 8.4 Command to reach the bin subfolder.

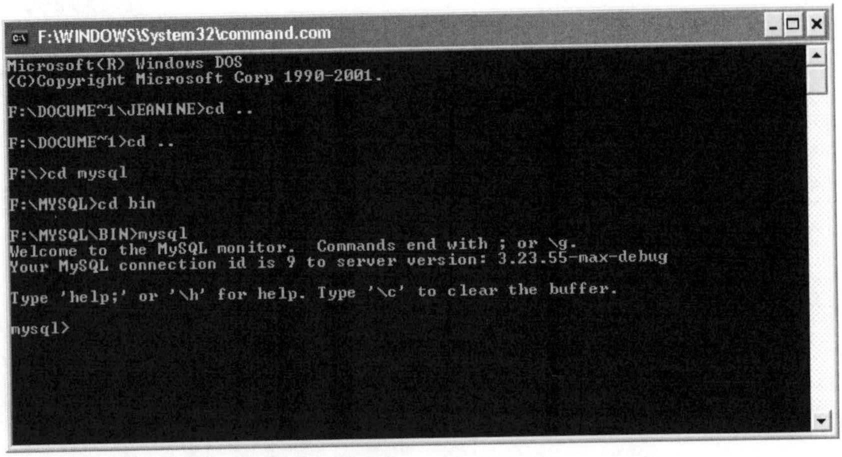

FIGURE 8.5 Commands to invoke MySQL.

This is the point at which the different options for doing MySQL on the server in different ways or doing it on your own computer all come together.

From now on, all commands are MySQL statements. Most of what will be shown are MySQL versions of the SQL statements described in the previous chapter. You need to put a semicolon to close each statement. Because the semicolon is required, you can spread a statement over several lines.

Your screens will not be exact copies of ours, but you should be able to see a resemblance and understand the pattern. If you type in the command:

```
show databases;
```

you will see any databases that you have created (or have been created for you). A typical screen is shown in Figure 8.6.

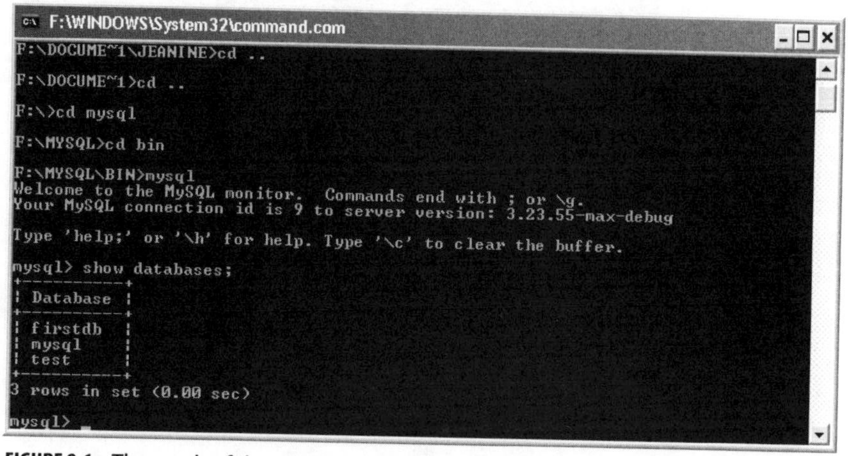

FIGURE 8.6 The result of the show databases command.

Notice that there are several databases returned as a table with a heading. This is the format for any recordset returned by SQL statements in MySQL. Notice also that MySQL returns a message indicating the number of rows in the set and the time taken.

To put us now on a similar footing, here is an example of a potentially dangerous command:

```
drop database test;
```

It might be appropriate during development if a situation occurs when it makes sense to start over.

The result is shown in Figure 8.7.

You can use the show command to confirm that the database was dropped. Now let us create a new database, called test by the command:

```
create database test;
```

The resulting screen is shown in Figure 8.8.

Now at the risk of annoying you, try now to create a table for a product catalog. The fields are to be:

- **Product identifier**: Use an integer to be generated by the DBMS.
- **Product name**: Use a text field. This field cannot be omitted.
- **Description**: Use a text field.
- **Cost**: Use a numeric field to hold two decimal places and a number up to 9999.

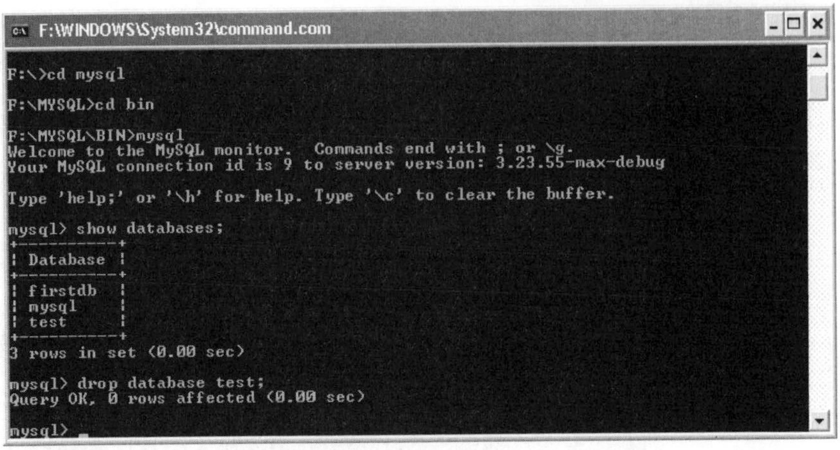

FIGURE 8.7   The drop database command.

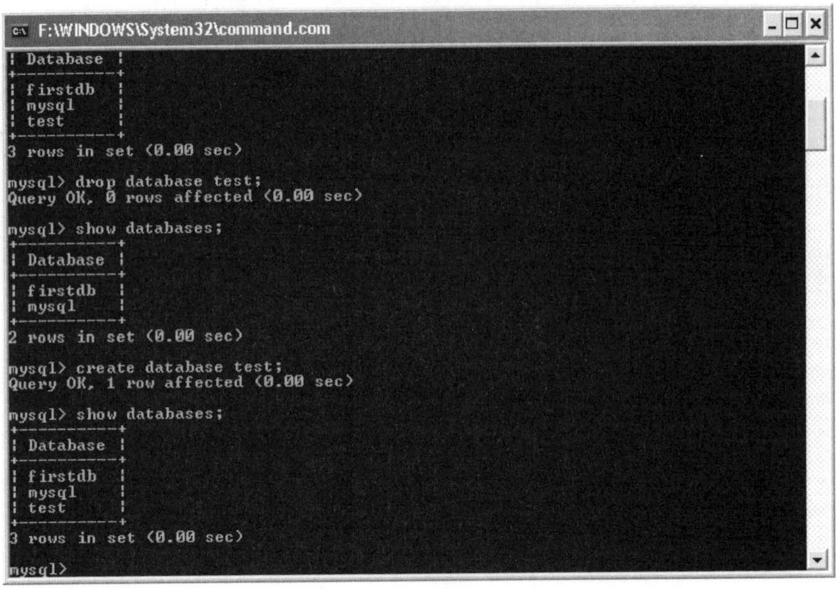

FIGURE 8.8   The create database test command.

You need to specify field names and field information. For field names, we suggest concise, but understandable names, all lowercase, using an underscore if you want to use two words. Some DBMSs allow blanks in field names, but then you need to use other symbols to delimit the name—it is easier to avoid that complexity. Some systems store tables as distinct files. If this is true, then you need to worry if the operating system is case-sensitive with respect to file-names. UNIX systems are; Windows systems are not. To avoid potential confusion, use all lowercase.

The field information includes the data type. The terms used for data type differ among DBMS products, but all products support the types indicated for this example.

The screen shot in Figure 8.9 shows an error.

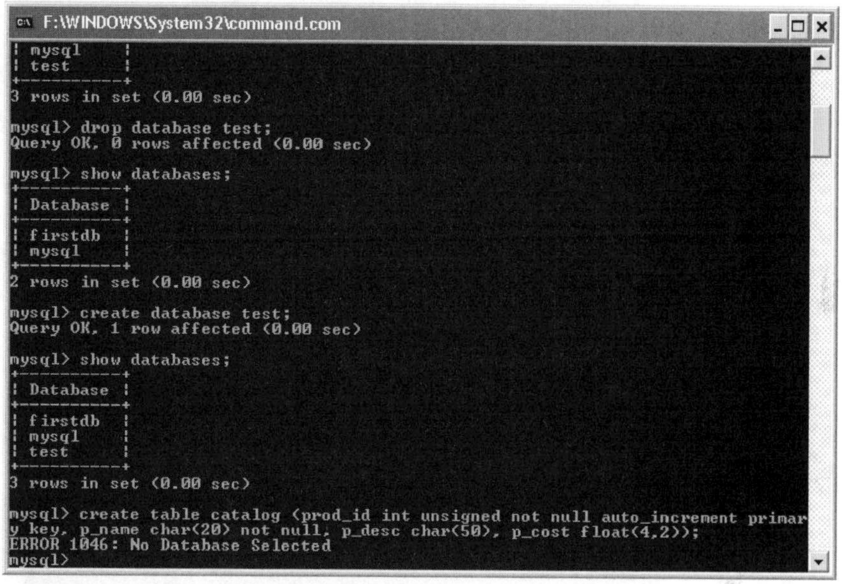

FIGURE 8.9   A MySQL command with an error.

Even though you would think that MySQL would "know" that you wanted to use the database you just created, you need to enter the command:

```
use test;
```

This produces the result shown in Figure 8.10.

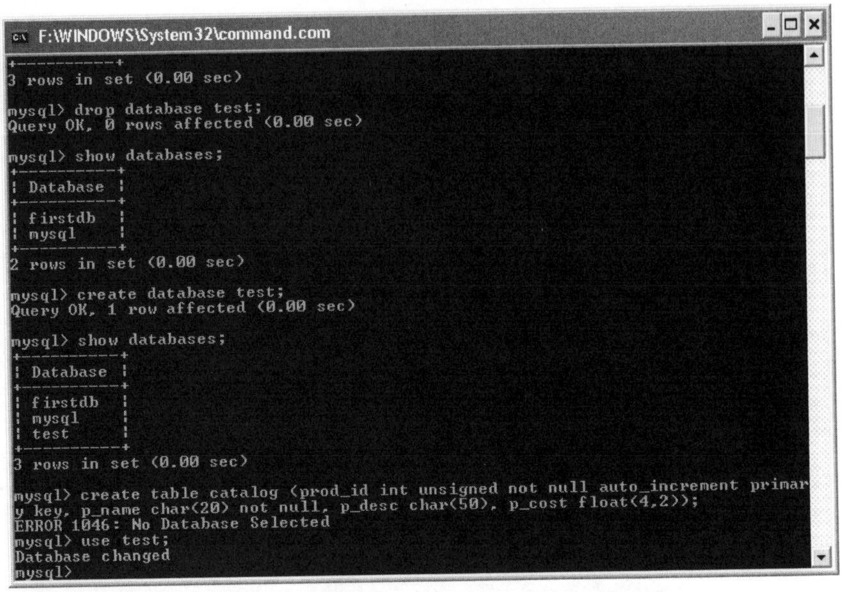

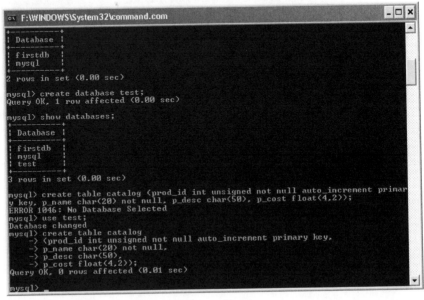

FIGURE 8.10 The use test command.

Now you can re-enter the create table command. Notice how the command is spread over several lines for clarity in the screen shown in Figure 8.11.

FIGURE 8.11 Multiline create command.

To check that a table was actually created, you can type in the command:

```
show tables;
```

as shown in Figure 8.12.

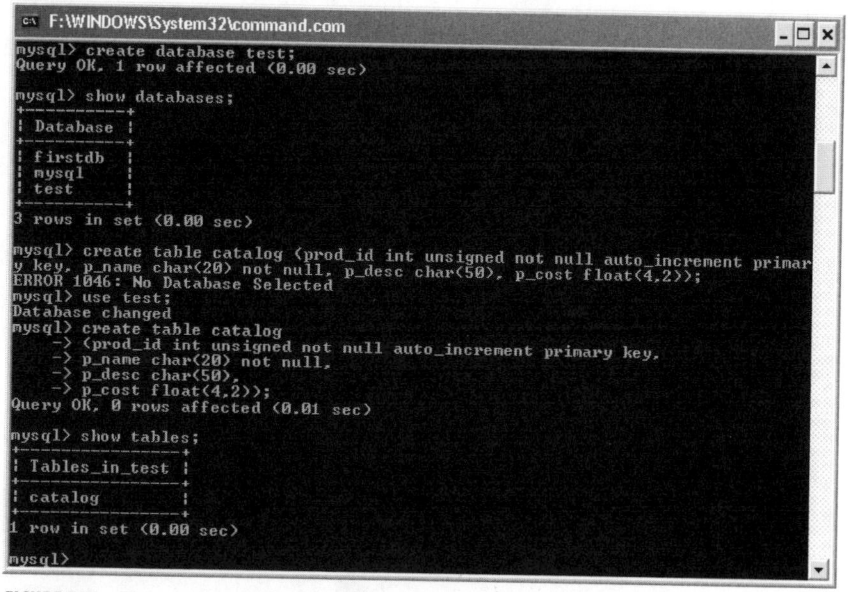

FIGURE 8.12   The show tables command, with the result.

Or, for information on a specific table (so far, there is just one table in the test database):

```
describe catalog;
```

The result is shown in Figure 8.13.

The default value for prod_id being NULL when the NULL column shows that NULL is not allowed is not a particularly good message. However, this is what MySQL returns. Let us enter some data. This is shown in Figure 8.14.

One record has been inserted. Note that what we have entered for a description is information that could be a way of categorizing models and, consequently, you can use if you want to redesign the table. Feel free to define products of your own choosing.

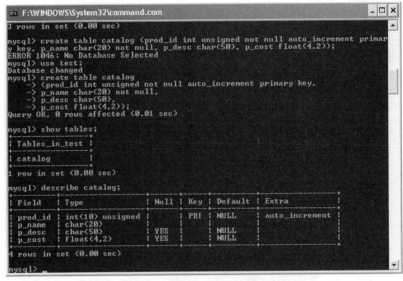

FIGURE 8.13   The `describe catalog` command, with the result.

FIGURE 8.14   An `insert` command.

Figure 8.15 shows an attempt to add two more entries, demonstrating different forms of the `insert` statement (and also making a mistake).

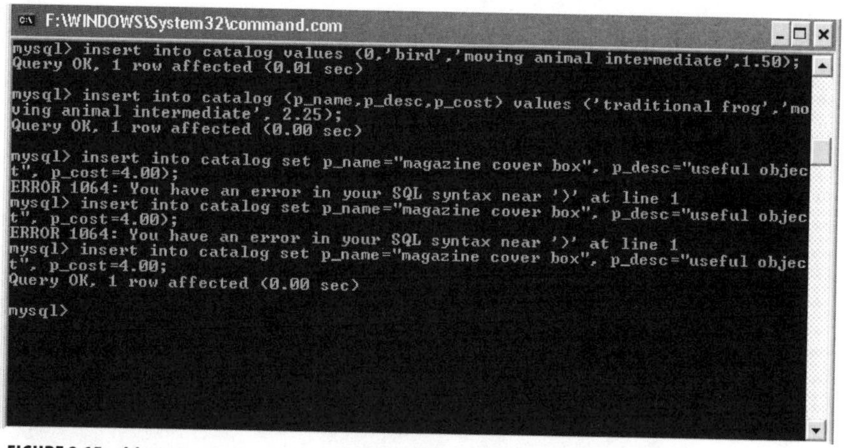

FIGURE 8.15   More `insert` commands, including an error.

The first form of `insert` listed all the fields in the order in which they were created. The second type allowed you to specify for which fields you were supplying values. Since we could leave out the prod_id field, this allowed us to get away with slightly less typing. This was the format used to input the traditional frog. The third form of `insert` allows you to enter field name and field value pairs. This might be advantageous when interpreting information that has been passed to the program in an unspecified order. However, we made a mistake by typing an extraneous parenthesis. We correct this error by typing the statement again without the extra parenthesis.

At this point, it is appropriate to show another feature of MySQL, which makes the command-line approach tenable. You can use a source file for your SQL statements. Get out of MySQL by typing:

```
quit;
```

Then close the command prompt window by clicking on the small X in the upper-right corner.

Open Notepad and enter the code:

```
insert into catalog
set p_name='traditional crane',
   p_desc='animal intermediate',
   p_cost=4.00;
insert into catalog
values (0, 'magazine cover box', 'useful object
simple',1.00);
```

Save this file in the mysql/bin folder under the name *input.txt*. The choice of file name is up to you.

You did not have to exit MySQL, but we want to show how to resume work. Click on Start and then Run, and, making sure that it indicates command, click OK. You need to get back to the mysql/bin folder and start MySQL again. Then, you need to indicate that you are using the test database. Finally, you will use the source command to indicate the use of a file for SQL input. The whole sequence of commands is shown in Figure 8.16.

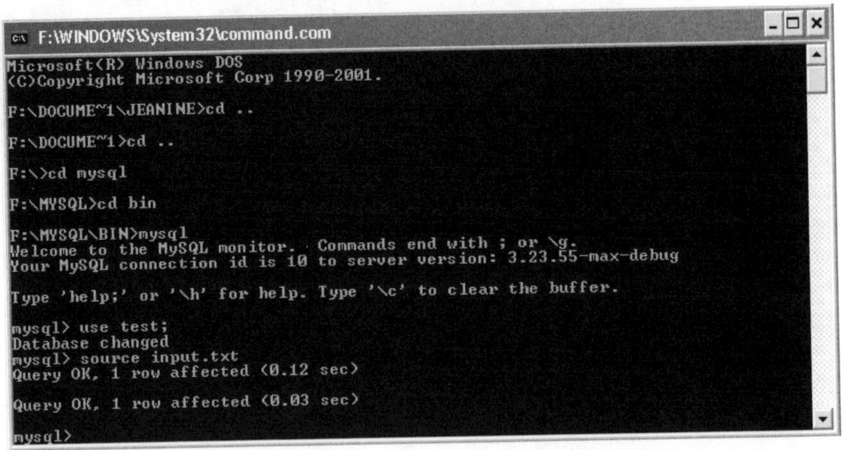

FIGURE 8.16   Starting MySQL, issuing a use command, and obtaining commands from a source file.

How do we see what is now in the table? You should be able to guess the answer. It is the `select` statement. To display all the fields of all the records in the catalog table of the database currently in use, type:

```
select * from catalog;
```

The screen shot of the result is shown in Figure 8.17.

The results display a problem, although not a MySQL error: the magazine cover box is entered twice. This would seem to be a redundant record. In fact, the two magazine cover box entries are not redundant, because the system-generated prod_id fields are different (as well as the costs). However, we do not want the fifth record, and we can demonstrate use of the `delete` command to remove this record:

```
delete from catalog where prod_id=5;
```

We then use the `select` command again as shown in Figure 8.18.

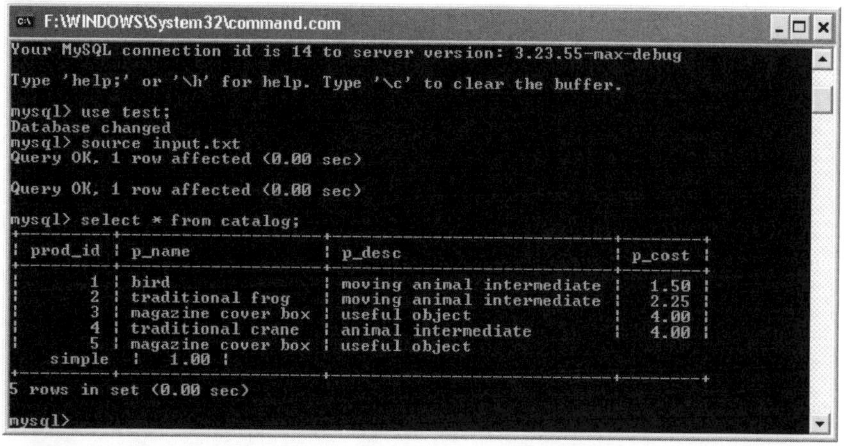

FIGURE 8.17 Select command with result.

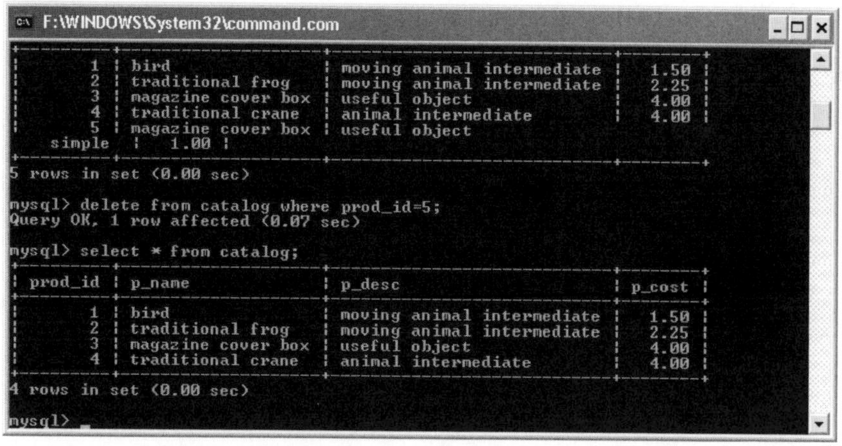

FIGURE 8.18 Contents of catalog table shown before and after deletion of a record.

The grant command establishes privileges for the designated user on a designated machine identified by a password to do all or a specified set of commands to the indicated tables of a database. The PHP scripts can all use the same username. The computer is "localhost." During development, assuming the database is named orders, you could enter:

```
grant all on orders.* to
curley@localhost identified by 'z4196q5';
```

where z4196q5 represents some hard-to-guess pattern. This information will be used in the PHP code to establish the connection to the database for all the scripts. Later, when everything is working, you systematically could determine what each script actually needs and establish a different set of privileges. For example:

```
grant select, update on orders.customers to
groucho@localhost identified by 'b4t2d66';
```

You can also enter:

```
revoke alter, create, delete, drop on orders.*
from curley@localhost;
```

Access

Now we move on to MS Access. You probably already have a copy of MS Access on your computer. Open it and choose the option to create a new database using a Blank Access database as shown in Figure 8.19.

FIGURE 8.19   Microsoft Access window for creating a new database.

You will be presented with the usual window for saving a file. Change the name of the file: we used "test." You will then see the window in Figure 8.20.

Access databases include tables and other parts of an application such as queries, forms, and reports. Since this database is to be used in a Web application, we focus here just on creating the tables. Click on Enter to accept the option of creating a table in Design view. You will see the window in Figure 8.21.

The task now is to enter in the field names, data types, and descriptions (of the field). This is how you would proceed to create for Access a table similar to the one just described for MySQL.

Type in prod_id into the first Field Name and press Enter. The first choice of data type, Text, will pop up. However, an arrow indicating a drop-down

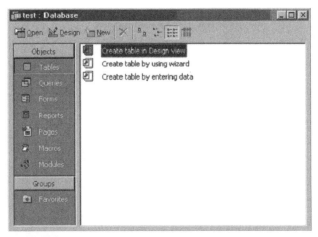

FIGURE 8.20   Access window for creating a table.

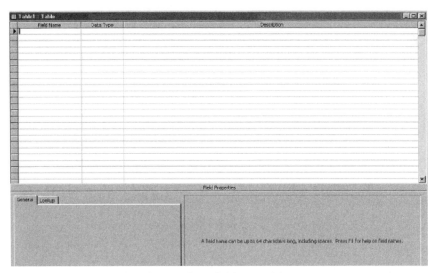

FIGURE 8.21   Access window for specifying fields in a table.

menu also appears. Click on it to see choices for the data type as shown in Figure 8.22.

Select the choice AutoNumber. For this, and other datatypes, the lower left-hand part of the window has more information about the database as shown in Figure 8.23.

The next step for this field is to tell Access that it is the primary key. You do this by clicking on the key icon on the toolbar as shown in Figure 8.24.

It is good practice to enter something into the Description field, although there is not much else to say about this particular field. Move on to the next

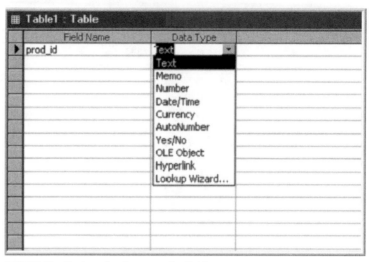

FIGURE 8.22 Options for data type for field.

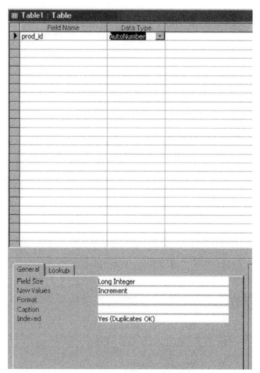

FIGURE 8.23 Window for defining field
information, when datatype is AutoNumber.

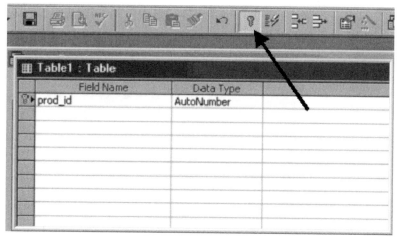

FIGURE 8.24   Specifying a field as a primary key; arrow indicates icon.

field by pressing the Tab key. This time, press Enter to accept the choice of Text. You will see the screen in Figure 8.25.

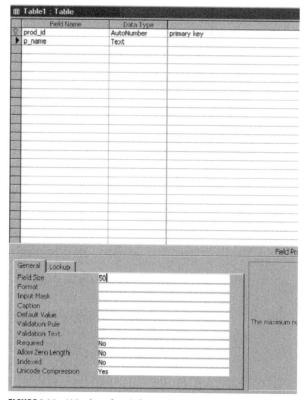

FIGURE 8.25   Window for defining field when data type is Text.

Change the Field Size to 20 and the Required Field to Yes. Tab to the Description field. If you are doing this work for an organization, it would be appropriate to indicate how the field values are assigned. Figure 8.26 shows a
description.

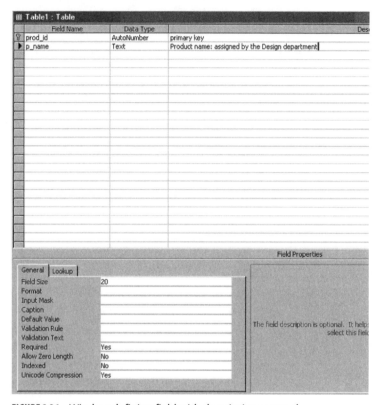

FIGURE 8.26   Window defining field with description entered.

Figure 8.27 shows the definition of the p_desc field.
Notice that we did not change the default Field Size of 50, nor the setting
that the field is not required.
The last field is the product cost. Access provides a currency data type as
shown in Figure 8.28.

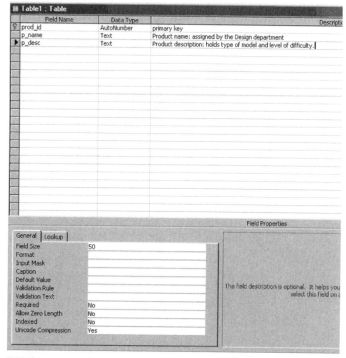

FIGURE 8.27   Window for defining fields: three fields defined.

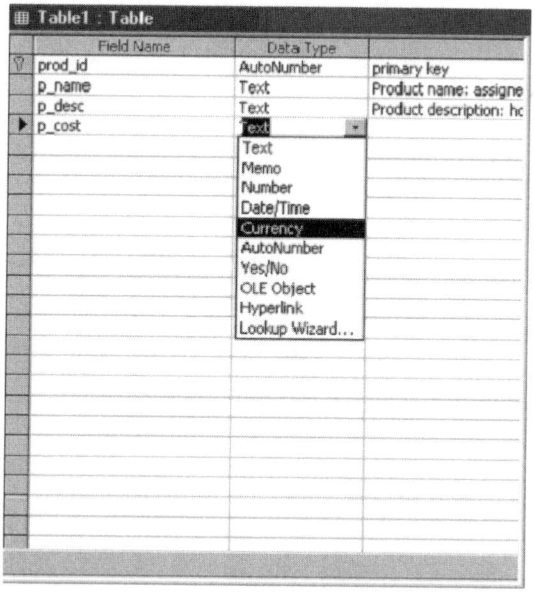

FIGURE 8.28   Partial screen shot of window defining field, showing currency option.

Figure 8.29 shows the table with the four fields defined.

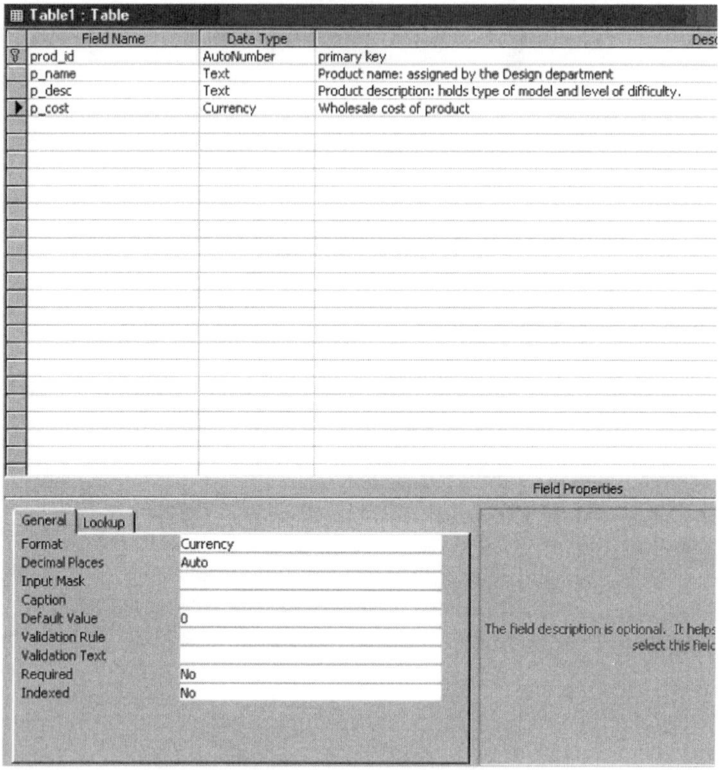

FIGURE 8.29   Screen show showing four fields defined.

You need to save what you have done. Click on File and then Save As to get the window shown in Figure 8.30.

FIGURE 8.30   Window to save and name table.

Change the file name Table1 to catalog and click OK.

At the bottom of the screen as shown in Figure 8.31, you will see the minimized icon for the database.

FIGURE 8.31   Icon to return to database.

Click on this to see the window in Figure 8.32.

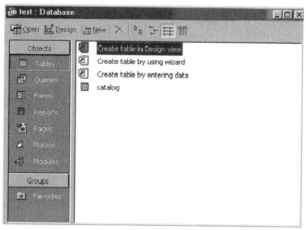

FIGURE 8.32   Window showing option to create another table or work with catalog table.

The catalog table is now listed under the Create options. Click on this to enter data into the catalog table. You will see a window customized for the table you just defined as shown in Figure 8.33.

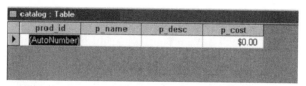

FIGURE 8.33   Window to enter records into the catalog table.

You can enter data, using the Tab key to move from field to field. Do not enter anything into the AutoNumber field. You will notice that values will appear. Use the products of your own imagination. Figure 8.34 shows data in the table.

prod_id	p_name	p_desc	p_cost
1	bird	moving animal i	$1.50
2	traditional frog	moving animal i	$2.25
3	magazine cover	useful object sir	$1.00
(AutoNumber)			$0.00

catalog : Table

FIGURE 8.34 The catalog table with sample data.

Access provides a mechanism sometimes referred to as query-by-example for specifying a query. From the database window, click on Queries and choose Create query in Design view as shown in Figure 8.35.

FIGURE 8.35 Window with options for specifying queries.

You will have a chance to add tables to the query. Since there is only one table, you have no choice except the one catalog table. Click Add, and then close as shown in Figure 8.36.

You will then see the screen shown in Figure 8.37.

The idea here is to put together a query by citing fields in the table or tables that have been added to the area at the top of the window. You can specify criteria. If you double-click on p_name and then p_cost, and then type in >1 or

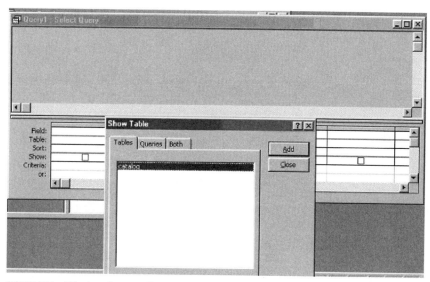

FIGURE 8.36   Window for specifying queries.

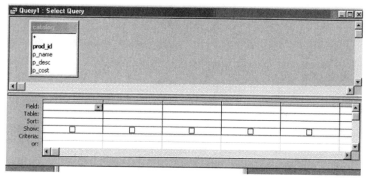

FIGURE 8.37   Screen showing start of process of defining a query graphically.

whatever a test would be for our data that selects only some of the records, the query will resemble Figure 8.38.

Run the query by clicking on the exclamation mark on the top toolbar as indicated in Figure 8.39.

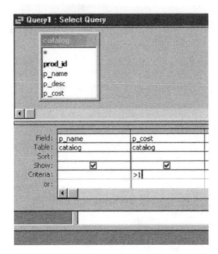

FIGURE 8.38 Screen shot showing process of defining query.

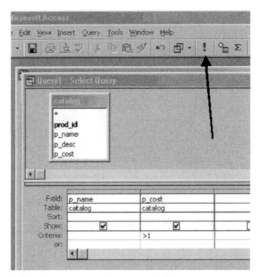

FIGURE 8.39 Arrow shows symbol to execute query.

Figure 8.40 shows the results of executing the query.

You can take the time to experiment making queries this way. One benefit is that the system will produce the SQL statement for you. Click on the View command and choose SQL View as shown in Figure 8.41.

You will see a window with the SQL statement corresponding to the query you designed as shown in Figure 8.42.

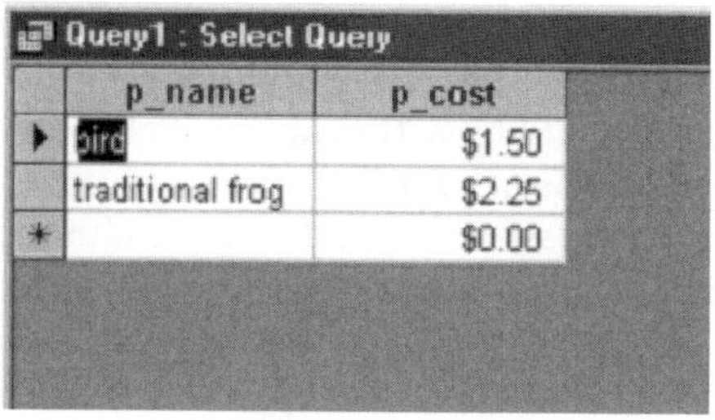

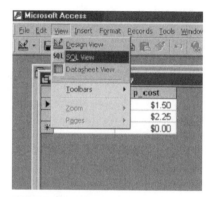

FIGURE 8.40   Results of query against
sample data.

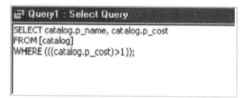

FIGURE 8.41   Option to obtain SQL
representation of query.

```
Query1 : Select Query
SELECT catalog.p_name, catalog.p_cost
FROM [catalog]
WHERE (((catalog.p_cost)>1));
```

FIGURE 8.42   SQL statement representing
query generated graphically.

REFLECTION

For both MySQL and Access, we have gone beyond what is necessary for a
database that will be accessed in a Web application using middleware. The
exact steps you take will depend on a variety of factors. The application, with
its database, already might exist and your task might be to port it to the Web.
You might find it useful to do some "batch" loading of records into the database working with the databases directly. You also might choose to use utilities
such as MyCC to create a new or modify an existing MySQL database. Chapter
16 identifies several critical issues to scale up your application.

It will help your understanding of databases in general, and MySQL and Access in particular, if you now reflect on what these two DBMS products have in common and how they differ. Certainly, the command interface of MySQL and the graphical user interface of Access is a big difference. The terminology for data types is another difference, although both products could produce essentially the same database. Continue to make these comparisons as you learn more about the use of the databases with PHP and ASP, respectively.

In the next chapter, you will learn about connecting to a database using PHP and ASP, and how to do simple insert and select queries.

EXERCISES, QUESTIONS, AND PROJECTS

1. Add additional tables to the test database in MySQL. Use show tables and describe *tablename* to confirm what you have done.
2. Create a source file to insert several records into the tables. Use select queries to confirm what you have done.
3. Add additional tables to the test database in Access.
4. Insert records into the tables. Make up a query in design view making use of two tables.
5. Using the general description of SQL statements in the previous chapter, use the SQL alter statement to add a new field called category to the catalog database in MySQL. Use describe catalog to confirm what you have done.
6. Assuming your description fields were similar to the ones here, use the SQL update statement to change the description fields to omit the "simple" and "intermediate" terms, and put that information into the category field.
7. In Access, change the values of fields in existing records, and add new records. Remember to save your work.
8. Go online and find out about the other data types supported by MySQL and Access.

CONNECTING TO THE DATABASE

T he purpose of this chapter is to explain how a middleware program such as a PHP or ASP script can access a database located on the server, perform insertions, and request information using simple select queries. This chapter will also address common problems and demonstrate debugging techniques. The next chapter will continue with more complex examples.

BACKGROUND

To understand the significance of the material covered in this chapter, you need to recall what middleware—that is, PHP or ASP/JavaScript—programs are; namely, programs running on the server computer in response to a request from a client computer. The server software makes the determination that the file is not a regular HTML file, but instead a PHP or ASP file. This leads to the file being interpreted by the PHP or ASP interpreter, again part of the server support system. The challenge for the interpreter that is covered in this chapter is how to do something other than just interpret PHP and ASP; namely, access (read from and write to) a database. The middleware program has to perform the same operations on a database that are done by the database management system (DBMS) in the stand-alone mode described in the previous chapter. The way the middleware program accomplishes the task is by making a connection to what is called the *driver* of the DBMS, namely MySQL or Access. This allows the DBMS functions to be invoked under program control to do SQL queries.

This chapter will cover how you can write PHP or ASP scripts to make these connections, and how you write the code to compose SQL statements and pass them to the DBMS. You have read about SQL and practiced writing SQL statements "on paper." You have also written them in command mode to access MySQL. You have done the equivalent of making SQL statements using the graphical user interface of Access. Now you will create SQL statements as character strings. These character strings will be arguments for PHP functions or ASP methods.

CONCEPTUAL EXPLANATION

The power of middleware is that the "making a connection to the DBMS" mentioned in the previous section actually is simple to program. However, you will need to make arrangements with your service provider before you proceed. In this chapter, we will describe the procedures we have designed for students at our institution.

What do you need to specify to set up the mechanisms for the middleware program to pass arguments to DBMS software? When you think about it, you should arrive at the following list:

- The name of the DBMS software. You are specifying the driver to be used by your program.
- The name and location of the specific database.
- Information relating to permissions, if required, such as user and password.

One more item of information you might have thought of concerns the mode of access. This specifies what you are going to do with the database; for example, just read it, or read and write. This might need to be specified explicitly so the system can protect the data from two people or, rather, two programs attempting to write at the same time. It is related to locking the database and will be discussed later in the chapter.

The presence of the first two as distinct items might be puzzling, but it is necessary. The commands need to specify in some way that it is a MySQL database or an Access database, in addition to "being told" the name and location of the specific database. You might think that there is some other program that will go to the database, see what type it is, and then go fetch the right software, but that is not how things work. The two systems, PHP and ASP, divide the specification of this information in different ways and also provide alternatives. This all contributes to the complexity. However, in each case, you need to write only a few lines of code. The standard practice is to put those lines of code in a separate file. Both PHP and ASP have a feature for including one file in another file. All your PHP or ASP scripts for a particular database will have calls to include the connection-making file.

Connecting with PHP

The PHP system has libraries for several DBMS products, including MySQL. For the other DBMSs, PHP has a set of functions making use of the Open Database Connectivity standard (ODBC). Since the text focuses on PHP and MySQL, you will use the MySQL functions. This is telling the system what DBMS you will be using. The command for making the connection is:

```
$link=mysql_connect($host,$user,$password);
```

where $host will indicate the host computer making the connection; $user, the user; and $password, the password. You could use constants in place of the variables. Recall the discussion in the previous chapter on the use of MySQL's grant statement. These relate to values set up by someone working on the server computer directly using the grant command. The value of $host would be "localhost." It definitely is not the client computer, because the connection is not made to the client computer but the server computer itself running the PHP program. At our college, our procedure is to use the same user IDs and passwords as the students use to upload their files using a File Transfer Protocol (FTP) program such as ws-ftp.

Notice that no mention has been made of the database. You have two options, and for one of those options, there again are two options. A PHP command exists to name the database:

```
$result=mysql_select_db($DBname);
```

will attempt to select a database for future commands, using the name in the variable $DBname. It will use the last opened link. The command returns and assigns to the variable indicated on the left-hand side of the assignment statement either true or false, depending on the success of the operation. It is a good idea to check these values and take appropriate action when operations fail. The appropriate action would be to return a message to the person on the client computer that the transactions cannot continue. The alternative is to have an ugly error message appear later in the process.

The other way to name the database is for you to specify the link:

```
$result=mysql_select_db($DBname,$link);
```

Assuming the firstdb is the name of your databases, you could also use a constant string:

```
$result=mysql_select_db("firstdb");
```

All the MySQL databases are kept in the same place on the server so there is no need to specify a path.

Alternatively, you can wait to specify the database until later when you make your queries. For example, the following command:

```
$result = mysql_db_query($DBname,$query, $link);
```

would specify the database named in the variable $DBname, pass along the query held in a string in the variable $query, and making use of the connection named in the variable $link.

Connecting with ASP

Let us move on to the ASP system, where, again, there are multiple ways to accomplish the same tasks. The ASP system provides a mechanism similar to what has just been described for PHP in which you specify the information directly in the program. However, it also supports a mechanism using what are called *data source names*, or DSNs. These DSNs are a way to package the DBMS information and the file and path to the specific database information in one place. You need to contact your Internet service provider (ISP) to find out if you need to use a DSN or use the other mechanism, called *DSN-less*, that will be described later.

If you are doing development work on your own computer, using Internet Information Server (IIS) or some other software, you can use the DSN method. You can define your own DSN on your computer by clicking on Start/Control Panel/Administrative Tools as shown in Figure 9.1.

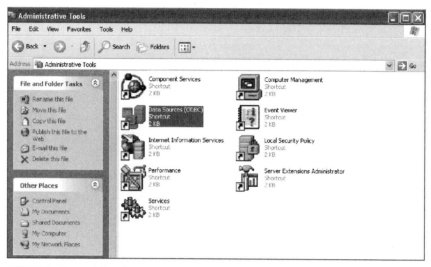

FIGURE 9.1   Control Panel.

Next, click on ODBC Data Sources. You will see something like Figure 9.2. Click on the System DSN tab. You now will see something like Figure 9.3. Yours might have no entries.

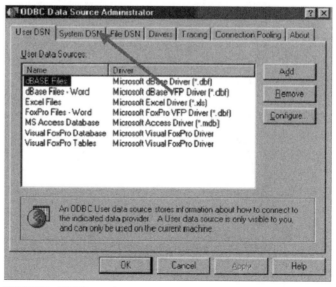

FIGURE 9.2   ODBC panel.

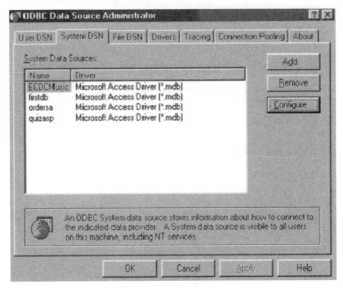

FIGURE 9.3   System Data Sources already set up.

To make a DSN, click the Add... button. What you see depends on what drivers you have loaded on your computer. It will look something like Figure 9.4.

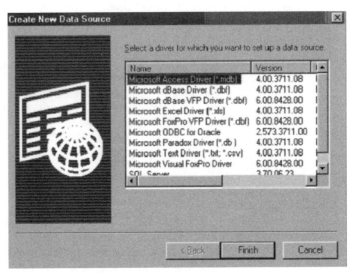

FIGURE 9.4   Panel to create a new data source.

Select the driver. In the case of Access, it is the one highlighted here. Click Finish. You will now have a chance to name the database, using the window shown in Figure 9.5.

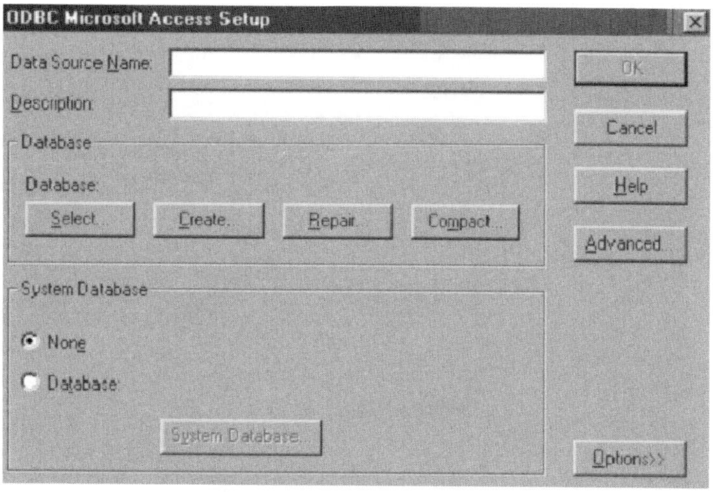

FIGURE 9.5   Panel to enter data for DSN.

First, however, give the data source name and a description of the database. The first two text boxes already are filled in the screen shot as shown in Figure 9.6.

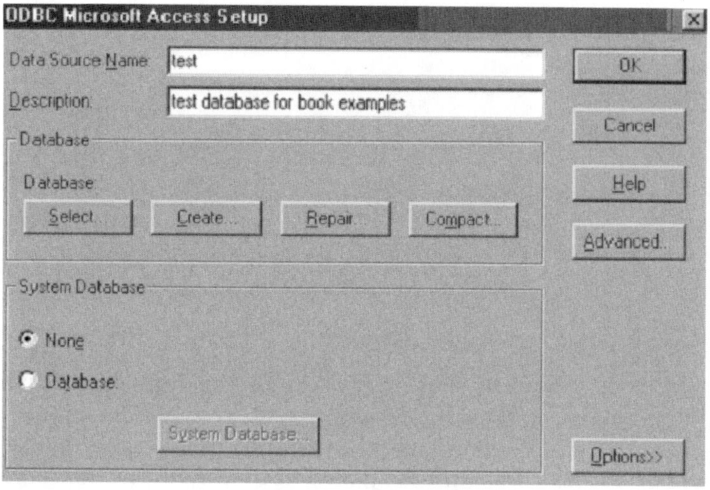

FIGURE 9.6   Form for DSN with test entries.

Now, click Select to see the usual Windows window for locating a file. Notice that you have the option to create a database. The screen shot in Figure 9.7 appears after browsing to a folder.

Select the database you want, and click OK. You will see something like the window shown in Figure 9.8.

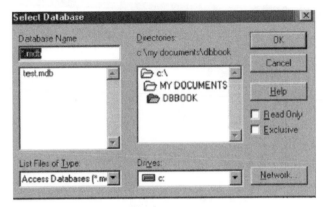

FIGURE 9.7   Window to select file.

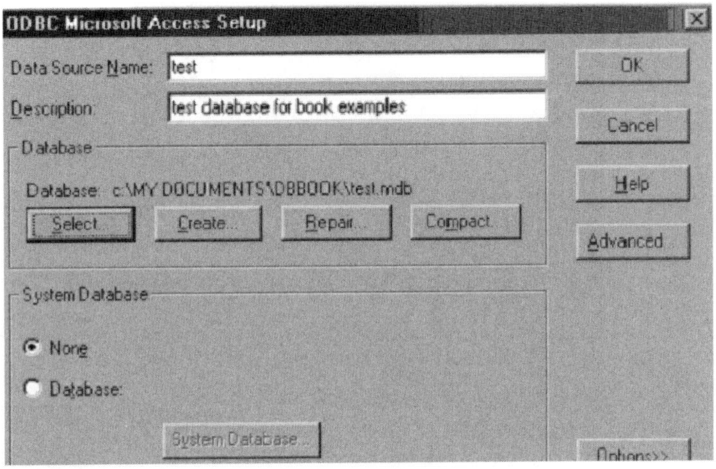

FIGURE 9.8   Form after selecting actual file.

Click OK, and from now on, you can use the DSN name you indicated in your commands. We will use `firstdb` or `test` in our examples. Your Internet Service Provider might give you a DSN to use.

The ASP and JavaScript system requires that you define the variables before using them. In this case, this means that you need to use the `CreateObject` method of the `Server` object to create an object of type `ADODB.Connection`. You will see this construction several more times. The code is:

```
Conn=Server.CreateObject("ADODB.Connection");
```

At this point, `Conn` is a variable holding a connection object. To make the connection for using the database defined by a DSN, you use the following code:

```
DSN="DSN=firstdb";
Conn.Open(DSN);
```

Notice that the variable called DSN is not the string "firstdb," but the string "DSN=firstdb." Conn is an object of type ADODB.Connection. All objects of this type have a method named Open. The Open method can take as a parameter a DSN.

Now let us turn to the DSN-less way. Again, you will follow the directions of your service provider. At our institution, we use the DSN-less way. Specifically, the students create their own Access databases, including specifying the tables. They then upload the databases using FTP.

To set up a DSN-less connection, you still need to create an object of type ADODB.Connection, and you do it the same way. However, now, you will prepare a string to use with the Open method. The string will hold information on the DBMS driver and the database itself. It is called a *connection string*.

```
strConnect =
"Driver={Microsoft Access Driver (*.mdb)};"
+ "DBQ=" + Server.MapPath("firstdb.mdb") ;
  Conn=Server.CreateObject("ADODB.Connection");
  Conn.Open (strConnect, "admin", "") ;
```

The string used for the Open specifies two parameters by name: Driver and DBQ. The Driver parameter is what is indicated between the curly brackets. The DBQ parameter must be the path to the firstdb database. The way we get the path is through use of the MapPath method of the Server object. The second parameter to the Open method names a user; we use "admin." The third parameter could contain a password. For industrial applications, you will probably choose a DBMS other than MS Access, and you will follow the procedures for passwords.

As promised, this is not a large amount of code, but it makes sense to put it in a file by itself to be included by all the files needing access to the database. Using this technique, you have just one place to go to if there are changes.

The PHP system has the include command for bringing one file into another file. When the statement is executed, the named file is brought into the calling file. If you have the statement within an if clause and control never goes to the clause, then the include operation will not happen. The PHP system has an alternative, the require command. This causes the named file to be included even if the section of code with the require statement is not executed. Use of include could conceivably save time by preventing loading of another file when it is not necessary. ASP has an include mechanism also, but it is not a statement but part of a comment. You will see examples of all these commands in the *Examples* section. In either case, you will need to name the file to be included and give it an extension. One practice is to use the extension .inc to remind you that this is not a file used by itself, but one included in other files. This reminder is beneficial. However, an alternative is to use the extension .php or .asp. This will prevent the file from being examined by someone browsing the Web. Since you might be putting password information here, you would not want others to see the files.

Making Queries

Continuing the explanation of the use of databases, assume that you have written the program to make the connection to an existing database with tables already defined. You now want to write code to insert a record or query the database using a select statement. The items of information you need to specify are:

- The connection already established
- The database name if that is not part of the connection and has not been specified already
- The query

The differences between PHP and ASP should now be familiar to you. The PHP code makes use of one of the commands in the MySQL library, and it has been mentioned already:

```
$result = mysql_db_query($DBname,$query, $link);
```

This assumes that the variables listed as the parameters have all been set to the database name, the query string, and the link, respectively. The $result variable will be assigned the result code indicating success or failure for an insert query. For a select query, the $result variable will hold what the query returns in the special data type called a *recordset*.

The ASP code is different depending on whether the query is a select or something else. For an insert, the command is:

```
result = Conn.Execute(query)
```

where Conn is the ADODB.Connection object already created and opened with the database specified. However, if the query is going to return a recordset, you will need to write the code to create an object of ADODB.Recordset. The code for this is:

```
rs=Server.CreateObject("ADODB.RecordSet");
rs.Open (query, Conn);
```

where query is a string holding the select statement, and Conn is, as before, the connection object. The Open method of the recordset can have two more parameters. The third parameter, which is optional, specifies the type of cursor, the internal pointer, to be used for the recordset. The significance of this is that you cannot use the default of zero if you want to find out the number of rows returned by the query. The fourth parameter specifies the locking mechanism.

The PHP and ASP systems handle locking in distinct ways. Locking is when you indicate that other programs are not to make use of the database or to make only limited (read-only) use. The PHP/MySQL system provides the SQL commands `Lock` and `Unlock` to lock a table from any other access and then restore access. The ASP system lets you specify a mode of access for the connection. For example:

```
Conn.Mode = 3;
```

specifies read and write access, without locking out any other access. Other modes include read only, write only, and modes that lock out other programs from reading or from writing. The ASP system also allows you to set up locking conditions at the time of opening the recordset. The statement:

```
rs.Open(query, Conn, 2, 3);
```

will set the cursor condition to provide going back and forth through the rows of the recordset and not lock out other users except at the moment that you update the recordset. For your information, much of the online ASP documentation makes use of a set of constants called ADOVBS. For example, `adOpenDynamic` is 2, and `adLockOptimistic` is 3. If you go to an online source, you might see the following in place of the previous line:

```
rs.Open(query, Conn, adOpenDynamic, adLockOptimistic);
```

If you looked in the code surrounding this line, you probably would not find the definitions of `adOpenDynamic` and `adLockOptimistic`. Instead, the example is making use of the ADOVBS constants. You can download a copy of the file from the Web and include it (or, more exactly, put in an `include` command to bring in the file). Since these are the only two we use, we use the actual values. An argument can be made that the named constants make the code more readable.

The recordset object requires special commands to get at the individual rows. In PHP, these will be commands from the library for MySQL. For ASP/JavaScript, you will use methods of the recordset object.

The last thing you need to do is close the connection to the database. The PHP and ASP systems both have commands to do this. Closing the connection frees up systems resources so it is a good thing to do.

Before closing this section, it is time to mention that you can and most probably will make mistakes when you develop applications! Programming problems, named *bugs* by Grace Murray Hopper, one of the pioneers of computing, can be sorted into two categories: problems that the system detects, and problems that it does not detect. In the first case, processing will stop and you will see some message produced by the PHP or ASP interpreter saying that you have an error. The message often contains a line number, although the problem might have occurred prior to that point in the code. Although seeing these messages can be annoying, this actually is the good case. In the second case, the system "finds no fault" with the coding in your scripts. However, the results are not what you intended. This situation is complicated by the basic nature of middleware in which processing is occurring in three different places: interpreting the PHP or ASP script, invoking the DBMS driver programs, and displaying the HTML. These situations require you to examine the results and, if they are not what you want, study all your scripts to discover the location of the problem.

It is possible for you to write code that will test the return values given by the DBMS software. You need to devise the appropriate action if such an event occurs, but it is generally better for you to generate a suitable display for the people using your application than for them to see a systems error message. This is sometimes referred to as *error catching* or *error trapping*, although those terms sometimes are reserved for more elaborate mechanisms than what is shown here.

One general recommendation is to proceed incrementally in your development: divide tasks into smaller tasks, and get the smaller ones working. You also need to make sure you test your application adequately. This means you need to take on the role of your customers and imagine what data they might enter into forms. Many programming systems have elaborate tools for debugging. With middleware, you are more on your own, but this might change over time. One technique you might need to use when a problem occurs is to put in statements that display the state of variables at different stages in the process. These strategies will be demonstrates in the examples that follow.

EXAMPLES

This section includes sample code in PHP and ASP for a simple database application. To further your understanding of middleware development, even though the examples are contrived, you will see examples of code that would never be included in a "real" application, and code with mistakes, which we will debug.

ON THE CD

The project demonstrated here is a catalog of favorite TV shows. The CD-ROM contains the code for the projects in the folder named chapter9code. This project is developed further in the next chapter.

MySQL and PHP

The steps suggested for the PHP project are:

1. Make arrangements with your ISP/Web host for you to have access to a MySQL database.
2. Write the connection code script. This will be an included file. The `require` function will be used in the other files to include the connection script.

3. Write the script to create the table for the database. This will be a test of the included file.
4. Run the `create table file` again. This will be a test of the internal error catching.
5. Write a script to insert a specific TV show. This is what is termed "throw-away code." It would not be part of the "real" application, but it will demonstrate the basics of insertion.
6. Write a script that displays the contents of the database.
7. Write a script that generates a form for a new entry to the favorites table and the handler for the form. Test the program with different titles and descriptions.

Let us assume that a database has been created on the server with the name firstdb and you have access to it as user id='curley' and password='12345'. The host will be "localhost", because this access will be in PHP scripts run on the same server as the database. Create the following file, with the appropriate changes in user ID and password:

```php
<?php
$host="localhost";
$user="curley";
$password="12345";
$DBname="firstdb";
$link=mysql_connect($host,$user,$password);
?>
```

The code in this file does not use $DBname, but it sets it and also sets $link. These will be the two values used in the code in the files that include this file.

Save this file with the name openfirstdb.php. Upload this file to your folder on the server.

Now you need to write the script to create a table, the only table, in the database. The following script will do the job (after you make the change to go to the name of your folder on the server instead of the name of our folder on our server):

```php
<html>
<head>
<title>Creating favorite table </title>
</head>
<body>
<h3> Creating the favorites table for firstdb </h3>
<br>
<?php
print ("about to make connection");
require("openfirstdb.php");
$tname = "favorites";
$fields =
```

```
"favorite_id INT UNSIGNED NOT NULL  AUTO_INCREMENT";
$fields = $fields .
"PRIMARY KEY, title char(50) NOT NULL, ";
$fields = $fields . "description char(50) NOT NULL";
$query="CREATE TABLE $tname ($fields)";
if (mysql_db_query($DBname,$query,$link)) {
   print ("The table, $tname, was created");
   print (" successfully.<br>\n");
}
else {
   print ("The table, $tname, was not created.");
   print (" <br>\n");
}
mysql_close($link);
?>
</body></html>
```

This code makes the assumption that `$link` has been defined to be the connection to the database. The `if` construction will let you know if the table was successfully created, because the function call `mysql_db_query` returns true or false based on what happens in the MySQL driver performing this query.

It is possible to avoid defining `$tname` and `$fields` as separate variables. In fact, you could even avoid defining `$query` and put everything in the `mysql_db_query` statement. The approach chosen here is to use simpler statements even if there are more of them rather than more complex statements. If you have any problems, PHP displays a line number, and so you are better off with more lines.

You could use a more general approach to the task of creating tables:

Function for creating a table of a given name and with specified fields
> *Construct query using arguments to function*
> *Invoke query, use if test to check success*

(end of function)
Make connection
Construct string representing field definitions
Call function with table name and field string
Close connection

The code for this approach is the following:

```
<?php
function createtable($tname,$fields) {
global $DBname, $link;
$query="CREATE TABLE $tname ($fields)";
if (mysql_db_query($DBname,$query,$link)) {
   print ("The table, $tname, was created");
```

```
    print ("  successfully.<br>\n");
}
else {
print ("The table, $tname, was not created. <br>\n");
    }
}
?>
<html>
<head><title>Creating favorite table </title>
</head>
<body>
<h3> Creating the favorites table for firstdb </h3>
<br>
<?php
print ("about to make connection");
require("openfirstdb.php");
$tname = "favorites";
$fields = "favorite_id INT UNSIGNED NOT NULL";
$fields = $fields . " AUTO_INCREMENT PRIMARY KEY, ";
$fields = $fields . "title char(50) NOT NULL, ";
$fields = $fields . "description char(50) NOT NULL";
createtable($tname, $fields);
mysql_close($link);
?>
```

This last script makes use of a function for creating the table. The statement:

```
global $DBname, $link;
```

tells the PHP interpreter to use the existing values for these variables and not define new variables, what are called *local variables*, for use just within the function. So, why go to the trouble of defining and using a function when it does seem to be more trouble? The answer is not clear-cut. This particular example, with just one table, does not justify using a function. However, in later applications, you will have a database with more than one table, and you can copy this one.

Upload this file to the server and try it out. You should see the message that the table was successfully created. If it does not work, check your code and consult with your server support crew. Assuming that your problems do not involve permissions, you might be able to find a problem by adding `print` statements to your script. For example, put in the line:

```
print("The query is: $query");
```

right before the `if` statement with the call to `mysql_db_query`. You will see the query in the HTML statement. If there is a problem with the query, you probably will be able to detect and fix it.

Moving on, run the create table script again. What happens? Hopefully, you will get the message that the table was not created. This is because the MySQL system notices that you already have a table by the name of "favorites" and will not let you create another one. This is a good result. It shows that the if test works both ways.

Now you will write a script for putting a single, specific record into the database. The TV show *ER* was chosen because it was the shortest possible name. Please make your own selection. The code with explanation is given in Table 9.1.

TABLE 9.1   PHP Script to Enter Specific Record into Favorites Table

`<html><head><title>Input and submit favorites to firstdb database </title></head><body>`	HTML tags
`<?php`	Start PHP
`require("openfirstdb.php");`	Connecting code
`$tname="favorites";`	Set name of table
`$title="ER";`	Set name of specific show
`$description="medical drama";`	Set description
`$query = "INSERT INTO $tname VALUES('0', '$title', '$description')";`	Set the query
`$result = mysql_db_query($DBname, $query, $link);`	Invoke the query
`if ($result) {`	Check result
`    print("The favorite was successfully added. \n"); }`	Print message indicating success
`else {print ("The favorite was NOT successfully added.  \n");}`	Print message indicating failure
`mysql_close($link);`	Close connection
`?>`	End PHP
`</body></html>`	Closing HTML tags

Notice the presence of the single quotation marks in the query statement. The MySQL software requires the quotation marks. Again, you can avoid using variables and put everything into one statement, but the complexity of the syntax makes this a better tactic for avoiding typos. Upload and try this program. Again, if you have problems, check the value of $title, $tname, and $query using print statements. The most likely error is a typo involving the punctuation.

If the program displays the message that the favorite was successfully added, you really cannot be certain that your program works! All you know is that it did not fail with a system error. To determine for sure that you have made an entry to the database, you need to write a script to display the contents. This is the next step.

The plan for the *showfavorites* script will be to use the simplest `select` query: select * from favorites. This will produce a recordset made up of one row for each record in the table. You will use special functions for working with recordsets, to be explained later in the context of the script. The script starts out like the previous ones, with HTML and then with PHP. The `require` command is used to connect to the database.

```
<html>
<head>
<title>Showing the contents of the favorites table
</title></head>
<body>
<h1>Favorite shows <br></h1>
<?
  require("openfirstdb.php");
```

The next lines of code set up and then make the query to the database. The $rs variable holds the recordset.

```
$sq ="SELECT * from favorites";
$rs = mysql_db_query($DBname,$sq,$link);
```

The rows (there is probably just one row at this point) are to be displayed as rows of an HTML table. Your code needs to output the HTML to start the table. This means the <table> tag and the first row holding heading information.

```
print("<table><tr><td> Titles</td>");
print("<td>Descriptions</td> </tr> ");
```

Now you need to get a row of the recordset, extract from it the title and description fields, and display each of these with <td> and </td> tags of a new row of the table. The function to "get" a row is mysql_fetch_array. Recordsets are special things that come with an implicit pointer to the current row. The mysql_fetch_array function does two things: it returns the current row as an array, and it advances the pointer to the next row. If there are no more rows, the function returns a value that an `if` statement or a `while` statement interprets as false. This means that you can use a `while` loop to go through the rows of the recordset.

The array is an associative array. This means that the elements can be extracted using the names of the fields. The array has three elements, but the code ignores the favorite_id element. You do need to print out the tag to start the row and the tag to end it. It is not strictly necessary, but it is useful to print out this HTML with line breaks for every row of the recordset (which is also every row of the HTML table). The command to do that is:

```
print("\n");
```

The "\n" is the ASCII code for line break. Try your script without this and you will see what its function is.

The rest of the *show favorites* script follows:

```
while ($row=mysql_fetch_array($rs)) {
  print("\n");
  print("<tr><td>");
  print($row["title"]);
  print("</td><td>");
  print( $row["description"]);
  print("</td> </tr>");
}  // end while
print("</table>");
?>
</body>
</html>
```

Upload this file and test it. You should now modify your script for adding a specific favorite to add another favorite. Upload and run it, and then run the *showfavorite* script again. You now have a system for inserting entries into the database and displaying them. However, it does require the services of someone who can write PHP. You will fix that in the next step: creating a script for showing the table, and creating a form for users to enter a new favorite title and description into the database.

Before continuing, you might want to try and write this script yourself. You now know how to do it, making use of the previous scripts in this chapter and copying parts of the state capital quiz in a prior chapter. Think about what you need for this task:

1. A script that presents a form and then serves as the handler for the form. The state capital quiz scripts serve as models.
2. The code that extracts form input data. Again, the state capital quiz scripts demonstrate how this is done.
3. Code for inserting something in a database. The script in this chapter in which we inserted ER is one model. You need to create a query that has constant parts, and parts that are variables that arise from form data.
4. Code for displaying the contents of a table in the database. This is the *show* script developed earlier in this section.

The code for *saddfavorites.php* is provided in Table 9.2.

Hopefully, you will copy this script accurately and get it working. Try it with different favorites. If you run into difficulty, continue reading to the end of this section.

TABLE 9.2   PHP Script to Handle and Display Form to Make Insertion of Favorite

`<html><head><title>Input and submit favorites to firstdb database </title></head>`	Usual HTML tags and text
`<body>`	HTML body tag
`<?php`	Start PHP
`require("openfirstdb.php");`	Function to include the script for connecting to the database
`if (@($submitted)) {`	If test to see if this is for handling the form or presenting the form. The true clause is handling the form. The @ prevents an error message if $submitted has not been set
`$valuesx = " VALUES ('0','" . $title . "', '" . $description . "')";`	Uses form data to define the variable $valuesx
`$query="INSERT INTO favorites " . $valuesx;`	Defines $query. This could have been combined with the prior step
`print("Insert query is: " . $query);`	Just in case there are any problems, displays the query. Remove when everything is working
`$result = mysql_db_query($DBname, $query, $link);`	Invokes the MySQL software to do the query. $result will be a return code
`if ($result) {`	Check return code
`print("The favorite was successfully added. \n");`	True clause causes a successful message to be displayed
`}`	Closes the true clause
`else {`	Start of else (not successful) clause
`print ("The favorite was NOT successfully added.  \n");`	Print that favorite was not added
`}`	End else clause
`$submitted = FALSE;`	Set $submitted to false for next time
`mysql_close($link);`	Close link to database
`print ("<a href=\"saddfavoriter. php\">Submit another favorite </a> ");`	Display link (a tag) to enter new favorite. Note direction of slashes
`} //ends if submitted`	Ends the true clause checking if this is the handler
`else {`	Start else clause: this is the clause to display the form

(continues)

TABLE 9.2   PHP Script to Handle and Display Form to Make Insertion of Favorite (*continued*)

`?>`	Get out of PHP
`<h1>Add a title to the databank of favorite shows.  </h1>`	Regular HTML. You could use a `print` statement
`<?`	Resume PHP code
`$sq ="SELECT * from favorites";`	Define `$sq` as constant query to get all of favorites table
`print("<h3>Favorites</h3> ");`	Print heading
`$rs = mysql_db_query($DBname,$sq,$link);`	Perform the `select` query. `$rs` will be a recordset
`print("<table><tr><td> Titles</td> <td>Descriptions</td> </tr> ");`	Print HTML tags for start of table
`print("\n");`	Put a line break in the HTML source
`while ($row=mysql_fetch_array($rs)) {`	Start `while` loop, which extracts a row at a time from the recordset. This will fail when recordset is exhausted (no more rows, that is, no more records)
`print("\n");`	Put a line break in the HTML source
`print("<tr><td>");`	Print starting row, and starting `td` tags
`print($row["title"]);`	Print the title field of the record
`print("</td><td>");`	Print the closing `td` tag and a starting `td` tag
`print($row["description"]);`	Print the description field of the record
`print("</td> </tr>");`	Print closing `td` and closing `tr` tags
`}  // end while`	End the `while`
`print("</table>");`	Print the closing table tag
`?>`	End PHP code
`<form action="saddfavoriter.php" method="POST"> `	Regular HTML for a form: `form` tag
`Title of show <input type=text name="title" size=50>  `	Input tag for title
`Description <input type=text name="description" size=50>  `	Input tag for description
`<input type=hidden name="submitted" value="True"> `	Input tag for hidden item: this will be the `$submitted` that is checked to see if a form has been submitted
`<input type=submit name="submit" value="Submit favorite!"> `	Input tag for Submit button

TABLE 9.2   *(continued)*

`</form>`	Prints the closing `form` tag
`<?`	Start PHP
`}  //ends else clause for submitting form`	Ends the `else` clause (of the `if(@$submitted)` test
`?>`	End PHP
`</body>`	Regular HTML close `body` tag
`</html>`	Regular HTML close `HTML` tag

Examples of Errors

To demonstrate what errors can look like, make an error on purpose. Suppose that someone entered the preceding script but made the following two typos:

Change the line outputting the title field to have an extra closing parenthesis:

```
print($row["title"]));
```

Omit the line printing the closing table tag:

```
print ("</table>");
```

If you named this file saddfavoritesbug.php, uploaded and invoked it, you would see the error message indicated in the next two lines.

```
Parse error: parse error, unexpected ')' in
D:\inetpub\wwwroot\jeanine\saddfavoritesbug.php on line 32
```

Count down 32 lines and you will reach (no surprise) the line with the extra parenthesis. This is a very common error. Get into the practice of matching opening and closing parentheses, curly brackets, and tags. Hopefully, if something like this happens, you would examine the statement and notice that the opening and closing parentheses do not match. Fix this error and try again. This time, the problem is subtler. You might see something like Figure 9.9.

This would vary with different browsers. In this case, the table is misplaced. Instead of being before the form, it is after the form. Sometimes it is helpful to look at the HTML source. You, using a browser to navigate to a PHP or ASP file, cannot examine the file itself. However, you can invoke View

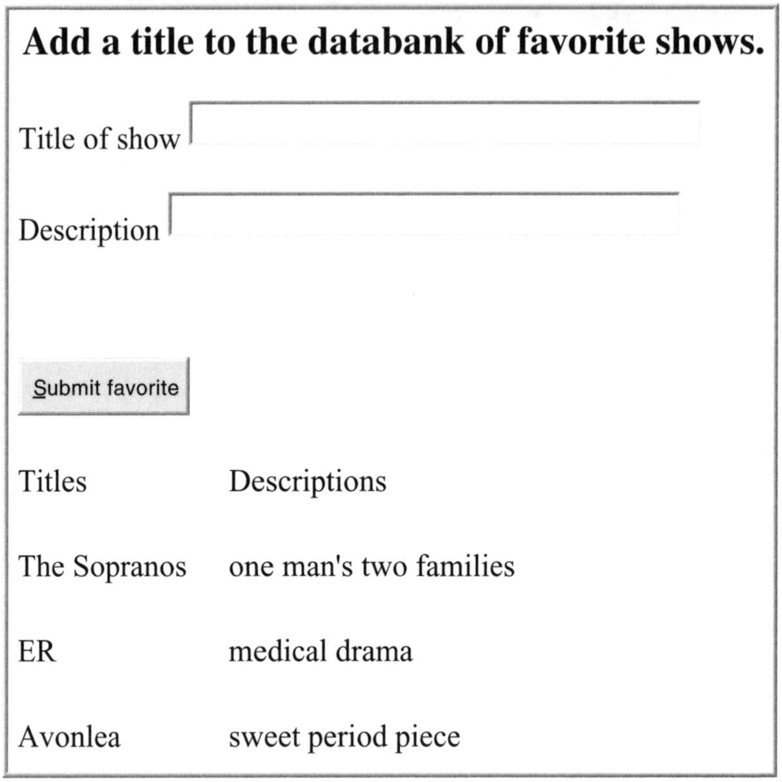

FIGURE 9.9   Screen capture showing misplaced table.

Source to look at the HTML that the middleware produces. For this example, it would be the following:

```
<html>
<head>
<title>Input and submit favorites to firstdb database
</title>
</head>
<body>
<h1>Add a title to the databank of favorite shows.
<br></h1>
<h3>Favorites</h3>
<br>
<table>
<tr><td> Titles</td> <td>Descriptions</td> </tr>
<tr><td>The Sopranos</td>
<td>one man's two families</td> </tr>
```

```
<tr><td>ER</td><td>medical drama</td> </tr>
<tr><td>Avonlea</td><td>sweet period piece</td>
</tr>
<form action="saddfavoritesbug.php" method="GET"><br>
Title of show <input type=text name="title" size=50>
<br>
Description <input type=text name="description"
size=50> <br>
<input type=hidden name="submitted" value="True"><br>
<input type=submit name="submit" value="Submit
favorite!"><br>
</form>
</body> </html>
```

Note that we have added line breaks to make it more readable.

Again, hopefully, after noticing the misplaced table in the display, when you examine the HTML source (the HTML produced by the PHP script), you will notice the absence of the closing tag </table>. Fix this and try again.

Access and ASP

Now we turn to the ASP example. The ASP project has similar, but not exactly the same, steps as the PHP project.

1. On your own computer, create an Access database. Put a couple of records into the table. Upload it to the server.
2. Write the code for connecting to the database. You will use the DSN-less method.
3. Test the connection code by writing a simple show program.
4. Write a script for inserting a specific new record into the table. This is throwaway code.
5. Write a form and the handler for the form for inserting new favorites. This will make use of the prior scripts. Test with different examples.
6. It will turn out that problems arise in the ASP case when the input contains symbols such as apostrophes. We will debug and fix the problem.
7. Download the database and examine the records. You can make additions, deletions, and changes to the records. Upload the modified file back to the server. This option is more reasonable for Access than for MySQL, given the graphical user interface of Access.

The first step repeats what was described in the previous chapters. Create a database with a single table, called favorites, with three fields:

- favorite_id
- title
- description

You can enter a couple of records. Upload it to the server. The second step is to create the file that will establish the connection:

```
<%
Conn = Server.CreateObject("ADODB.Connection");
Conn.Mode = 3  ;
strConnect = "Driver={Microsoft Access Driver
(*.mdb)};" + "DBQ=" + Server.MapPath("firstdb.mdb") ;
Conn.Open (strConnect, "admin", "") ;
%>
```

The connection mode establishes that you will be doing reading and writing. The `Server.MapPath` is a way to obtain the complete path to the file. The connection is opened setting the user to be `"admin"` and with no password. You might need to consult with your service provider. Name the file *sopenconn.asp* and upload it to the server.

To show all the records in the database, you will send the `select * from favorites` query to the database and then display the results by putting the information in each row of the recordset into `td` elements. The commands for manipulating the recordset are different for ASP than for PHP, but the effects are the same. The recordset has an implicit pointer. The code advances the pointer by the method `move`. So, if result holds the recordset:

```
result.move(1);
```

advances to the next record. The property:

```
result.EOF
```

will be true if you have reached the end of the recordset, and false, otherwise. Table 9.3 shows the code with explanation.

TABLE 9.3   ASP Script for Showing Favorites

`<%@ Language=JavaScript %>`	Set language to JavaScript
`<html><head><title>Show favorites</title></head>`	HTML
`<body>`	HTML
`<!- #include file="sopenconn.asp"  ->`	Call to include the connection file. Note that it is in the form of a comment
`<%`	Start ASP
`var query="Select * from favorites";`	Define variable query to be the select query
`Response.Write("query is: " + query);`	Display it. Remove when everything works

TABLE 9.3   *(continued)*

`var result = Server.CreateObject` `("ADODB.RecordSet");`	Define the variable `result` to hold a recordset
`result.Open(query,Conn);`	The open method of a recordset is what acquires the records from the database
`Response.Write("<table>");`	Display HTML opening table tag
`while (!result.EOF) {`	Start while loop. The loop body will be executed if result is not at the end
`Response.Write("\n");`	Output a line break to the HTML

`Response.Write("<tr><td> " +`
`result.fields.item("title") +`
`"</td> <td>");`
	Output the title item of the fields at the current record (row) of result with the appropriate table tags

`Response.Write(result.fields.item` `("description") + "</td></tr>");`	Output the description item of the fields of the current record of result, with appropriate table tags
`result.move(1);`	Advance the pointer for `result`
`}`	Close the `while`
`Response.Write(" </table>");`	Output the closing table tag
`Conn.Close();`	Close the connection
`%> </body> </html>`	End ASP and then output the closing HTML tags

The next step is to write a script that inserts a specific title. Hopefully, the following should be clear to you. The `insert` query is sent to the database using the `Execute` method of the `connection` object:

```
Conn.Execute(query)
```

In this example, instead of using an assignment statement to put the result in a separate variable, the call is used directly as the condition to an `if` statement.

```
<%@ Language=JavaScript %>
<html>
<head>
<title>Input specific title
</title>
</head>
<body>
<!- #include file="sopenconn.asp"  ->
<%
var fields = " (title, description) ";
var valuesx = " VALUES ('The Princess Bride','silly')";
```

```
var query="INSERT INTO favorites " + fields + valuesx;
Response.Write("Insert query is: " + query);
if (Conn.Execute(query))
  {
   Response.Write
   ("<br>Title was successfully entered.  <br>");
  }
else
  {
   Response.Write("Title was NOT entered.<br>");
  }
Conn.Close();
%>
</body>
</html>
```

At this point, as in the previous case, you could attempt to do the next step on your own: prepare a script to both display the contents of the favorites table and a form for adding a new title, and handle the form by taking the form data and making the insertion. You have the scripts from the state capital quiz, the script just explained for adding a specific title, and the PHP script to use as models.

Table 9.4 shows the script with explanation.

TABLE 9.4   ASP Script for Inputting a New Favorite

`<%@ Language=JavaScript %>`	Set language to JavaScript
`<html><head><title>Input and submit favorites to firstdb database </title></head><body>`	Usual HTML
`<!- #include file="sopenconn.asp"  ->`	Include file with connection code
`<%`	Start ASP
`var submitted=String(Request.Form ("submitted"));`	Define variable submitted from form data. The function `String` ensures that the data is a string and testable. It can still be undefined
`if (submitted !="undefined") {`	`if` test to see if the invocation is to handle the form or display it. True clause is for handling the form
`  var title = String(Request. Form("title"));`	Defines title from form data
`  var description= String(Request. Form("description"));`	Defines description from form data
`  var valuesx = " VALUES ('"+title+"', '" + description +"')";`	Defines `valuesx` from the variables from form data

TABLE 9.4   (*continued*)

`var fields = " (title, description) ";`	Defines fields as a constant
`var query="INSERT INTO favorites " + fields + valuesx;`	Puts it all together to be the query
`Response.Write("Insert query is: " + query);`	Writes out query just in case there are problems. Remove this line when everything works
`if (Conn.Execute(query))`	Sends the query to the database and does a check. True clause means the insertion was successful
`{Response.Write(" Title was successfully entered.  ");}`	Displays message indicating success
`else {Response.Write("Title was NOT entered. "); }`	else clause: displays message indicating failure
`Conn.Close();`	Close the connection
`Response.Write("<a href=\"saddfavorite. asp\"> Submit another title </a>  ");`	Outputs the HTML for a link to enter a new title
`}  // ends if form was submitted.`	Ends true if clause
`else {`	Start else clause (need to display form)
`%>`	Close ASP
`<h1>Add a title to the databank of favorite shows.  </h1>`	Regular HTML: heading
`<%`	Start ASP
`var sq ="SELECT * from favorites";`	Define sq to be the select query
`Response.Write("<h2>Favorites</h2>");`	Output heading
`rs=Server.CreateObject ("ADODB.RecordSet");`	Define rs to be a recordset object
`rs.Open (sq,Conn);`	The Open method gets the data into the recordset
`Response.Write("<table><tr><td> Titles</td> <td>Descriptions</td> </tr> ");`	Output the HTML for the start of the table
`while (!(rs.EOF)){`	while test: it will loop until the end of the recordset
`Response.Write("<tr><td>" + String(rs.fields.item("title"))+ " </td><td>"+ String(rs.fields.item ("description"))+ "</td> </tr>");`	Output HTML tags, title field, and description field
`rs.move(1);`	Advance the implicit pointer to the next record of the recordset

(continues)

TABLE 9.4 ASP Script for Inputting a New Favorite *(continued)*

`}  // end while`	End the while
`Response.Write("</table>");`	Output the closing table tag
`%>`	End ASP
`<form action="saddfavorite.asp" method="POST"> `	Regular HTML: the opening form tag
`Title of show <input type=text name="title" size=50>  `	The text and input tag for the title
`Description <input type=text name="description" size=50>  `	The text and input tag for the description
`<input type=hidden name="submitted" value="True"> `	The input tag for the hidden submitted value
`<input type=submit name="submit" value="Submit favorite!"> `	The tag for the Submit button
`</form>`	Closing form
`<%`	Start ASP
`}  //ends else clause for submitting form`	Close the else clause for the test on if a form was submitted
`%>`	Close ASP
`</body> </html>`	Closing HTML tags

Example of Problem Input

You are done, following along the path the text has shown you. However, if you now try to enter a title such as *The Sopranos* with the description set to "one man's two families," you will see the following lines on the screen, starting with a debugging message we included in the script.

```
Insert query is: INSERT INTO favorites (title, description) VALUES
   ('The Sopranos', 'one man's two families')
Microsoft OLE DB Provider for ODBC Drivers error '80040e14'
[Microsoft][ODBC Microsoft Access Driver] Syntax error (missing
   operator) in query expression ''one man's two families')'.
/jeanine/saddfavorite.asp, line 14
```

The first line is the "just in case" line indicated in the explanation column. It is not part of the error message. This is an indication that the error was detected at runtime, not before. At this point, since you have already tested this script with other entries, it is safe to assume that your code does not have any syntax (punctuation) problems.

Examine the query as displayed by your code. Do you see the problem? The 14th line contains the call to execute the query. The error message detects a syntax error. It turns out that the problem is that the description field has an apostrophe, otherwise known as a single quotation mark, and quotation marks have special meaning to MySQL. Now the question is, what to do about it? You cannot count on the users of your application avoiding special characters such as single quotation marks. The solution is to use a pair of functions called escape and unescape. What they do is put escape symbols in front of all special characters. You need to insert code to "escape" the data coming from the form, and then "unescape" the data coming from the database before displaying it.

The new script in shown in Table 9.5, with calls to the escape and unescape functions.

TABLE 9.5   ASP/JavaScript Using escape and unescape

`<%@ Language=JavaScript %>`	Choose language
`<title>Input and submit favorites to firstdb database</title></head><body>`	Usual HTML
`<!- #include file="sopenconn.asp"  ->`	Include connecting code
`<%`	Start ASP
`var submitted=String(Request.Form ("submitted"));`	Acquire form data holding submitted flag
`if (submitted !="undefined") {`	if test: has form been submitted
`var title = escape(String(Request. Form("title")));`	Acquire form data for title, escaping the contents
`var description =  escape(String (Request.Form("description")));`	Acquire form data for description, escaping the contents
`var valuesx = " VALUES ('"+title+"', '" + description +"')";`	Compose what will be values part of insert query
`var fields = " (title, description) ";`	Create part of query designating fields
`var query="INSERT INTO favorites " + fields + valuesx;`	Create query
`Response.Write("Insert query is: " + query);`	Debugging statement
`if (Conn.Execute(query))`	Execute query and test success
`        {        Response.Write(" Title was successfully entered.  ");}`	When successful, write out message
`else { Response.Write("Title was NOT entered. ");}`	When not successful, write out message
`Conn.Close();`	Close connection
`Response.Write("<a href=\ "saddfavoritefix.asp\">"); Response.Write(" Submit another favorite </a>");`	Write out link to add another favorite.

(continues)

TABLE 9.5 ASP/JavaScript Using escape and unescape (*continued*)

`Response.Write("  ");`	Write out line break
`}`	Ends if form was submitted
`else {`	Begins clause for displaying form
`%>`	End ASP
`<h1>Add a title to the databank of favorite shows.  </h1>`	Heading
`<%`	Restart ASP
`var sq ="SELECT * from favorites";`	Define query to get all the favorites
`    Response.Write("<h2>Favorites</h2>");`	Write out heading
`    rs=Server.CreateObject ("ADODB.RecordSet");`	Create a `recordset` object
`rs.Open (sq,Conn);`	Invoke query
`Response.Write("<table><tr><td> Titles</td> <td>Descriptions</td> </tr> ");`	Write out `table` tags
`while (!(rs.EOF)) {`	while statement: iteration over all favorites in recordset
`Response.Write("<tr><td>");`	Write out `table` tags
`Response.Write( unescape(String (rs.fields.item("title")))+ " </td><td>"+ unescape(String(rs.fields. item("description")))+ "</td> </tr>");`	Extract title and then description from recordset, unescaping each one, write out with `table` tags
`  rs.move(1);`	Advance to next record in recordset
`}`	End while iteration
`Response.Write("</table>");`	Write out ending `table` tag
`%>`	Close ASP
`<form action="saddfavoritefix.asp" method="POST"> `	HTML form tag, with action this script
`Title of show <input type=text name="title" size=50>  `	HTML for title input
`Description <input type=text name= "description" size=50>  `	HTML for description input
`<input type=hidden name="submitted" value="True"> `	Input tag for submitted flag
`<input type=submit name="submit" value="Submit favorite!"> `	Input tag for Submit button
`</form>`	Form end
`<%`	Restart ASP

TABLE 9.5   *(continued)*

}	End `else` clause for submitting form
%>	End ASP
</body> </html>	Closing HTML tags

Try the new script with titles and descriptions that contains characters such as single and double quotation marks and slashes. This problem demonstrates the necessity to test your application with varied data.

You might now ask why this problem was not discussed in the PHP case. The answer is that it did not appear on our system because PHP supports a feature named "magic quotes." Specifically, if the php.ini file in the server code has magic_quotes_qpc on, PHP automatically will escape the quotes and other special characters. You can run a script with the `phpinfo()` function:

```
<?
phpinfo();
?>
```

and check the setting of magic_quotes_gpc. If it is not set to on and if you are not in a position to convince the server crew to accommodate you, you can use the PHP functions that correspond to the ASP/JavaScript `escape` and `unescape`; namely, `addslashes` and `stripslashes`.

Returning to ASP and MS Access, the last step is to take advantage of the ease of use of Access to examine the database contents directly. Download the database from the server using the ws-ftp program or any equivalent. Open it using Access. Examine the records. In particular, notice the contents of any fields containing quotes or other special characters.

REFLECTION

This chapter demonstrated distinct differences between the PHP and the ASP systems, driven chiefly by the fact that PHP uses functions to provide system capabilities, and ASP uses objects. Please note that the PHP language does support programmer-defined objects. If and when you need to build large applications, you can make use of the object-making features of PHP to define your own objects. However, it is true that PHP provides the critical capabilities through function calls. In particular, PHP has a library of functions just for MySQL. The net effect of this is that most people find PHP simpler to use. Please take the time to notice the similarities between the PHP and ASP approaches. The similarities become more pronounced if you choose to use PHP with a DBMS for which there is not a library of functions.

This chapter represents the culmination of the preceding material. If you worked through the examples, you are now in a good position to plan and build a Web application making use of databases. You can put together the SQL statements you learned about in previous chapters with what you learned in this chapter to build new applications. The next several chapters will cover advanced features of applications, such as queries involving multiple tables, files, and cookies. After that, you can read the exposition on a shopping cart project and a quiz show project, which make use of the advanced features.

EXERCISES, QUESTIONS, AND PROJECTS

1. Enhance the favorites application to prevent redundant entries. You can decide whether that means redundant titles, or redundant titles and descriptions. You will need to do a select query and check the number of rows of the returned recordset.

2. Write scripts, in PHP and ASP, to display the contents of the favorites table, and present a form in which the user can designate an entry to delete from the table. You can choose to display the favorite_id for each record. The query to be sent to the database would take the form: "Delete from favorites where favorite_id=" followed by the number entered into the form surrounded by single quotes.

3. Build a slightly different favorites application by changing the description field to designate one of several predefined categories. Then, build a form and handler combination in which people can select the category desired for showing. Use a select with the distinct clause to get a list of distinct categories.

4. Go to the Web and find out about the ODBC library for PHP. You should then be able to write an application in which PHP script accesses an Access database.

5. Go to the Web and find out about using ASP with another DBMS, such as SQL Server.

6. Go to the Web and research the issue of DSN versus DSN-less connections. Your server crew might not give you a choice, but this will help you understand the issues, or at least the jargon.

CONNECTING TO A DATABASE: ADVANCED

The purpose of this chapter is to continue the study of using a database with middleware programming by demonstrating deleting and updating records in the database, and complex queries involving more than one table.

BACKGROUND

The previous chapter showed the benefits of middleware by demonstrating how to build a Web application giving visitors to a Web site the ability to add information to a database and to display the current database contents. This capability changes the Web from a static to a dynamic medium. However, this is only the start of what is possible.

The benefits of databases as opposed to simple files, also known as *flat files*, are demonstrated when the application requires operations other than the insertion of records and display of all records. This chapter will build on the prior ones and show you how to delete records, update information in records, and request customized views of the database contents.

The main thrust of this chapter is on the use of SQL. However, you also need to know how to generate the HTML to display information on the client computer and acquire input from the person sitting at the client computer. This will require new PHP and ASP/JavaScript coding techniques. The situation is a reminder of the general term for PHP and ASP: *middleware*. The PHP and ASP scripts operate in the middle: between the database management systems (DBMS) software on the server computer and the browser that interprets HTML on the client computer.

CONCEPTUAL EXPLANATION

This section presents the concepts behind several important facilities you might need to use in your database application. The following section contains examples of the code for the ASP and PHP implementations.

Alter, Delete, and Update

An unfinished piece of business remains from the last chapter. As you will recall, the single quote caused a problem, noticeable in the ASP system. The fix was to use so-called escape characters to indicate that the single quote was to be viewed as simple data and not with any special meaning. We had to call for escape characters explicitly in the ASP system. The escaping was done for us in PHP. Escaping also applied to blank spaces. In any case, this means that the data going into the text (char) fields in the database potentially were bigger than anticipated. This leads to the common situation that people decide after the initial design and, even, deployment of the project that the size of certain fields is inadequate. The SQL `Alter` query is the answer. The syntax is slightly different for Access versus MySQL.

You might decide that a show is no longer a favorite. This leads to the use of the SQL `Delete` command. Needless to say, you need to be very careful that your code is deleting only the record you want deleted. If your code contains the statement `delete from tablename`, the system does not assume you made a mistake because you did not specify a particular record. Instead, it deletes all records in the table.

The approach recommended here is to display a table listing all the titles in the favorites table. The table will contain special hyperlinks, namely HTML `<a ... >` tags containing as the value of the `href` attribute the name of a handler script with a query string that specifies the id number of the associated title. The person at the client computer sees the screen in Figure 10.1.

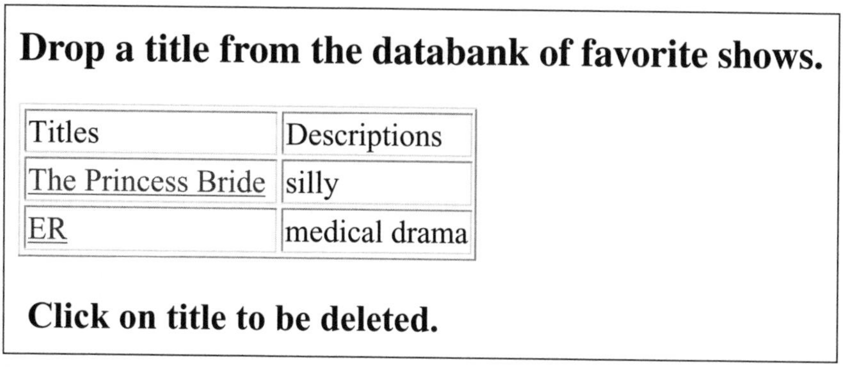

Drop a title from the databank of favorite shows.

Titles	Descriptions
The Princess Bride	silly
ER	medical drama

Click on title to be deleted.

FIGURE 10.1   Display of titles.

If he or she clicks *The Princess Bride* to indicate that it is to be deleted (which no one in my household would ever do), then the hyperlink taken would be something like the following:

```
href='sdropfavoritefancy.asp?whichid=1'
```

The number would be 1 if this was the first record entered into the database, but it could be something else. You do not need to know this number. Instead, your ASP or PHP code will generate the code for the table, including the visible titles and descriptions, and also including the `favorite_id` values that get positioned after `whichid` as part of the `href` attribute. The part of the attribute following the question mark is called the *query string*. In this situation, there is exactly one name=value set. If there were more information to send to the script, you would use ampersands to separate the sets.

This is a case of something that looks like a form but is not an HTML form, even though we call it *sdropfavoriteform* for both the ASP and PHP case.

However, you can think of *sdropfavoritefancy.asp* or *sdropfavoritefancy.php* as handler scripts. The coding in these scripts get the information from out of the query string data as they would get information from form data that is sent using the GET method.

A storyboard representing the deletion operation is shown in Figure 10.2.

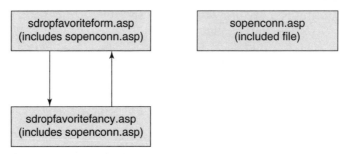

FIGURE 10.2 Storyboard for dropping title application.

The PHP version would be the same, except with PHP as the extension of the filenames.

In prior storyboards, you saw a distinction between links representing form handling and links based on hyperlinks. The link from *sdropfavoriteform* to *sdropfavoritefancy* is the <a> tag with the query string. The link from *sdropfavoritefancy* to *sdropfavoriteform* is a plain hyperlink for the user who wants to delete another title.

Besides insertion and deletion, you might decide that it is critical to provide a facility for changing the information in the database. The design will be very similar to the deletion case in that you create a table with links that have query strings. However, for the update operation, you need one more step. Therefore, there will be three scripts. The strategy is the same for ASP and PHP. The file extensions are omitted in this description:

- **supdate1**: A script presenting all the titles, with links containing query strings.

- **supdate2**: A script with a form with text boxes for new title and description. The original values for the textboxes will be the current data.

- **supdate3**: A script that actually does the update operation on the database.

The problem of the troublesome single quote reared again. This time, the problem was putting a string containing a quotation mark to be the original value for a form input tag. To put this precisely, the HTML form input tags have attributes named VALUE. The value of the VALUE attribute, is the thing on the other side of the equal sign. For this situation, for the example giving a description of the show, *The Sopranos*, this was:

```
one man's two families
```

The HTML ignored what came after the apostrophe.

A solution is presented that works for the apostrophe (single quote) case for both ASP and PHP. However, PHP has a function called `htmlspecialcharacters`, which is more powerful. See the *Exercises*.

The storyboard diagram for the update example is shown in Figure 10.3.

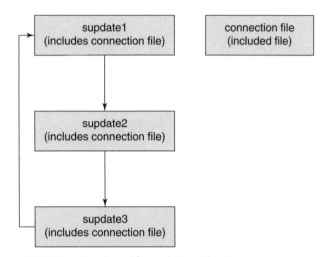

FIGURE 10.3   Storyboard for update application.

The diagram is in a slightly different style: without file extensions and with the connection file described conceptually rather than by filename. This is done on purpose. Storyboards are for your benefit, so define your own conventions to make them work for you.

You will see in the code examples later in the chapter that the connection is closed at the end of each script and then re-opened in the next script. You might ask if this is not a waste of time. It is true that the closing and opening does take system resources. However, think about what is occurring for each script. The middleware script prepares an HTML file for a person to view. The person will take time reading the display and, perhaps, clicking to choose a record to update and, later, typing in the new values. This is an enormous amount of time for the system to keep a connection open. The connections could be limited in number. The person could walk away. The closing makes sense. However, this is a more complex question and is the topic for advanced database design. For example, it could be that you want to check that the data has not been changed since the previous read operation. Some ideas on this issue will be discussed in Chapter 16, "Scaling Up Your Application."

To demonstrate the composition of joins involving more than one table, we will need to define a database with more than one table. The sample to be presented here is to add to the favorites database two more tables: a table containing warnings and a table for categories of warnings. This is intended to reflect the TV and movie practice of issuing a warning if a show has violence, sex, foul language, and/or adult themes. The categories table will contain two fields: an identifier number and a description. The warnings table will contain three fields: the identifier for the favorite that bears the warning, the identifier for the category of warning, and a reason for the warning.

The warnings table does not have a primary key. You could decide to establish that the combination of the favorite identifier and the category identifier uniquely define the warning record. This would be a concatenated primary key, which is allowed by both MySQL and Access. However, this would mean that you could not have multiple warnings for the same show in the same category. In any case, this example shows you that a table does not have to have a primary key.

Following the practice taken early, it is suggested that you use a different approach for PHP/MySQL and for ASP/Access. For PHP/MySQL, you will see scripts for creating the two additional tables. Since the categories table has a limited number of records, you can copy the code for inserting a specific favorite to write a script for inserting the four warning categories mentioned already. In contrast, for ASP/Access, you can download the database to your own computer. You do this in order not to lose any existing data. You then use Access as before to create two new tables. Use the Create in Design View option. You can then click on the newly created categories table and insert four records.

Use of Stand-Alone Access

The Access stand-alone system also has a feature for defining relationships. In the new database, there is a relationship between the warnings and the favorites tables, and the warnings and the categories table. A warning record contains as foreign keys, a `favorite_id` field and a `cat_id` field. Specifying this relationship "tells" the Access system to check that data being placed in the foreign key fields must be valid primary keys for the corresponding tables. The system does what are called *referential integrity checks*. As a side benefit, you can also get Access to draw the ER diagram for you. This will be demonstrated later.

Now we get to the design for inserting warning records in the system. This will follow the model for updates. Specifically, you will see in the next section (and should try to implement for yourself), the following three scripts:

- **swarning1**: A script that presents all the favorites in a table. The entries will be links with query strings holding the id information.
- **swarning2**: A script that presents a form. The form has a set of radio buttons with the category possibilities. It also has a text box in which to type in the reason for giving this warning. Lastly, the form has the favorite_id value as hidden data to be passed on to the script handler for this form.
- **swarning3**: A script to perform the `insert` operation.

Please note that this application, the update application, and the delete operation could all be done using the technique of one script being the form and the handler. The approach taken here follows the principle that several small tasks are easier than one complex task. However, this approach does mean that you need to deal with several scripts at a time.

More SQL

The last set of applications deal with presentation of information. Since the application now has warnings, we need to develop a way to show the warnings. Here are three distinct facilities you could provide:

- Display all warnings.
- Display all favorites and show the count of warnings.
- Allow the user to select a warning category and display all warnings (with title and description of favorite along with the reason given in the warning). The text implements this feature using two scripts.

The first two scripts are basically "constants." They do not require any input from the user. They contain fixed SQL statements.

The challenge for the second task is to include the favorites that do not have any warnings indicated by a count of zero. The technique for doing this is to use what is called a LEFT JOIN in SQL. The term comes from the fact that you are joining two tables using some condition, but if there is not a match for something in the left table, SQL will build a row anyway, putting a null in the locations where there were no values. You will make use of an SQL aggregate function, COUNT, which will not add in anything for any null fields.

The third task does ask the user to select a category. It can be modeled after the first *swarning2* scripts, which display a way to select a category, and the display scripts.

The next section shows details on these features using both ASP and PHP. Do feel free to try to write the scripts on your own.

EXAMPLES

This section contains the scripts for the tasks described in the previous sections. Please note that the scripts often contain `print` or `Response.Write` statements useful for debugging. You should include them when you try to replicate these examples. You would remove them from any code used for real operations. Do not, either in your experiments or for real projects, copy the style here of squeezing statements together. It is done here to simplify the explanations. Do put in comments and blank lines.

ON THE CD

The application described in this chapter builds on the favorites applications started in Chapter 9, "Connecting to the Database." You will find the code for this chapter on the CD-ROM in the folder named chapter10code. You will need the *openfirstdb.php* and *sopenconn.asp* files from the chapter9code folder.

Altering Field Sizes

The scripts to modify the size of the title field are similar for PHP and ASP/JavaScript, one obvious difference is that the term is "char" for MySQL and "text" for Access. These are programs that are run exactly one time.

The PHP script is shown in Table 10.1.

TABLE 10.1   PHP Script to Alter Field Size

`<html><head><title>Alter table</title></head><body>`	Usual HTML start
`<?php`	Start PHP
`require("openfirstdb.php");`	Include connection code
`$query="Alter table favorites modify title char(30)";`	Define $query
`print("alter query is: $query");`	For debugging
`$result = mysql_db_query($DBname,$query, $link);`	Send query to MySQL
`if ($result) {`	Do check on return code
`    print("The table was successfully altered.  \n"); }`	Positive result
`else {`	Start of else clause
`    print ("The table was NOT successfully altered.  \n");}`	Negative result
`mysql_close($link);`	Close connection
`?>`	End PHP
`</body></html>`	HTML close

The ASP/JavaScript *alter* script is shown in Table 10.2.

TABLE 10.2   ASP/JavaScript to Alter Field Size

`<%@ Language=JavaScript %>`	Set JavaScript as language
`<html><head><title>Alter table</title></head><body>`	Usual HTML start
`<!- #include file="sopenconn.asp"  ->`	Include connection code
`<%`	Start ASP
`var query="Alter table favorites alter column title text(30)";`	Define query
`Response.Write("alter query is: " + query);`	Debugging
`if (Conn.Execute(query))`	Send query to Access and do check on return value

TABLE 10.2   *(continued)*

`{Response.Write(" Table column` `changed.  ");}`	Positive result
`else {Response.Write("Table column was` `not changed. "); }`	Negative result
`Conn.Close();`	Close connection
`%> </body> </html>`	Close ASP and HTML close

Deleting Records

For a change, here are the ASP/JavaScript scripts first for the delete function. After reading this script, you can see if you can do the PHP one by yourself.

Recall that the technique is to use two scripts. For the first (Table 10.3), your code will produce a table with hyperlinks that link to the second script. The second script (Table 10.4) is a handler script that makes use of an id inserted in the query string.

TABLE 10.3   ASP/JavaScript Script to Display Titles

`<%@ Language=JavaScript %>`	Set JavaScript as the language
`<html><head><title>Form for selecting a` `favorite for deletion </title>` `</head><body>`	Usual HTML start
`<h1>Drop a title from the databank of` `favorite shows.  </h1>`	HTML for heading
`<!– #include file="sopenconn.asp"  –>`	Include connection code
`<%`	Start ASP
`var sq ="SELECT * from favorites";`	Define sq to hold query
`rs=Server.CreateObject` `("ADODB.RecordSet");`	Create a recordset object
`rs.Open (sq,Conn);`	Invoke query
`Response.Write("<table border='1'><tr>` `<td> Titles</td> <td>Descriptions</td>` `</tr> ");`	Output HTML for start of table
`while (!(rs.EOF)){`	while loop: will iterate through the recordset: once of each record (favorite) in the table
`Response.Write("<tr><td>");`	Output start of row, and first td item

(continues)

TABLE 10.3   ASP/JavaScript Script to Display Titles (*continued*)

`Response.Write("<a href=` `'sdropfavoritefancy.asp?whichid=");`	The contents of this item will be a HTML `<a>` element. This is the beginning of that element, with the `href` a link including the start of a query string
`Response.Write(rs.fields.item` `("favorite_id"));`	Output the `favorite_id` field of this favorite to be the rest of the query string
`Response.Write("'>");`	Output a closing single quote and a closing pointy bracket to complete the `<a>` tag
`Response.Write(unescape(String` `(rs.fields.item("title"))));`	Output the title field of this favorite. Need to remove any escape characters
`Response.Write("</a>");`	Output the closing `</a>` tag
`Response.Write(" </td><td>"+unescape` `(String(rs.fields.item` `("description"))));`	Output the table tags and then the description field of this favorite. Need to remove any escape characters
`Response.Write("</td> </tr>\n");`	Output closing table tags: for item and for row. The `\n` is a line break for the HTML source
`rs.move(1);`	ASP code to advance to the next record of the recordset
`}  // end while`	End `while`
`Response.Write("</table>");`	Output closing `table` tag
`Response.Write("Click on title to` `be deleted.");`	Output instructions
`Conn.Close();`	Close connection
`%>`	End ASP
`</body></html>`	Closing HTML

Table 10.4 shows the handler. It performs the deletion, using the id field sent over via the query string.

TABLE 10.4   ASP/JavaScript Script to Delete Specified Title

`<%@ Language=JavaScript %>`	Set JavaScript as the language
`<html><head><title>Delete favorites from firstdb database </title></head><body>`	Usual HTML start
`<!— #include file="sopenconn.asp"  —>`	Include connection code
`<%`	Start ASP
`   var whichid = parseInt(Request.QueryString("whichid"));`	Set the variable `whichid` to be value sent over via the query string
`   var query="DELETE FROM favorites where favorite_id=" + whichid;`	Set the query variable to be the `delete` query made by concatenating the fixed part with the favorite identifier
`   Response.Write("delete query is: " + query);`	Debugging
`  if (Conn.Execute(query))`	Execute (send over to Access) the `delete` query and do a test on the result
`     {Response.Write(" Title was successfully deleted.  ");}`	Positive outcome
`  else {Response.Write("Title was NOT deleted. "); }`	Negative outcome
`  Conn.Close();`	Close connection
`Response.Write("<a href=\"sdropfavoriteform.asp\"> Remove another title</a>  ");`	Output a link to let the user go back and remove another title
`%>`	Close ASP
`</body> </html>`	Usual HTML close

Now at this point, you could try writing the PHP scripts by yourself. You use the ASP scripts for this task and any PHP scripts from the previous chapter as models. Table 10.5 shows the script for presenting the titles, and Table 10.6 shows the script that performs the deletion.

TABLE 10.5   PHP Script to Display Titles

`<html><head><title>Dropping favorite </title></head><body>`	Usual HTML start
`<h1>Drop a title to the databank of favorite shows.  </h1>`	Heading
`<?`	Start PHP
`require("openfirstdb.php");`	Include connection code

(continues)

TABLE 10.5   PHP Script to Display Titles *(continued)*

`$sq ="SELECT * from favorites";`	Define query
`print("<h3>Favorites</h3> ");`	Output another heading
`$rs = mysql_db_query($DBname,$sq,$link);`	Invoke the query

`print("<table border='1'><tr><td>`
`Titles</td> <td>Descriptions</td>`
`</tr> ");`
	Output `table` tags

`print("\n");`	Output line break for the HTML
`while ($row=mysql_fetch_array($rs)) {`	`while` loop: this will iterate through the records (rows) of the recordset
`  print("\n");`	Output line break
`  print("<tr><td>");`	Output `table` tags for start of row and first item
`  print("<a href='sdropfavoritesfancy.` `php?whichid=");`	Output the start of the a tag
`  print($row["favorite_id"]);`	Output the `favorite_id` field
`  print("'>");`	Output the rest of the a tag, including a single quote and a closing pointy bracket
`  print($row["title"]);`	Output the title field of this favorite
`  print("</a>");`	Output closing a tag
`  print("</td><td>");`	Output `table` tags to close this item and start the next one
`  print($row["description"]);`	Output the description field of this favorite
`  print("</td> </tr>");`	Output `table` tags to close the item and the row
`  } // end while`	End the `while`
` print("</table>");`	Output closing tag for table
` print("Click on favorite to be` `deleted.");`	Output instructions
`?>`	Close PHP
`</body> </html>`	Usual HTML close

TABLE 10.6   PHP Script to Drop the Specified Title

`<html><head><title>Drop favorites from` `firstdb database </title></head><body>`	Usual HTML start
`<?php`	Start PHP
`  require("openfirstdb.php");`	Include connection code

TABLE 10.6   *(continued)*

`$query="DELETE from favorites where favorite_id='$whichid'";`	Define query as concatenation of fixed part with the identifier sent over via the query string
`print("Delete query is: $query  ");`	Debugging
`$result = mysql_db_query($DBname, $query, $link);`	Invoke query
`if ($result) {`	If test on return value
`print("The favorite was successfully deleted. \n");}`	Positive result
`else { print ("The favorite was NOT successfully deleted.  \n");}`	Negative result
`mysql_close($link);`	Close connection
`print ("<a href=\"sdropfavoritesform. php\">Drop another favorite </a> ");`	Output instructions
`?>`	Close PHP
`</body></html>`	Usual HTML close

Updating Records

The task of updating the title and/or description fields of the favorites records is modeled on the delete example, except that it is suggested that you use three scripts. The first presents the user with all the favorites. The second provides the user with a form in which to update the selected favorite. The third script does the updating. Again, the first set of scripts will be for ASP/JavaScript.

The first script (Table 10.7) is for the user to choose what is to be updated: this is not an HTML form, although the user might think of it as one. It resembles the script used for the delete case.

TABLE 10.7   ASP/JavaScript Displaying Titles for Updating

`<%@ Language=JavaScript %>`	Set the language
`<html><head><title>Form for selecting a favorite for update </title></head><body>`	Usual HTML start
`<h1>Drop a title from the databank of favorite shows.  </h1>`	HTML header
`<!– #include file="sopenconn.asp"  –>`	Include connection code
`<%`	Start ASP
`var sq ="SELECT * from favorites";`	Define query

(continues)

TABLE 10.7   ASP/JavaScript Displaying Titles for Updating (*continued*)

`rs=Server.CreateObject ("ADODB.RecordSet");`	Set `rs` to be a recordset
`rs.Open (sq,Conn);`	Invoke the query
`Response.Write("<table border='1'><tr> <td> Titles </td> <td>Descriptions</td> </tr> ");`	Output tags for start of table
`while (!(rs.EOF)){`	while loop: will iterate through the records of the recordset
`Response.Write("<tr><td>");`	Output table tags
`Response.Write("<a href='supdate2.asp?whichid=");`	Output start of a tag, with query string
`Response.Write(rs.fields.item ("favorite_id"));`	Output the `favorite_id` field
`Response.Write("'>");`	Output close of a tag
`Response.Write(unescape(String(rs. fields.item("title"))));`	Output the title field of the favorite. Need to remove any escape characters
`Response.Write("</a>");`	Output the closing a tag
`Response.Write(" </td><td>"+unescape (String(rs.fields.item("description"))));`	Output the table tags and the description field of the favorite. Need to remove any escape characters
`Response.Write("</td> </tr>\n");`	Output table tags and line break
`rs.move(1);`	Advance to next record
`}  // end while`	Close while
`Response.Write("</table>");`	Output closing table tags
`Response.Write("Click on title to be changed.");`	Output instructions
`Conn.Close();`	Close connection
`%>`	End ASP
`</body></html>`	Usual HTML close

The next script (*supdate2.asp* shown in Table 10.8) "knows" what favorite is to be updated. It presents a form for making the updates. The original contents of the title and description fields are placed in the text boxes. Notice the use of the slash as an escape character for the double quotation marks. This is to ensure that any single quotation marks in the contents of the title or the descriptions are interpreted as content, not as special characters.

The final script (*supdate3.asp* shown in Table 10.9) does the work of making the change to the database. The identifier for the record to be updated has been carried over in a hidden form input.

TABLE 10.8   ASP/JavaScript for Performing Update of Specified Title

`<%@ Language=JavaScript %>`	Set language
`<html><head><title>Update favorites from firstdb database </title></head><body>`	Usual HTML
`<!– #include file="sopenconn.asp"  –>`	Include connection code
`<%`	Start ASP
`  var whichid = parseInt(Request.QueryString("whichid"));`	Set whichid variable from query string
`  var query="Select * FROM favorites where favorite_id=" + whichid;`	Define query using the whichid variable
`  Response.Write("select query is: " + query);`	Debugging
`  rs=Server.CreateObject ("ADODB.RecordSet");`	Set rs to be a recordset
`  rs.Open (query,Conn);`	Invoke the query
`  Response.Write("<form action= 'supdate3.asp'>\n");`	Output start of form
`  Response.Write("Title: <input type= 'text' name='title' value=\""+unescape (rs.fields.item("title"))+"\">");`	Output input tag with current value of title. Note use of slashes to "escape"; namely, make JavaScript ignore the quotation marks
`  Response.Write("Description: <input type='text' name='desc' value=\""+unescape(rs.fields.item ("description"))+"\" size='30'>");`	Output input tag with current value of description. See above
`  Response.Write("<input type='submit' value='Update'>");`	Output Submit button
`  Response.Write("<input type='hidden' name='whichid' value='" + whichid + "'>");`	Output a hidden tag so the whichid value will be sent along to the next script
`  Response.Write("</form>");`	Output close of form
`  Response.Write("  Change fields and click on Update button. ");`	Output instructions.
`  Conn.Close();`	Close connection
`%>`	End ASP
`</body> </html>`	Usual HTML close

TABLE 10.9   ASP/JavaScript to Perform the Update of the Favorite

`<%@ Language=JavaScript %>`	Set language
`<html><head><title>Complete update of a favorite </title></head><body>`	Usual HTML
`<!– #include file="sopenconn.asp"  –>`	Include connection code
`<%`	Start ASP
`  var whichid = parseInt(Request ("whichid"));`	Set whichid (in this script) to be value sent over from last script
`  var title = escape(String(Request ("title")));`	Set title from form input. Need to escape any special values user has typed
`  var desc = escape(String(Request ("desc")));`	Set desc from form input
`  var query1="Update favorites set title='" + title +"', ";`	Define query is pieces. This is because of the complex syntax
`  var query2= "description = '" + desc + "'";`	Set description field to value of desc
`  var query3= "where favorite_id=" + whichid;`	Set the `favorite_id` field to value of whichid
`  var query = query1 + query2 + query3;`	Combine parts to make the complete query
`  Response.Write("update query is: " + query + " ");`	Debugging
`  if (Conn.Execute(query)) {`	Invoke query and do test
`    Response.Write("Favorite updated successfully."); }`	Positive outcome
`  else {Response.Write("Favorite not updated."); }`	Negative outcome
`  Conn.Close();`	Close connection
`  Response.Write("<a href='supdate1.asp'> Update another favorite.</a>");`	Output link to let user go back and update another field
`%>`	Close ASP
`</body> </html>`	Usual HTML close

Now is the time for you to see if you can do the PHP version on your own. Recall that there are three scripts. The first script lets the user select a favorite to be updated. It is shown in Table 10.10.

TABLE 10.10   PHP Script to Display Titles for Updating

`<html><head><title>Form for selecting a favorite for update </title></head><body>`	Usual HTML opening
`<h2>Select a title from the databank of favorite shows.  </h2>`	HTML heading
`<?`	Start PHP
`require("openfirstdb.php");`	Include the connection code
`$query="Select * FROM favorites";`	Define the variable `$query` to be the query
`print("select query is: " . $query);`	For debugging
`$rs = mysql_db_query($DBname,$query, $link);`	Invoke the query
`print("<table border='1'><tr><td> Titles </td> <td>Descriptions</td> </tr> ");`	Output table tags
`while ($row=mysql_fetch_array($rs)){`	while loop: will iterate through all the records (rows) of the recordset `$rs`
`print("<tr><td>");`	Output row table tags
`print("<a href='supdate2.php?whichid=");`	Output start of a tag, with `href` holding link and start of query string
`print($row["favorite_id"]);`	Output favorite_id for this record to be part of the query string
`print("'>");`	Output close of a tag
`print($row["title"]);`	Output title field of this record
`print("</a>");`	Output closing a tag
`print(" </td><td>".$row["description"]);`	Output table tags plus the description field of this record
`print("</td> </tr>\n");`	Output closing table tags plus line break for the HTML
`}  // end while`	Close of `while` loop
`print("</table>");`	Output closing `table` tag
`print("Click on title to be changed.");`	Output instructions
`mysql_close($link);`	Close connection
`?>`	End PHP
`</body></html>`	Usual closing HTML

The second script is shown in Table 10.11. It uses the `favorite_id` passed in the query string to build a form.

TABLE 10.11   PHP Script to Enter Update Information

`<html><head><title>Update favorites from firstdb database </title></head><body>`	Usual HTML opening
`<?php`	Start PHP
`  require("openfirstdb.php");`	Include connection code
`  $query="Select * FROM favorites where favorite_id=$whichid";`	Define $query to be query made by concatenating fixed parts with the favorite_id passed in via the query string
`  $rs = mysql_db_query($DBname,$query, $link);`	Invoke the query
`  $row=mysql_fetch_array($rs);`	Fetch the first (and presumably only) row of the recordset
`  print("<form action='supdate3.php'>");`	Output form header tag
`  print("Title: <input type='text' name='title' value=\"");`	Output start of input tag for title. It will contain the current title. Note the slash in front of the double quote
`  print($row["title"]);`	Output the title field for this favorite
`  print("\">");`	Output close of input tag, including "escaped" double quote
`  print("Description: <input type='text' name='desc' value=\"");`	Output start of input tag for description. See above treatment for title
`  print($row["description"]);`	Output the description field for this favorite
`  print("\" size='40'>");`	Output close of input tag. Give it expanded size
`  print("<input type='submit' value='Update'>");`	Output Submit button
`  print("<input type='hidden' name='whichid' value='$whichid'>");`	Output as a hidden input tag element the $which value
`  print("</form>");`	Output form close
`  print("  Change fields and click on Update button. ");`	Output instructions
`  mysql_close($link);`	Close link
`?>`	End PHP
`</body> </html>`	Usual HTML close

The third and final script (shown in Table 10.12) does the updating of the record in the database.

TABLE 10.12   PHP Script to Perform Update of Title

`<html><head><title>Complete update of a favorite </title></head><body>`	Usual HTML start
`<?php`	Start PHP
`require("openfirstdb.php");`	Include connection code
`$query1="Update favorites set title='$title', ";`	Will define query in three parts due to complex syntax. This part gets in form input for title
`$query2= "description='$desc' ";`	This step uses form input for description.
`$query3= "where favorite_id=$whichid";`	This step uses form input for the id, which was passed in the hidden input tag
`$query = $query1 . $query2 . $query3;`	Define $query as the concatenation of these three string variables
`print("query is $query  ");`	Debugging
`$result = mysql_db_query($DBname,$query, $link);`	Invoke query
`if ($result) {`	If test to check return value
`    print("Update successful. \n"); }`	Positive outcome
`else { print ("Update not successful.  \n");}`	Negative outcome
`mysql_close($link);`	Close connection
`print("<a href='supdate1.php'>Update another favorite.</a>");`	Output link to give user a chance to do another update
`?>`	Close PHP
`</body> </html>`	Usual HTML close

Creating New Tables Using PHP

Now we begin the programming to enhance the application with two new tables. As before, given the command-line interface for MySQL, it is suggested that you use PHP scripts to add the new tables. Since there are two tables to define, you can appreciate that defining a `createtable` function is a useful thing to do. Table 10.13 shows the script to define the new tables.

TABLE 10.13 PHP Script for Defining New Tables

`<?php`	Start PHP
`function createtable($tname,$fields) {`	Define function called createtable. It has two parameters
`global $DBname, $link;` and `$link`	Set up to use global values for $DBname and $link
`$query="CREATE TABLE $tname ($fields)";`	Define $query
`if (mysql_db_query($DBname,$query, $link)) {`	Invoke query and test for success
`    print ("The table, $tname, was created successfully. \n");    }`	Positive outcome
`else { print ("The table, $tname, was not created.  \n");}`	Negative outcome
`}`	End of function definition
`?>`	End PHP
`<html><head><title>Creating new tables</title></head><body>`	Usual HTML start
`<h3> Creating the added tables for firstdb </h3>  `	HTML heading
`<?php`	Start PHP
`require("openfirstdb.php");`	Include connection code. This sets the global variables to be used in the createtable function
`$tname = "warnings";`	Set $tname for warnings table
`$fields = "favorite_id INT NOT NULL, cat_id INT NOT NULL, reason char(50)";`	Set $fields. The table has three fields. It does not have a primary key
`createtable($tname, $fields);`	Call createtable function
`$tname = "categories";`	Set $tname for categories table
`$fields="cat_id INT NOT NULL AUTO_INCREMENT PRIMARY KEY, cat_desc char(50)";`	Set $fields. This table has two fields
`createtable($tname,$fields);`	Call createtable function
`mysql_close($link);`	Close connection
`?>`	End PHP
`</body> </html>`	Usual HTML close

The categories table has a limited number of entries, so instead of creating scripts for adding categories (see the *Exercises*), Table 10.14 shows an execute one-time only script to "populate" the table with four records.

TABLE 10.14   PHP Script for Populating the Categories Table

`<html><head><title>Adding entries to categories table</title> </head> <body>`	Usual HTML start
`<h3> Categories</h3>  `	HTML heading
`<?php`	Start PHP
`require("openfirstdb.php");`	Include connection code
`$tname="categories";`	Set name of table
`$query="INSERT INTO $tname VALUES('0','Violence')";`	Set $query
`$result = mysql_db_query($DBname,$query, $link);`	Invoke query
`if ($result) {`	Check result
`    print("The violence category was successfully added. \n"); }`	Positive result
`else {print ("The violence category was NOT successfully added.  \n");}`	Negative result
`$query="INSERT INTO $tname VALUES('0','Sex')";`	Repeat for next category
`$result = mysql_db_query($DBname,$query, $link);`	Invoke query
`if ($result) {`	Check result
`    print("The sex category was successfully added. \n"); }`	Positive result
`else {print ("The sex category was NOT successfully added.  \n");}`	Negative result
`$query="INSERT INTO $tname VALUES('0','Language')";`	Repeat for next category
`$result = mysql_db_query($DBname,$query, $link);`	Invoke query
`if ($result) {`	Check result
`    print("The language category was successfully added. \n"); }`	Positive result
`else {print ("The language was NOT successfully added.  \n");}`	Negative result
`$query="INSERT INTO $tname VALUES('0','Adult Themes')";`	Repeat for next category
`$result = mysql_db_query($DBname,$query, $link);`	Invoke query
`if ($result)`	Check result.
`{print("The adult themes was successfully added. \n"); }`	Positive result
`else {print ("The adult themes was NOT successfully added.  \n");}`	Negative result
`mysql_close($link);`	Close connection
`?>`	End PHP
`</body></html>`	Usual HTML close

Using Access to Create New Tables

Now we turn to the ASP system, specifically Access. It has been suggested that you add the new tables and populate the categories table all in stand-alone mode. You need to download the database from the server. You define the new tables the same way you defined the original table, favorites.

Assuming you have the three tables defined, you can use the Access system to specify the relationships between the tables. See Figure 10.4. Click on Tools.

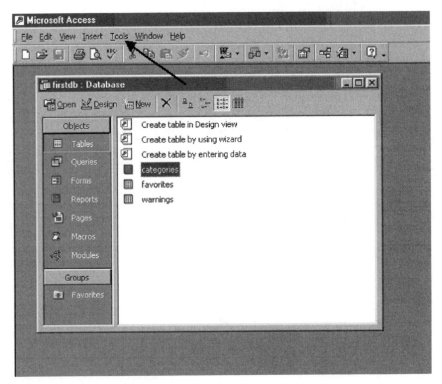

FIGURE 10.4   Access window.

Now, click on Relationships to see the drop-down menu shown in Figure 10.5.

After clicking on Relationships, you see the Window shown in Figure 10.6. Click on View.

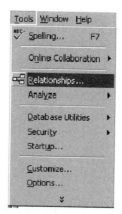

FIGURE 10.5 Options under Tools.

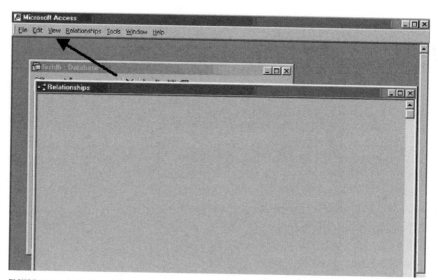

FIGURE 10.6 Relationships window: see arrow pointing to view.

Then, click on Show Table. You get yet another window as shown in Figure 10.7.

Select and then click on Add for all three of the tables. You will see the window in Figure 10.8.

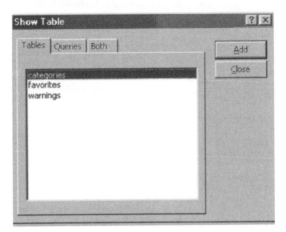

FIGURE 10.7   Show Table window.

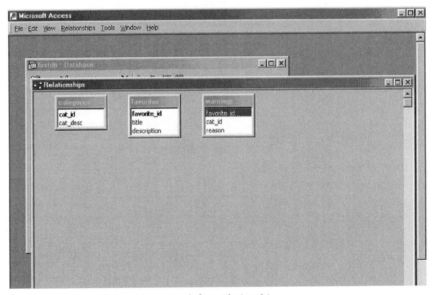

FIGURE 10.8   Tables showed to use to define relationship.

Now click on Relationships and then Edit Relationships. The screen in Figure 10.9 is displayed. Click Create New....

You will see the window shown in Figure 10.10 for specifying the table names and field names.

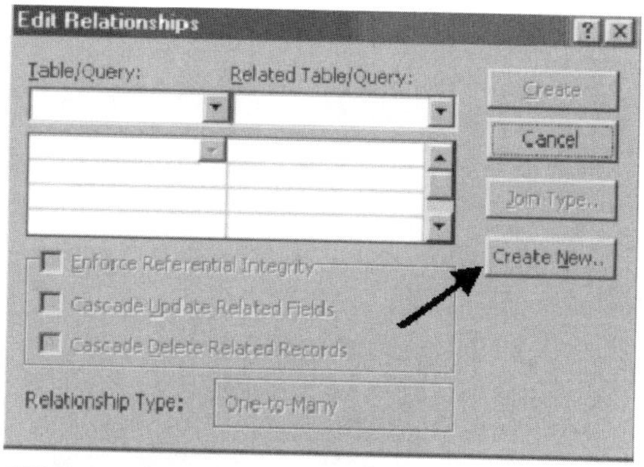

FIGURE 10.9 Edit Relationships window.

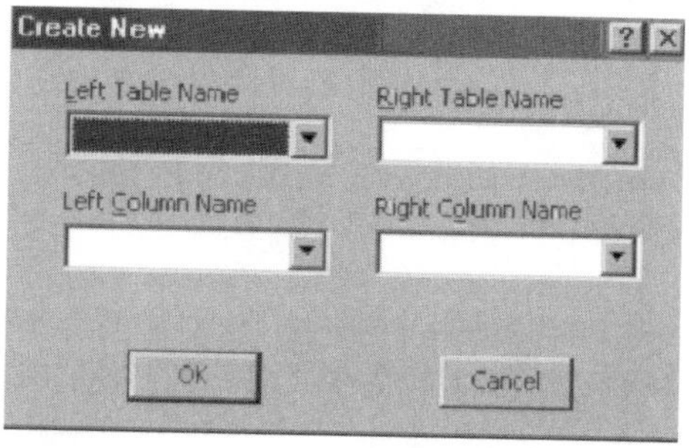

FIGURE 10.10 Window to define relationships by specifying tables and fields.

The downward arrows list the tables you have added to the Relationships window and, once you select a table, the table's field names. Figure 10.11 is a completed window for one relationship.

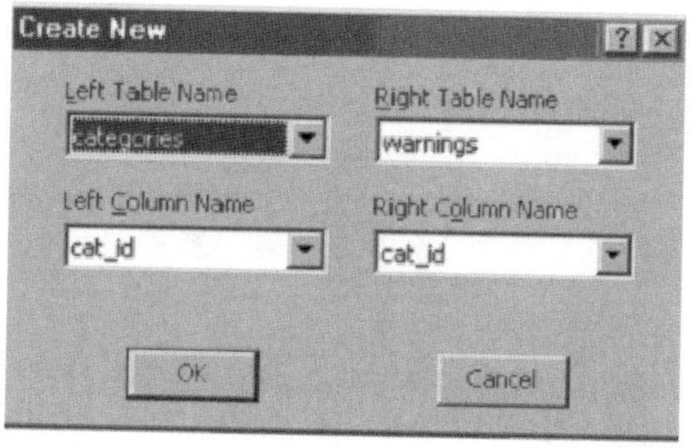

FIGURE 10.11 Completed entry to specify new relationship.

Click OK. You then see the window in Figure 10.12.

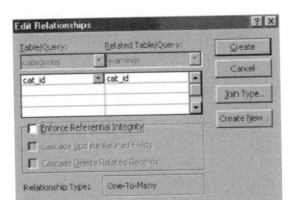

FIGURE 10.12 Window to edit information on relationship.

Click the box next to Enforce Referential Integrity and then on Create. You will see something like what is shown in Figure 10.13.

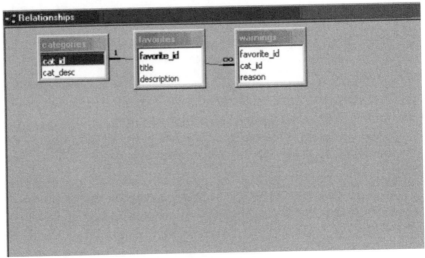

FIGURE 10.13 Relationship shown as partially hidden line.

The line connecting categories and warnings goes behind the favorites. You can click and drag the categories table to be on the other side of the warnings table. This makes the diagram look much better as shown in Figure 10.14.

Now repeat this process to establish the relationship between favorites and warnings. This is based on the fields named favorite_id. You will see Figure 10.15 holding a complete ER diagram.

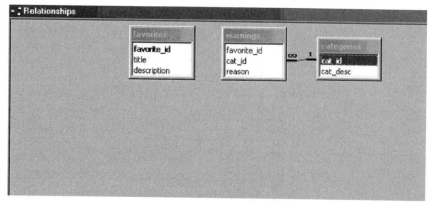

FIGURE 10.14   Relationship shown after moving table symbols.

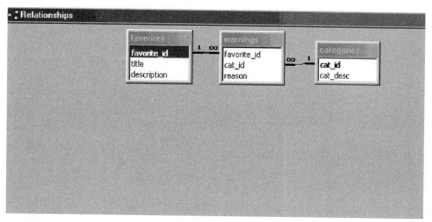

FIGURE 10.15   Diagram showing two relationships.

Upload the database to the server.

Inserting Records and Displaying Information

Now, having added tables to the database, you need to implement the scripts to use the tables. What are described here are scripts to add a warning to a selected favorite show, and scripts to display the warnings three different ways.

The logic to insert a warning follows the model of updating the favorites table. The PHP scripts are shown first and then the ASP scripts.

The *swarning1.php* script is shown in Table 10.15.

TABLE 10.15   PHP Script for Adding a Warning

`<html><head><title>Adding warning</title></head><body>`	Usual HTML
`<h1>Favorites </h1>`	HTML heading
`<?`	Start PHP
`require("openfirstdb.php");`	Include connection code
`$sq ="SELECT * from favorites";`	Define query
`$rs = mysql_db_query($DBname,$sq,$link);`	Invoke the query, setting $rs to be a recordset
`print("<table border='1'><tr><td>Titles</td> <td>Descriptions</td></tr> ");`	Output the table tags
`print("\n");`	Output a line break for the HTML
`while ($row=mysql_fetch_array($rs)) {`	while loop: this will iterate through all the records (rows)
`print("\n");`	Output a line break
`print("<tr><td>");`	Output table tags
`print("<a href='swarning2.php?whichid=");`	Output the start of an a tag
`print($row["favorite_id"]);`	Output the favorite_id to be passed along via the query string
`print("'>");`	Output the close of the a tag
`print($row["title"]);`	Output the title field for the favorite
`print("</a>");`	Output the close of the a tag
`print("</td><td>");`	Output table tags
`print($row["description"]);`	Output the description field of the favorite
`print("</td> </tr>");`	Output the table tags
`}  // end while`	End the while loop
`print("</table>");`	Output the closing table tag
`print("Click on favorite to add a warning.");`	Output instructions
`?>`	Close PHP
`</body> </html>`	Usual HTML close

The next script (*swarning2.php* shown in Table 10.16) "knows" the favorite for which the warning is to be inserted. It generates a form containing an input textbox for the user to enter a reason and a set of radio buttons for selecting the category of the warning.

TABLE 10.16   PHP Script for Adding Warning to Specified Favorite Title

`<html><head><title>Add warning concerning favorite</title></head><body>`	Usual HTML start
`<?php`	Start PHP
`  require("openfirstdb.php");`	Include connection code
`  $query="Select * FROM favorites where favorite_id=$whichid";`	Define query using the favorite_id passed along via the query string
`  $rs = mysql_db_query($DBname,$query, $link);`	Invoke the query setting $rs
`  $row=mysql_fetch_array($rs);`	Fetch the first and only row of $rs
`  print("Title: " . $row["title"]);`	Output the title
`  print(" Description: ". $row["description"]);`	Output the description
`  ?>`	End PHP (This is done to illustrate going out of and into PHP)
`<form action="swarning3.php">`	The form tag
`<?`	Re-start PHP
`print("Reason for warning: <input type='text' name='reason'>");`	Output input tag for user to enter the reason
`$query="Select * from categories";`	Define $query to be a query to get all the categories
`$rs = mysql_db_query($DBname,$query, $link);`	Invoke the query
`while ($row=mysql_fetch_array($rs)) {`	while loop: will iterate through all the categories
`print("<input type='radio' name='cat' value='" . $row['cat_id']."'>" . $row['cat_desc']);`	Output radio button with value the cat_id and the text next to the radio button cat_desc
`}`	End while loop
`  print("<input type='submit' value='Insert Warning'>");`	Output Submit button
`  print("<input type='hidden' name='whichid' value='$whichid'>");`	Output as hidden tag the favorite_id value
`  print("</form>");`	Output close of form
`  print("  Enter reason, choose category and click on Insert Warning button. ");`	Output instructions
` mysql_close($link);`	Close connection
`?>`	End PHP
`</body> </html>`	Usual HTML close

The last script (*swarning3.php* shown in Table 10.17) does the actual insertion using the information passed from the form in *swarning2.php*. If for some reason the favorite identifier or the category identifier did not point to existing records in their respective tables, the update operation would fail. Presumably that could not occur based on how these values are calculated. However, in an application involving multiple users, this could conceivably happen.

TABLE 10.17   PHP Script to Insert Warning for Favorite

`<html><head><title>Insert warning for a favorite </title></head><body>`	Usual HTML start
`<?php`	Start PHP
`require("openfirstdb.php");`	Include connection code
`$query = "INSERT ignore into warnings values ($whichid,$cat,'$reason')";`	Define query using data passed from the previous script
`print("query is $query  ");`	For debugging
`$result = mysql_db_query($DBname,$query, $link);`	Invoke query
`if ($result) { print("Update successful. \n"); }`	Check return: this is positive outcome
`else { print ("Update not successful.  \n");}`	Negative outcome
`mysql_close($link);`	Close connection
`print("<a href='swarning1.php'>Add another warning</a>");`	Output link so user can go back to previous script to enter another warning
`?>`	Close PHP
`</body> </html>`	Usual HTML close

To display all the warnings with the titles, descriptions, reasons and category description, you need to create a query joining all three tables. This is a constant query. That is, no user input is required. However, it is a complex one. All three tables are being used. The `where` clause joins the tables together. Alternatively, you could use `on` clauses. The PHP script is shown in Table 10.18.

TABLE 10.18   PHP Script to Display All Warnings

`<html><head><title>Favorites with warnings </title> </head> <body>`	Usual HTML start
`<h2>Favorites with warnings </h2> `	HTML heading
`<table border='1'>`	Start of table

TABLE 10.18   *(continued)*

`<tr><td>Category</td><td>Titles </td>`
`<td>Descriptions </td><td>Reason</td>`
`</tr>`
	Table tags continued

`<?php`	Start PHP
`require("openfirstdb.php");`	Include connection code
`$query="Select c.cat_desc, f.title,` `f.description, w.reason ";`	Define query. This time use the ability to concatenate onto an existing string
`$query .=" from favorites as f, warnings` `as w, categories as c ";`	Uses the .= operator to add on
`$query .="where c.cat_id = w.cat_id and` `f.favorite_id = w.favorite_id ";`	Add on more
`$query .=" order by c.cat_desc";`	Add on more
`$result=mysql_db_query($DBname, $query,` `$link);`	Invoke query
`while ($row=mysql_fetch_array($result)) {`	while loop: will iterate through each record in the recordset
`  print ("<tr><td>");`	Output table tags
`  print($row['cat_desc']);`	Output the category description field
`  print("</td><td>");`	Output table tags
`  print($row['title']);`	Output the title field
`  print("</td><td>");`	Output table tags
`  print ($row['description']);`	Output the description field
`  print("</td><td>");`	Output table tags
`  print($row['reason']);`	Output the reason field
`  print("</td></tr>");`	Output the table tags closing the last item and the row
`  }`	Close of while loop
`mysql_close($link);`	Close connection
`?>`	End PHP
`</table>`	Closing table tag
`</body></html>`	Usual HTML close

Your users might want to see warning information displayed in a different way. The following script shows all favorites with a count of the number of warnings for each favorite. You use one of the same conditions as in the previous case, but in the form of an on condition. Notice that you do not need to mention the categories table. In this script, if a favorite does not have any warnings, it still is included in the display. The trick to getting such records is to use the SQL facilities `left join`. The SQL uses the `group by` clause, as explained in the previous section, to aggregate all the records with a single favorite_id. The summary function count uses a field that will have null entries for any records from the other table that do not have matches. The count function does not "count" these records. If you used `count(*)`, it would produce a count of 1 for such records. At this point, we apologize for naming the description field of the categories table `cat_desc`. The `desc` that you see in the query refers to descending order. This program (shown in Table 10.19) gives the favorites with the most warnings first and ends with any favorites with no (0) warnings.

TABLE 10.19   PHP Script to Display All Favorites with Counts of the Warnings

`<html><head><title>Current Favorites </title> </head> <body>`	Usual HTML start
`<h2>Favorites with warnings </h2>`	HTML heading
`<table border='1'>`	Table tag
`<tr><td>Titles </td> <td>Descriptions </td><td>Number of warnings</td> </tr>`	Table tags for top of table
`<?php`	Start PHP
`require("openfirstdb.php");`	Include connection code
`$query="Select f.title, f.description, count(w.favorite_id) as cnt ";`	Define query. It will be done over several statements
`$query .=" from favorites as f left join warnings as w ";`	Add on to query
`$query .="on f.favorite_id=w.favorite_id group by f.favorite_id ";`	Add on to query
`$query .=" order by cnt desc";`	Add on to query
`$result=mysql_db_query($DBname, $query, $link);`	Invoke the query
`while ($row=mysql_fetch_array($result)) {`	While loop: this will iterate over each row in the recordset. This will be each favorite with the common title and description values and the calculated cnt field with the count
`  print ("<tr><td>");`	Output table tags
`  print($row['title']);`	Output the title field
`  print("</td><td>");`	Output table tags
`  print ($row['description']);`	Output the description field

TABLE 10.19   *(continued)*

`print("</td><td>");`	Output table tags
`print($row['cnt']);`	Output the cnt field
`print("</td></tr>");`	Output table tags
`}`	Ends while loop
`mysql_close($link);`	End connection
`?>`	End PHP
`</table>`	Closing table tag
`</body></html>`	Usual HTML close

The last PHP scripts give the user a chance to select the category for the warnings. Two scripts are used. The first script (shown in Table 10.20) presents the categories as radio buttons in a form.

TABLE 10.20   PHP Script Presenting Chance to Select Category

`<html><head><title>Pick category of warning and show any favorites</title></head><body>`	Usual HTML start
`<h2>Pick category </h2> `	HTML heading
`<form action="spickcat2.php">`	HTML form tag
`<?php`	Start PHP
`require("openfirstdb.php");`	Include connection code
`$query="Select * from categories";`	Define $query
`$rs = mysql_db_query($DBname,$query, $link);`	Invoke query setting $rs
`while ($row=mysql_fetch_array($rs)) {`	While loop: this will iterate over each category in the categories table
`print("<input type='radio' name='cat' value='" . $row['cat_id']."'>" . $row['cat_desc']);`	Output a radio button with value the identifier for the category and text next to the radio button the category description
`}`	End of while loop
`print("<input type='submit' value='Show all favorites with the warning'>");`	Output submit button tag
`print("</form>");`	Output close of form
`mysql_close($link);`	End connection
`?>`	End PHP
`</body> </html>`	Usual HTML close

The second script, the handler shown in Table 10.21, displays all the favorites with warnings in the selected category. Notice that the script includes several links for the user to choose among for a follow-up operation.

TABLE 10.21   PHP Script to Show Favorites with Warnings in Selected Category

`<html><head><title>Current Favorites </title> </head><body>`	Usual HTML start
`<?php`	Start PHP
`require("openfirstdb.php");`	Include connection code
`$query="Select f.title, f.description, w.reason ";`	Define $query. This will be done in parts
`$query .=" from favorites as f, warnings as w, categories as c ";`	Add on
`$query .="where c.cat_id = w.cat_id and f.favorite_id = w.favorite_id ";`	Add on
`$query .=" and c.cat_id=$cat";`	Add on. The $cat is the value passed in from the form script
`$result=mysql_db_query($DBname, $query, $link);`	Invoke query
`?>`	End PHP
`<table border='1'>`	Table start
`<tr><td>Titles </td> <td>Descriptions </td><td>Reason</td></tr>`	First row of table
`<?`	Start PHP
`while ($row=mysql_fetch_array($result)) {`	While loop: this will iterate over records returned in recordset $result. This will be all the warnings within the category requested
`  print ("<tr><td>");`	Output table tags
`  print($row['title']);`	Output title field
`  print("</td><td>");`	Output table tags
`  print ($row['description']);`	Output description field
`  print("</td><td>");`	Output table tags
`  print($row['reason']);`	Output reason field
`  print("</td></tr>");`	Output table tags
`  }`	End while loop
`  mysql_close($link);`	Close connection
`?>`	End PHP
`</table>`	Table closing tag
`<ul>`	HTML unordered list

TABLE 10.21   *(continued)*

`<li><a href="showfavoriteswithwarnings.`
`php">Show all favorites with`
`warnings</a>`
	Link to show all the warnings

`<li><a href="showfavorites.php">Show` `all favorites</a>`	Link to show all the favorites

`<li><a href="showallfavoriteswith`
`warningcounts.php">Show favorites with`
`count of warnings </a>`
	Link to show favorites with warning counts

`<li><a href="spickcategory1.php">Show`
`favorites with warnings in one`
`category </a>`
	Link to request a new category of warnings to be displayed

`</ul>`	End unordered list
`</body></html>`	Usual HTML close

Turning to the ASP system, here is the implementation for inserting warning. The strategy is the same: use three scripts and follow the update model. You can try to implement these scripts on your own using the PHP scripts just described and the ASP update scripts.

Table 10.22 shows *swarning1.asp*.

TABLE 10.22   ASP/JavaScript for Showing Favorites for Adding a Warning

`<%@ Language=JavaScript %>`	Define language
`<html><head><title>Show favorites` `</title></head><body>`	Usual HTML start
`<!– #include file="sopenconn.asp" –>`	Include connection code
`<%`	Start ASP
`var query="Select * from favorites";`	Define query
`var result = Server.CreateObject` `("ADODB.RecordSet");`	Define result to hold a recordset
`result.Open(query,Conn);`	Invoke query
`Response.Write("<table border='1'>");`	Output table tag
`Response.Write("<tr><td> Titles` `</td><td>Descriptions</td></tr>");`	Output first row of table
`while (!result.EOF) {`	While loop: it will iterate until recordset is exhausted
`  Response.Write("\n");`	Output line break in the HTML source
`  Response.Write("<tr><td><a href=` `'swarning2.asp?whichid=");`	Output table tags plus start of a tag with start of query string

(continues)

TABLE 10.22   ASP/JavaScript for Showing Favorites for Adding a Warning (*continued*)

`Response.Write(result.fields.item` `("favorite_id"));`	Output favorite_id field
`  Response.Write("'>");`	Output close of a tag

`  Response.Write(unescape(result.`
`fields.item("title")) +`
`"</a></td> <td>");`
	Output title field. Note use of unescape to remove any escape characters

`Response.Write(unescape(result.fields.` `item("description")) + "</td></tr>");`	Output description field
`  result.move(1);`	Advance to next record in recordset
`}`	Close of `while` loop
`Response.Write(" </table>");`	Output table closing tag
`Conn.Close();`	Close connection
`%> </body> </html>`	End ASP and usual HTML closing tags

The next script, *swarning2.asp* shown in Table 10.23, presents a form in which the user can select the category for the warning by selecting one of a set of radio buttons and enter a reason for the warning.

TABLE 10.23   ASP/JavaScript for Adding a Warning for a Specified Favorite Title

`<%@ Language=JavaScript %>`	Define language
`<html><head><title>Enter warning` `</title></head> <body>`	Usual HTML start
`<!— #include file="sopenconn.asp"  —>`	Include connection code
`<%`	Start ASP
`var whichid = parseInt(Request.` `QueryString("whichid"));`	Get the favorite_id, which was passed along via the query string
`var query="Select * FROM favorites` `where favorite_id="+ whichid;`	Define query using the `whichid` variable
`var result = Server.CreateObject` `("ADODB.RecordSet");`	Define result to hold a recordset. (Note: there is only one row in this recordset)
`result.Open(query,Conn);`	Invoke the query
`var title=result.fields.item("title");`	Define title to be the title item. (It is the field of the record, but the terminology fields.item is what is used in ASP.)
`var desc=result.fields.item` `("description");`	Define desc to be the description item
`Response.Write("Title: " + title);`	Output title
`Response.Write(" Description: "+ desc);`	Output description
`Response.Write("<form action=` `'swarning3.asp'>");`	Output form tag

TABLE 10.23 *(continued)*

`Response.Write("Reason for warning:` `<input type='text' name='reason'>");`	Output input tag for user to enter a reason
`query="Select * from categories";`	Set query to be a new query string
`var rs = Server.CreateObject` `("ADODB.RecordSet");`	Define a new variable for this new recordset
`rs.Open(query,Conn);`	Invoke the query
`while (!rs.EOF) {`	`While` loop: it will iterate through all the categories

`Response.Write("<input type='radio'`
`name='cat' value='" +rs.fields.item`
`("cat_id")+"'>");`
	Output input radio tag holding the category id for the value

`Response.Write(rs.fields.item` `("cat_desc"));`	Output the category description to be the text next to the radio button
`rs.move(1);`	Advance to the next category
`}`	Close `while` loop
`Response.Write("<input type='submit'` `value='Insert Warning'>");`	Output submit button
`Response.Write("<input type='hidden'` `name='whichid' value="+whichid+">");`	Output hidden tag to hold the value of the favorite_id
`Response.Write("</form>");`	Output form close
`Response.Write("  Enter reason,` `choose category and click on Insert` `Warning button. ");`	Output instructions
`Conn.Close();`	Close connection
`%> </body> </html>`	Close ASP and usual HTML close

The last of the three scripts, *swarning3.asp* shown in Table 10.24, completes the process by making the insertion into the warnings table.

TABLE 10.24   ASP/JavaScript to Perform Actual Insertion of Warning

`<%@ Language=JavaScript %>`	Define language
`<html><head><title>Complete insertion` `</title></head><body>`	Usual HTML start
`<!— #include file="sopenconn.asp"  —>`	Include connection code
`<%`	Start ASP
`var whichid = parseInt(Request.` `QueryString("whichid"));`	Define `whichid` from the hidden form input. This is the favorite_id

(continues)

TABLE 10.24   ASP/JavaScript to Perform Actual Insertion of Warning (*continued*)

`var cat = parseInt(Request("cat"));`	Define cat from the form input
`var reason = escape(String(Request("reason")));`	Define reason from the form input. Note that it needs to be "escaped"
`var fields = "(favorite_id, cat_id, reason)";`	Define fields. This is to cut down on the complexity of the next line
`query = "INSERT into warnings "+fields+" values (" + whichid+", " + cat+", '"+reason+"')";`	Define query
`if (Conn.Execute(query))`	Invoke query and do if test to check on outcome
`    {Response.Write(" Warning was successfully entered.  ");}`	Positive outcome
`  else {Response.Write("Warning was NOT entered. "); }`	Negative outcome
`  Conn.Close();`	Close connection
`Response.Write("<a href=\"swarning1.asp\"> Submit another warning.</a>  ");`	Output link to go back and submit another warning
`%> </body> </html>`	Close ASP. Usual HTML close

The ASP scripts for the display of the warning information follow. Table 10.25 shows the script displaying all the titles with warnings.

TABLE 10.25   ASP/JavaScript for Displaying All Titles with Warnings

`<%@ Language=JavaScript %><html><head> <title>Current Favorites </title> </head> <body>`	Define language and Usual HTML start
`<h2>Favorites with warnings </h2> `	HTML heading
`<table border='1'>`	Start of table
`<tr><td>Category</td><td>Titles </td> <td>Descriptions </td><td>Reason</td> </tr>`	First line of table
`<!— #include file="sopenconn.asp"  —>`	Include connection code
`<%`	Start ASP
`var query="Select c.cat_desc, f.title, f.description, w.reason ";`	Define query. It is done in steps because of complexity
`query +=" from favorites as f, warnings as w, categories as c ";`	Add on. Note use of synonyms (single letters)
`query +="where c.cat_id = w.cat_id and f.favorite_id = w.favorite_id ";`	Add on. These are the two joining conditions

TABLE 10.25   *(continued)*

`query +=" order by c.cat_desc";`	Add on. This is the order condition
`var result = Server.CreateObject` `("ADODB.RecordSet");`	Create result to hold a recordset
`result.Open(query,Conn);`	Invoke the query
`while (!result.EOF) {`	`While` loop: this will iterate until the result is exhausted
`  Response.Write("\n");`	Output a line break
`  Response.Write("<tr><td> " + unescape` `(result.fields.item("cat_desc")));`	Output table tags plus the cat_desc field
`  Response.Write("</td> <td>");`	Output table tags
`Response.Write(unescape(result.fields.` `item("title")));`	Output the title field
`  Response.Write("</td> <td>");`	Output table tags
`Response.Write(unescape(result.fields.` `item("description")));`	Output the description field
`  Response.Write("</td> <td>");`	Output table tags
`Response.Write(unescape(result.fields.` `item("reason")));`	Output the reason field
`  Response.Write("</td></tr>");`	Output table tags
`  result.move(1);`	Advance to the next record
`}`	Close `while` loop
`Response.Write(" </table>");`	Output the closing table tag
`  Conn.Close();`	Close the connection
`%> </body> </html>`	Close ASP and usual HTML close

The next script (shown in Table 10.26) is the ASP file to display all favorites with count of warnings. The SQL in this program is slightly different from the PHP version. The SQL of Access does not allow the synonym cnt to be used in the order by clause. The SQL of Access also requires all the fields for grouping to be named in the group by clause, and all fields named in the group by clause to be among the selected fields.

TABLE 10.26   ASP/JavaScript for Displaying All Favorites with Counts of the Warnings

`<%@ Language=JavaScript %>`	Define language
`<html><head><title>Current Favorites` `</title> </head> <body>`	Usual HTML start
`<h2>Favorites with warnings </h2> `	HTML header

(continues)

TABLE 10.26   ASP/JavaScript for Displaying All Favorites with Counts of the Warnings (*continued*)

`<table border='1'>`	HTML table tag
`<tr><td>Titles </td> <td>Description </td><td>Number of Warnings</td> </tr>`	Table tags for first row
`<!– #include file="sopenconn.asp"  –>`	Include connection code
`<%`	Start ASP
`var query="SELECT f.title, f.description, count(w.favorite_id) AS cnt ";`	Define query. This will be done over several steps. Note the synonym cnt. This will be used later
`query +=" FROM favorites AS f LEFT JOIN warnings as w ";`	Add on to the query. This part defines the join as a left join, meaning the non-matched records will be represented in the final recordset
`query +=" ON f.favorite_id = w.favorite_id GROUP BY f.title, f.description ";`	Add on. This includes the group by clause. (Note that both `f.title` and `f.description` need to be mentioned)
`query +=" ORDER BY count(w.favorite_id) DESC";`	Add on. This includes the order by clause. Note that the complete expression for the aggregate function is cited. The desc stands for descending order
`var result = Server.CreateObject ("ADODB.RecordSet");`	Create result to hold a recordset
`result.Open(query,Conn);`	Invoke the recordset
`while (!result.EOF) {`	While loop: this will iterate over the records, namely one for each favorite
`Response.Write("\n");`	Output a line break
`Response.Write("<tr><td> ");`	Output table tags
`Response.Write(unescape(result.fields. item("title")));`	Output the title field
`Response.Write("</td> <td>");`	Output table tags
`Response.Write(unescape(result.fields. item("description")));`	Output the description field
`Response.Write("</td> <td>");`	Output table tags
`Response.Write(unescape(result.fields. item("cnt")));`	Output the cnt field. This is the synonym for the count aggregate operation defined in the query
`Response.Write("</td></tr>");`	Output table tags
`result.move(1);`	Advance to the next record

TABLE 10.26   *(continued)*

`}`	Close the `while` loop
`Response.Write(" </table>");`	Output table close
`Conn.Close();`	Close the connection
`%> </body> </html>`	End ASP and usual HTML close

The next scripts for the ASP system give the user a chance to select the category of warnings. The first script, shown in Table 10.27, presents a form with radio buttons as before.

TABLE 10.27   ASP/JavaScript for Displaying Categories

`<%@ Language=JavaScript %>`	Define language
`<html><head><title>Pick category of warning and show any favorites</title> </head><body>`	Usual HTML start
`<h2>Pick category </h2> `	HTML header
`<form action="spickcat2.asp">`	Form tag
`<!– #include file="sopenconn.asp"  –>`	Include connection code
`<%`	Start ASP
`query="Select * from categories";`	Define query to get all categories
`var rs = Server.CreateObject ("ADODB.RecordSet");`	Define `rs` to hold a recordset
`rs.Open(query,Conn);`	Invoke query
`while (!rs.EOF) {`	While loop: this will iterate until `rs` is exhausted
`Response.Write("<input type='radio' name='cat' value='" +rs.fields.item ("cat_id")+"'>");`	Output radio button. The value will be the cat_id
`Response.Write(rs.fields.item ("cat_desc"));`	Output cat_desc next to radio button
`rs.move(1);`	Advance to next category
`}`	End `while` loop
`Response.Write("<input type='submit' value='Show all favorites with this warning'>");`	Output Submit button
`Response.Write("</form>");`	Output end of form
`Conn.Close();`	Close connection
`%> </body> </html>`	End ASP and usual HTML close

The handler for the form, shown in Table 10.28, presents the favorites with warnings of the specified category. It differs from the PHP version. See the *Exercises* section for a challenge.

TABLE 10.28   ASP/JavaScript to Display Favorites with Warnings in Specified Category

`<%@ Language=JavaScript %>`	Define language
`<html><head><title>Current Favorites </title></head><body>`	Usual HTML head
`<h2>Favorites with warnings </h2> `	Heading
`<table border='1'>`	Table tag
`<tr><td>Titles </td> <td>Descriptions </td><td>Reason</td> </tr>`	Table first row
`<!– #include file="sopenconn.asp"  –>`	Include connection code
`<%`	Start ASP
`var cat = parseInt(Request("cat"));`	Define cat from form input
`var query="Select f.title, f.description, w.reason ";`	Define query. This will be done in several steps
`query +=" from favorites as f, warnings as w, categories as c ";`	Add on
`query +="where c.cat_id = w.cat_id and f.favorite_id = w.favorite_id ";`	Add on
`query +=" and c.cat_id=" + cat;`	Add on. This includes the cat_id value passed in from form on prior script
`var result = Server.CreateObject ("ADODB.RecordSet");`	Define result to hold a recordset
`result.Open(query,Conn);`	Invoke query
`while (!result.EOF) {`	While loop: will iterate over all records
`Response.Write("\n");`	Output line break
`Response.Write("<tr><td>");`	Output table tags
`Response.Write(unescape(result.fields. item("title")));`	Output title field
`Response.Write("</td> <td>"); Response. Write(unescape(result.fields.item ("description")));`	Output table tags and description field
`Response.Write("</td> <td>");`	Output table tags
`Response.Write(unescape(result.fields. item("reason")));`	Output reason field
`Response.Write("</td></tr>");`	Output table tags

TABLE 10.28   *(continued)*

`result.move(1);`	Advance to next record
`}`	Close `while` loop
`Response.Write(" </table>");`	Output table close
`Conn.Close();`	Close connection
`%> </body> </html>`	End ASP and Usual HTML close

REFLECTION

This chapter revolved around a small database application that still managed to require a variety of SQL and PHP and ASP programming features. One lesson that you could learn from this is that when you are developing an application, it is possible to test your logic and design on a small system. You need not and should not enter in all your data before you have tested the basics. Your test system needs to have some variety of data, but it does not need large numbers of records.

As in the last chapter, special characters—for example, the single quotation mark—required special handling. This was discovered just because the test data originally used contained an apostrophe. This means you need to include special characters in your testing.

You probably ran into pesky syntax bugs involving single and double quotation marks, opening and closing parentheses, curly brackets and tags. Techniques to employ for debugging include:

- Use of `print` and `Response.Write` to output query statements and any other variable that might be questionable.
- Dividing steps into multiple steps (such as construction of a string for a complex query). Error codes from PHP and ASP are given in terms of line numbers.
- Examination of the HTML source.

This chapter also exposed some differences in the SQL for MySQL versus the SQL for Access. If you do go from one system to another and find that something fails to work, your best bet is to go online to find an answer.

The logic for the ASP and PHP systems is the same. Moreover, the logic of one task carries over to another task. Try to see the similarity between tasks so you can copy sections of code from script to script and build on your experience for new applications.

EXERCISES, QUESTIONS, AND PROJECTS

1. Create a script, with the necessary SQL `select` query, to display the favorites ordered by title.

2. Implement the deletion operation using just one script.
3. Create a script that displays the favorite titles not using a table; for example, using the HTML unordered list tags.
4. After adding the two additional tables, create a script, with the necessary SQL select query, to display all the favorites, with different orderings.
5. Complete the ASP script for displaying the warnings for a given category to include the links shown in the PHP version. In each case, add a link to add a new warning.
6. Create scripts to allow a user to add a new category of warning.
7. Since the design allows for multiple warnings for the same favorite in the same category, modify the display so that the title and description are not repeated in the case of multiple warnings. (Hint: you will use a variable to hold the current title and current description and check these values as you are creating the HTML table.)
8. Create a script that will display all favorites that do not have any warnings.
9. Create a set of scripts that allows your customer to choose a category of warning and see a display of all favorites that do *not* have any warnings in that category.
10. Go online and find out about the `htmlspecialchars` function for PHP. You also can try to find an ASP/JavaScript analogous feature.

11

REGULAR EXPRESSIONS

T he goal of this chapter is to introduce regular expressions and demonstrate their use in middleware programming. This will include comparing regular expression processing and the LIKE operator in SQL.

BACKGROUND

The origin of regular expressions, a system for defining patterns of character strings, lies in theoretical computer science; namely, the theory of formal languages. Regular expressions also served a practical function by being incorporated in the earliest UNIX editors.

Regular expressions can serve two overlapping roles in middleware projects. A common function of a PHP or ASP script is to validate text data submitted by the person at the client computer. Regular expressions are an exact match for this role. Regular expressions also can be used to manipulate character strings, extract parts, and/or replace parts. An example of this will be shown in the next chapter in which the address for a file is calculated using the address for the script itself.

After learning about regular expressions, you might want to use them for doing searches in the database. Standard SQL supports a facility for what can be called *inexact* or *incomplete matches*: the LIKE operator. For example, you can check if a field contains a string by combining the given string with wildcard characters. The LIKE operator does not accept regular expressions. In addition, MySQL has an operator called REGEXP that checks a field of a table against a regular expression pattern.

CONCEPTUAL EXPLANATION

The first parts of this section will be independent of PHP, ASP, or, indeed, any specific implementation of regular expressions. Next, we cover the specific implementations of regular expressions using PHP and ASP/JavaScript. Lastly, there is a discussion of SQL and patterns.

Basic Patterns and Groupings

A regular expression defines a pattern of character strings. Once the pattern is defined, you can use functions in PHP, methods in ASP, and commands in other programming systems to determine if a given string matches the pattern.

Regular expressions are made up of constants, classes of characters, and notation for defining logical combinations, groupings, and position. The fact that you can use the notation to build regular expressions out of component parts is what gives this technology its power.

An example of a regular expression is any string of characters. The following is a regular expression:

```
bird
```

As given, this pattern will match any string that contains the characters "bird" anywhere in the string.

You can combine two regular expressions to produce a third expression that matches on either of the constituent parts.

```
(bird)|(frog)
```

will match any string that contains either 'bird' or 'frog' or both.

For any pattern, you can specify a new pattern made up by repeating the base pattern any number of times, including no times at all.

```
c(a)*t
```

will match a string that contains a 'c' followed by any number of a's followed by a 't'. So, the following patterns would match:

```
ct
cat
caat
caaaaaaaaaaaaaaaat
```

The following patterns would not match:

```
cxt
coat
```

There are other combination notations. A plus stands for one or more repetitions.

```
c(a)+t
```

This would not match ct, but would match cat, caat, and so on.

A question mark stands for zero or one repetition. To specify an exact range of possible repetitions, you use curly brackets:

```
(cat){2,5}
```

would match on:

```
catcat
catcatcat
catcatcatcat
catcatcatcatcat
```

You can specify that the pattern must start at the start of the string by using the caret symbol:

```
^cat
```

would match the following strings:

```
cat
cat and not dog
cat cat cat
```

but would not match:

```
The dog chased the cat.
```

Similarly, you can specify that the pattern must be at the end of the string by using the dollar sign:

```
cat$
```

would match:

```
The dog chased the cat
```

If you needed to check for an exact match, you would use:

```
^cat$
```

To check that the string contained only dog or cat, use the regular expression:

```
^(dog)|(cat)$
```

Fixing the pattern to start or end the string is called *anchoring*.

Character Sets

You can specify a set of characters using square brackets.

```
[0-9]
```

specifies one of the 10 numerals.

```
[a-z]
```

specifies the lowercase letters.

```
[a-zA-Z]
```

specifies all letters.

A period specifies exactly one character. So the string:

```
c.t
```

would match any string containing the character c, followed by exactly one character, followed by a t. These include:

```
cat
cot
cit
c2t
```

You can combine all these features. To specify any number of letters, you would use:

```
[a-zA-Z]*
```

You also can specify that a character not be in a set by using the caret symbol inside the square brackets:

```
[^a-z]
```

stands for any character that is not a lowercase letter.

You can combine patterns sequentially:

```
(cat)+(dog)+
```

matches a string with one or more instances of the string cat followed by one or more instances of the string dog.

The particular implementation of regular expressions can have classes of characters predefined for you.

What do you do if you need to match one of the special symbols such as period or dollar sign? The answer is to put a slash in front of the special symbol. If you need to use a slash, you must use two slashes.

In addition to determining if a regular expression has a match within a given string, you might want to replace the matched parts with other strings. For example, you construct the regular expression to represent common misspellings and then replace the mistakes with the proper spelling. Most implementations of regular expressions include facilities for replacement. The replacements can be complex: replacing certain groups in the pattern but not others.

Role of Validation

While it is important, even critical, that scripts check data submitted by users, it is wrong to focus on checking as the only way to ensure valid input. The design of the interface should make it easy for people to do the right thing and difficult to do the wrong thing before their input reaches the validation code. Consider the task of asking customers or clients to enter a date. One approach would be to present a text field in a form. However, a better approach, and the one that appears to be prevalent on the Web today, is to present three pull-down menus with the full names of the months, numbers for the day of the month, and the years that are appropriate for the question. This makes special sense for a global audience, since people in the United States use a month/day/year format, and people in many other places use day/month/year or year/month/day. It also makes sense to force a person to pick this year or later if the date is to be something like a credit card expiration. Restricting what your user can do is a good tactic. In the examples given for adding a warning to the database for a favorite show, the interface required clicking on the name of the show, not typing a name into a text field. Of course, if the list of favorites was very long, scrolling through all the shows might take too much time. However, you still would want to try to design something that does not require people to type an unrestricted entry.

One fault that you might want to avoid in your validation code is to stop the validation as soon as you find the first error. It might not always be possible, but you should try to tell the person doing input all the problems all at once. The method shown in the *Examples* section uses what can be called "okay so far" coding. The code defines a variable to be true. After each check, if the input fails, this variable is set to be false and a message is output to the HTML document describing the specific error. The variable might be set to false several times. After all the checks, if the variable is still true, then processing can continue.

It is as important to test the validation code as any other code in your application. This means that you need to submit data with errors and, moreover, combinations of good and bad input.

Regular Expressions in PHP

The PHP system has several regular expression functions. The `ereg` and `eregi` functions return true or false, depending on whether a pattern is found in a string or not. The difference between the two is that `eregi` is not case-sensitive. If:

```
$source = "cats and dogs";
$pattern = "dog";
$pattern1="^dog";
```

then:

```
ereg($pattern,$source)
```

would return true, but:

```
ereg($pattern1,$source)
```

would return false since the string dog is not at the start of the tested string. If:

```
$source1 = "Cats and Dogs";
```

then:

```
ereg($pattern,$source1)
```

would return false because of the upper case D. However:

```
eregi($pattern,$source1)
```

would return true.

The PHP system also has functions for finding parts of strings using regular expressions and replacing them. The call:

```
ereg_replace($pattern,"kittens",$source);
```

would return a new string with the value: "cats and kittens". A common way of using ereg_replace would be:

```
$source =
ereg_replace($pattern, $replacement ,$source);
```

where $replacement holds a correction for piece of the string matched to the pattern in $pattern.

The eregi_replace acts like the ereg_replace function, except that the initial matching is done with upper- and lowercase treated as being the same.

Regular Expressions in JavaScript

The regular expression facility for the ASP examples in this text is the JavaScript facility. The ASP objects do not provide any special function relating to regular expressions.

JavaScript has a distinct notation for regular expressions. The slash is used to start and end a regular expression in place of the quotation marks for strings. The following are two variables defined as regular expressions:

```
var pattern = /dog/;
var patterni = /dog/i;
```

The i at the end in the definition of `patterni` indicates that matches are to be done independent of upper- and lower-case.

Assume the following:

```
var source = "cats and dogs";
var source1 = "Cats and Dogs";
```

All strings have `match()` and `replace()` methods. The following:

```
source.match(pattern)
```

will return true.

```
source1.match(pattern)
```

will return false because of the capital D. However:

```
source.match(patterni)
```

and

```
source1.match(patterni)
```

will both return true since the `patterni` indicated a case-insensitive case.

Strings in JavaScript have another method for replacing parts of strings matched by regular expressions.

```
source1 = source1.replace(patterni,"kittens");
```

would set source1 to be "Cats and kittens".

SQL Operators: LIKE and REGEXP (in MySQL)

The SQL standard provides the LIKE operator for specifying a limited set of matches. Specifically, LIKE accepts two so-called wildcard symbols. The underscore stands for any single character, and the percent sign stands for one or more of any character. To return all records in which the field named firstname starts with "Jea," use the SQL query:

```
SELECT * from tablename where firstname LIKE 'Jea%'
```

To select only records in which the field named code has values of exactly three characters, use:

```
SELECT * from tablename where code LIKE '___'
```

The long dash is exactly three underscore symbols.

To return all records in which the field named desserts contains "chocolate," use:

```
SELECT * from tablename where desserts LIKE 'chocolate'
```

This last query will return records with desserts field such as:

```
chocolate
chocolate cake
dark chocolate candy
```

MySQL supports an additional operator, REGEXP, that uses regular expressions. Its use will be demonstrated in the *Examples* section. This is an example of how the open-source development process can make enhancements to standard techniques. However, it is not standard SQL.

EXAMPLES

ON THE CD

Let us consider several common items of information that could be input by a person sitting at the client computer. The projects demonstrated here involve using regular expressions to validate user input and regular expressons and other patterns to find records in databases. The CD-ROM contains the code for the projects in the folder named chapter11code.

A postal zip code for the United States consists of five digits, or five digits followed by a hyphen and then four more digits. A regular expression for a zip code needs to do the following:

- Anchor the pattern at the start with the caret.
- Define a sub-pattern that specifies exactly five digits.
- Define a sub-pattern that specifies a hyphen followed by exactly four digits. This sub-pattern is to be present zero or one time, requiring the question mark symbol.
- Anchor the pattern at the end with the dollar sign.

With this reasoning, the regular expression for a zip code is:

```
^[0-9]{5}(-[0-9]{4})?$
```

A common input type is the specification of quantity for an order. Assume that this is input as a string as opposed to a drop-down box or a component that allows the user to click to increase a quantity. The reasoning used to generate this pattern is:

- Anchor the pattern at the start with the caret
- Require one digit from 1 to 9
- Define the sub-pattern as zero to any number of digits
- Anchor the pattern at the end with the dollar sign

With this reasoning, the regular expression is:

```
^[1-9][0-9]*$
```

Suppose you want to detect the presence of one of several possible words in a string. Perhaps you need to design a form for customer complaints, and you want to direct all complaints about "quality" and "performance" to one specific department. You would do a regular expression check using the pattern:

```
(quality)|(performance)
```

In this example, you probably would choose to make the test case-insensitive and, consequently, use the appropriate function in PHP or the i following the slash in JavaScript.

For a last example, suppose you want to check for a credit card number that is four groups of four numbers. You have decided to permit either 16 contiguous numbers or four groups of four numbers separated by a blank or by hyphens. People need to choose one or the other—they cannot put in eight numbers and a blank and then eight more. The reasoning to generate this pattern is:

- Anchor the pattern at the start with the caret.
- Define as one sub-pattern 16 digits.
- Define as a sub-pattern four digits. Combine it with a sub-pattern of a blank or a hyphen repeated to get the full 16 digits plus three intervening symbols.
- Make the two previous sub-patterns alternates using the | symbol.
- Anchor the pattern at the end with the dollar sign.

The resulting regular expression is:

```
^([0-9]{16})|( [0-9]{4}( |-)[0-9]{4}( |-)[0-9]{4}( |-)[0-9]{4})$
```

Validation in PHP

The form shown in this example includes name, number of tickets, zip code, and a destination, given via a drop-down menu. The number of tickets and the zip code are validated using the regular expressions discussed in the previous section. However, the name also requires validation. Specifically, this script, as is typical, will check to make sure that this field is not blank. It is not a rigorous validation, but the situation does often occur that someone submits a form and leaves out information, so you need to incorporate checking for this situation in your code.

The destination value is not validated. A legal value is always sent to the handler because there is a default value. However, the message produced by the system tells the person what destination was selected. In most applications involving money transactions, the customer is given a chance to confirm the information, so if the default value was not correct, the customer could correct the information.

The application consists of an HTML form script and a handler script. The HTML form script will be the same for both the PHP and ASP/JavaScript versions, except for the file specified in the action attribute of the form tag. The PHP script for displaying the form, with explanation, is shown in Table 11.1.

TABLE 11.1   PHP Script to Display Form

`<html> <head><title>Travel</title> </head><body>`	Usual HTML
`<h1>Travel</h1>   <p>`	Heading
`<hr>`	Horizontal rule
`<form action="midt.php" method=get>  `	Directs the form input to the midt.php file
`Name: <input type=text name="name">  `	Input file for the name
`Number of tickets: <input type=text name="ticketno">  `	Input file for the number of tickets
`Zip code (5 digit or 5+4 format): <input type=text name="zip">  `	Input file for the zip code
`Select destination  `	Text preceding drop-down menu
`<select name="state">`	Start of drop-down menu
`    <option value="NY">NY</option>`	NY option
`    <option value="NJ">NJ</option>`	NJ option
`    <option value="IL">IL</option>`	IL option
`</select> `	End of drop-down menu
`<input type=submit value='SEND'><input type=reset value='RESET'>`	Submit button tag
`</form> </body> </html>`	Usual HTML close

The HTML produces the form, shown in Figure 11.1 with the fields filled in.

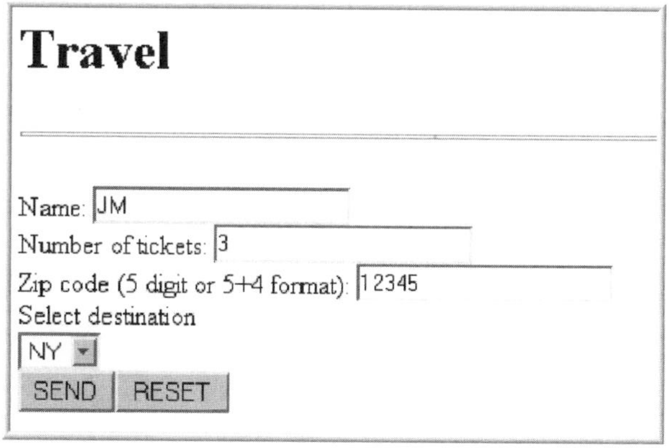

FIGURE 11.1   Travel form filled in.

The PHP handler is shown in Table 11.2.

TABLE 11.2   PHP Script for Server-Side Validation of Form Data

`<html> <head><title>ticket checker</title></head><body>`	Usual HTML start
`<?php`	Start PHP
`$ticketchk="^[1-9][0-9]*$";`	Define the pattern to check for a number greater than 0
`$zippattern="^[0-9]{5}(-[0-9]{4})?$";`	Define the pattern for a zip code: 5 digits plus option of 5-4
`$oksofar=true;`	Start the $oksofar variable to be true
`if ($name=="") {`	Check if name is empty string
`    $oksofar=FALSE;`	This is a problem. Flip $oksofar to false
`    print(" Please enter a name. ");}`	Output an error message
`if (!eregi($ticketchk,$ticketno)){`	Compare the number of tickets input with the pattern. If it does not match...
`    $oksofar=FALSE;`	This is an error. Flip $oksofar
`    print(" Please enter number of tickets. ");}`	Output an error message
`if (!eregi($zippattern,$zip)) {`	Compare the zip code inputted with the pattern. If it does not match...
`    $oksofar=FALSE;`	This is an error. Flip $oksofar
`    print (" Zip code given, $zip, is not in standard format.");`	Output an error message
`}`	End if
`if ($oksofar) {`	Check $oksofar—is it still true
`    if ($ticketno==1){`	Do test to determine if ticketno is 1 or not
`    print (" <font size=12><b>Thank you, $name.  You bought a ticket to $state.</b></font>");}`	Print out message for buying one ticket
`else {`	Else (it was more than 1)
`    print (" <font size=12><b>Thank you, $name.  You bought $ticketno tickets to $state.</b></font>");}`	Print out message for more than one ticket
`}`	End if checking $oksofar
`?>`	Close PHP
`</body> </html>`	Usual HTML close

When the SEND button is clicked in the HTML form properly filled out as shown, the screen shown in Figure 11.2 appears.

Thank you, JM.
You bought 3 tickets to NY.

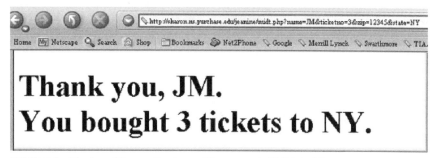

FIGURE 11.2 Display of Screen Capture of Response to Validated Data

Examine the query string up in the location field to see the values actually sent to the handler. Notice that NY is sent as the state value, even though it was not clicked. It is the default. The handler correctly determines that the input is valid and prints a message.

What if the input indicated in Figure 11.3 was typed into the form?

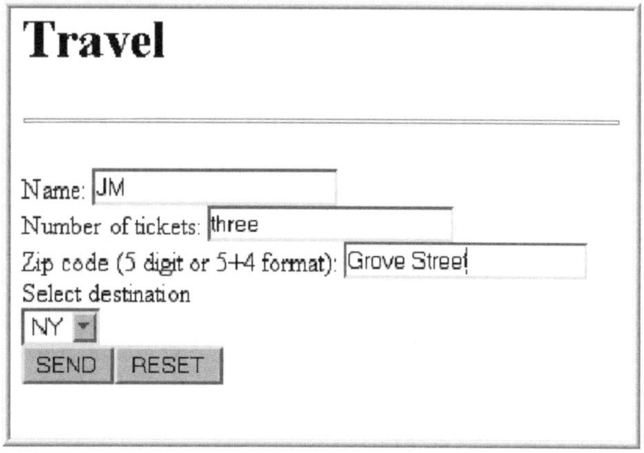

Travel
Name: JM
Number of tickets: three
Zip code (5 digit or 5+4 format): Grove Street
Select destination
NY
SEND
RESET

FIGURE 11.3 Form with incorrect data.

The response by the handler is shown in Figure 11.4.

The handler has detected the two errors. The message concerning the number of tickets could be improved.

Please enter number of tickets.
Zip code given, Grove Street, is not in standard format.

FIGURE 11.4   Response in case of errors.

Validation in ASP/JavaScript

The same application will be shown using JavaScript. The HTML form is identical to the one just shown for PHP, except for the form tag, which, in this case, points to an ASP file:

```
<form action="midt.asp" method=post> <br>
```

The handler for checking the data is shown in Table 11.3.

TABLE 11.3   ASP/JavaScript Script to Validate Form Data

`<%@ Language=JavaScript%>`	Sets JavaScript as language
`<html><head><title>ticket checker</title></head><body>`	Usual HTML open
`<%`	Start ASP
`var name=String(Request.Form("name"));`	Extract form input to define name
`var ticketno=String(Request.Form ("ticketno"));`	Extract ticket number input
`var zip=String(Request.Form("zip"));`	Extract zip code input
`var state=String(Request.Form("state"));`	Extract state input
`var ticketchk=/^[1-9][0-9]*$/;`	Define pattern to check ticket number
`var zippattern=/^[0-9]{5}(-[0-9]{4})?$/;`	Define pattern to check zip code
`var oksofar=true;`	Set oksofar to start as true
`if (name==""){`	Check if name was not given
`    oksofar=false;`	Flip oksofar to be false
`    Response.Write(" Please enter a name. ");`	Output error message
`}`	End if test
`if (!ticketno.match(ticketchk)) {`	Check ticket number
`    oksofar=false;`	Flip oksofar

TABLE 11.3   *(continued)*

`    Response.Write (" Please enter number of tickets. ");`	Output error message
`}`	End `if` test
`if (!zip.match(zippattern)) {`	Check zip code
`    oksofar=false;`	Flip `oksofar`
`    Response.Write (" Zip code given, "+zip+", is not in standard format.");`	Output error message
`}`	End `if` test
`if (oksofar) {`	Check if `oksofar` still true
`    if (ticketno==1){`	Check if just 1 ticket (NOTE this is two equal signs to check equality)
`    Response.Write (" <font size=12><b>Thank you, "+name+".  You bought a ticket to "+state+".</b></font>");}`	Output appropriate message for one ticket
`else {`	`Else` other possibility: more than one ticket
`    Response.Write (" <font size=12><b>Thank you, "+name+".  You bought "+ticketno+" tickets to "+state+".</b></font>");}`	Output appropriate message for more than one ticket
`}`	Close `else` clause
`%>`	End ASP
`</body></html>`	Usual HTML end

SQL Queries

The previous examples make use of the PHP language and JavaScript. You might decide that you want to make an SQL query in which you want to find records based on a pattern match of field values instead of equality or inequality. For example, users might want to search for the warnings in the database that contain a specific word, but could contain other things. The form to request this information is shown in Figure 11.5.

If you filled out the form as indicated in Figure 11.6, you might expect to get a response with all the shows having any warnings containing the "problem" item. Figure 11.7 shows the response.

The reason field contained the "problem," but did not exactly match it.

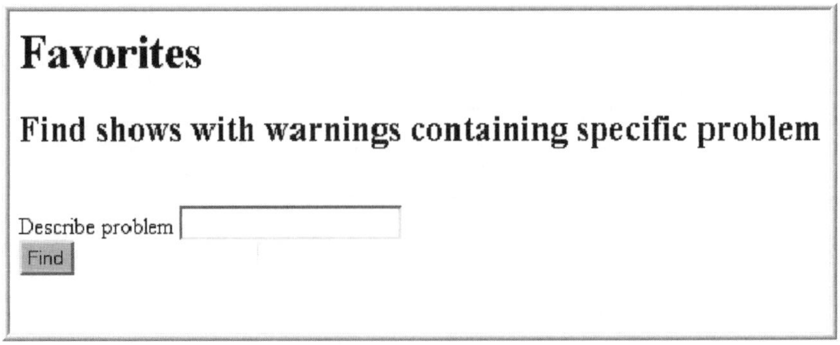

Favorites

Find shows with warnings containing specific problem

Describe problem [   ]
[Find]

FIGURE 11.5 Screen capture requesting problem term.

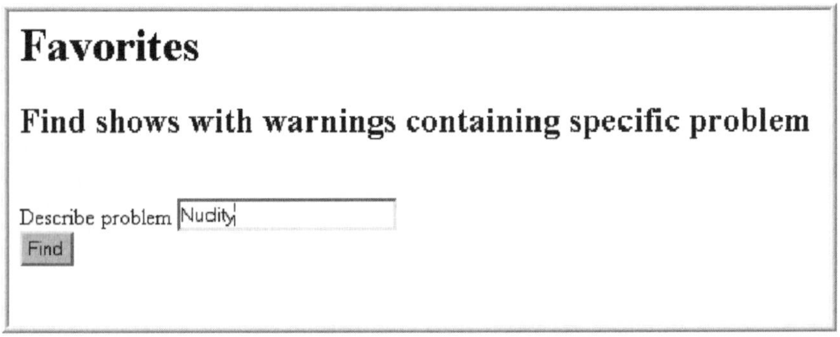

Favorites

Find shows with warnings containing specific problem

Describe problem [Nudity   ]
[Find]

FIGURE 11.6 Problem entered into form.

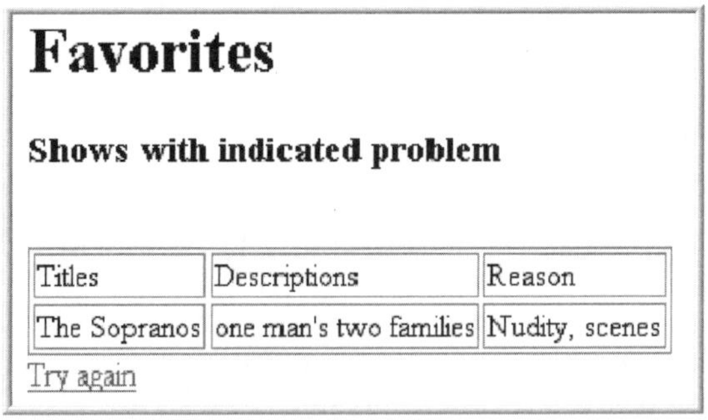

Favorites

Shows with indicated problem

Titles	Descriptions	Reason
The Sopranos	one man's two families	Nudity, scenes

Try again

FIGURE 11.7 Screen capture for response for warnings containing the problem term.

The SQL standard provides the `LIKE` operator and its two wildcards: percent sign for any number of any character, and underscore for exactly one character. In addition, MySQL provides `REGEXP` for regular expression matching. The next two sections demonstrate the use of these operators in the PHP/MySQL system and the ASP/JavaScript Access system. The critical component of these two alternatives is the database. MySQL provides more functionality than Access, so to get the response just described, you need to do some work.

MySQL `LIKE` and `REGEXP`

The following script accepts input from the person sitting at the client computer and uses the text in an SQL statement using the `LIKE` operator. The `Select` query requests title, description, and reason fields from shows that have warnings with reasons that match the data. The records from the recordset produced are displayed.

The code needs to detect the situation of no records matching. This requires use of the PHP function `mysql_num_rows`. Because this test needs to be done after the query, you need to resist the temptation to output the HTML with the initial table tags at the very start of the script.

This script will serve to handle the form and display the form so it contains an `if` statement checking if the form has been submitted using a hidden input tag.

Since the query is complex, the code in Table 11.4 constructs the query in three steps and also displays it. This is all for the purposes of easy debugging. You can change it once your script is working.

TABLE 11.4   PHP Script to Find Warnings with Specified Term

`<html><head><title>Find shows with certain warnings</title></head> <body>`	Usual HTML start
`<h1>Favorites </h1>`	Heading
`<?`	Start PHP
`if (@$submitted) {`	Check if this is the handling part of the script
`include("openfirstdb.php");`	Include the code that makes connection to the database
`$sq ="SELECT f.title, f.description, w.reason ";`	Construct the query in several steps
`$sq = $sq . " from favorites as f, warnings as w where f.favorite_id = w.favorite_id ";`	Add to query

(continues)

TABLE 11.4   PHP Script to Find Warnings with Specified Term *(continued)*

`$sq = $sq . " and w.reason LIKE '$problem'";`	Add to query
`print("Query is $sq ");`	Print out query for debugging purposes
`$rs = mysql_db_query($DBname,$sq,$link);`	Perform the query to get a recordset in `$rs`

`if (mysql_num_rows($rs)==0) {print ("No warnings match: $problem. Use a more general pattern.");`
`    }`
`else {`
	Check for no matches. If so, print out a message

`print("<h3>Shows with indicated problem</h3> ");`	Output heading
`print("<table border='1'><tr><td> Titles</td> <td>Descriptions</td>");`	Output table tags
`print("<td>Reason</td> </tr> ");`	More table tags
`print("\n");`	Output line break for the HTML
`while ($row=mysql_fetch_array($rs)) {`	While loop to iterate through the recordset of matches. This will stop when no more rows; that is, records in the recordset
`print("\n");`	Output line break for the HTML
`print("<tr><td>");`	Output table tags
`print($row["title"]);`	Output the title
`print("</td><td>");`	Output table tags
`print($row["description"]);`	Output the description
`print("</td><td>");`	Output table tags
`print($row["reason"]);`	Output the reason
`print("</td> </tr>");`	Output table tags closing off row of table
`    }  // end while`	End of while
`print("</table>");`	Output closing table tag
`} // ends else, rows in recordset`	End the `else` clause for it not being the case that there were no records. There were records
`mysql_close($link);`	Close connection
`$submitted = false;`	Reset the `submitted` variable
`print("<a href='sfindwarnings.php'>Try again </a>");`	Output a hyperlink to allow user to try again

TABLE 11.4   *(continued)*

`}`	End the `if form was submitted` clause
`else {`	Start the *else* clause: form needs to be shown
`?>`	Close PHP
`<h2>Find shows with warnings containing specific problem </h2> `	Straight HTML heading
`<form action="sfindwarnings.php">`	Form tag
`Describe problem <input type='text' name='problem'>  `	Input tag for problem string
`<input type='hidden' name='submitted' value='true'>`	Hidden input tag
`<input type='submit' value='Find'>`	Button
`</form>`	Close form
`<?`	Restart PHP
`}`	Close `else` clause
`?>`	Close PHP
`</body> </html>`	Usual HTML close

If you try this script and want to check for a word contained in the reason field of a record in warnings, you will need to type in the wild card percent sign symbol before and after the term. Try this script with your database using terms that are contained in the reason fields. In our example, using "Nudity" would not return any records. In contrast, typing in "%Nudity%" would. You would need to use the next script or do some other manipulation of the user input to get the results indicated in the previous screen shots.

The MySQL system supports the operator `REGEXP`. Let us modify the script to make use of this operator. The one difference from the preceding example would be the definition of the query:

```
$sq ="SELECT f.title, f.description, w.reason ";
$sq = $sq . " from favorites as f, warnings as w";
$sq = $sq . " where  f.favorite_id = w.favorite_id ";
$sq = $sq . " and w.reason REGEXP '$problem'";
```

In this case, the test for a specific word within the reason field of warning would be indicated just by the word because that is the default for regular expressions. The user would not need to put percent sign symbols for wild cards. Knowledgeable users could use this facility for more general regular expression queries.

Access LIKE

The Access database supports the standard SQL LIKE operator. However, do check the documentation for your version of the Access product; previous versions might have used symbols other than % and _ for the wildcard.

As was the case with the PHP script, it is important for this application to be able to check if a recordset contains no records. The recordset object does have a method for this purpose: RecordCount. However, this method will not return a valid number unless the recordset has been opened with a third parameter holding a value different from the default value.

```
result.Open(sq,Conn, 1)
```

The third parameter is for the cursor. The default value assumes that the code will read the recordset once from the start until the end. A way of remembering to use this parameter if you need to get a count of the records is to consider that counting the records involves going through the entire recordset. However you think about it, you need to use the open method this way. The code is shown in Table 11.5.

TABLE 11.5   ASP/JavaScript to Find Warnings with Specified Term

`<%@ Language=JavaScript %>`	Set the language
`<html><head><title>Find shows with certain warnings</title></head><body>`	Usual HTML start
`<h1>Favorites </h1>`	Heading
`<!- #include file="sopenconn.asp"  ->`	Include the code for making the connection
`<%`	Start ASP
`var submitted=String(Request ("submitted"));`	Extract the hidden input indicating submitted
`if (submitted != 'undefined') {`	If test to check if the form has been submitted
`var problem = String(Request("problem"));`	Extract the form input
`sq ="SELECT f.title, f.description, w.reason ";`	Define the query taking several statements
`sq = sq + " from favorites as f, warnings as w where f.favorite_id = w.favorite_id ";`	Add to the query
`sq = sq + " and w.reason LIKE '" + problem+"'";`	Add to the query
`Response.Write("Query is "+sq+" ");`	Output the query for debugging

TABLE 11.5   (*continued*)

`var result = Server.CreateObject ("ADODB.RecordSet");`	Create a variable object of type `recordset`
`result.Open(sq,Conn, 1);`	Need cursor setting to be one in order to get a valid RecordCount
`if (result.RecordCount==0) { Response. Write("No warnings match: $problem. Use a more general pattern."); } else {`	If test to check if there were no records meeting the `LIKE` condition. If so, output a message. Start `else` clause
`%>`	End ASP
`<table border='1'>`	Straight HTML for table
`<tr><td>Titles </td> <td>Descriptions </td><td>Reason</td> </tr>`	Continue with table tags
`<%`	Restart ASP
`while (!result.EOF) {`	`While` loop: will iterate until result recordset is at the end.
`Response.Write("\n");`	Output line break for the HTML
`Response.Write("<tr><td>");`	Output table tags
`Response.Write(unescape(result.fields. item("title")));`	Output the title. Needs to have an escape character removed
`Response.Write("</td> <td>");`	Output table tags
`Response.Write(unescape(result.fields. item("description")));`	Output the description
`Response.Write("</td> <td>");`	Output table tags
`Response.Write(unescape(result.fields. item("reason")));`	Output the reason field
`Response.Write("</td></tr>");`	Output table tags
`result.move(1);`	Advance to the next record in the recordset
`}`	End the `while`
`Response.Write(" </table>");`	Output table close
`} // ends else, when rows in recordset`	End the else
`Conn.Close();`	Close the connection
`Response.Write("<a href='sfindwarnings. asp'>Try again </a>");`	Output a hyperlink to allow the user to try again
`}`	Close the `if` clause for the handle of form
`else {`	Start else clause: need to display form

(*continues*)

TABLE 11.5   ASP/JavaScript to Find Warnings with Specified Term *(continued)*

`%>`	Close ASP
`<h2>Find shows with warnings containing specific problem </h2> `	Heading
`<form action="sfindwarnings.asp">`	Form tag indicating the handler script (the name of this script)
`Describe problem <input type='text' name='problem'>  `	Input tag for problem
`<input type='hidden' name='submitted' value='true'>`	Hidden input tag
`<input type='submit' value='Find'>`	Button
`</form>`	Close form
`<%`	Restart ASP
`}`	Close of `else` clause for the display of the form
`%>`	Close ASP
`</body> </html>`	Usual HTML close

The Access database does not have an operator for SQL conditions with the function of MySQL's `regexp`. Please note that VBScript does support `regexp` as an object type for regular expressions, so you might see `regexp` in ASP/VB-Script programs.

It probably would be appropriate to take any user input and surround it with the wildcard percent sign symbols. This would be done in the `var` statement defining the variable problem:

```
var problem = "%" + String(Request("problem"))+"%";
```

With this manipulation (some would use the term *massaging*) of the data entered by the user, the script probably would produce the effects intended.

REFLECTION

As a technology with a long history and with steady use, numerous resources exist online and in books on regular expressions. You can and should develop sufficient understanding that you can decode a suggested regular expression to determine if it fits your needs. The ability to create your own regular expressions will grow as you make use of them in your work.

If the `LIKE` operator appears to be a poor substitute for regular expressions, you have the option of using MySQL. However, the `LIKE` operator might be sufficient for most operations involving information already in databases. Information in the fields of records is not generally of the free-form character that gives rise to the need for general searches. You do have the ability to use your knowledge of the LIKE or the REGEXP operators to modify any user input.

Interface design and validation procedures require and deserve your attention. The technical tools are available; the hard work is determining what you need to do.

EXERCISES, QUESTIONS, AND PROJECTS

1. Test your version of the tickets application thoroughly, including the difference in response to one or more than one ticket. You also can try to improve the error message for numbers.

2. Select a musical group of your choice. Create a regular expression that will recognize a string containing the first name of any of the members of the group. Modify that regular expression to recognize a string containing only the first name. Create a new regular expression that will recognize first, last, or first and last names.

3. Suppose that you want to limit the quantity field to being less than a certain amount. Define a regular expression to check that the input is a whole number greater than zero and less than 1,000.

4. Define a regular expression for dollars and cents. You will need to provide for two possible patterns: nothing to the right of the decimal point, or exactly two digits. You might also choose to accept strings with or without dollar signs.

5. Do research if necessary and define a regular expression for another currency, such as euros or British pounds or yen.

6. Go online and find candidate regular expressions for a valid URL. Decipher and compare the results.

7. Go online and find candidate regular expressions for a valid e-mail address. Decipher and compare the results.

12

FILES

The purpose of this chapter is to explain the use of middleware for reading and writing ordinary files. It also will cover uploading files in PHP.

BACKGROUND

Before there were database management systems (DBMSs), designers and developers of computer applications made use of *files*. A file is a collection of information used by computer programs. Files come in different types, indicated by the extensions. You are probably familiar with word processing files, image files, and spreadsheet files. For the score-keeping application shown in this chapter, the file is a set of records, with each record containing a name and a score. The other application explained in this chapter is the uploading of image files that illustrate products. Similar code could be used for files of any type.

Files can be the appropriate choice for an application if the organization of data is simple or, strangely enough, very complex. The score-keeping application fits the criteria of being a simple application. It does not require multiple tables with fields in one table pointing to records in another, and the potential size of the list is small. If the structure of the data is complex in a way that cannot be represented by tables and relationships, then you might be better off using files. For example, an application in which records contain arbitrary pointers to other records might be best implemented using files as opposed to databases.

A benefit of using files over databases is that they do not require the purchase or installation of software. An aspect of using files that is both positive and negative is that you can design any structure you want. This is a positive feature because there are no constraints on how you solve the challenges of your application. However, it is negative because there are no standards. In general, files are designed to work with a single program or small set of programs. Sharing and re-use are limited. Typically, databases are used with multiple applications done by different people and teams within an organization. New applications arise that make use of existing databases.

CONCEPTUAL EXPLANATION

In this chapter, we will address reading and writing of text files, using a file holding the names and scores of players, and uploading of files, such as image files used to show products.

Files and Records

Text files hold lines of text. Using the terminology of files, a record in the text file corresponds to a line when the file is viewed in any text editor program, such as Notepad in Windows.

Because each file has its own structure, the middleware programs must be able to operate at the file, line, or character level. The PHP system provides functions for reading the entire file at once, reading one line at a time, or reading one character at a time. Moreover, PHP provides a facility to read and print out the entire file with one instruction. The ASP system provides methods to the `TextStream` object for reading the entire file, reading a line at a time, or reading a certain number of characters. Each system, by functions or methods, provides ways to skip characters or lines to get to a specified point in the file.

The internal structure of a line does not matter to the file handling functions in the scripts. In the example described in this chapter, each line (record) of the file will be a name followed by a comma and then a number in character form. This represents the name of a player and a score. To extract information from a record, your code makes use of the comma. Both PHP and ASP have facilities that generate arrays from strings based on specification of a delimiter. In PHP, the explode function takes as arguments a string representing the delimiter and an original string and produces an array.

```
$items = explode(",",$original);
```

In ASP, the split method of string objects does the same job:

```
items = original.split(",");
```

If `$original` or `original` consisted of:

```
Tom, 98
```

then `$items` and `items` would be arrays with two elements:

```
"Tom"
"98"
```

Reading and Writing Text Files with PHP and ASP

The examples in this chapter show how to read and write to a text file. More specifically, the code reads in all the existing records, displays them, and then allows the person at the client computer to enter new information. The new information is appended (added) as a new record to the file. It is generally necessary to specify how a file is to be used by indicating what is called the *mode of use*. Although different systems define mode in different ways, the general categories are:

- Read
- Write data to the file from the beginning, erasing any existing information
- Append (add) data to the end of what is already in the file

Establishing the mode of access is done as part of what is called the *open operation*. The act of opening a file is analogous to establishing the connection in databases. The system sets up links and reserves buffer space for the subsequent file operations. As with databases, your code should release these system resources by issuing a call to close the file, after it is done accessing it.

Although as you would expect by this time, the coding for the PHP and ASP systems appears different for handling files but supports similar functionality. The ASP system uses methods of objects: the `Scripting.FileSystemObject` and a file stream object created by use of a method of the file system object. The `Scripting` object is a Windows object as opposed to an ASP object. This is of no practical significance, except that you might come across this when using other Windows tools. The methods used in this chapter are `ReadLine`, `write`, `FileExists`, `OpenTextFile`, `AtEndofStream`, and `close`. The ASP methods and properties for file handling, including some not used in this chapter, are shown in Table 12.1.

TABLE 12.1   ASP Methods and Properties for File Handling

`AtEndOfStream`	Property holding condition of being at the end or not
`Close()`	Closes the connection to the file
`FileExists(fp)`	Checks if a file as specified by the path `fp` exists
`OpenTextFile(fp,mode,cop,fop)`	Establishes a connection to the specified file for mode access, with options `cop` and `fop`
`Read(nc)`	Read `nc` characters
`ReadAll()`	Read the entire file (similar to PHP's `file`)
`ReadLine()`	Reads in one line from file stream
`Write(s)`	Writes the string `s` to the file
`WriteLine(s)`	Writes out the string `s` and adds an end-of-line character
`Skip(nc)`	Skip `nc` characters
`SkipLine(nl)`	Skip `nl` lines

The PHP used in this chapter are the simple functions `fopen`, `file` (for reading in the whole file), `fwrite`, and `fclose`. The PHP functions for file handling are shown in Table 12.2.

Table 12.2   PHP Functions for Files

`file($fp)`	Reads in the file at `$fp`
`fopen($fp,mode)`	Establishes connection with file for mode access. Returns value to be used by later commands

Table 12.2   *(continued)*

`fread($fp, nc)`	Read in nc characters
`fgets($fp, nc)`	Read in until reach end-of-line character or nc characters or until the end-of-the-file, which ever comes first
`fwrite($op,$s)`	Writes the string $s to the file opened
`fseek($fp,nc)`	Goes (seeks) to the point nc characters into the file
`flock($fp, type)`	Controls if or how the file can be used by others. A setting of type=1 allows other readers; type = 2 prevents shared use; a setting of 3 releases an existing lock
`fclose($op)`	Closes connection to the file

To demonstrate to you that the systems can work together, both the ASP and PHP score-keeping application uses the same file. That is, you can invoke the ASP code to add a record to the file, and then, when you invoke the PHP code, you will see the file with the new information added. You also can do the reverse: add a record using the PHP script and see it using the ASP script. Independently of ASP or PHP, you can examine the file. Since the suggested file extension is "txt" and not ASP or PHP, you can view the file using a browser or download it. This should make sense to you: the file does not retain any connection with the ASP or PHP programs.

The single file used for both systems is located in the same folder as the ASP and PHP scripts. Each script will calculate the location of the file using functions and methods, respectively, for determining the address of the script itself. The calculation will be done using regular expressions to remove the part of the URL that points to the script and replace it with the name and extension of the file.

Since file handling might involve things that you cannot tightly control, you will need to think about detecting errors. For example, what if someone has removed the file from the server computer? Your code must take the correct action and not display a cryptic error for your customers. The PHP script uses the @ operator to prevent an error on opening the file, and then checks if a file was opened. The ASP script uses the `FileExists` method.

Uploading a File Using PHP

The task described here and in a later chapter is that of uploading an image file that shows a product for the online store. An ordinary customer would not perform this task, but employees of the store would. You, as the system designer and builder, might choose to implement adding new product information as part of the Web application, and this could involve the uploading of images of the product.

The uploading file task is more problematical than you might suppose. This is because uploading an unknown file to a server is a risky operation for the operators of the server. The upload operation requires modifying the directory of the server. Letting a program change the directory provides an opening for a hacker to do considerable damage. In addition, the uploaded file might prove to be a problem. What if the uploaded file was a substitute for an existing file used by the system or by another user? The PHP system does provide functions for uploading files, and tools are available for ASP. However, you will need to check with your server administration to see if you can incorporate such code in your application. This chapter will show the PHP solution.

Programming the uploading operation as performed in the PHP system consists of several subtasks. You must code a form suitable for uploading files. The form in which the person sitting at the client computer specifies the file to be uploaded requires the:

```
ENCTYPE="multipart/form-data">
```

attribute in the form tag. The input tag is of type "file."

In the part of the script that handles the form input, your code must copy the file to its proper location. This means that you need to calculate an address similar to what is required for reading and writing files.

EXAMPLES

ON THE CD

This section contains PHP and ASP implementations of a use of files for keeping scores, and a PHP implementation for uploading files such as image files illustrating products. The projects demonstrated here involve the use of files. The CD-ROM contains the code for the projects in the folder named chapter12code.

Simple Score-Keeping Example

The demonstration of reading and writing to files will use a text file with records consisting of a name and a number in character format. The two fields will be separated by commas. An example of such a file is the following:

```
Jeanine,98
Aviva,101
Daniel,110
Mike,140
Ted,134
Judy,200
Mike,300
Mike,300
Willie,200
Willie,200
JM,132
```

This file could be the scores for a game. There is no attempt to order the scores (see the *Exercises* section). The script displays the entire contents of the file using a table for formatting. The script displays a form in which your user can type in a player name and a score and submit this information to the file. The term *handle* is taken from the slang used in game playing. Figure 12.1 shows the screen displayed with the existing scores plus the form to enter a name and score.

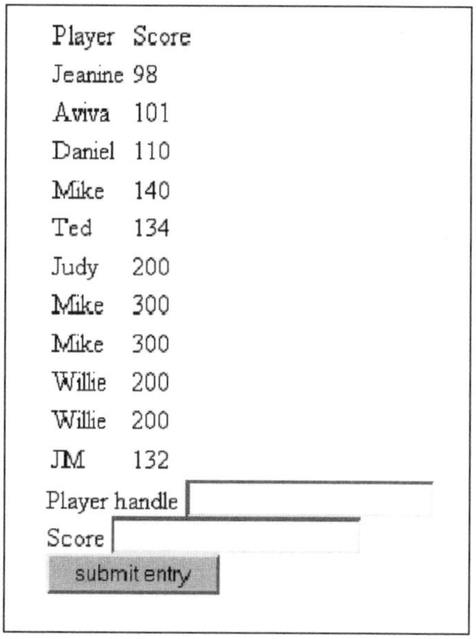

FIGURE 12.1   Display of scores plus form.

Because the code in these examples is not lengthy, and also to give you examples of both approaches, the examples in this chapter return to the technique of using one script to be both the presenter of a form and the script that handles the form.

The file resides in the same folder as the script. If you have chosen to place your PHP scripts in one folder and your ASP scripts in another, you will need to make an adjustment, either in your practice or in your coding to get the correct string containing the file address.

The outline for the PHP and the ASP files is the same:

HTML starting tags
Variables set to generate the file address
displayfile function
handleform function
displayform function

Main body: if test checking if form has been submitted

> *If submitted, call handleform. Check return code and display appropriate message*
>
> *Else (not submitted): displayfile. Check return code and display appropriate message. Call displayform.*

HTML closing tags

In both cases, you will see that the scripts go into and out of PHP or ASP independently of the bracketing defined by the function definitions and the `if` and `else` clauses. You might find this lack of proper nesting disconcerting, but this is standard practice for middleware programming.

Reading and Writing to a File Using PHP

In this operation, the script does the bulk of the work in the functions. The `displayfile` function and the `handleform` function each open and close the file. You might ask, "why not open the file, do all the processing, and then close it?" The reason to avoid this approach is that it is best to open and close the file as quickly as possible. This would allow more users to access the file.

What is done outside and prior to the function definitions or function calling code is generating the file address. The built-in variable `$PATH_TRANSLATED` furnishes the address of this script. The code uses regular expressions to remove the filename to produce what is named `$stub`, signifying that it is the stub of the address. The next statement concatenates the name of the file. The resulting `$filen` variable is declared as global in each of the functions so code inside the function can access the variable already defined. The code is shown in Table 12.3.

TABLE 12.3   PHP Code for Displaying and Then Adding to File

`<html><head><title>File reading & writing</title> </head><body>`	HTML tags
`<?php`	Start PHP
`$abspath = $PATH_TRANSLATED;`	Define $abspath using a built-in PHP variable giving the path to this script
`$stub=ereg_replace("\\filetest.php", "\\",$abspath);`	Use the regular expression to take off the name of this script
`$filen = $stub . "scores.txt";`	Add the filename scores.text to the stub produced in the prior line
`function displayfile() {`	displayfile function header
`global $filen;`	Specify that $filen is to be the global variable

TABLE 12.3   *(continued)*

`$open = @fopen($filen,"r");`	Attempt to open the file for reading. The @ will prevent an error triggered by a missing file
`if ($open) {`	If test to check if a file was opened
`?>`	Leave PHP temporarily
`<table>`	HTML table tag
`<tr><td>Player </td> <td> Score </td> </tr>`	HTML for first line of table
`<?`	Get back into PHP
`    $filecontents = file($filen);`	Read the entire file into `$filecontents`
`    for ($n=0;$n<count($filecontents); $n++) {`	For loop: it will iterate for as many elements as there are in `$filecontents`
`        $record = explode(",", $filecontents[$n]);`	Based on comma as the delimiter, define `$record` to be the array based on the parts of the `$nth` element in `$filecontents`
`        print ("<tr><td>".$record[0]. "</td>");`	Output the first part (it will be the name) as an item in the table
`        print ("<td>".$record[1]. "</td></tr>\n");`	Output the second part (it will be the score) as an item in the table. Output a line break for the HTML
	Close the `for` loop
`    print("</table>");`	Output the closing table tag
`    fclose($open);`	Close the file
`    $ok = TRUE;`	Set `$ok` to be true to be the return value
`    }`	Close if a file was opened
`else {$ok = FALSE;}`	The `else` clause: a file was not opened: set `$ok` to false
`    return $ok;`	Return `$ok`
`    }`	Ends the definition of the function `displayfile`
`function handleform(){`	handleform file function header
`    global $player;`	Specify that `$player` is to be the global variable. It is a value sent from the form.
`    global $filen;`	Specify `$filen` as the global variable. It was set at the start of this script

(continues)

TABLE 12.3   PHP Code for Displaying and Then Adding to File *(continued)*

`global $score;`	Specify that `$score` is to be the global variable. It is a value sent from the form
`$open=@fopen($filen,"a");`	Open the file for appending to the end
`if ($open) {`	If test: was a file opened
`    fwrite($open,"$player,$score\n");`	Write out a string holding the two values from the form, separated by a comma and ending in a line break character
`    fclose($open);`	Close the file
`    $ok=TRUE;`	Set the variable to be used as a return value to true
`}`	Ends if the file open was okay
`else {$ok=FALSE; }`	The `else` clause: the file open was not okay
`return $ok;`	Return the return code variable
`}`	Ends the function definition
`function displayform() {`	`displayform` function header
`    ?>`	Leave PHP temporarily
`<form action="filetest.php" method=get>`	HTML form tag
`Player handle <input type=text name='player'>`	Specify tag for player's name
`  Score <input type=text name='score'> `	Specify tag for score
`<input type=hidden name='submitted' value = 'TRUE'>`	Set up a hidden tag to use to check if form has been submitted
`<input type=submit name='submit' value='submit entry'>`	Tag for the Submit button
`</form>`	HTML form close
`<?`	Restart PHP
`}`	Ends definition of `displayform` function
`if (@$submitted) {`	This is the body of the script. The `if` test to see if the form has been submitted or needs to be displayed
`    if (handleform()) {`	Positive clause: this is a call to the `handleform` function. An `if` tests checks its return value
`        print("entry made");`	Positive: output that an entry was made

TABLE 12.3 *(continued)*

`}`	Close positive clause
`else {print ("entry not made");`	Negative (on return of handleform): output that an entry was not made
`}`	Close negative clause
`}`	Close the clause on the form being submitted
`else {`	`Else`: need to display the existing data in the file and then display the form
`if (!displayfile()){`	Call `displayfile`. If it is the case that it returned a false value—
`print ("NO PLAYER SCORES ");}`	Output no player scores, meaning no file found
`displayform();`	Call to `displayform`
`}`	Close `else` clause for test of `if` submitted
`?>`	Close PHP
`</body> </html>`	Closing HTML tags

Reading and Writing to a File Using ASP

The ASP script shown here uses the `ReadLine` method. This method is called to prepare the output for each row of the HTML table. The overall structure of the script including the function definitions is similar to the PHP script. As was the case with the PHP script, there is code at the start to define the address (`filepath`) to the scores.txt file. In this case, the built-in variable to obtain the path to the script is one of the `ServerVariables` collection of the `Request` object.

The ASP system uses two objects for file handling: a file system object and a file stream object. The `OpenTextFile` method of the file system object can be used with one, two, three, or four parameters:

```
fso.OpenTextFile(filepath, mode, create_option,
    format_option);
```

In the code that follows, the method is used two times. The first time there is just the first parameter, indicating that the mode is the default, which is 1 for read. The second time, the first two parameters are specified. The mode is set to 8, indicating the append mode for adding lines at the end of the file. The value of the mode for writing a file, meaning erasing anything already there, is 2. The `create_option` specifies what is to be done if the file does not exist. A value of false, the default, means to do nothing. A value of true means to create the file. A format_option of 1 means Unicode. This might become more important in the future. A `format_option` of 2 means to use the system default. The default format is 0 for ASCII. The code is shown in Table 12.4.

TABLE 12.4   ASP/JavaScript for Displaying and Then Adding to a File

`<html> <head><title>File reading & writing </title> </head><body>`	HTML tags
`<%@ Language=JavaScript %>`	Set JavaScript as language
`<%`	Start ASP
`var abspath=String(Request.ServerVariables("PATH_TRANSLATED"));`	Define a string to be the address of this script
`var filepath=abspath.replace (/\\\w*\.asp/,"\\") + "scores.txt";`	Using the `replace` method for any string, create the `filepath` for the scores.txt file
`function displayfile() {`	The header for `displayfile` function
`fso=new ActiveXObject("Scripting.FileSystemObject");`	Define `fso` to be a file system object
`if (!fso.FileExists(filepath)) {`	Check if the file exists and
`  return(false); }`	if it does not, return false
`Else {`	Start the other clause: the file does exist
`file_stream=fso.OpenTextFile(filepath);`	Set `file_stream` to be a `file_stream` object connecting to the desired file
`%>`	End ASP temporarily
`<table>`	HTML table tag
`<tr><td>Player </td> <td> Score </td> </tr>`	HTML for first row of table
`<%`	Restart ASP
`ok = false;`	Set ok to false. If things go well, this will be set to true
`while (!file_stream.AtEndOfStream) {`	While loop: this will iterate until the end of the file is reached
`  ok = true;`	Set ok to true
`  record = file_stream.ReadLine();`	Read in one line of the file. The variable record is a string
`  recorda = record.split(",");`	Make `recorda` an array holding the two parts of the line from the file
`  Response.Write("<tr><td>" + recorda[0]+ "</td>");`	Output what is the player name as a table item

TABLE 12.4 *(continued)*

`Response.Write("<td>"+recorda[1] + "</td></tr>\n");`	Output what is the score as a table item
`}`	End the `while` loop
`Response.Write("</table>");`	Output the table close
`file_stream.close();`	Close the file
`return ok;`	Return ok as the return code
`}`	End the `ELSE` (there was a file)
`}`	End the definition of `displayfile`
`function handleform(){`	The `handleform` function header
`ok = true;`	Set ok to true
`var player = String(Request ("player"));`	Extract the player form data
`var score = String(Request ("score"));`	Extract the score form data
`fso=new ActiveXObject ("Scripting.FileSystemObject");`	Define fso to be a file system object
`file_stream=fso.OpenTextFile (filepath, 8); // 8 for append`	Define `file_stream` to be a file stream object connecting to the file address held in filepath. The 8 indicates append
`file_stream.Write(player + "," + score + "\n");`	Write out the data as a string with a comma separating the two items and a line break at the end
`return ok;`	Return ok
`}`	End the definition of `handleform`
`function displayform() {`	The `displayform` function
`%>`	End ASP temporarily
`<form action="filetest.asp" method=get>`	HTML form tag
`Player handle <input type=text name='player'>`	Player input tag
`  Score <input type=text name= 'score'> `	Score input tag
`<input type=hidden name='submitted' value = 'TRUE'>`	Set up submitted as hidden form input
`<input type=submit name='submit' value='submit entry'>`	Set up Submit button
`</form>`	HTML form end

(continues)

TABLE 12.4   ASP/JavaScript for Displaying and Then Adding to a File *(continued)*

`<%`	Restart ASP
`}`	End definition of `displayform` function
`var submitted = String(Request ("submitted"));`	Main body of file: extract the submitted form input
`if (submitted!="undefined") {`	Check if form submitted
`    if (handleform()) {`	If form was submitted, call handleform. Do an `if` test on the return value
`        Response.Write("entry made");`	Positive case (true return by handleform): output entry made
`    }`	End positive case
`    else {Response.Write ("entry not made");`	Negative case: output that entry was not made
`    }`	End negative case
`}`	End form being submitted
`else {`	`Else` clause: form wasn't submitted
`    if (!displayfile()){`	Call `displayfile`. If the return value was false—
`        Response.Write ("NO PLAYER SCORES ");}`	Output that there was no player scores
`    displayform();`	Call displayform function
`}`	Close the `else` clause on submitted
`%>`	End ASP
`</body> </html>`	HTML closing tags

Uploading Files Using PHP

The uploading of an entire file based on user information is considered more threatening to system integrity than accepting individual pieces of information and storing them in files or databases. However, situations exist in which you might want to provide this function. For example, the shopping cart application described later in this text provides a way for users (store employees) to add a product to the online catalog. Product information includes a picture of the product, and the picture is held in an image file.

The script is a stand-alone file for uploading any file. The person at the client computer indicates the file using a form as shown in Figure 12.2.

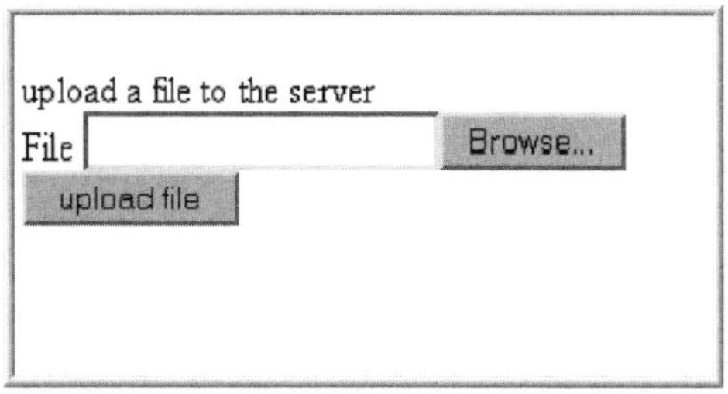

FIGURE 12.2   Form for specifying file to upload.

The organization of the script is:

HTML tags
If form submitted (indicated by definition of $file)
   Print out messages
   Generate address for file within same folder as script
   Copy file over from a temporary location to this folder
   Print out messages depending on success of copy operation
In any case, display form.

The form will get displayed again after the upload. This is different from the other situations in which an `if/else` construction either handled the form input or displayed the form.

The filename used on the system is obtained from the file specified by the user. One way of adding some security to this procedure would be for the script to create the filename. This would prevent a malicious user from uploading a substitute for a file used by the system for another purpose.

The file begins with the usual HTML opening tags and then starts PHP:

```
<html>
<head><title>File upload test </title>
</head>
<body>
<?php
```

The `$file` in the next line refers to form input. This HTML form is shown a little later. If the value is defined, indicating that the file has been submitted using the form, then the true clause for the `if` is executed.

```
if (@$file) {
```

The presence of a form input tag of type "file" creates the `$file_name` and the `$file_size` variables with the name of the file as on the client computer and the size of the file. The code in this script outputs this information. In some applications, you might choose not to bother the user with this information.

```
print ("uploading file named $file_name <br>");
print ("File size is $file_size <br>");
```

The next lines of code are similar to that shown for the reading and writing to an existing file. The code is determining a place for the file to be placed.

```
$abspath = $PATH_TRANSLATED;
$stub=ereg_replace("\\fileupload.php","\\",$abspath);
$fullname = $stub . $file_name;
print ("fullname is: $fullname.<br>");
```

The next step is to copy the file to its designated home. At this point in the execution of the script, the file is in a temporary area and will not be accessible unless it is copied. The call to the copy function is done within an if test.

```
if (copy($file,$fullname)) {
    print ("file successfully uploaded. <br>");    }
else {  print ("file could not be copied.");    }
```

The unlink operation removes the connection to the temporary file.

```
unlink($file);
```

The bracket ends the clause for the true condition on the existence of $file; that is, the handling of the form data.

```
}
```

The next part of the script displays the HTML form. The user is given the chance to specify a file to be uploaded to the server, starting with a message:

```
print ("<br>upload a file to the server<br>\n");
```

The form can be expressed using plain HTML so PHP coding is ended.

```
?>
```

The form tag has what probably is a new attribute to you: the ENCTYPE. This is required when the form data is something in addition to plain text as input in textboxes, radio boxes, and so on.

```
<form action='fileupload.php' method=POST
ENCTYPE="multipart/form-data">
```

The file type of input form does what you would suppose it to do: provide a way for a user to specify a file. The next input tag sets up the Submit button, and the rest of the HTML is the usual closing up of form, body, and html.

```
File <input type=file name="file"><br>
<input type=submit name="submit" value="upload file">
</form> </body> </html>
```

As you can see in Figure 12.3, a Browse button comes "for free" along with the ENCTYPE attribute and the input type=file tag. Click on it and you will see the usual Windows browsing windows. For example, here is a screen capture after clicking on the Browse button. A file named dragon.jpg was selected. The next step is to click on the Open button shown in Figure 12.3.

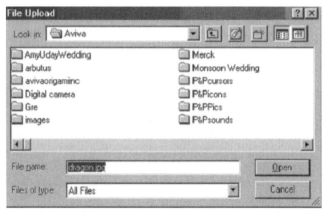

FIGURE 12.3   Window to browse and specify file for uploading.

Figure 12.4 shows the resulting message.

You can see the messages produced by the file handling part of the script followed by the display of the form.

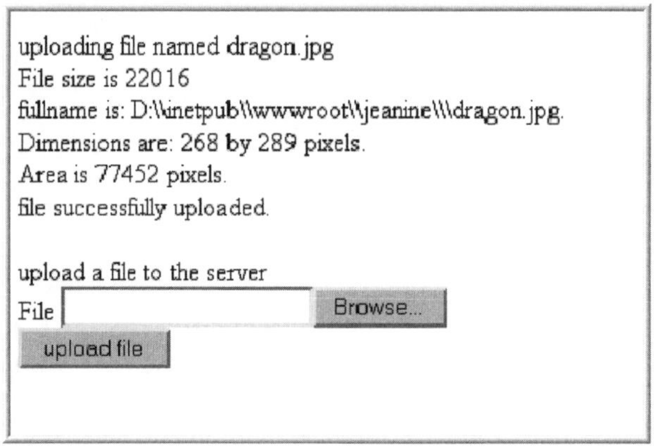

FIGURE 12.4 Screen showing message plus form for new upload.

REFLECTION

Files can be the appropriate choice for many applications. This can be in place of or in addition to databases.

At this point, it would be natural if you concluded that the PHP system offers more functionality and in a simpler, more direct way than the ASP system. However, it could be argued that the ASP system provides more protection of your system. It also is true that ASP provides the generality of working with JavaScript or VBScript, and we have "stacked the decks" somewhat by using MySQL for which there is a library of PHP functions. The open-source supporters would say that PHP (and MySQL, Linux, and Apache, the server software) together provide all the protection that you would want and in a way that you can design and configure for yourself. As you continue studying this book and when you finish it, you might want to go online to investigate comparisons of these two approaches. A goal of this text is to provide you knowledge and experience in both systems as well as the background to learn other middleware software and better understand any debate on which software is superior.

EXERCISES, QUESTIONS, AND PROJECTS

1. Design a new application involving reading and appending records to a file. Make your application have at least three fields, separated by a character other than a comma.
2. Try to read a remote file using PHP or ASP. You need to put in a complete file path. Note: on our systems, this worked in PHP but not using ASP.
3. Redo the scripts in this chapter, changing the PHP script to read in a line at a time using the `fgets` function, and changing the ASP script to use the `ReadAll` method.

4. Go back to the state capital quiz application and enhance the application to keep score. You would need to ask the player for a name ("handle"). You also need to include a new command to end the session, computing the score and adding a record consisting of name, date, and score to a file. You also need to have a way to present the scores.
5. Using the basic scripts provided in this chapter or what you have done in the previous exercise, produce scripts that just keep the five top scores. You need to order them and then only add a score if it is justified as being in the top five.
6. Go online and find out ways to upload files using ASP. Note that some products that cost money do provide services such as additional security.

COOKIES AND SESSION VARIABLES

The goal of this chapter is to describe the use and application of cookies and session variables.

Background

The design of the original World Wide Web was to support sharing of information among scientists using what are termed *stateless protocols*. The browser program on the client computer sends requests to the server software on the server computer. Each request was and is handled independently. The server software does not "know" (the "know" is in quotes as an excuse for using such an anthropomorphic term) if a request is from a client computer that has made a request recently or has never made a request before this one. Similarly, no information entered or calculated about the particular site visitor is retained from previous visits or passed on to another Web page on the same site. This design simplifies the workings of the Web, but does not support the requirements of complex applications such as e-commerce.

Here are two examples of situations in which the site builders would want to retain information.

An online application might involve multiple Web pages. One example of this is online shopping. The customers move from catalog pages to specifying details of the order, to catalog pages again, and then to the check-out page. The technical term for this is *transaction*. The system designer wants to maintain all the information and then execute the complete transaction. For these situations, the information needs to persist for the duration of the time the visitor is seeing the pages belonging to the application.

Many sites require the visitor to log on to the system. Since most of us "belong" in this way to many sites, this means remembering multiple sets of logon ID and passwords. The owners of Web sites would like to simplify the process for their clients. As a gesture of good will, in addition, the owners want to greet each visitor with a personalized welcome. This greeting could, of course, include a customized marketing appeal. For this situation, the site owners want to access the information each time a visitor returns to one of the Web pages on the site.

Cookies were developed to address these types of situations. The term *cookies* is intended to be a term of innocence and fun. Cookies are small files located on the client computer. These files are written by a specific Web site and used only by code on that Web site. They last for the duration of an invocation of a browser or for a fixed amount of time, which could be days or months.

Session variables are more elaborate mechanisms to hold information over the course of a visit to one or more Web pages located on a single server. The bulk of the session data is kept on the server computer.

You can choose to set your browser to refuse cookies. It is, after all, your computer, and you might not like the idea of someone writing a file to one of your drives. There is a limitation to the number and size of cookies that can be written by any one Web site, and the total number of cookies. For this reason, if you are designing a Web site, you cannot depend on cookies being present.

CONCEPTUAL EXPLANATION

As indicated already, cookies are small files associated with each browser, holding information written by a Web site. A cookie holds:

- The name of the Web site and two additional fields (path and domain) indicating the extent of this Web site, specifically what files might have access to the cookies
- A flag indicating if the cookie is only to be sent over secured lines
- An expiration time
- The name of the cookie
- The value of the cookie

A cookie is intended to be read by the same site that created it. However, the mechanism provides for refining or expanding the specification of the site. If the site holding the Web page setting the cookie is sharon.ns.purchase.edu, you can specify a path so that only Web pages from within that path can read the cookie. Since the author shares this Web site with all her students, the specification /jeanine/ would mean that only pages from the jeanine folder and its subfolders could access the cookie, not any of the students who are assigned other folders; for example, sharon.ns.purchase.edu/jdoe. There also is a mechanism for expanding the access. Suppose there is another server machine named www.ns.purchase.edu. The cookie setting functions and methods provide a way to specify a domain. The domain setting .purchase.edu would allow Web pages contained in www.ns.purchase.edu to access the cookie.

The expiration time is to be expressed in the number of seconds from January 1, 1970. The functions and methods described later provide this information.

The value of the cookie can be a simple text string or an array of information.

Examining Cookies

To demystify cookies, try the following:

Click on Search in Windows XP or its equivalent on your platform. Type `cookies*` into the place for the name as shown in Figure 13.1.

The result will be similar to what is shown in Figure 13.2.

FIGURE 13.1   Search window.

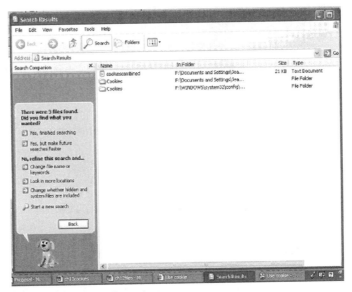

FIGURE 13.2   Results of search.

Clicking on the Cookies folder, you will see something similar to the screen shown in Figure 13.3.

Internet Explorer keeps each cookie as a distinct file. You can see an indication of the Web sites that produced the cookies in the terms following the @ sign. Click on one.

Keep in mind that these files are not intended for humans to read, but you can get a sense of what the cookie files contain. After you create cookies, you can use this same procedure to see what you have created.

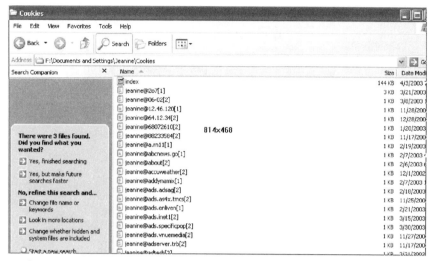

FIGURE 13.3   Internet Explorer Cookies folder. Web browser © 2003 Microsoft Corp.

If you use Netscape, the screen shot shown in Figure 13.4 shows how to find the Cookie Manager under Tools.

FIGURE 13.4   Netscape Tools drop-down menu showing Cookie Manager. Web browser © 2003 Netscape.

The screen shot shown in Figure 13.5 indicates the cookies managed by Netscape on this computer. The particular cookie shown was created using one of the scripts described later in this section.

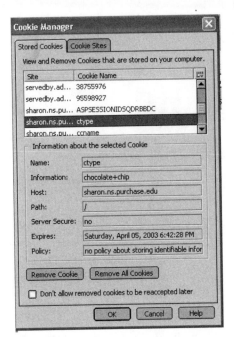

FIGURE 13.5   Cookie Manager in Netscape.

Cookie Mechanics

Setting cookies involves the intricacies of the Web protocols. However, in this as in everything else, the middleware software of PHP and ASP masks the complexity. One issue is critical, however. The cookie information is transferred from server to client computer using what is called the *HTTP header*. This means that it must be sent before anything else is sent to the client. In the *Examples* section, you will see a common error in which this was not done.

The PHP and ASP procedures for setting cookies resemble the PHP and ASP procedures for everything else. The PHP system uses the function `setcookie` to create a cookie. This function has optional parameters for setting the expiration, path, domain, and security flag. To access a cookie, you only need to refer to it by name preceded by a dollar sign. You remove a cookie by setting the expiration time to a time in the past. In some circumstances, setting a cookie to the empty string would be an appropriate act.

The ASP system uses the `cookies` collection of the `Response` object to create a cookie, and the `cookies` collection of the `Request` object to set a cookie. A collection is sometimes called an *associative array*. Elements in the array are cited by name. Setting the expiration time, path, domain, or security flag requires setting properties of the cookie element. To set the expiration time, you need to convert the time as produced by the JavaScript functions to the variant datatype expected by ASP. The method `getVarDate()` performs this operation.

Sessions

Both PHP and ASP provide a specialized mechanism for session information. This is information maintained for each visitor while the visitor is viewing Web sites on a single server. This information will not persist after the browser is closed. The PHP and ASP statements perform the same function of storing information, but in distinct ways. Using PHP, sessions are started (and restarted). In PHP, specific variables are registered as session variables. The ASP system has a `Session` object, which has a `Contents` collection. It holds key and value pairs. Using ASP, you store a value under a specific name, also known as the *key*, in the `Session.Contents` collection. In both PHP and ASP systems, the information is kept on the server computer. However, to distinguish one user's session information from another, a session identifier is generated and stored as a cookie if the browser has been set up to accept cookies. If that is not the case—that is, if the browser is not accepting cookies—the PHP system uses the query string to pass on the session identifier. If your code includes certain tricks such as redirection using the header function, you will need to make an adjustment. The ASP system does not have a similar fallback mechanism. If the user does not want to have cookies, the ASP session system will not work.

The PHP terminology for sessions can be misleading. The command:

```
session_start();
```

will do one of two things. If no session exists for this visitor for this server, PHP will start a session, generating the session ID to be stored in a cookie or passed along as part of the query string in the links on the page. However, if a session does exist, the `session_start` function restores the values of any variables registered as session variables. The function:

```
session_register('cart');
```

registers the variable named $cart to be a session variable. This involves saving this information on the server computer for use by code in any Web page associated with the session id. You then use $cart as you would any other variable. Session variables can be arrays or objects and can be quite large.

The command:

```
session_unregister('cart');
```

will free the space used to store the variable called $cart. Since session variables do take up space, it might be appropriate to do this.

If the PHP system determines that cookies are disabled, it creates a constant, SID, holding the session identifier in the format of a query string. The PHP system does the job of passing along this identifier when any links are made from one Web page on the server to another on the same server.

Another mechanism exists for jumps from one page to another, called *re-direction*. The command:

```
header("Location: next.php");
```

causes another Web page to be sent to the browser without the person at the client computer needing to click on a link. This often is used to signal a change of Web sites or when checking passwords. A problem arises of how to make use of re-direction compatible with sessions when the browser has disabled cookies. This solution is to put the session identifier in the header statement. The PHP constant SID is available for this purpose. This can be used to pass along the session ID information in situations such as the following:

```
header("Location:next.php?=" . SID);
```

Again, the PHP system will take care of the normal hyperlinks from Web page to Web page on a server site.

The ASP system Session object has properties in addition to the Content collection. These include SessionId, holding the generated session ID, and Timeout. The Timeout can be reset.

The Session object also has a StaticObjects collection for all objects created by <object> tags (e.g., Micromedia Flash movies).

In PHP, you store information by registering a variable of a certain name as a session variable, and use the variable as you would any other variable. In ASP, you define a member of the Contents collection:

```
Session.Contents("mycart") = cart;
```

Here, the example uses "mycart" just to emphasize that it can be a different name. Because Contents is the default collection, you can also use:

```
Session("mycart") = cart;
```

Your code reads session information by accessing the collection. Assuming that cart was itself an array, then:

```
len = Session("mycart").length;
for (i=0; i<len; i++) {
  Response.Write(Session("mycart")[i] + "<br>");
}
```

would display the elements of what was the array cart one item to a line.

You will need to check the server settings for both PHP and ASP to confirm that you can use sessions.

EXAMPLES

The quiz and origami store examples contain practical uses of cookies and session variables and are described in the next chapters. In Chapter 16, "Scaling Up Your Application," you will read about using session variables to implement a password system. In this chapter, the examples are short and designed to encourage you to implement them and try them in various combinations. The scripts explained here show the use of cookies and sessions. The CD-ROM contains the code for the projects in the folder named chapter13code.

The setting of cookies is independent of ASP versus PHP, but not independent of a browser. The examples described here all make use of a form in which the user enters a name and a type of [dessert] cookie. Examples of cookies are things you eat, such as chocolate chips or lemon squares. Two computer cookies are set when the form is submitted: one named 'cname' for the username, and the other named 'type'. The scripts *cookies.asp* and *cookies.php* each set the two cookies to persist only as long as the browser is open. The scripts *cookies5min.asp* and *cookies5min.php* each set the cookies to last for five minutes. The time interval of five minutes was chosen to give you enough time to exit the browser or go to another Web site, but not too long to try your patience. The intent is for you to perform two tests for each of the four scripts:

- Execute the script, exit the browser, and then invoke the same browser again within five minutes.
- Execute the script, do something else for more than five minutes, and return to the page of the script. You might need to force the browser to reload the page, which sometimes is a problem.

In the first case, the values of the cookies the name and the type of cookie, will not appear if the script last used was *cookies.asp* or *cookies.php*. The two values will appear if the script was *cookies5min.asp* or *cookies5min.php*. In contrast, if you invoke one of the five-minute scripts first and then *cookies.asp* or *cookies.php*, you will see the last set of values. The form is shown in Figure 13.6.

FIGURE 13.6   Form to enter information to be stored as cookie. Web browser
© 2003 Netscape

Filling in the cookie, you will see something like what is in Figure 13.7.
Clicking on the send info button will produce the response Web page in Figure 13.8.

Now we will examine the scripts for these pages. The first pair of scripts (one for ASP and one for PHP) produce cookies that last only as long as the browser is open. These are called *cookies without expiration*. This terminology

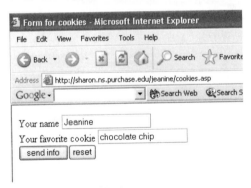

FIGURE 13.7   Form filled in.

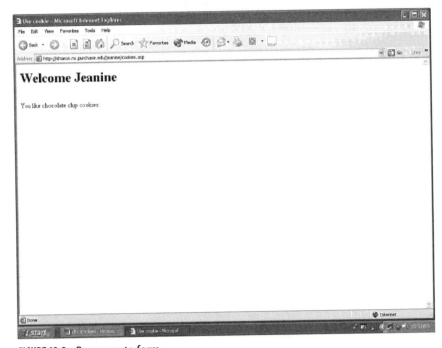

FIGURE 13.8   Response to form.

does not mean that they never expire; it means, again, that they last as long and only as long as the browser is open. The second set of scripts sets an expiration time for the cookies. The expiration time chosen is quite short: five minutes. However, it is not associated with the running of the browser.

Cookies Without Expiration

The *cookies.asp* script, shown in Table 13.1, both handles the form data and displays the form for the user to enter data.

TABLE 13.1 ASP/JavaScript for Displaying Form and Handling Form

Code	Description
`<%@ Language=JavaScript %>`	Sets JavaScript as language
`<%`	Starts ASP
`var submitted=String(Request.Form("submitted"));`	Extracts submitted form data
`if (submitted !="undefined") {`	Checks if form has been filled out
`    sname=String(Request("cname"));`	Set variable with form data
`    stype=String(Request("type"));`	Set variable with form data
`Response.Cookies("ccname") = sname;`	Define cookie named "ccname" (or, to use the collection terminology, with the key "ccname") to be the value of `sname`
`Response.Cookies("ctype") = stype;`	Define cookie named "ctype" (key "ctype") to be the value of `stype`
`    %>`	Close ASP
`<html><head><title>Use cookie </title></head>`	Normal HTML start
`<body>`	HTML body tag
`<h1> Welcome`	HTML
`<%`	Start ASP
`Response.Write (sname + "</h1>\n");`	Write out information given by form
`Response.Write (" You like "+ stype +" cookies.");`	Write out information given by form
`    %>`	Close ASP
`<body>`	HTML
`</html>`	HTML
`<%    }`	Restart ASP to close off true `if` clause
`else { %>`	Start `else` clause and close ASP
`<html><head><title>Form for cookies </title></head> <body>`	Normal HTML
`<form action="cookies.asp" method=post>`	Start form. Action handler is this script
`Your name <input type=text name='cname' value='<%fromcookiename= Request.Cookies("ccname");`	Input tag. This code will display the customer name data if it has been stored as a cookie. A local variable is used to hold the value

(continues)

TABLE 13.1   ASP/JavaScript for Displaying Form and Handling Form *(continued)*

`Response.Write` `(fromcookiename);%>'>`	The variable is sent to the browser. If there was no cookie sent, nothing will be displayed
` `	Line break
`Your favorite cookie <input` `type=text name='type'`	Input tag

`value='<%fromcookietype=Request.Cookies`
`("ctype");Response.Write`
`(fromcookietype); %>'>`
	A local variable is set with the value from the cookie and written out

` `	Line break
`<input type=hidden name='submitted'` `value=TRUE>`	Input tag for hidden value to indicate the form has been submitted
`<input type=submit value='send` `info'><input type=reset value='reset'>`	Input tag for the submit button
`</form>`	Form closing tag
`</body>`	Body closing tag
`</html>`	HTML closing tag
`<% }     %>`	Restart ASP to close `Else` clause

The *cookies.php*, shown in Table 13.2, follows the same overall structure as the ASP file for the form handler and form. For the PHP case, you need to use the @ operator to suppress an error message in the case when no variable, including no cookie, exists.

TABLE 13.2   PHP Script for Displaying Form and Handling Form

`<?php`	Start PHP
`if (@($submitted)) {`	Check for is this form handler or form display
`setcookie("ccname",$cname);`	Set a cookie named "ccname" to be the value of $cname, which is one of the form inputs
`setcookie("ctype",$type);`	Set a cookie named "ctype" to be the value of $type, which is one of the form inputs
`?>`	Close PHP
`<html><head><title>Use cookie` `</title></head>`	Normal HTML
`<body>`	HTML

TABLE 13.2   *(continued)*

`<h1> Welcome`	HTML
`<?`	Restart PHP
`print ("$cname! </h1>\n");`	Display response
`print (" You like $type` `cookies.");`	Display response
`?>`	Close PHP
`</body>`	Body close tag
`</html>`	HTML close tag
`<?    }`	Restart PHP. Closing bracket for the `if true` clause on `if submitted`
`else { ?>`	Else clause. End PHP
`<html><head><title>Form for` `cookies </title></head> <body>`	HTML
`<form action="cookies.php"` `method=post>`	Form tag
`Your name <input type=text` `name='cname'`	Input tag
`value='<?print (@$ccname); ?>'>`	Use $ccname for value of value attribute. Will use cookie if it exists. The @ prevents an error warning message
` `	Line break
`Your favorite cookie <input` `type=text name='type'`	Input tag
`value='<? print (@$ctype); ?>'>`	Use $ctype for value of value attribute. Will use cookie if it exists. The @ prevents an error warning message
` `	Line break
`<input type=hidden name='submitted'` `value=TRUE>`	Input tag for hidden submitted variable

`<input type=submit`
`value='send info'><input type=reset`
`value='reset'>`
	Button labeled send info

`</form>`	Close form
`</body>`	Close body
`</html>`	Close HTML
`<? }`	End PHP. Closing bracket for the `else` clause
`?>`	Close PHP

Cookies with Expiration

To set a cookie with an explicit expiration time, ASP uses a property of the values in the Cookies collection; namely, the expires property. The first step is to determine the time. This is done using the JavaScript function for Date, which returns date and time. The next step for this example is to modify this value by FIVE minutes. This is done using methods of JavaScript date objects: getMinutes and setMinutes. The setMinutes method will do the right thing if the new value of minutes also changes the hours and day. Lastly, the calculated expiration must be converted to be the datatype expected by ASP. The expires property must be set with a time value in what ASP calls the *Variant datatype*. Most of the time, datatypes seem to take care of themselves, but this is one of the times when coding is necessary to change the datatype explicitly. The conversion (also called *cast*) from the JavaScript date datatype to Variant is done by the getVarDate method.

Here is the code for setting the cookies with an expiration time of five minutes from now:

```
var later=new Date();
later.setMinutes(later.getMinutes()+5 );
Response.Cookies("ccname") = sname;
Response.Cookies("ccname").expires
  = later.getVarDate();
Response.Cookies("ctype") = stype;
Response.Cookies("ctype").expires = later.getVarDate();
```

The PHP command to set a cookie to have an explicit expiration is the same command but with an additional parameter. The time() function returns a value of the current time. You need to add what you want to this value. For this example, it is written 5 times 60 just to make the five minutes clear. The PHP system does the correct thing with addition. The call to setcookie is:

```
setcookie("ccname",$cname,time()+5*60);
setcookie("ctype",$type, time()+5*60);
```

Common Error

The setting of a cookie is done in the HTTP header. This means it must be done before anything is sent to the client. The following script would cause an error because the html tags at the start cause a header to be generated:

```
<html><head><title>Form for cookies
</title></head> <body>
<?php
if (@($submitted)) {
  setcookie("ccname",$cname);
  setcookie("ctype",$type);
  ?>
  <html><head><title>Use cookie </title></head>
```

```
    <body>
    <h1> Welcome
    <?
    print ("$cname! </h1>\n");
    print ("<br>You like $type cookies.");
      ?>
    </body>
    </html>
    <?       }
else { ?>
  <form action="cookies.php" method=post>
  Your name <input type=text name='cname'
  value='<?print (@$ccname); ?>'>
  <br>
  Your favorite cookie <input type=text name='type'
 value='<? print (@$ctype); ?>'>
  <br>
  <input type=hidden name='submitted' value=TRUE>
  <input type=submit value='send info'>
  <input type=reset value='reset'>
  </form>
  </body>
  </html>
  <? }       ?>
```

The PHP system would display the screen shown in Figure 13.9.

Warning: Cannot add header information - headers already sent by (output started at

D:\inetpub\wwwroot\jeanine\cookiesbad.php:3) in

D:\inetpub\wwwroot\jeanine\cookiesbad.php on line **5**

Warning: Cannot add header information - headers already sent by (output started at

D:\inetpub\wwwroot\jeanine\cookiesbad.php:3) in

D:\inetpub\wwwroot\jeanine\cookiesbad.php on line **6**

Welcome Jeanine!

You like chocolate chip cookies.

FIGURE 13.9 Screen shot showing warning messages.

Examine Cookies

Once you have these scripts working, you should repeat the steps outlined previously to examine the cookies. The screen shot in Figure 13.5 shows the cookie ctype stored by Netscape 7.

Netscape 6.2 stores its cookies in a file called cookies.txt. There would be entries such as:

```
sharon.ns.purchase.edu    FALSE    /    FALSE    1036259442         ctype
    chocolate+chip
sharon.ns.purchase.edu    FALSE    /    FALSE    1036259442    ccname
    Jeanine
```

after running either of the *cookies5min.asp* or *cookies5min.php*.

In the case of Internet Explorer 6, the cookie file would be:

```
ctype
chocolate+chip
sharon.ns.purchase.edu/
1536
1142620928
29526132
2953848224
29526131
*
ccname
Jeanine
sharon.ns.purchase.edu/
1536
1142620928
29526132
2953848224
29526131
*
```

The values other than the cookie name, value, server, and time (the 1142620928) are used in some way by Internet Explorer and not necessary to decipher.

Session

The following examples show the use of session data. This time, the saved data includes a color for setting the background color (bgcolor) of the Web pages and displaying the time the session began. All of this also could have been done using cookies.

The example uses two scripts for two Web pages. The first presents and handles a form as shown in Figure 13.10.

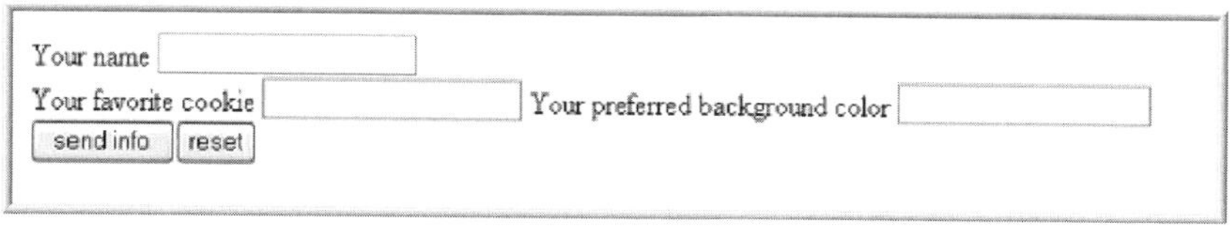

FIGURE 13.10   Form for obtaining information.

After filling in the form, the screen would look like Figure 13.11.

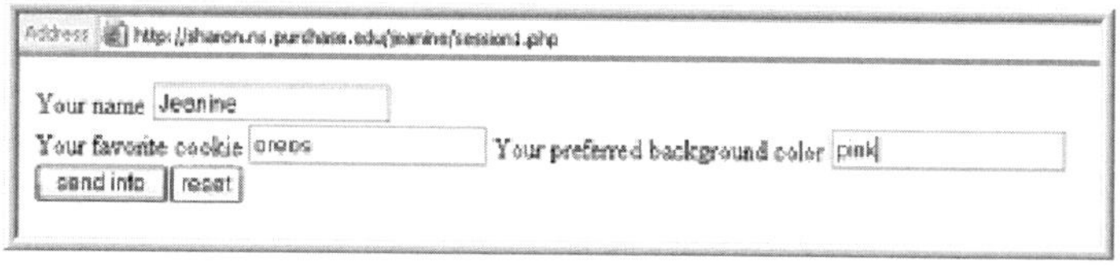

FIGURE 13.11   Filled-in form.

After clicking the send info button, you would see the screen shown in Figure 13.12.

FIGURE 13.12   Screen showing response.

Notice the form data in the query string shown in the Address field. It contains the form data. The Next page hyperlink is provided to go to the second page. This Web page will make use of the session information. It is shown in Figure 13.13.

Notice the query string in the Address field this time: it contains a rather complex string of letters and numbers that is the session ID. Notice also the color (shade in this black-and-white book) of the page.

The PHP script for the first page (*session1.php*) is shown in Table 13.3.

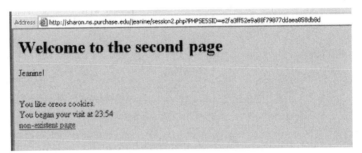

FIGURE 13.13   Shot of follow-up screen.

TABLE 13.3   PHP Script for Setting Session Variables

`<?php`	Start PHP
`if (@($submitted)) {`	If test for handler or form
`    session_start();`	Start the session
`session_register('cname');`	Register the variable named cname as a session variable
`session_register('type');`	Register type
`    Session_register('bcolor');`	Register bcolor
`    $starttime = time();`	Determine the current time
`      session_register('starttime');`	Register starttime as a session variable
`    ?>`	Close PHP
`    <html><head><title>Use session values </title></head>`	Normal HTML
`    <body>`	Normal body
`    <h1> Welcome`	Heading
`    <?`	Re-start PHP
`    print ("$cname! </h1>\n");`	Display form input
`    print (" You like $type cookies.");`	Display form input
`        ?>`	End PHP
`      <a href="session2.php">Next page </a>`	Hyperlink to next page
`    </body>`	Body close
`    </html>`	HTML close
`    <?    }`	Restart PHP. Close If submitted clause

TABLE 13.3   (*continued*)

`else { ?>`	Else clause. End PHP
`<html><head><title>Form for session data </title></head> <body>`	HTML opening tags
`<form action="session1.php">`	Form tags
`Your name <input type=text name='cname'>`	Input tag
` `	Line break
`Your favorite cookie <input type=text name='type'>`	Input tag
`Your preferred background color <input type=text name='bcolor'>`	Input tag
` `	Line break
`<input type=hidden name='submitted' value=TRUE>`	Input tag for submitted
`<input type=submit value='send info'><input type=reset value='reset'>`	Input tag for Submit button
`</form>`	End form
`</body>`	End body
`</html>`	End html
`<? }    ?>`	Restart PHP to close off `else` clause and then end PHP

The *session2.php* script is shown in Table 13.4. Note that the session_start function actually re-establishes the session. Any session variables are reinstated with the values set in previous Web pages.

TABLE 13.4   PHP Script Following Script Setting Session Variables

`<? session_start();?>`	PHP: re-establish session. End PHP
`<html><head><title>Follow on page using session data </title></head>`	Normal HTML
`<body bgcolor="<?print($bcolor);?>">`	Normal HTML. Use session variable to set `bgcolor` of page
`<h1> Welcome to the second page </h1>`	Heading
`<?`	Restart PHP
`print ("$cname! </h1>\n");`	Display session variable
`print (" You like $type cookies.");`	Display session variable

(*continues*)

TABLE 13.4 PHP Script Following Script Setting Session Variables *(continued)*

`print(" You began your visit at $starttime");`	Display session variable
`?> `	End PHP. Line break
`<a href="session3.php">non-existent page </a>`	One more link: this is to demonstrate that you could go to yet another page
`</body></html>`	Ending HTML tags

The time as displayed in the previous scripts is not too meaningful. An improvement would be the following:

```
$darray = getdate($starttime);
$dhrs = $darray{"hours"};
$dmins = $darray{"minutes"};
if (strlen($dmins)<2) {$dmins = "0".$dmins;}
print("<br>You began your visit at $dhrs:$dmins");
```

The `if` statement is necessary to prevent 2 hours and 5 minutes from appearing as 2:5 when you want 2:05.

The ASP session scripts follow the same format as the PHP scripts. This is one case in which the ASP code is simpler because there is no analog to PHP's `session_start`. Since the start time is used here just for display, the code shows the use of the JavaScript date object method `toString`.

The first ASP script is shown in Table 13.5.

TABLE 13.5 ASP Script Setting Session Variables

`<%@ Language="JavaScript" %>`	Set language as JavaScript
`<%`	Start ASP
`var submitted=String(Request ("submitted"));`	Extract form data
`if (submitted != "undefined") {`	If test for handler versus form
`    cname=String(Request("cname"));`	Set cname variable from form data
`    ctype = String(Request("type"));`	Set ctype variable from form data
`    bcolor =String(Request("bcolor"));`	Set bcolor data from form data
`    var starttime = new Date();`	Determine current time
`Session("cname")=cname;`	Set session value for "cname" to be value of cname variable
`Session("ctype")=ctype;`	Same for ctype
`Session("bcolor")=bcolor;`	Same for bcolor

TABLE 13.5   *(continued)*

`Session("starttime")= starttime.toString();`	Set session value for "starttime" to be `starttime` converted to a string
`%>`	End ASP
`<html><head><title>Set session values </title></head>`	Normal HTML tags
`<body>`	Body tag
`<h1> Welcome`	Heading
`<%`	Restart ASP
`Response.Write(cname+"! </h1>\n");`	Write out `cname`
`Response.Write(" You like "+ ctype+" cookies.");`	Write out `ctype`
`%>`	End ASP
`<a href="session2.asp">Next page </a>`	Hyperlink to next page
`</body>`	Body close
`</html>`	HTML close
`<%    }`	Restart ASP to close `If` clause
`else { %>`	`Else` clause. End ASP
`<html><head><title>Form for session data </title></head> <body>`	Normal HTML
`<form action="session1.asp" method="get">`	Form tag
`Your name <input type=text name='cname' >`	Input tag
` `	Line break
`Your favorite cookie <input type=text name='type' > `	Input tag
`Your preferred background color <input type=text name='bcolor'>`	Input tag
` `	Line break
`<input type='hidden' name='submitted' value=TRUE>`	Input tag for hidden variable `submitted`
`<input type='submit' value='send'>`	Button
`</form>`	End form
`</body>`	End body
`</html>`	End HTML
`<% }    %>`	Re-open ASP to close `Else` clause. Close ASP

The *session2.asp* script that is the next page that makes use of the session information is shown in Table 13.6.

TABLE 13.6   ASP Script Following Script that Sets Session Variables

`<%@ Language="JavaScript" %>`	Set JavaScript as language
`<%`	Start ASP
`var bcolor = Session("bcolor");`	Extract bcolor from session
`var cname = Session("cname");`	Extract cname
`var ctype = Session("ctype");`	Extract ctype
`var starttime=Session("starttime");`	Extract starttime
`%>`	End ASP
`<html><head><title>Follow on page using session data </title></head>`	Normal HTML
`<body bgcolor="<%Response.Write (bcolor);%>">`	Body tag: break into ASP to get value of bcolor. End ASP
`<h1> Welcome to the second page </h1>`	Heading
`<%`	Start ASP
`Response.Write(cname+"! </h1>\n");`	Write out cname
`Response.Write(" You like "+ ctype+" cookies.");`	Write out ctype
`Response.Write(" You began your visit at " + starttime);`	Write out time
`%> `	End ASP. Line break
`<a href="session3.asp">non-existent page </a>`	Hyperlink to show you can go to another page
`</body></html>`	Closing HTML tags

REFLECTION

After studying this chapter on cookies and sessions, it is important to recall the main focus of the text: databases. Databases provide ways other than cookies or sessions for builders of Web applications to retain information on the visitors to the site, or at least the ones willing to invest the time and have the trust to enter information into the system. Similarly, you have seen the trick of passing information in the query string of an address cited in a hyperlink. You now have the tools of data bases, query strings, cookies, and session information to use in your application, individually or in combination.

When deciding on whether to use sessions, you will need to estimate the upper limit on concurrent visitors to your Web site and consult with the server administration.

EXERCISES, QUESTIONS, AND PROJECTS

1. After studying the session example, create ASP and PHP scripts that generate cookies that specify the look of a page, starting with the background color. You can also specify the color of the `text`, `link`, `vlink`, and `alink` text.
2. Create cookies that last a different amount of time than five minutes.
3. Create ASP or PHP scripts to record as cookies ID and password information to save people from re-entering information into a form.
4. Using a file (see the previous chapter), create an ASP or PHP set of scripts that accepts an ID and password pair of fields and compares them to sets kept in the file. If there is a match, set a session variable such as `pwokay` to `true`. Check this value in other scripts, and if it is not set, return to the script to enter ID and password. The PHP command for this is `header ("Location: pw.php")`, assuming `pw.php` is the script with the form to enter ID and password. The ASP command is `Response.Redirect ("pw.asp")`, assuming `pw.asp` is the corresponding script.

SHOPPING CART

The goal of this chapter is to present detailed scripts for creating a shopping cart used to order products from an online store.

BACKGROUND

The requirements of e-commerce are among the main driving forces for middleware technology. Online stores need to access and modify information in databases and create customized Web pages to present information to customers. Product information, including image files to showcase new products, needs to be uploaded to keep the online catalog current. The shopping process usually involves customers viewing multiple Web pages, a process that can be eased by using cookies and/or session information. The shopping cart covered in this chapter will be described using the entity-relationship, process, and storyboard design tools. The scripts use the features of SQL, PHP and MySQL, and ASP/JavaScript and Access that you learned about in earlier chapters.

CONCEPTUAL EXPLANATION

The first part of any shopping cart is the product offerings where customers can view their choices. Figure 14.1 shows an example of the product offerings for an Origami model store.

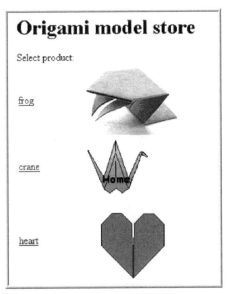

FIGURE 14.1   Initial screen for origami store.

Once customers have viewed the product selection, they can choose the one they are interested in purchasing by clicking on the product name as seen in Figure 14.1. They now have the option to select how many frogs they want to purchase using the screen shown in Figure 14.2.

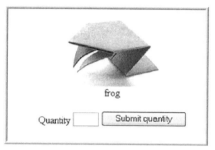

FIGURE 14.2 Screen to specify quantity.

After entering in a quantity and clicking the Submit quantity button, the customers would be able to review their order, as shown in Figure 14.3.

Shopping cart

Product ID	Product Name	Quantity	Total cost
1	frog	5	1.25
TOTALS		5 items	$1.25

Checkout (submit order)!   More shopping!

FIGURE 14.3 Contents of the shopping cart.

The last part of the transaction typically involves the customer checking out and supplying the pertinent order and payment information, as shown in Figure 14.4.

This quick example obviously does not include all the necessary forms for a real transaction, but it does provide the basic idea of how a shopping cart functions on many online stores.

Shopping Cart Design

The design of the shopping cart begins with the design of the database. The initial requirement is to define tables for products, customers, and orders.

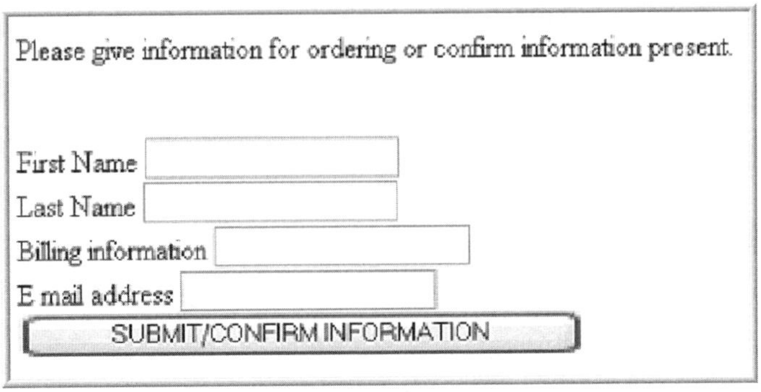

Please give information for ordering or confirm information present.

First Name
Last Name
Billing information
E mail address

SUBMIT/CONFIRM INFORMATION

FIGURE 14.4   Form to enter customer information.

Because the shopping process needs to allow for multiple products per order, a fourth table needs to be defined for ordered items. The entity-relationship diagram in Figure 14.5 shows the tables, the fields in the tables, and the relationship between the tables.

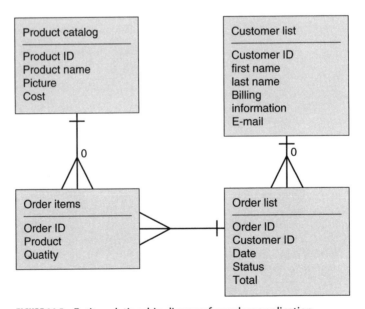

FIGURE 14.5   Entity-relationship diagram for orders application.

The shopping cart is only a subset of the many processes required for an e-commerce site. The processes described here include:

- Ordering products by viewing the items for sale and adding them to a virtual shopping cart

- Performing a checkout operation, including supplying name and payment information
- Adding new products to the database

Figure 14.6 shows the data flow for these processes.

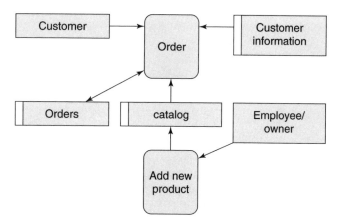

FIGURE 14.6   Process diagram for the shopping cart.

Both an orders and an ordered items data store could be shown, but that is a greater level of detail than is needed for defining the processes. The main point to convey is that there are two processes being implemented, each involving a different agent. The application stores three types of information: product information in something usually called a *catalog*, information on orders, and information on customers. Therefore, adding a new product requires two operations: creating and uploading an image file for the product, and using the *inputproducts* script to add a new record to the catalog table in the database.

The storyboard for our PHP implementation is shown in Figure 14.7. The storyboard indicates that two scripts are contained in other scripts: the script establishing a connection to the database, and a script with a function for displaying the cart contents. This information is kept in a session variable. The heavy arrows represent linkages made by form action attributes. As indicated previously, dividing an application into several scripts is a good practice. However, you need to realize that the particular division is arbitrary. For example, the choice was made to make the *submitorder* script present a form, and be the handler for the form. You could decide to do things differently. Making the code that displays the cart functions a file by itself is a good practice, since otherwise you would need to repeat the code in each of the *shoppingcart* and *submitorder* files.

The storyboard for our ASP implementation would be similar, but not identical. The *createtables* script is not present. The *fileupload* script would be mentioned in the storyboard, but possibly with the php extension included

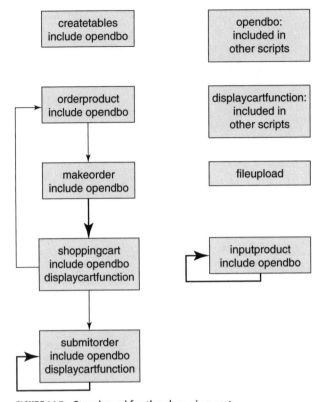

FIGURE 14.7 Storyboard for the shopping cart.

because it is different from the others. To put it another way, the ASP implementation relies on two functions being carried out independent of the ASP
scripts:

- The database and the database tables are created offline in Access and the
  entire database uploaded to the Web site.
- The image files are uploaded using a PHP script.

Session Information

The PHP and the ASP implementations each make use of sessions to hold the
items ordered along with the quantity of each item ordered. The PHP session
variable, named $cart, is an associative array. This is an array holding values
stored by arbitrary keys as opposed to indices. To iterate through the cart, the
code uses the foreach construction:

```
foreach (@$cart as $pid => $qty) {
```

which starts a loop in which each key/value pair is extracted from `$cart`. Within the body of the loop, the code references the key/value pair by `$pid` for the key and `$qty` for the value. You can use the `foreach` feature for any associative array, not just session variables.

The ASP coding needs to perform a similar job, although the terminology and the syntax are different. The data is stored in the `Session.Contents` collection. The term *collection* is what ASP calls an *associative array*. The expression `Session.Contents.Count` returns the number of key/value pairs. With this information, you can write the JavaScript for a loop:

```
for (i=0; i<Session.Contents.Count; i++)
```

that can be used to iterate over all the key/value pairs in the collection. Within this loop, the statement:

```
itemn = Session.Contents.key(i);
```

will assign a key (in this situation a product ID) to the variable `itemn`, and then:

```
… Session(itemn)…..
```

can be used to refer to the corresponding value (in this situation, the associated quantity). The latter is shorthand for:

```
… Session.Contents(itemn)…
```

EXAMPLES

The coding for these two implementations is similar to what you studied in previous chapters. The following are statement-by-statement explanations.

ON THE CD

You will find the code for the two shopping cart applications on the CD-ROM in the folder named chapter14code. This folder contains a subfolder named images with image files for several origami models.

The PHP and MySQL Implementation

The *opendbo.php* file is included (using the `require` function) in all the scripts to establish the connection to the database. The calculated `$link` value and the `$DBname` value will be used in the script that requires `opendbo.php` and are declared as `global` variables. The script is shown in Table 14.1.

TABLE 14.1   PHP Script to Establish Connection to Database

`<?php`	Start PHP
`global $DBname, $link;`	Make these two global
`$host="localhost";`	Set $host
`$user="curley";`	You will need to change this
`$password="12345";`	You will need to change this
`$DBname="orders";`	You might need to change this
`$link=mysql_connect($host,$user, $password);`	Establish the connectiono
`mysql_select_db($DBname,$link);`	Select the database
`?>`	End PHP

For the PHP/MySQL system, define the tables using a script: *createorderta-bles* as shown in Table 14.2.

TABLE 14.2   PHP Script for Creating the Tables for the Shopping Cart

`<?php Start PHP  function createtable ($tname,$fields) {`	Function for creating tables
`global $DBname, $link;`	Use global values
`$query="CREATE TABLE ".$tname." (".$fields.")";`	Defines the query using the parameter values
`if (mysql_db_query($DBname,$query, $link)) {`	Execute the MySQL operation. Check if it succeeded
`   print ("The table, $tname, was created successfully. \n");`	Print success message
`   }`	Close out true clause
`else {`	Start `else` clause
`   print ("The table, $tname, was not created.  \n");`	Print out not a success (for example, if the table was already created)
`   }`	End `else` clause
`}`	End definition of function
`?>`	Close PHP
`<html><head><title>Creating order project tables </title> </head>`	Normal HTML
`<body>`	HTML
`<?php`	Start PHP
`require("opendbo.php");`	Include the connecting script
`$tname = "customers";`	Set name of table, first to be defined

TABLE 14.2   *(continued)*

`$fields="id INT UNSIGNED NOT NULL AUTO_INCREMENT PRIMARY KEY, fname char(30), lname char(30), billing TEXT, emailaddress char(50), pass char(30)";`	Set definition of fields
`createtable($tname, $fields);`	Call function to create the customers table
`$tname="orders";`	Set name of table
`$fields="id INT UNSIGNED NOT NULL AUTO_INCREMENT PRIMARY KEY, customer_id INT UNSIGNED NOT NULL, o_date DATE, status ENUM('open','set','billed', 'shipped'), total FLOAT(2)";`	Set definition of fields
`createtable($tname,$fields);`	Call function to create orders table
`$tname="catalog";`	Set name of table
`$fields="id INT UNSIGNED NOT NULL AUTO_INCREMENT PRIMARY KEY, p_name CHAR(30), picture CHAR(50), cost FLOAT(2)";`	Set definition of fields
`createtable($tname,$fields);`	Call function to create orders table
`$tname="ordereditems";`	Set name of table
`$fields="order_id INT UNSIGNED NOT NULL, p_id INT UNSIGNED NOT NULL, quantity INT NOT NULL";`	Set definition of fields
`createtable($tname,$fields);`	Call function to create orders table
`mysql_close($link);`	Close link
`?>`	End PHP
`</body>`	HTML
`</html>`	HTML

The *inputproducts.php* script, shown in Table 14.3, lets authorized staff add a product to the catalog. This script is a form handler and a display of the form.

The previous script created a new database record containing a field with the address of a product image file. Table 14.4 shows the code for uploading an image file to the server, *fileupload.php*. See Chapter 12, Files, for more explanation and to the CD-ROM folder for Chapter 12 for the code for *fileupload.php*.

ON THE CD

TABLE 14.3   PHP Script to Add a New Product to the Catalog Table

`<html><head><title>Adding products to catalog table db</title> </head>`	HTML
`<body>`	HTML
`<?php`	Start PHP
`require("opendbo.php");`	Include connecting script
`$tname = "catalog";`	Set table name
`// need sign in procedure`	Comment indicating a place to improve this process
`if (@($submitted)) {`	Is this the form handler
`    $p_name = trim($p_name);`	Trim the inputted product name
`    $picture= trim($picture);`	Trim the inputted name of the image file
`    $pattern="(http://)?([[:alnum:] \.,-_?/&=])\.((gif)\|(jpg))$";`	Prepare a regular expression pattern to check if this is a good file address including being an appropriate file extension for images
`    if (!eregi($pattern,$picture)){`	Perform the check
`      print ("Please submit a valid address for a picture. ");`	Print a message indicating the need to submit a valid image file address
`      print ("Use the BACK function on your browser to return to the form.");`	Print instructions
`    }`	Close clause for bad picture address
`    else {`	Else clause
`      $picture = AddSlashes($picture); // should check for valid address`	Add escaping for slashes in the file name
`      // should check $cost to be valid number`	Possible improvement
`      $query = "INSERT INTO $tname values ('0','".$p_name."', '".$picture."', ".$cost.")";`	Create insert query
`      $result = mysql_db_query($DBname, $query, $link);`	Perform insert query
`      if ($result) {`	Check if good result
`        print("The product was successfully added. \n");`	Print out message
`      }`	End clause
`      else {`	Start `else` clause

TABLE 14.3 *(continued)*

`print ("The product was NOT successfully added.  \n");`	Print out message for no success
`}`	End clause
`$submitted = FALSE;`	Reset to allow new submission
`mysql_close($link);`	Close link
`print ("<a href=\"inputproducts. php\">Submit another product. </a> ");`	Display link to return to script again.
`} //ends if good URL`	Ends if clause for good picture file address
`} //ends if submitted`	Ends if handler
`else {`	Start else for displaying form
`print ("<h1>Add a product to the catalog  \n </h1> ");`	Print heading
`print ("<form action= \"inputproducts.php\" method=post>\n");`	Print form tag
`print ("Name of product <input type=text name=\"p_name\" size=30> \n");`	Print input tag for product name
`print ("File name of picture <input type=text name=\"picture\" size=50> \n");`	Print input tag for picture file address
`print ("Cost of product <input type=text name=\"cost\" size=6> \n");`	Print input tag for cost
`print ("<input type=hidden name=\"submitted\" value=\"True\ "> \n");`	Print input tag for submitted flag
`print ("<input type=submit name=\"submit\" value=\"Submit product!\"> \n");`	Print button tag
`print ("</form> \n");`	Print end of form
`}`	Close the `else` clause
`?>`	End PHP
`</body> </html>`	HTML

TABLE 14.4   PHP Script for Uploading Image File to Illustrate a Product

`<html><head><title>File upload test </title> </head><body>`	HTML
`<?php`	Start PHP
`if (@$file) {`	Check if this is to handle the form (previous examples used a special form input value named submitted)
`    print ("uploading file named $file_name  ");`	Print message letting the person know what is going on
`    print ("File size is $file_size  ");`	Print message on file size
`    $abspath = $PATH_TRANSLATED;`	Set the variable to be the path to the current script
`    $stub=ereg_replace("\\fileupload. php","\\",$abspath);`	Modify the variable to take out the name of the current script
`    $fullname = $stub . $file_name;`	Add in the filename. This is the line you might need to alter for your application
`    print ("fullname is: $fullname. ");`	Debugging message, letting user know where the file was placed
`    $size=GetImageSize($file);`	Use PHP command to extract information on file. This only makes sense for image files
`    print ("Dimensions are: ".$size[0]." by ".$size[1]." pixels.  ");`	Print out file information
`    $area = $size[0]*$size[1];`	Compute area
`    print ("Area is $area pixels. ");`	Print out area
`    if (copy($file,$fullname)) {`	This contains the critical step: copying the file to the proper place. Check if successful…
`        print ("file successfully uploaded.  ");}`	Print out message
`    else { print ("file could not be copied."); }`	Else clause: problem in copying file
`    unlink($file);`	End connection to the file in temporary storage
`}`	Close clause that this was handler
`print (" upload a file to the server \n");`	Print out heading

TABLE 14.4   *(continued)*

`?>`	End PHP
`<form action='fileupload.php' method=POST ENCTYPE="multipart/ form-data">`	Form tag. The ENCTYPE is required for forms that have a file as one of the inputs
`File <input type=file name="file"> `	Input tag for file. This will generate a Browse button
`<input type=submit name="submit" value="upload file">`	Input tag for Submit button
`</form>`	End form
`</body>`	End body
`</html>`	End HTML

Now it is on to implementing ordering products. The *orderproduct.php* script is the first of four scripts that accomplishes the task for accepting and recording an order. An order is represented in the database by one record in the orders table, and one or more entries in the `ordereditems` table. The *orderproduct* script presents the products as a table. Each row of the table holds a product name and a product picture. The name is a hyperlink with the `href` attribute of the `<a>` tag set to `makeorder.php` followed by a question mark and the product ID. The *orderproduct* script, shown in Table 14.5, uses the `currentcustomer` cookie, if it is defined, to greet a returning customer by name.

TABLE 14.5   Initial PHP Script to Display Products to Customer

`<html><head><title>Presenting products </title> </head><body>`	HTML start
`<h1>Origami model store </h1> <p>`	HTML heading
`<?php`	Start PHP
`require ("opendbo.php");`	Include connecting script
`if (@$currentcustomer) {`	If current customer is defined via a cookie (this will be the ID)
`print("currentcustomer id is: $currentcustomer ");`	Debugging message
`$query="SELECT fname FROM customers where id=$currentcustomer";`	Define query to find customer's name
`$result=mysql_db_query($DBname,$query, $link);`	Invoke query
`$Num_past = mysql_num_rows($result);`	Compute number returned

(continues)

TABLE 14.5   Initial PHP Script to Display Products to Customer *(continued)*

`if ($Num_past!=0) {`	If the number isn't zero
`$fname=mysql_result($result,0,` `'fname');`	Take the first one (there should only be one)
`print("Welcome back, $fname! ");`	Print customized welcome message
`}`	Close if customer found
`}`	Close if cookie defined
`?>`	End PHP
`Select product:`	HTML
`<table>`	Start table
`<?php`	Start PHP
`$query="Select * from catalog";`	Define query
`$result=mysql_db_query($DBname, $query,` `$link);`	Invoke query to get all the products
`while ($row=mysql_fetch_array` `($result)) {`	While loop to iterate through the products
`print ("<tr><td><a href=` `makeorder.php");`	Start of printing to make the table item be an <a> tag with a call to *makeorder.php*…
`print ("?p_id=");`	…with a query string carrying as p_id…
`print($row['id']);`	…the value of the id field of the record
`print(">");`	Close <a…> tag
`print($row['p_name']);`	Print out the name of the product
`print("</a></td>");`	Print out </a> tag and close table datum element
`print("<td><img src=\"");`	Print out next table datum: start of img tag
`$picture=$row['picture'];`	Store the value of the picture field of the record in a variable
`print("../images/$picture");`	Continue with img tag: the src value will be in the images folder, a folder parallel (subfolder of parent folder) of this script
`print("\"></td></tr>");`	Print closing table datum and table row tags
`}`	Close of `while` loop
`print ("</table>");`	Print </table> tag to end the table
`mysql_close($link);`	Close link to database

TABLE 14.5 *(continued)*

?>	End PHP
</body> </html>	Closing HTML

The *orderproduct* script invokes the *makeorder* script, shown in Table 14.6, with a query string holding the ID of the product that the customer has clicked. The customer is given a chance to enter the quantity of the product.

TABLE 14.6 **Present Individual Product for Customer to Enter Quantity**

`<html><head><title>Presenting products </title> </head><body>`	Starting HTML
`<?php`	Start PHP
`require("opendbo.php");`	Including connecting to database
`?>`	End PHP
`<h1>Indicate quantity and confirm order </h1>`	HTML header
`<p>`	Paragraph
`<?`	Start PHP
`$query="Select * from catalog where id=$p_id";`	Define query to get the record in the database corresponding to the $p_id value from the query string sent over by the call from orderproducts
`$result=mysql_db_query($DBname,$query, $link);`	Invoke query
`$p_name=mysql_result($result,0,"p_name");`	Define product name variable
`$picture=mysql_result($result,0, "picture");`	Define picture file name variable
`$cost=mysql_result($result,0,"cost");`	Define cost variable
`print ("<center><img src=\"../images/ $picture\">");`	Print out tags to display picture
`print(" ");`	Print line break
`print("$p_name");`	Print out product name
`?>`	End PHP
`<form action=shoppingcart.php method=get>`	HTML for form: note that this does not require any PHP
`Quantity <input type=text size=3 name="quantity">`	Field for quantity

(continues)

TABLE 14.6   Present Individual Product for Customer to Enter Quantity *(continued)*

`<input type=submit value="Submit quantity" >`	Submit button
`<input type=hidden name=productid value='`	Start of HTML to define a hidden variable to carry along the `productid`
`<? print($p_id);`	Restart PHP to output the `$p_id` value
`?>`	End PHP
`'>`	Need this quotation mark after `$p_id` value
`</form> </body> </html>`	Closing HTML

The *makeorder* script calls the *shoppingcart* script, shown in Table 14.7, which makes use of the `cart` session variable. The latest product ordered with the quantity is added to `cart` as a key/value pair. The total contents of the shopping cart—that is, everything ordered so far—is displayed. The customer is given the option of clicking on either of two links: one to continue shopping, and the other to check out.

TABLE 14.7   PHP Script to Display Current Shopping Cart

`<?php`	Start PHP
`if (!session_is_registered("cart")) {`	Check if cart is not yet registered as a session variable
`  $cart = array();`	Initialize $cart to be an empty array
`  session_register("cart");`	Register "cart" as a session variable
`}`	End the clause to initialize the cart
`?>`	Close PHP
`<html><head><title>Shopping Cart</title>`	HTML tags
`<?`	Start PHP
`require("displaycartfunction.php");`	Include the file holding the function to display the cart
`?>`	Close PHP
`</head>`	HTML tag
`<body>`	HTML body
`<?php`	Start PHP
`require("opendbo.php");`	Make connection to database
`?>`	Close PHP
`<h1>Shopping cart</h1>`	HTML heading
`<p>`	Paragraph

Chapter 14   Shopping Cart   **313**

TABLE 14.7   *(continued)*

`<?`	Start PHP
`if (@$productid){`	If a `$productid` is defined
`  $cart[$productid] = $quantity;`	Set the value in the associative array `$cart` for this product ID to be the `$quantity` value
`}`	
`displaycart();`	Call the `displaycart` function
`?>`	Close PHP
`<hr>`	Horizontal rule
`<a href="submitorder.php"> Checkout (submit order)! </a>    `	Link to complete order by going to `submitorder` script
`<a href="orderproduct.php"> More shopping! </a>`	Link to more shopping by going to `orderproduct`
`</body> </html>`	Closing HTML

The *shoppingcart.php* script and the *submitorders.php* script each have calls to the require function to include the *displaycartfunction.php* shown in Table 14.8.

TABLE 14.8   Script to Display the Contents of the Shopping Cart

`<?php`	Start PHP
`//assumes that opendbo called, and session started when call is made.`	Comment? on context of call
`function displaycart() {`	Function header
`  global $cart, $DBname, $link, $totalprice;`	Function will use the global values set outside of the function
`  print ("<table>");`	Print table tag
`  print ("<tr><td> Product ID </td> <td> Product Name </td><td> Quantity </td> <td> Total cost </td> </tr>");`	Print table tags for column headings
`  $items = 0;`	Initialize `$items`. This will hold the number of products ordered
`  $totalprice = 0.00;`	Initialize `$totalprice`. This will hold the dollar total
`  foreach (@$cart as $pid => $qty) {`	A loop to iterate through all the key/value pairs in the `$cart` array
`    $items += $qty;`	Increment the number of items by the `$qty` value. This is equivalent to `$items=$items + $qty;`

(continues)

TABLE 14.8   Script to Display the Contents of the Shopping Cart *(continued)*

`$query="Select * from catalog where id=$pid";`	Define the query to get the record for the product with ID equal to `$pid`
`$result = mysql_db_query($DBname, $query, $link);`	Invoke the query
`$item_price = mysql_result($result,0, "cost");`	Set a variable with the item's cost
`$item_name = mysql_result($result,0, "p_name");`	Set a variable with the item's name
`$item_total_price = $item_price * $qty;`	Calculate the cost for the number of items ordered
`$totalprice += $item_total_price;`	Add this value to the variable holding the total
`$item_total_pricef = number_format ($item_total_price,2);`	Prepare a formatted string with the total (two decimal places)
`print ("<tr><td> $pid </td> <td> $item_name </td><td> $qty </td> <td> $item_total_pricef </td> </td> ");`	Print out the results
`}`	End the foreach iterating over each item in the cast
`$totalpricef = "$" . number_format ($totalprice,2);`	Prepare a formatted string for the over all total
`print("<tr> <td> TOTALS </td> <td> </td> <td> $items items</td><td> $totalpricef </td></tr>  </table>");`	Print out the totals
`}`	End the definition of the function
`?>`	End PHP

The *shoppingcart.php* script contains a link to the *submitorders.php* script, shown in Table 14.9, for immediate checkout or the *ordersproduct* script for more shopping. The *submitorders.php* script presents a form and handles the form An If test determines which of the two to do.

TABLE 14.9   PHP Script to Display and Handle Form for Customer Data

`<?php`	Start PHP
`session_start();`	Re-start the session
`require("opendbo.php");`	Include the connection to the database
`require("displaycartfunction.php");`	Include the `displaycartfunction` code

TABLE 14.9 *(continued)*

`$today = Date("Y-m-d");`	Set $today to be the date in Year-month-day format
`if (!@$submitconfirm) {`	If form not yet submitted
`  print ("Please give information for ordering or confirm information present. ");`	Print out instructions
`  print ("<form action=\"$PHP_SELF\" method=post> ");`	Print out form tag. Notice the use of $PHP_SELF to indicate this script
`  $ofname=""; $olname=""; $obilling=""; $oemail="";`	Initialize several variables to empty strings. They will be used as is if there is not a currentcustomer cookie
`  if (@$currentcustomer)`	Check if there is a currentcustomer cookie (which would hold a customer ID)
`  {$query="SELECT * from customers where id=$currentcustomer";`	Define a query to get that customer's record
`  $result=mysql_db_query($DBname, $query,$link);`	Invoke the query
`  $Num_past = mysql_num_rows($result);`	Find out the number of records
`  if ($Num_past>0) {`	If there is at least one record (there would be zero or 1 since IDs are unique)
`  $obilling=mysql_result($result,0, "billing");`	Get the billing information
`$olname = mysql_result($result,0, "lname");`	Get the customer name
`  $oemail=mysql_result($result,0, "emailaddress");`	Get the mail information
`  print ("<input type=hidden name=oldcustomer value=TRUE>");`	Print out hidden input tag holding a variable that flags that the form has information from a current customer
`  print(" INFO OKAY <input type= \"radio\" name=\"choices\" value=\"OKAY\" CHECKED >");`	Print out radio buttons: the information is either okay, which is the default
`  print (" CHANGE MY INFO <input type=\"radio\" name=\"choices\" value=\"CHANGE\" >");`	… radio button indicating change, which the customer clicks if he or she puts in new information

(continues)

TABLE 14.9   PHP Script to Display and Handle Form for Customer Data *(continued)*

`print (" NEW CUSTOMER <input type=\"radio\" name=\"choices\" value=\"NC\"> ");`	Radio button for a new customer
`}`	Ends clause for customer in database
`}`	Ends clause for existence of cookie
`print ("First Name <input type=text name='fname' value='".$ofname."'> ");`	Print out input tag. There might or might not be a displayed value
`print ("Last Name <input type=text name='lname' value='".$olname."'> ");`	Print out input tag as above
`print ("Billing information <input type=text name='billing' value='".$obilling."'> ");`	Print out input tag as above
`print ("E mail address <input type=text name='email' value='".$oemail."'> ");`	Print out input tag as above
`print ("<input type=hidden name='submitconfirm' value=TRUE>");`	Print out a hidden input tag to flag that form has been submitted
`print ("<input type=submit name='submit' value='SUBMIT/CONFIRM INFORMATION'>");`	Print out the Submit button
`print ("</form>");`	Print out the form end tag
`}`	Ends clause for displaying form
`else {`	`Else` (handle form)
`if (!@$oldcustomer) {`	If it was not a case of an old customer
`$query="INSERT INTO customers VALUES ('0','".$fname;`	Define query to add a new record
`$query=$query."','".$lname."','".$billing."','".$email."','X')" ;  // X for pass now`	Construction of query takes two statements
`$result=mysql_db_query($DBname, $query,$link); //need error handling.`	Invoke query
`$currentcustomer=mysql_insert_id();` ... `inserted.`	The `mysql_insert_id` function returns returns the id of the record just
`setcookie("currentcustomer", $currentcustomer); //sets permanent cookie`	Set the cookie to be this new value
`}`	End if not old customer

TABLE 14.9   *(continued)*

`else {`	Start clause for it being the case of an old customer
`    if (@$choices=='CHANGE') {`	If the customer changed information
`        $query="UPDATE customers set` `fname='".$fname ;`	Create a query for changing (updating) the information
`        $query = $query . "', lname=` `'".$lname."', billing='".$billing;`	Continue construction of query

`        $query = $query . "',`
`emailaddress='".$email ."' where`
`id=$currentcustomer";`
	Continue

`        mysql_db_query($DBname,$query,` `$link);`	Invoke query
`    }`	End old customer/new information clause
`    else if (@$choices=='NC') {`	Start clause for choice to make new customer
`        $query="INSERT INTO customers` `VALUES ('0','".$fname;`	Create query

`        $query=$query."','".$lname."',`
`'".$billing."','".$email."','X')" ;`
`// X for pass now`
	Continue constructing query

`        $result=mysql_db_query($DBname,` `$query,$link); //need error handling.`	Invoke query
`        $currentcustomer=mysql_insert_id();`	Obtain ID of record just created
`        $duration = 90 * 24 * 60* 60;` `//90 days`	Time period for this cookie will be 90 days

`        setcookie("currentcustomer",`
`$currentcustomer, time()+$duration);`
`//sets long term`
	Set cookie with duration parameter

`    }`	End if changed to new customer
`  }`	End `else` clause for it being an old customer
`print("Welcome, $fname  ");`	Print out welcome
`print ("Today is $today  \n");`	Print out date
`print ("Here is your order.<hr>");`	Print out heading
`displaycart();`	Invoke `displaycart` function to display the whole cart

(continues)

TABLE 14.9   PHP Script to Display and Handle Form for Customer Data *(continued)*

`print ("<hr> We are billing it using the following information:   $billing ");`	Print out information on billing
`$query = "INSERT INTO orderlist VALUES ('0', '";`	Start construction of query to insert record into the orderlist table
`$query = $query . $currentcustomer."', '".$today."', 'set',".$totalprice.")";`	Continue construction
`mysql_db_query($DBname, $query, $link);`	Invoke query
`$orderid=mysql_insert_id();`	Obtain ID of record just created
`foreach ($cart as $pid=>$qty) {`	Use foreach to iterate over cart to insert insert records into the ordereditems table
`    $query="INSERT INTO ordereditems values ('".$orderid."','".$pid."',".$qty.")";`	Create the query
`    mysql_db_query($DBname,$query,$link);`	Invoke query
`}  //ends the foreach`	End iteration through cart
`session_unregister('cart');`	Unregister the cart session variable
`unset($cart);`	This returns any space used by $cart
`session_destroy();`	Stop the session
`}`	Ends handling of form—the else clause on if submitconfirm
`?>`	Close PHP
`</body> </html>`	Closing HTML tags

The ASP and Access Implementation

The ASP implementation bears the same relationship to the PHP implementation as prior projects. Our suggestion is to create the database with all the tables in stand-alone mode; that is, directly in Access. This means that there is no ASP file that corresponds to the *createtables.php* file.

The *openconn.asp* script shown in Table 14.10, holds the code for connecting to the database named *orders.mdb* located in the folder as these scripts. It is of the DSN-less type.

TABLE 14.10   The ASP/JavaScript Script to Connect to the Database

`<%`	Start ASP
`Conn = Server.CreateObject("ADODB.` `Connection");`	Create connection object
`Conn.Mode = 3  ;`	Set mode to read/write

`strConnect = "Driver={Microsoft Access`
`Driver (*.mdb)};" + "DBQ=" +`
`Server.MapPath("orders.mdb") ;`
	Define the connection string to point to the appropriate driver and database

`  Conn.Open (strConnect, "admin", "") ;`	Make the connection, using a general user and no password
`%>`	Close ASP

The *inputproduct.asp* file, shown in Table 14.11, is used to input products.

TABLE 14.11   The ASP/JavaScript Script for Inputting a New Product

`<%@ Language=JavaScript %>`	Set language
`<html><head><title> Adding products to` `catalog table </title></head><body>`	HTML
`<!— #include file="openconn.asp" —>`	Include file to establish connection
`<%`	Start ASP
`var submitted=String(Request.Form` `("submitted"));`	Extract from form input the variable that flags if this is form or handler
`if (submitted !="undefined") {`	Check submitted
`    var pname=String(Request.` `Form("pname"));`	Extract pname from form input
`    var picture=String(Request.` `Form("picture"));`	Extract picture file name from form input
`    var cost=Request.Form("cost");`	Extract cost
`  if (picture=="") {`	Check if picture not given
`      Response.Write("Please submit` `a valid address for a picture. ");`	Error message
`      Response.Write("Use the` `browser BACK to return to the` `form. ");`	Instructions to return to form
`    }`	End clause
`  else {`	Else
`        queryf = "(p_name,` `picture, cost)";`	Part of setting up insert query

(continues)

TABLE 14.11   The ASP/JavaScript Script for Inputting a New Product *(continued)*

`queryv = " VALUES ('" + pname + "','" + picture +"', " + cost + ")";`	Part of setting up insert query
`query="INSERT INTO catalog " + queryf + querytv;`	Part of setting up insert query
`if (Conn.Execute(query))`	Execute query and do IF test
`{Response.Write (" Product was successfully entered.  ");}`	Write out success
`else {Response.Write("Product was NOT entered. ");`	Write out failure
`}`	End clause
`Conn.Close();`	End connection
`Response.Write("<a href= \"inputproducts.asp\">Another product? </a>  ");`	Display a link to go to submit another product
`}`	Ends if good picture
`} // ends if submitted`	Ends if handling form
`else {`	Else: present form
`%>`	Stop ASP
`<h1>Add product to the catalog </h1>`	HTML heading
`<form action="inputproducts.asp" method="POST"> `	Form tag
`Product name <input type=text name="pname" size=50>  `	Input field for product name
`Picture file <input type=text name="picture" size=50>  `	Input field for picture file name
`Cost <input type=text name="cost" size=6> `	Input field for cost
`<input type=hidden name="submitted" value="True"> `	Input field for submitted, which works as a flag indicating form is to be handled
`<input type=submit name="submit" value="Enter product!"> `	Submit button
`</form>`	Form close tag
`<%`	Restart ASP
`}`	Close `else` clause for submitting form
`%>`	End ASP
`</body> </html>`	HTML closing tags

Now we get to the set of scripts for ordering products. The first one is *orderproduct.asp*, shown in Table 14.12.

TABLE 14.12   The ASP/JavaScript Script for Ordering Products

Code	Description
`<%@ Language=JavaScript %>`	Set language
`<!-- #include file="openconn.asp" -->`	Include file for connecting to the database
`<html><head><title>Presenting Products</title><head><body>`	HTML starting tags
`<h1>Origami model store </h1>`	Heading
`<%`	Start ASP
`currentcustomer = String(Request.Cookies("currentcustomer"));`	Extract cookie holding currentcustomer
`if (currentcustomer!="") {`	If cookie was set
`    query="SELECT fname FROM customers WHERE customer_id="+currentcustomer;`	Creating query to get that customer record
`    result=Server.CreateObject("ADODB.RecordSet");`	Create recordset object
`    result.Open(query,Conn);`	Invoke query
`    fname=String(result.fields.item("fname"));`	Extract the `fname` field from that record
`    Response.Write("Welcome back, "+fname+" ");`	Display customized greeting
`    }`	End if cookie set
`%>`	End ASP
`Select Product:`	Instructions
`<table>`	HTML table tag
`<%`	Start ASP
`query="SELECT * from catalog";`	Define query
`rs=Server.CreateObject("ADODB.RecordSet");`	Create recordset object
`rs.Open(query,Conn);`	Invoke query
`while (!rs.EOF) {`	While loop to iterate through all the items in the catalog
`    Response.Write("<tr><td><a href=makeorder.asp?p_id=");`	Start to display, as first item in row of table, an a tag, with the `href` value for the link *makeorder.asp* plus the start of a query string

(continues)

TABLE 14.12   The ASP/JavaScript Script for Ordering Products (*continued*)

`Response.Write(rs.fields.item` `("p_id"));`	The rest of the query string is the product identifier
`Response.Write(">");`	Close up the `<a>` tag
`Response.Write(rs.fields.item` `("p_name"));`	Write out the product name as the visible part of the link
`Response.Write("</a></td><td>` `<img src=");`	Output the `</a>` tag along with more table tags and the start of an img tag
`Response.Write(rs.fields.item` `("picture"));`	Output the picture file
`Response.Write("></td></tr>");`	Output the table tags closing up the row
`rs.move(1);`	Advance in the record set
`}`	Close up the `while` loop
`Response.Write("</table>");`	Output the closing table tag
`Conn.close();`	Close the connection to the database
`%>`	End ASP
`</body></html>`	HTML tags

The *orderproduct* script contains tags with links to the *makeorder.asp* script. A query string holds the product ID value for the link the customer clicks. The *makeorder* script, shown in Table 14.13, allows the customer to indicate the quantity.

TABLE 14.13   The ASP/JavaScript Script for Specifying the Quantity

`<%@ Language=JavaScript %>`	Set language
`<!- #include file="openconn.asp" ->`	Include code to connect to database
`<!- #include file="moneyformat.asp" ->`	Include code to format money
`<html><head><title>Input quantity` `</title></head><body>`	HTML tags
`<h1>Indicate quantity and confirm order` `</h1><p>`	HTML heading
`<%`	Start ASP
`p_id = Request("p_id");`	Extract the product ID from the query string
`query="Select * from catalog where` `p_id=" + p_id;`	Create query for selecting that record

TABLE 14.13   (*continued*)

`result=Server.CreateObject("ADODB.RecordSet");`	Create a recordset object
`result.Open(query, Conn);`	Invoke query
`p_name=String(result.fields.item ("p_name"));`	Extract product name
`picture=String(result.fields.item ("picture"));`	Extract picture filename
`cost=result.fields.item("cost");`	Extract cost
`Response.Write("<center><img src= '"+picture+"'>");`	Write out HTML to display image
`Response.Write(" ");`	Write out line break
`Response.Write(p_name);`	Write out product name
`Response.Write("<i> price @ item </i> ");`	Write out text
`Response.Write(money(cost));`	Write out cost formatted as money
`%>`	End ASP
`<form action=shoppingcart.asp method=post>`	Form field. The script indicated to handle the form is *shoppingcart.asp*
`Quantity <input type=text size=3 name= "quantity"> `	Quantity field
`<input type=submit name=submit value="Submit Quantity">`	Submit button
`<input type=hidden name=productid value='`	The productid is passed along as an additional form value
`<%`	Start ASP
`Response.Write(p_id);`	Write out product ID
`%>`	End ASP
`'>`	Output quotation mark to follow product ID
`</form>`	End form
`</body>`	End body
`</html>`	End HTML

The *moneyformat* script, shown in Table 14.14, does not add a dollar sign, but does make sure that the amount is given with two decimal places.

TABLE 14.14   The ASP/JavaScript Script Holding the Function for Formatting Money

`<%`	Start ASP
`function money( raw) {`	Function definition header. The parameter is named raw
`var thirdd = 0.0050000001;`	Set third to be used for rounding up
`var dandc = "" + ( raw + thirdd );`	The dandc is set by first adding raw and thirdd as numbers and then concatenated with the empty string to produce a string
`var dp = dandc.indexOf ( '.' );`	Find the decimal point
`var zeros;`	The variables zeroes will be used later
`if ( dp < 0 ) {`	If there is no decimal point
`dandc = dandc + '.00'; }`	…concatenate two zeros to the end of dandc
`else {`	Else (there was a decimal point)
`dandc = dandc.slice ( 0, dp + 3 );`	If there are two or more decimal places, this reduces the string to extend just two places past the decimal point
`zeros = 3 - ( dandc.length - dp );`	Zeros will be greater than zero only if the string had less than two decimal places
`for ( var i=0; i<zeros; i++ ) {`	For loop: if zeros is greater than zero
`dandc = dandc + '0';    }`	Add zero to the end, as needed
`}`	End for loop
`return dandc;`	Return dandc
`}`	End function
`%>`	End ASP

The *shoppingcart.asp*, shown in Table 14.15, script displays all items bought so far and gives the customer a chance to complete the order (checkout) or return for more shopping.

TABLE 14.15   The ASP/JavaScript Script Displaying the Shopping Cart

`<%@ Language=JavaScript %>`	Set language
`<!- #include file="openconn.asp" ->`	Include file to make connection to database

TABLE 14.15   *(continued)*

`<!– #include file="displaycartfunctions.` `asp" –>`	Include file with function to display the cart
`<html><head><title> Start or add to` `shopping cart </title> </head><body>`	HTML tags
`<%`	Start ASP
`npid = String(Request.Form` `("productid"));`	Extract product ID from form input
`nqty = parseInt(Request.Form` `("quantity"));`	Extract quantity from form input
`Session(npid) = nqty;`	Add to the session information a key/value pair, with the key being the product ID and the value being the quantity
`tqty=0`	Initialize variable holding total quantity of items to zero
`totalcost = 0.00;`	Initialize variable holding total cost to zero
`displaycart();`	Call `displaycart` function
`Conn.close();`	Close connection
`%>`	Close ASP
` `	Line break
`<a href="orderproduct.asp"> Enter new` `item </a>`	Link for more shopping
` `	Line break
`<a href="submitorder.asp"> Complete` `order </a>`	Link to complete order
`</body></html>`	Closing HTML tags

The *displaycartfunctions* script, shown in Table 14.16, holds the one function `displaycart`.

TABLE 14.16   The ASP/JavaScript Script Holding the `displaycart` **Function**

`<!– #include file="moneyformat.asp"  –>`	Include the `moneyformat` function
`<%`	Start ASP
`function displaycart() {`	Function header
`rs=Server.CreateObject` `("ADODB.RecordSet");`	Create a `recordset` object
`    Response.Write("<hr>");`	Output horizontal rule

(continues)

TABLE 14.16   The ASP/JavaScript Script Holding the displaycart Function *(continued)*

`Response.Write("<table>");`	Output table tag
`Response.Write("<thead>");`	Output more table tags
`Response.Write("<th>Name <th> Unit Cost <th> Quantity <th> Cost <TBODY>");`	Table column headings
`for (i=1; i<=Session.Contents. Count;i++) {`	For loop to iterate through the Session.Contents
`itemn = Session.Contents. key(i);`	Set itemn to be a key value
`query="Select p_name, cost from catalog where p_id=" + itemn;`	Create a query to get that record
`rs.Open(query, Conn);`	Invoke the query
`pn=String(rs.fields.item ("p_name"));`	Extract the product name
`pc=parseFloat(rs.fields. item("cost"));`	Extract the cost and convert to a decimal number
`rs.Close();`	Close the recordset (it may be re-used)
`pqty=parseInt(Session(itemn));`	Obtain the quantity from the Session information. Convert to be an integer
`tqty=tqty+pqty;`	Add to the running total quantity variable
`ptotal = pc*pqty;`	Compute the cost
`totalcost=totalcost+ptotal;`	Add to the running total cost variable
`Response.Write("<tr><td>" + pn + " </td>");`	Output table tags plus the product name
`Response.Write("<td>" + money(pc) + "</td>");`	Output table tags plus the formatted (unit) cost
`Response.Write("<td>" + pqty + " </td>");`	Output table tags plus the quantity
`Response.Write("<td>" + money(ptotal) + " </td>\n </tr>");`	Output the formatted total cost for this product
`}`	Close loop through shopping cart
`Response.Write("<tr> <td> Totals </td> <td> </td> <td>"+ tqty +"</td><td>");`	Output as the last row of the table the totals
`Response.Write("<b>$ " +money(totalcost));`	Continue outputting last row

TABLE 14.16   (continued)

`Response.Write("</b></td></tr>` `</table>");`	Finish up last row
`}`	Close function definition
`%>`	Close ASP

The script that actually stores the order information in the database is *submitorders.asp*, shown in Table 14.17. It first displays a form and requests that the customer confirm, change, or enter new customer information. The same script then handles the form information.

TABLE 14.17   **The ASP/JavaScript Script to Collect and Handle Customer Information**

`<%@ Language="JavaScript" %>`	Set language
`<!- #include file="openconn.asp" ->`	Include connecting to database
`<!- #include file="displaycartfunctions.` `asp" ->`	Include code to display shopping cart
`<%`	Start ASP
`dx= new Date();`	Define dx as a date object holding today's date
`today = dx.getDate()+"-"+ dx.getMonth()` `+"-"+dx.getFullYear();`	Define today as a string with formatted information from dx
`var submitted=String(Request.` `Form("submitted"));`	Extract submitted flag to check if this
`if (submitted =="undefined") {`	Check if handler or form. The positive if test is to display the form
`  Response.Write("Please confirm or` `give new information. ");`	Output instructions to customer
`  Response.Write("<form action=` `\"submitorder.asp\" method=post> ");`	Output form header
`  ofname=""; olname=""; obilling="";` `oemail="";`	Initialize variables to be used in the display
`  currentcustomer = String(Request.` `Cookies("currentcustomer"));`	Extract cookie value
`  if (currentcustomer!="") {`	Check if cookie was set
`  query="SELECT * FROM customers WHERE` `customer_id="+currentcustomer;`	Define query to get this customer's record from the database
`  result=Server.CreateObject` `("ADODB.RecordSet");`	Define a recordset object
`  result.Open(query,Conn);`	Invoke query

(continues)

TABLE 14.17   The ASP/JavaScript Script to Collect and Handle Customer Information (*continued*)

`ofname=String(result.fields.item("fname"));`	Set `ofname` with the value from the database
`olname=String(result.fields.item("lname"));`	Set `olname` with the value from the database
`obilling=String(result.fields.item("billing"));`	Set `obilling` with the value from the database
`oemail=String(result.fields.item("emailaddress"));`	Set `oemail` with the value from the database
`Response.Write("<input type=hidden name=oldcustomer value='TRUE'>");`	Write out as a hidden tag that there was information from an "old'" customer
`Response.Write(" Okay<input type=\"radio\" name=\"choices\" value=\"OKAY\" CHECKED >");`	Write out as radio button with the default, that the information was okay
`Response.Write("Change<input type=\"radio\" name=\"choices\" value=\"CHANGE\"  >");`	Write out as radio that the information needed to change (but for the same, "old," customer)
`Response.Write("New Customer<input type=\"radio\" name=\"choices\" value=\"NC\" >");`	Write out as radio button the choice that this is a new customer
`}`	Close `if` clause for cookie existing
`Response.Write(" First Name <input type=text name='fname' value='" +ofname + "'> ");`	Output input tag for first name. The value showing is taken from `ofname`. It is empty if the cookie did not exist
`Response.Write("Last Name <input type=text name='lname' value='" + olname + "'> ");`	Output input tag for last name
`Response.Write("Billing <input type=text name='billing' value='" + obilling + "'> ");`	Output input tag for billing
`Response.Write("Email <input type=text name='email' value='" + oemail + "'> ");`	Output input tag for e-mail
`Response.Write("<input type=hidden name='submitted' value='TRUE'>");`	Output as hidden form tag the submitted value
`Response.Write("<input type=submit name='submit' value='SUBMIT/CONFIRM INFORMATION'>");`	Output Submit button
`Response.Write("</form>");`	Output form close

TABLE 14.17 *(continued)*

`}`	End clause for the situation to present the form
`else`	`Else` clause: form handler
`{oldcustomer=Request.Form ("oldcustomer");`	Extract `oldcustomer` value. This is the hidden value indicating if there was an "old customer"
`fname=String(Request.Form ('fname'));`	Extract `fname` value
`lname=String(Request.Form ('lname'));`	Extract `lname`
`billing=String(Request.Form ('billing'));`	Extract `billing`
`email=String(Request.Form ('email'));`	Extract e-mail
`if (oldcustomer!='TRUE') {`	If there was *not* an old customer
`fieldsx = "(fname, lname, billing, emailaddress)";`	Start to prepare query to insert a new customer record
`valuesx = " ('" + fname +"','" + lname + "','" + billing + "','" + email+ "')";`	Continue with preparation of query
`query="INSERT INTO customers "+ fieldsx + " VALUES " + valuesx;`	Define query
`Conn.Execute(query);`	Execute query
`query="SELECT max(customer_id) as maxid from customers";`	This produces the id of the record just added to the table
`rs=Server.CreateObject("ADODB. RecordSet");`	Define a new recordset
`rs.Open(query, Conn);`	Invoke query
`currentcustomer=rs.fields. item("maxid");`	This is the ID of the customer whose record was just inserted (added)
`}`	Ends if not old customer; i.e., new customer
`else {`	`Else` (old customer)
`currentcustomer = String (Request.Cookies("currentcustomer"));`	Extract the current customer ID from the form
`choices = Request.Form ("choices");`	Extract the value of choices
`if (choices=="CHANGE") {`	If choices indicates a change

(continues)

TABLE 14.17   The ASP/JavaScript Script to Collect and Handle Customer Information
(*continued*)

`query="UPDATE customers  set fname ='"+fname+"', lname='" +lname;`	Start creation of the query to update (change) the customer information
`query= query+"', billing= '"+billing+"', emailaddress= '"+email+"'";`	Continue with query
`query= query +" where customer_id ="+currentcustomer;`	Complete creation of query
`Conn.Execute(query);`	Invoke query
`}`	Ends change info but same `currentcustomer`
`else if (choices=='NC') {`	Else if new customer
`fieldsx = "(fname, lname, billing, emailaddress)";`	Start to prepare query for insertion
`valuesx = " ('" + fname +"', '" + lname + "','" + billing + "', '" + email+ "')";`	Continue preparing query
`query="INSERT INTO customers "+ fieldsx + " VALUES " + valuesx;`	Complete query
`Conn.Execute(query);`	Invoke query
`query="SELECT max(customer_id) as maxid from customers";`	Define query to obtain the ID for the record just inserted
`rs=Server.CreateObject("ADODB. RecordSet");`	Define new recordset
`rs.Open(query, Conn);`	Invoke query
`currentcustomer=rs.fields. item("maxid");`	Extract value. This is the ID for the record just created
`}`	Ends make new `currentcustomer`
`}`	Ends old customer
`Response.Write("Welcome, "+fname);`	Output greeting
`Response.Write(" Today is "+ today);`	Output date
`Response.Write(" Here is your order. <hr>");`	Output message
`tqty=0`	Initialize variable that will hold total quantity
`totalcost = 0.00;`	Initialize variable that will hold total cost
`displaycart();`	Call `displaycart`

TABLE 14.17   *(continued)*

`Response.Write("We are billing it using:  "+billing+" ");`	Output message on billing
`fieldsx="(customer_id, o_date, status, total)";`	Start to prepare query for insertion into orders table
`valuesx="('"+ currentcustomer+"', '"+ today+"','set',"+ totalcost+")";`	Continue
`query="INSERT INTO orderlist "+ fieldsx + " VALUES "+ valuesx;`	Complete query
`Conn.Execute(query);`	Invoke query
`query="SELECT max(order_id) as maxid from orderlist";`	Define new query to get ID of record just added to `orderlist`
`rs=Server.CreateObject("ADODB. RecordSet");`	Define new recordset
`rs.Open(query, Conn);`	Invoke query
`order_id=rs.fields.item("maxid");`	Extract value of `order_id`
`fieldsx="(order_id, p_id, quantity)";`	Start preparation of query for insertion into ordereditems table. This same string will be part of the query for each item
`for (i=1; i<=Session.Contents. Count;i++) {`	For loop: for each product ordered. The iteration is over the `Sessions.Contents`
`itemn = Session.Contents. key(i);`	Extract product ID
`pqty=parseInt(Session (itemn));`	Extract the associated quantity and convert to be integer
`valuesx = "("+order_id+", "+itemn+","+pqty+")";`	Continue with preparation of query
`query="INSERT INTO ordereditems "+fieldsx+ "VALUES "+valuesx;`	Complete definition of query
`Conn.Execute(query);`	Invoke query
`}`	Close for loop
`Conn.Close();`	Close connection
`Session.Abandon;`	Destroys all session variables; that is, the cart
`}`	Ends handling of form
`%>`	End ASP
`</body></html>`	Closing HTML tags

REFLECTION

The shopping cart application shows the use of many of the database and middleware software features you have learned about in this book. It also gives you a project to build on both to test and enhance your skills and produce an application to suit your requirements.

As you know from doing online shopping, the customer information should have some type of password control. Similarly, the ability to add new products should be restricted to authorized store personnel. You can use your HTML, PHP, and ASP knowledge (see the *Exercises* and also look ahead to Chapter 16, Scaling Up Your Application) to add features to this project.

EXERCISES, QUESTIONS, AND PROJECTS

1. Improve the look of the scripts. You might want to consult sources on stylesheets. However, keep in mind that your customers want to see the products and make their orders quickly.
2. Improve the display by changing either or both of the displaycart function and the money function. You might want to make the money function always return strings of a fixed size.
3. Change the code to support currencies other than dollars.
4. Add images to the final Web page presented to the customer: thumbnails of each product ordered.
5. Add fields to each of the tables and do validation using regular expressions. For example, check for credit card numbers of the format four groups of digits.
6. Design, program, and debug a set of scripts for the processes of shipping the orders and billing the customers. This would start with reading the orders and ordered items table.
7. Replace the use of cookies and sessions by the use of another table in the database. You might want to wait until completing the next chapter, which includes use of temporary tables.

15

QUIZ SHOW

T he goal of this chapter is to present in detail scripts for a quiz show application.

BACKGROUND

Education applications and games are a significant and growing area of the computer and Web industry. The requirements for these applications drive technology in the same way as e-commerce.

The United States state capital application featured in an earlier chapter demonstrated the use of PHP and ASP in quiz-type applications in which information was kept in array variables. The information was in files to be included using the PHP `require` function and the ASP `include` instruction. The quiz show application that is the focus of this chapter is based on the use of databases. The databases contain tables holding the questions, data on players and history of player performance. The application makes use of important features in SQL, PHP and MySQL, ASP/JavaScript, and Access.

CONCEPTUAL EXPLANATION

The critical aspect of the quiz show is the treatment of questions. A table in a database holds a set of questions. Each question has a category, the text of the question, an answer pattern, and a point or cost value. People inputting questions can specify anything as a category. To put it another way, there are no preset categories. Players are presented with a form (see Figure 15.1) in which they enter their names and pick a category. The drop-down list of categories is created dynamically from the distinct categories in the questions table.

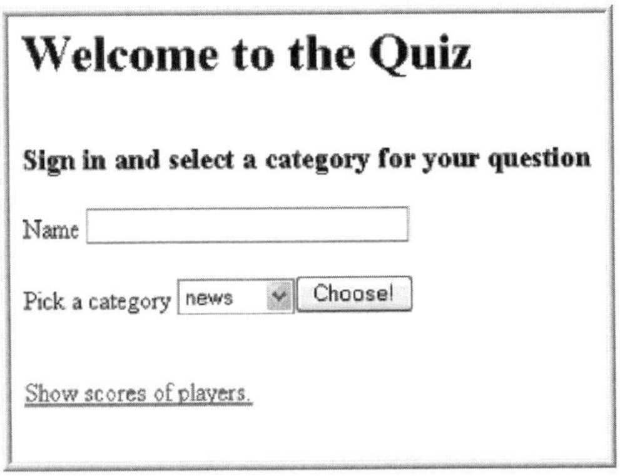

FIGURE 15.1   Initial screen for quiz show.

The game attempts to find a question to ask the player in the chosen category. The game keeps a history of the questions asked a player, whether the player's answer was correct or incorrect, and the date. The game has a policy concerning repeating questions. If a person has answered a question correctly, he or she will not be asked it again. If a player has been asked the question on a prior day and answered it incorrectly, the question is put into the pool of acceptable questions. The code selects a question at random from the pool of acceptable questions.

Figure 15.2 shows a screen with a question from the trivia category:

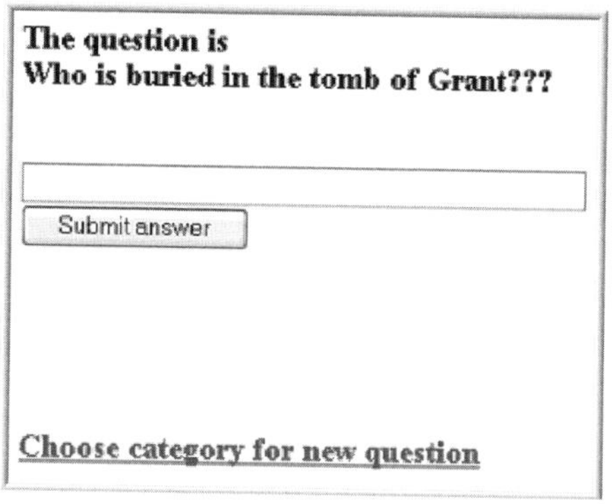

The question is
Who is buried in the tomb of Grant???

> Submit answer

<u>**Choose category for new question**</u>

FIGURE 15.2   Question from trivia category.

If the player types in a correct answer, the response is as shown in Figure 15.3.

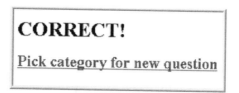

CORRECT!

<u>**Pick category for new question**</u>

FIGURE 15.3   Response to correct answer.

This background is enough to design the database for the application.

Quiz Show Design

The quiz show requires three tables: questions, players, and history. The questions table is also called the question databank. A question record contains more than just the question. One field in a question record is the text of a question; another field is a string that is an answer pattern. Using patterns provides flexibility in evaluating answers. The entity-relationship diagram in Figure 15.4 was previously shown in Chapter 1, "Introduction."

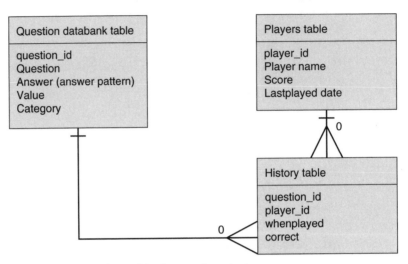

FIGURE 15.4   Entity-relationship diagram for quiz show.

The table that is called the question databank and the players table are not related directly. Instead, each of these tables has a relationship to the history table.

The implementation described in the code in detail supports two main processes: a player plays the game, and someone, called the editor, inserts questions, as shown in Figure 15.5. Two minor processes are showing all the scores and clearing the tables.

As was the case in the previous chapter, the level of detail shown in the process diagram can vary. Here, we have chosen to show the three tables of the database explicitly. The diagram shows all the processes, including the *cleartables* process used for debugging. The storyboard showing the relationships among the scripts is shown in Figure 15.6 for the PHP implementation.

The storyboard for the ASP implementation would be essentially the same. You can follow the procedure of the shopping cart example and create the tables using Access in stand-alone mode. You can also clear tables using Access. This would allow for more selective editing of the records. Our implementation puts the JavaScript for obtaining a random choice in a distinct file.

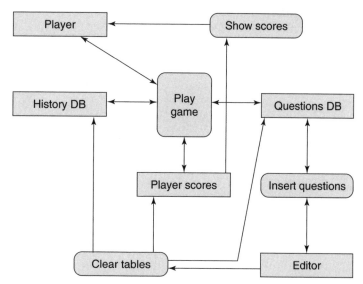

FIGURE 15.5   Process diagram for quiz show.

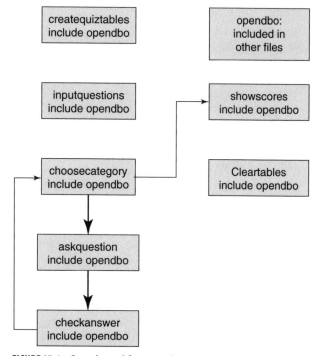

FIGURE 15.6   Storyboard for quiz show.

Temporary Tables and LEFT JOINS

The implementation makes use of a temporary table in the *askquestion* scripts to capture relevant past history on the player. MySQL provides an explicit mechanism for temporary tables. When using Access, the code erases everything in a table called *past* before populating it with records for the current player.

The *askquestion* scripts make use of a LEFT JOIN to identify questions that do not have the characteristic of having been asked on the current day or been answered correctly. Review the chapter on SQL if you need more examples of LEFT JOINs.

A question record in the questions table contains the answer as a regular expression pattern. The check is done using the PHP `eregi` function and the ASP/JavaScript string `search` method. This is a neat way to make the quiz performance more flexible and less obviously mechanical. However, it does require the person inputting questions to know how to design a regular expression.

EXAMPLES

The coding for these two implementations is similar to what you studied in previous chapters. Try to do some of the coding yourself. Statement-by-statement explanations are provided. Two other exercises you can attempt is to look at the column with the code and see if you can explain it yourself, or look at the explanation and see if you can write the code. One cautionary note: copy-and-paste is a good technique, but you must be careful when going back and forth between ASP and PHP that you remove or insert the dollar signs. You also need to extract form data explicitly in the case of ASP.

ON THE CD

You will find the code for the quiz show applications on the CD-ROM in the folder named Chapter15code.

The PHP and MySQL Implementation

The *opendbq.php* script, shown in Table 15.1, establishes the connection to the database and is included, using the PHP `require` function, in all of the other scripts. The example provided here, as in the previous case, has our values for user ID and password. You will need to insert your values.

TABLE 15.1   PHP Script to Establish Connection with Database

`<?php`	Start PHP
`global $DBname, $link;`	Set these values to be global so they can be used elsewhere, including in functions
`$host="localhost";`	Sets the host
`$user="curley";`	Sets the user

TABLE 15.1   *(continued)*

`$password="12345";`	Sets the password
`$DBname="quiz";`	Sets the database name
`$link=mysql_connect($host,$user,` `$password);`	Establish the connection
`mysql_select_db($DBname,$link);`	Set the database used. Later code may set this, also
`?>`	Close PHP

The *createquiztables.php* script, shown in Table 15.2, establishes all three tables for the quiz show application.

TABLE 15.2   PHP Script to Create the Tables for the Quiz Show Application

`<?php`	Start PHP
`function createtable($tname,$fields) {`	Function header for `createtable`. It will be called for each table
`global $DBname, $link;`	Uses the global values
`$query="CREATE TABLE ".$tname."` `(".$fields.")";`	Define query using values passed in as parameters
`if (mysql_db_query($DBname,$query,` `$link)) {`	Invoke the query and do an `if` test if it worked okay
`   print ("The table, $tname, was` `created successfully. \n");`	Print success message
`   }`	End clause
`else {`	Start `else` for unsuccessful query
`   print ("The table, $tname, was not` `created.  \n");`	Print message of no success (for example, table already created or bad user ID and password)
`   }`	End clause
`}`	End function definition
`?>`	Stop PHP
`<html><head><title>Creating quiz` `tables </title> </head><body>`	HTML
`<?php`	Start PHP
`require("opendbq.php");`	Include connecting code
`$tname = "questions";`	Set variable for table name to be `"questions"`

(continues)

TABLE 15.2   PHP Script to Create the Tables for the Quiz Show Application (*continued*)

`$fields = "question_id INT UNSIGNED NOT`
`NULL AUTO_INCREMENT PRIMARY KEY,`
`question char(50) NOT NULL, answerpattern`
`char(50) NOT NULL, category char(30) NOT`
`NULL, value INT NOT NULL";`
	Set variable for field definitions

`createtable($tname, $fields);`	Call function
`$tname = "players";`	On to the next table: set variable to `"players"`

`$fields ="player_id INT UNSIGNED NOT`
`NULL AUTO_INCREMENT PRIMARY KEY, name`
`char(50) NOT NULL, lastplayed DATE not`
`null, score INT NOT NULL";`
	Set field variable

`createtable($tname,$fields);`	Invoke function
`$tname = "history";`	On to last table: set variable to `"history"`

`$fields="question_id INT unsigned not`
`null, player_id INT unsigned not null,`
`whenplayed DATE not null, correct`
`TINYINT not null, primary key`
`(question_id, player_id) ";`
	Set field variable. Notice that correct (since it can be right or wrong) is set as a TINYINT

`createtable($tname,$fields);`	Call function
`mysql_close($link);`	Close link
`?>`	Stop PHP
`</body></html>`	Closing HTML tags

The *inputquestion.php* script, shown in Table 15.3, allows someone to enter new questions into the database. This script is a handler for a form as well as a presenter of a form, and has the usual check on whether or not the `submitted` variable has been set.

TABLE 15.3   PHP Script to Add Questions

`<html><head><title>Adding questions to` `quiz db</title> </head><body>`	Usual HTML
`<?php`	Start PHP
`require("opendbq.php");`	Include connecting code
`$tname = "questions";`	Set table name
`if (@($submitted)) {`	If test to see if form has been submitted. The @ prevents a warning message

TABLE 15.3   *(continued)*

`$question = trim($question);`	Remove white space (for example, blanks) from the question form input using the `trim` function
`$ans = trim($ans);`	Trim the answer
`$ans = AddSlashes($ans);` `$question = AddSlashes($question);`	Add in slashes to "escape" any special characters
`$cat = trim($cat);`	Trim category
`$value= trim($value);`	Trim value. (It could be appropriate to check that value is a number. Alternatively, see the *Exercises*)

`$query = "INSERT INTO $tname values`
`('0','".$question."', '".$ans."',`
`'".$cat."', '".$value."')";`
	Create the query. Note that the zero value is used as a placeholder. MySQL will insert the next number for the question ID

`$result = mysql_db_query($DBname,$query,` `$link);`	Invoke the query
`if ($result) {`	If test to check if the question was added successfully
`    print("The question was` `successfully added. \n");}`	Print positive message
`else {print ("The question was NOT` `successfully added.  \n");}`	Print negative message
`$submitted = FALSE;`	Set submitted to false to re-show the form
`mysql_close($link);`	Close the link
`print ("<a href=\"inputquestions.php\` `">Submit another question </a> ");`	Print an a tag to form a hyperlink allowing the user/question editor to submit another question
`}  //ends if submitted`	Ends the clause for handling the form
`else {`	Starts the clause for presenting a form
`print ("<h1>Add a question to the` `databank of questions  \n </h1> ");`	Print a heading
`print ("<form action=\"inputquestions.` `php\" method=post>\n");`	Print form tag
`print ("Text of question <input` `type=text name=\"question\"` `size=50> \n");`	Print input tag for question text

(continues)

TABLE 15.3   PHP Script to Add Question *(continued)*

`print ("Answer pattern <input type=text name=\"ans\" size=50> \n");`	Print input tag for answer pattern
`print ("Category <input type=text name=\"cat\" size=30> \n");`	Print input tag for category
`print ("Point Value <input type=text name=\"value\" size=6> \n");`	Print input tag for point value
`print ("<input type=hidden name= \"submitted\" value=\"True\"> \n");`	Print the hidden form input tag holding the submitted variable
`print ("<input type=submit name=\"submit\" value=\"Submit question!\"> \n");`	Print the tag for the Submit button
`print ("</form> \n");`	Print the form close
`}`	End the clause for displaying the form
`?>`	End PHP
`</body></html>`	End HTML

Now, after programming these preliminary scripts, it is time to start building the scripts implementing the asking of questions. The first one is called *choosecategory.php*. The code with explanation is provided in Table 15.4. The player enters his or her name and then chooses a category from the drop-down list. Because the handling of this form is fairly complex, it is implemented in a separate script as opposed to making this script both present a form and handle the input to the form.

TABLE 15.4   PHP Script for Signing In and Selecting a Category

`<html><head><title>Sign in and select category </title></head><body>`	Starting HTML
`<h1> Welcome to the Quiz </h1>  `	HTML heading
`<h3> Sign in and select a category for your question </h3>`	HTML
`<form action="askquestion.php" method=post>`	Form. Action (handler) is the *askquestion.php* script
`<p>Name <input type=text name='player' size=30`	Name input tag
`<?php`	Start PHP
`if (@$currentplayer) {`	Check if there is a cookie set for holding the `currentplayer`
`    print ("VALUE=$currentplayer>  ");}`	If so, print it out as the default value of the name input tag

TABLE 15.4   *(continued)*

`else { print ("> ");}`	Else (no cookie) just print out the end of the input tag. It will appear blank
`?>`	Close PHP
`<p>Category <select name='pickedcategory'>`	Start the `select` element that will produce the pull-down list of category names
`<?php`	Start PHP
`require ("opendbq.php");`	Bring in code to make connection to the database
`$query="SELECT DISTINCT category FROM questions";`	Create a query to get all the different category value; that is, the set of distinct values
`$categories = mysql_db_query($DBname, $query, $link);`	Invoke the query
`while ($row=mysql_fetch_array ($categories))`	While loop: this will iterate through the recordset named `$categories` set by invoking the query
`{ $cat=$row['category'];`	Extract the category (name)
`  print ("<option value=$cat>$cat </option> \n");`	Print it as an option
`}`	End the `while` loop
`mysql_close($link);`	Close the connection
`print ("</select>");`	Print out the close of the `select` element
`print ("<input type=submit name=submit value=\"Choose!\">  \n");`	Print out the tag to produce the button labeled `Choose!`
`print ("</form>");`	Print out the end of the form
`?>`	Close PHP
`<a href="showscores.php">Show scores of players. </a>`	An a tag with the option to show players' scores
`</body></html>`	Closing HTML

The *askquestion.php* script, shown in Table 15.5, is invoked as the handler of the form presented by *choosecategory.php*. That is, it is the file specified by the action attribute in the form tag. The *askquestion.php* script is the most complex one in this application. It sets a cookie using the player's name passed from the form. Notice that this is done before any HTML is output. It determines an acceptable question, making use of the past history of the player, a temporary table, and the LEFT JOIN construct. The temporary table is made using an SQL CREATE statement that incorporates a SELECT statement.

TABLE 15.5 **PHP Script that Finds Appropriate Question to Ask**

`<?php`	Start PHP
`setcookie("currentplayer",$player);`	Set a cookie for as long as the browser is open. This could be the cookie already set
`?>`	End PHP
`<html><head><title>Fetch appropriate question from category and ask </title></head><body>`	Standard HTML
`<?php`	Start PHP
`$today = Date("Y-m-d");`	Set $today to be today in year-month-day format
`print ("Today is $today  \n");`	Print out date
`require("opendbq.php");`	Include connecting code
`$query="SELECT name, player_id, lastplayed, score from players where name='".$player."'";`	Define query to get information on player. Note: this could be used to distinguish players with the same name. However, that is not done in this script. All players with the same name are batched together
`$result=mysql_db_query($DBname, $query, $link);`	Invoke query
`if (mysql_num_rows($result)==0) {`	If there is no such player
`    $query2 = "INSERT INTO players values ('0','".$player."','".$today."','0')";`	Create a query string to add a new player record
`    mysql_db_query($DBname,$query2,$link);`	Invoke the query
`    $query="SELECT player_id from players where name='".$player."'";`	Create query to get the player_id for the record just created
`    $result = mysql_db_query($DBname, $query, $link);`	Invoke this query
`    }`	End clause for no such player
`$player_id = mysql_result($result,0, "player_id"); // take first 0th record`	At this point, no matter what, $result holds a player record. Extract the player_id
`$query="CREATE temporary TABLE past (item_id INT)";`	Start to build a query string to create a temporary table named past
`$query=$query . " SELECT question_id FROM history where (player_id='". $player_id;`	Continue building query
`$query=$query . "' AND (whenplayed='". $today."' OR correct))";`	Finish definition of query

TABLE 15.5   (*continued*)

`$result=mysql_db_query($DBname,$query, $link);`	Invoke the query
`$query="SELECT * FROM past";`	Build a query to get a recordset from past
`$result = mysql_db_query($DBname,$query, $link);`	Invoke the query
`$Num_past = mysql_num_rows($result);`	Find out the number of rows in `$result` (also in past)
`print ("Number of past relevant actions is $Num_past  ");`	This is a debugging statement that could be removed
`if ($Num_past>0) {`	If there were relevant past statements
`    $sel = "SELECT questions. question_id, question, answerpattern, value from questions";`	Start to build a query (held in variable `$sel`) that contains questions that are not in past (that is, not allowed to be asked)
`    $sel =$sel . " LEFT JOIN past ON questions.question_id = past.question_id WHERE ";`	Continue definition
`    $sel = $sel . " category='" . $pickedcategory . "' AND past.question_id IS NULL";}`	Complete definition
`    else {$sel="SELECT question_id, question, answerpattern, value from questions ";`	Else clause: if there were no relevant past questions, then start to build a simpler querystring in `$sel`
`    $sel= $sel . " WHERE category= '" . $pickedcategory. "'";`	Finish definition of `$sel`
`    }`	End the `else` clause
`$result=mysql_db_query($DBname, $sel, $link);`	Invoke the query
`$NoR=mysql_num_rows($result);`	Find out number of rows
`print (" Number of appropriate questions is ".$NoR);`	This could be considered a debugging statement to remove
`if ($NoR==0) {`	If there are no appropriate questions
`print ("  No appropriate questions in databank. Pick new category.  \n");}`	…print out that message
`else`	Else (there was at least one appropriate question)

(*continues*)

TABLE 15.5 PHP Script that Finds Appropriate Question to Ask (*continued*)

`{ if ($NoR > 1) {`	If there is more than one appropriate question, need to make a random choice
`srand ((double) microtime()*1000000);`	Suggested way to seed pseudo-random number generator.
`$choice=rand(0,$NoR-1);`	$choice is a random number from 0 to one less than $NoR
`}`	End clause of more than one acceptable question
`else {`	Else: (only one acceptable question)
`$choice=0;}`	... set $choice to 0
`$question_id = mysql_result($result,` `$choice,"question_id");`	The $choice is used to extract question data from the $result recordset. Extract the question_id
`$question    = mysql_result($result,` `$choice,"question");`	Extract the question text
`$ans         = mysql_result($result,` `$choice,"answerpattern");`	Extract the answerpattern
`$value       = mysql_result($result,` `$choice,"value");`	Extract the value
`print ("<h3><p> The question is  ` `$question ???  \n");`	Print out the question
`print ("<form action=\"checkanswer.` `php\" Method=post> \n");`	Print out start of a form. The handler will be *checkanswer.php*. Note: method is post so player will not see the hidden form data
`print ("<input type=text name=player_ans` `size=50> \n");`	Print out the input tag for the player to enter his or her answer
`print ("<input type=submit name=submit` `value='Submit answer'> \n");`	Print out the tag to produce the Submit button
`print ("<input type=hidden name=ans` `value='$ans'> \n");`	Print out as a hidden value the answer pattern
`print ("<input type=hidden name=value` `value='$value'> \n");`	Print out as a hidden value the point value
`print ("<input type=hidden` `name=question_id value='$question_id'>` ` \n");`	Print out as a hidden value the question_id
`print ("<input type=hidden` `name=player_id value='$player_id'>` ` \n");`	Print out as a hidden value the player_id

TABLE 15.5   *(continued)*

`print ("<input type=hidden name=today value='$today'> \n");`	Print out as a hidden value today
`print ("</form>");`	Print out the end of form tag
`}`	Ends clause
`mysql_close($link);`	Close connection
`print ("<a href=\"choosecategory. php\">Choose category for new question </a>");`	Print out link to choose a new question
`?>`	End PHP
`</body></html>`	Closing HTML

The *checkanswer.php* script, shown in Table 15.6, handles the form presented by *askquestion.php*. It uses the PHP function for checking that a string, the answer submitted by the player, matches a regular expression, the answer pattern passed on as hidden data from the form. If there is a match, meaning the player is correct, the player record is updated with the score increased by the value of the question. In any case, a record is added to the history file.

TABLE 15.6   PHP Script for Checking Answer

`<html><head><title>Check answer </title> </head><body>`	Usual HTML
`<?`	Start PHP
`require("opendbq.php");`	Include connecting code
`$ans = StripSlashes($ans);`	Strip out the slashes from the answer pattern
`if (eregi($ans,$player_ans)) {`	If test on the result of a regular expression check
`    $corval='-1'; // anything non-zero stands for correct`	True clause: set `$corval` to –1, indicating a true value
`    print ("<h1> CORRECT! </h1><p>\n");`	Print a message
`    $query="UPDATE players set score = score + $value, lastplayed= '".$today."' where player_id='" .$player_id."'";`	Set query to update the player record with `playerid` matching the `$player_id` value passed from the form. Two changes are made: the score is increased by the `$value` passed from the form, and the date is changed to `$today` (also passed in from the form)

(continues)

TABLE 15.6   PHP Script for Checking Answer (*continued*)

`        }`	End the true clause
`else {`	Start the negative clause: incorrect answer
`    $corval='0'; //`	Zero stands for false
`    print ("<h1> WRONG! </h1> <p>\n");`	Print message
`    $query="UPDATE players set lastplayed='".$today."' where player_id='".$player_id."'";`	Set query to update players to change the lastplayed field to $today
`    }`	End the wrong answer clause
`mysql_db_query($DBname,$query,$link);`	Invoke the query
`$query="INSERT INTO history  values ('".$question_id."','".$player_id."', '".$today."','".$corval."')";`	Define new query string for inserting record into the history table
`mysql_db_query($DBname, $query,$link);`	Invoke query
`$query = "Select score from players where player_id='".$player_id."'";`	Define query to obtain player's score
`$result=mysql_db_query($DBname, $query,$link);`	Invoke query
`$score = mysql_result($result,0,"score");`	Extract score
`print ("<h2> The score is now " . $score. ".</h2> \n");`	Print score
`mysql_close($link);`	Close link to database
`?>`	End PHP
`<a href="choosecategory.php"><h2>Pick category for new question</h2> </a>`	Link to get a new question: link to *choosecategory.php* script
`</body></html>`	Closing HTML tags

The *showscores.php* script, shown in Table 15.7, does just that: show all the scores. It can be invoked directly or by using a link from *choosecategory.php*.

TABLE 15.7   The PHP Script to Display the Scores of All the Players

`<html><head><title>Show player scores</title> </head> <body>`	Usual HTML
`<?php`	Start PHP
`    require("opendbq.php");`	Include connecting code
`    $query="Select name, score from players order by score desc";`	Build query to get score information, in descending order (highest to lowest)

TABLE 15.7   *(continued)*

`$rs=mysql_db_query($DBname, $query, $link);`	Invoke query
`?>`	End PHP
`<table>`	Table tag
`<tr><td> Player Name </td> <td> Score </td> </tr>`	First row of table with column headings
`<?`	Start PHP
`while ($row=mysql_fetch_array($rs)){`	While loop: will iterate through the `$rs` recordset
`    print("<tr> <td>");`	Print table tags
`    print($row['name']);`	Print player name
`    print("</td><td>");`	Print table tags
`    print($row['score']);`	Print score
`    print("</td></tr>");`	Print table tags, ending row
`    }`	End while
`print("</table>");`	Print closing table tag
`?>`	End PHP
` `	Line break
`<a href="choosecategory.php">Choose category for new question </a>`	An a tag to go and choose a new category for a new question.
`</body> </html>`	Closing HTML tags

The *cleartables.php* script, shown in Table 15.8, is used to clear the tables as the user's request. To retain valid data, if the players or the questions table are cited for clearing, then the history table is also cleared. This is because the history table records point to each of these tables, and so the history table contents would be meaningless if the contents of either of these tables were deleted. In contrast, if the history table was deleted, the other two tables still would contain meaningful data. This script is a handler and also a form.

TABLE 15.8   PHP Script to Clear Tables

`<html><head><title>Get request and clear tables</title> </head><body>`	Usual HTML
`<?php`	Start PHP
`if ($submitted){`	If test for is this to be the handler
`  include("opendbq.php");`	Include the connecting code

(continues)

TABLE 15.8   PHP Script to Clear Tables *(continued)*

`if ($tname=='players' or $tname=='questions') {`	Do if test on $tname to check if the history table also needs to be cleared
`  $query="Delete from history";`	True clause: build the query to clear the history table
`  mysql_db_query($DBname, $query,$link);`	Invoke the query
`  }`	End the clause
`  $query="Delete from $tname";`	Build the query to delete the given table
`  mysql_db_query($DBname,$query,$link);`	Invoke the query
`  mysql_close($link);`	Close the link
`  Print("The records in the $tname table have been deleted. \n");`	Print a message
`}`	End the clause for handling a submitted form
`else {`	Else (clause for displaying the form)
`print ("<form action=cleartables.php method=post> \n");`	Print the form tag
`print ("<select name='tname'> \n");`	Print select tag
`print (" <option value='questions'> Questions (also history) </option> \n");`	Print as a first option Questions
`print (" <option value='history'>History of player actions </option> \n");`	Print as a second option History
`print (" <option value='players'>Players (also history) </option> \n");`	Print as a third option Players
`print ("</select> \n");`	End the select element to close off the options list
`print ("<input type=hidden name='submitted' value='TRUE'> \n");`	Print the hidden tag for the submitted value
`print ("<input type=submit value='Submit' name='submit'> \n");`	Print the tag for the Submit button
`print ("</form> \n");`	Print the form closing tag
`}`	End the clause for the form display
`?>`	End PHP
`<a href="choosecategory.php">Pick category of questions </a> <p><p>`	An a tag to go to pick a category for a new question
`<a href="inputquestions.php">Input new questions </a>`	An a tag to input new questions
`</body> </html>`	Closing HTML tags

The ASP and Access Implementation

The ASP implementation closely resembles the PHP implementation, with the exceptions noted previously. As has been suggested before, you might want to try to produce one or more of the ASP scripts on your own, using the PHP script and previous ASP scripts as models.

The *openconnquiz.asp* script, shown in Table 15.9, establishes the connection to the database. This file is included in all the other scripts. Note that the connection mode is set to be read/write in this script.

TABLE 15.9   ASP/JavaScript Script to Establish Connection to Database

`<%`	Start ASP
`Conn = Server.CreateObject ("ADODB.Connection");`	Create connection object
`Conn.Mode = 3  ;`	Set mode
`strConnect = "Driver={Microsoft Access Driver (*.mdb)};" + "DBQ=" + Server.MapPath("quizasp.mdb") ;`	Define a connection string that holds the driver and specific filename for the database
`  Conn.Open (strConnect, "admin", "") ;`	Open the connection, using standard values for user and password
`%>`	End ASP

The *inputquestions.asp* script, shown in Table 15.10, allows a user to add questions to the questions table. The script serves as a handler of a form and a presenter of a form.

TABLE 15.10   ASP/JavaScript Script to Add a New Question

`<%@ Language=JavaScript %>`	Define the language
`<html><head><title>Input and submit questions to quizasp db </title></head><body>`	Standard HTML
`<!– #include file="openconnquiz.asp"  –>`	Include the connecting code
`<%`	Start ASP
`var submitted=String(Request.Form ("submitted"));`	Extract the submitted flag
`if (submitted !="undefined") {`	If the form has been shown
`  var question = String(Request.Form ("question"));`	Extract the question text passed as form data
`  var ans = String(Request.Form("ans"));`	Extract the ans text

(continues)

TABLE 15.10   ASP/JavaScript Script to Add a New Question *(continued)*

`var valuex = parseInt(Request.Form ("value"));`	Extract the point value
`var cat = String(Request.Form("cat"));`	Extract the category
`var fields = " (question, answerpattern, category, points) ";`	Begin formation of the insert query. The fields part is constant
`var valuesx = " VALUES ('"+question+"', '" + ans +"', '" + cat +"', " + valuex +")";`	Form the values part of the query
`var query="INSERT INTO questions " + fields + valuesx;`	Build the complete query
`Response.Write("Insert query is: " + query);`	For debugging, display the query
`if (Conn.Execute(query))`	Execute the query. Do a check
`{Response.Write(" Question was successfully entered.  ");}`	Display the message that the question was successfully entered
`else {Response.Write("Question was NOT entered. "); }`	Display the message that the question was not successfully entered
`Conn.Close();`	Close the connection
`Response.Write("<a href= \"inputquestions.asp\"> Submit another question </a>  ");`	Display a link to this script to submit another question
`}  // ends if form was submitted.`	End the clause for handling a form
`else {`	Start the clause to display the form
`%>`	End ASP
`<h1>Add a question to the databank of questions.  </h1>`	HTML heading
`<%`	Start ASP
`var sq ="SELECT * from questions";`	Create a query (sq) to get all the questions
`Response.Write("Questions in database  ");`	Display a heading
`rs=Server.CreateObject("ADODB. RecordSet");`	Create a recordset object
`rs.Open (sq,Conn);`	Invoke the query
`while (!(rs.EOF)){`	While loop: iterates through all the questions. (See *Exercises* section)
`Response.Write(" " + String (rs.fields.item("question"))+ " Category: "+ String(rs.fields.item ("category"))+ " ");`	Display questions, outputting line breaks in between

TABLE 15.10   (*continued*)

`rs.move(1);`	Advance to next record
`}  // end while`	End while
`%>`	Close ASP
`<form action="inputquestions.asp" method="POST"> `	Form tag
`Text of question <input type=text name="question" size=50>  `	Input tag for question text
`Answer pattern <input type=text name="ans" size=50>  `	Input tag for answer pattern text
`Category <input type=text name="cat" size=30>  `	Input tag for category
`Value <input type=text name="value" size=6> `	Input tag for value. Note: "value" is our name for this input
`<input type=hidden name="submitted" value="True"> `	Input tag for the submitted flag
`<input type=submit name="submit" value="Submit question!"> `	Tag for submit button
`</form>`	End form
`<%`	Start ASP
`}`	Close clause for presenting form
`%>`	Close ASP
`</body> </html>`	Close HTML

The *choosecategory* script, shown in Table 15.11, is the first of three scripts for playing the game. The *choosecategory* script contains a form that is handled by `askquestion` as specified by the action attribute of the form. The code checks if a session value has been set with the name of the current player and, if so, displays it as the value of an input box.

TABLE 15.11   Initial ASP/JavaScript for Signing In and Selecting a Category

`<%@ Language=JavaScript %>`	Set language
`<html><head><title>Sign in and select category </title></head><body>`	Usual HTML
`<h1> Welcome to the Quiz </h1>  `	Heading
`<h3> Sign in and select a category for your question </h3>`	Instructions

(*continues*)

TABLE 15.11 **Initial ASP/JavaScript for Signing In and Selecting a Category** *(continued)*

`<form action="askquestion.asp" method=post>`	Form tag
`<p>Name <input type=text name='player' size=30`	Player name tag
`<%`	Start ASP
`currentplayer=String(Session ("currentplayer"));`	Extract session value
`if (currentplayer != "undefined") {`	Check if the session value was defined
`    Response.Write("VALUE= "+ currentplayer+"> ");`	If so, display this as the value for the input tag
`    }`	Close the clause
`else {`	Start the `else` clause
`    Response.Write("> ");`	Simply close the input tag
`    }`	Close the clause
`%>`	Close ASP
`<p>Pick a category <select name=pickedcategory>`	Instructions to player and select tag, which starts the pull-down list
`<!- #include file="openconnquiz.asp" ->`	Include the connecting code
`<%`	Start ASP
`query="SELECT DISTINCT category FROM questions";`	Build a query to get the distinct categories
`rs=Server.CreateObject ("ADODB.RecordSet");`	Create a `recordset` object
`rs.Open(query,Conn);`	Invoke the query
`while (!(rs.EOF))`	`While` loop: iterates over recordset holding categories
`{ cat=String(rs.fields.item ("category"));`	Extract the category value
`  Response.Write("<option value="+cat +">"+cat+"</option> \n");`	Display the category as an option
`  rs.Move(1);`	Advance to the next category
`}`	Close `while` loop
`Conn.close();`	Close connection
`Response.Write("</select>");`	Output closing select (ending the pulldown list)
`Response.Write("<input type=submit name=submit value=\"Choose!\">  \n");`	Output input tag for submit button: in this case, the label is `"Choose!"`

TABLE 15.11   (*continued*)

`Response.Write("</form>");`	Output end of form tag
`%>`	Close ASP
` `	Line break
`<a href="showscores.asp">Show scores of players. </a>`	An a tag to allow player to go to *showscores* script
`</body></html>`	Closing HTML

The *askquestion.asp* script, shown in Table 15.12, uses the information passed from the *choosecategory* script to find a question. This script must apply the policies of the game concerning appropriate questions: a player is not asked any question answered correctly or asked the same day. This requires use of a LEFT JOIN. The ASP script uses a permanent table as a temporary table: all old records are deleted.

TABLE 15.12   ASP/JavaScript for Choosing an Appropriate Question

`<%@ Language=JavaScript %>`	Set language
`<%`	Start ASP
`player=String(Request.Form("player"));`	Extract from the form data the player name
`Session("currentplayer")=player;`	Set the session value currentplayer to be this name
`pickedcategory=String(Request.Form ("pickedcategory"));`	Extract category
`Response.Write(" The selected category is: "+pickedcategory);`	Display the category. This could be considered a debugging statement
`%>`	Close ASP
`<html><head><title>Fetch appropriate question from category and ask </title></head><body>`	Standard HTML
`<%`	Start ASP
`dx= new Date();`	Get the date
`today = dx.getDate()+"-"+ dx.getMonth()+"-"+dx.getFullYear();`	Create today with a formatted form of the date. This will be used for immediate display and to compare with records from the history table
`Response.Write(" Today is "+today+"  \n");`	Create today with a formatted form

(*continues*)

TABLE 15.12 ASP/JavaScript for Choosing an Appropriate Question (*continued*)

`Response.Write("Here is your question, "+player+". ");`	Display customized instruction
`%>`	Close ASP
`<!- #include file="openconnquiz.asp"  ->`	Include the connecting code
`<!- #include file="random.asp" ->`	Include code to get random question
`<%`	Start ASP
`query="SELECT name, player_id, lastplayed, score from players where name='"+player+"'";`	Build the query to get player information
`rs=Server.CreateObject ("ADODB.RecordSet");`	Create a `recordset` object
`rs.Open(query,Conn, 1, 3);`	Invoke the query. Need the locking and cursor settings to obtain the count of records.
`if (rs.RecordCount==0) {`	If no information (meaning this player has not played)
`    query2 = "INSERT INTO players (name, lastplayed, score) values ('"+player+"', '"+today+"','0')";`	Build a query to insert a new record into the players table
`    Conn.Execute(query2);`	Execute the query
`    query="SELECT player_id from players where name='"+player+"'";`	Build a query to obtain the `player_id` of the record just created
`rs1=Server.CreateObject ("ADODB.RecordSet");`	Create a `recordset` object
`    rs1.Open(query, Conn, 1, 3);`	Invoke the query
`player_id=String(rs1.fields.item ("player_id"));`	Extract the `player_id` and store in variable
`    }`	Close clause for no prior record for player
`else {`	Start `else` clause
`    player_id = String(rs.fields. item("player_id")); // take first 0th record`	Extract the `player_id` from the recordset
`    }`	Close clause
`query="DELETE * from past";`	Form a query to delete the records from past
`Conn.Execute(query);`	Execute query

TABLE 15.12   *(continued)*

`query= "SELECT question_id FROM history where (player_id="+player_id;`	Start formation of query to get questions from history that were answered correctly or asked today
`query= query + " AND (whenplayed= #"+today+"# OR correct=Yes))";`	Continue forming query
`rs = Server.CreateObject ("ADODB.Recordset");`	Create `recordset` object
`rs.Open(query, Conn, 1, 3);`	Execute query
`NoR=rs.RecordCount;`	Obtain count of records
`if (NoR>0) {`	If there were prior relevant questions
`query= "SELECT question_id FROM history where (player_id="+player_id;`	Start building query that will populate the past table
`query= query + " AND (whenplayed= #"+today+"# OR correct=Yes))";`	Continue
`    query="INSERT into past "+query;`	Continue
`    Conn.Execute(query);`	Execute the query to populate the past table
`    sel = "SELECT questions.question_id, question, answerpattern, points from questions";`	Start to form another query (in the `sel` string) that will pick up all questions...
`    sel =sel + " LEFT JOIN past ON questions.question_id = past.question_id WHERE ";`	Using the `LEFT JOIN` mechanism
`    sel = sel + " category='" + pickedcategory + "' AND past.question_id IS NULL";`	Questions that are in the category and not in the past table (by the `past.question_id` being null after the LEFT JOIN)
`    }`	Close clause
`else {`	Start clause for no relevant past questions
`    sel="SELECT question_id, question, answerpattern, points from questions ";`	Start forming of `sel`
`    sel= sel + " WHERE category= '" + pickedcategory+ "'";`	Continue with `sel`
`    }`	Close the `else` clause
`rs3=Server.CreateObject("ADODB. RecordSet");`	Create yet another `recordset` object
`rs3.Open(sel, Conn, 1, 3);`	Invoke the query

(continues)

TABLE 15.12   ASP/JavaScript for Choosing an Appropriate Question (*continued*)

`NoR=rs3.RecordCount;`	Obtain the `recordcount`
`if (NoR==0) {`	Check if there were any appropriate questions
`Response.Write("  No appropriate questions in databank. Pick new category.  \n");`	If none, write out message
`}`	Close clause
`else`	`Else`
`{ if (NoR > 1) {`	Need to check if there was more than one question. If more than one, apply a random procedure to get question
`choice=rand(NoR-1);`	Invoke `rand` (in the *random.asp* file) to get choice
`Response.Write(" Choice is: "+choice);`	Debugging statement
`}`	Close clause for more than one
`else {`	Start `else` clause
`choice=0;}`	Set `choice` to zero for the situation with just one question
`rs3.Move(choice,1);`	Advance in the recordset choice positions, starting from the first record
`question_id = rs3.fields.item ("question_id");`	Extract the `question_id`
`question    = rs3.fields.item ("question");`	Extract the question text
`ans         = rs3.fields.item ("answerpattern");`	Extract the answerpattern text
`points      = rs3.fields.item("points");`	Extract the point value
`Response.Write("<h3><p> The question is   "+question+"???  \n");`	Display the question (text)
`Response.Write("<form action= \"checkanswer.asp\" Method=post>  \n");`	Output a form, with the action going to *checkanswer.asp*
`Response.Write("<input type=text name=player_ans size=50> \n");`	Output the input tag to hold the player's answer
`Response.Write("<input type=submit name=submit value='Submit answer'>  \n");`	Output the Submit button

TABLE 15.12   (*continued*)

`Response.Write("<input type=hidden name=ans value='"+ans+"'> \n");`	Output as a hidden tag the actual answer pattern (from the database)
`Response.Write("<input type=hidden name=pval value='"+points+"'> \n");`	Output as a hidden tag the points
`Response.Write("<input type=hidden name=question_id value='"+question_id +"'> \n");`	Output as a hidden tag the question_id. This is for use when creating and inserting the history record
`Response.Write("<input type=hidden name=player_id value='"+player_id+"'>  \n");`	Output as a hidden tag the player_id. Used in the history record
`Response.Write("<input type=hidden name=today value='"+today+"'> \n");`	Output as a hidden tag the today value. Used in the hidden record
`Response.Write("</form>");`	Output the close of form tag
`}`	End clause for appropriate questions
`Conn.Close();`	Close the connection
`Response.Write("<a href=\"choosecategory. asp\">Choose category for new question </a>");`	Output an <a> tag to choose a category and get a new question
`%>`	Close ASP
`</body></html>`	Closing HTML

The *checkanswer.asp* script, shown in Table 15.13, performs the check on the player's answer by comparing it to the value given in the database. The regular expression search method of string objects is used. The code makes an insertion into the history table and updates the player's record in the players table.

TABLE 15.13   ASP/JavaScript Script to Check Answer

`<%@ Language=JavaScript %>`	Set language
`<html><head><title>Check answer </title> </head><body>`	HTML
`<!- #include file="openconnquiz.asp"  ->`	Include the connecting code
`<%`	Start ASP
`ans=String(Request.Form("ans"));`	Extract ans from the form data. This is the database answer pattern
`player_ans=String(Request.Form ("player_ans"));`	Extract the player's answer

(*continues*)

TABLE 15.13 **ASP/JavaScript Script to Check Answer** (*continued*)

`pval=parseInt(Request.Form("pval"));`	Extract the points
`question_id=parseInt(Request.Form` `("question_id"));`	Extract the question_id
`today=String(Request.Form("today"));`	Extract the date
`player_id=String(Request.Form` `("player_id"));`	Extract the player_id
`if (player_ans.search(ans)>-1){`	Do the check. If it is correct, indicated by a return value greater than −1 (remember strings begin with zero)
`    corval='Yes'; //`	Access wants yes/no
`    Response.Write("<h1> CORRECT!` `</h1><p>\n");`	Write out result
`    query="UPDATE players set score` `= score + "+pval+", lastplayed=` `'"+today+"' where player_id="+player_id;`	Define a query to update the player's record: increment score and modify lastplayed field
`        }`	End clause
`else {`	Else clause: player got it wrong
`    corval='No';`	Set the variable
`    Response.Write("<h1> WRONG!` `</h1> <p>\n");`	Write out result
`    query="UPDATE players set` `lastplayed='"+today+"' where player_id=` `"+player_id;`	Define a query to update the player's record, just changing the lastplayed field
`        }`	End the clause
`Conn.Execute(query);`	Execute the query (could be either one)
`query="INSERT INTO history (question_id,` `player_id, whenplayed, correct) values` `("+question_id+","+player_id+",` `#"+today+"#,"+corval+")";`	Build a query to insert a record into the history file
`Conn.Execute(query);`	Execute the query
`Conn.Close();`	Close the connection
`%>`	Close ASP
`<a href="choosecategory.asp"><h2>Pick` `category for new question</h2> </a>`	An a link to pick a category for a new questions
`</body></html>`	Closing HTML

The *random.asp* code, shown in Table 15.14, could easily be incorporated into the calling routine.

TABLE 15.14   ASP/JavaScript File Defining the rand Function

`<%`	Start ASP
`function rand(number) {`	Function header
`    choice= Math.floor(Math.random()*(number+1))`	Use `Math` methods to get a choice between 0 and the number passed as a parameter (including both 0 and the number as possibilities)
`    return choice;`	Return the value
`}`	Close the function
`%>`	End ASP

The *showscores.asp* script, shown in Table 15.15, displays the scores of each player.

TABLE 15.15   The ASP/JavaScript Script for Displaying Scores

`<%@ Language=JavaScript %>`	Set the language
`<html><head><title>Show player scores</title> </head><body>`	Standard HTML
`<!– #include file="openconnquiz.asp"  –>`	Include the connecting code
`<%`	Start ASP
`rs=Server.CreateObject("ADODB.RecordSet");`	Create a recordset object
`query="Select name, score from players order by score desc";`	Create a query
`rs.Open(query, Conn);`	Invoke the query
`%>`	Close ASP
`<table><tr><td> Player Name </td> <td> Score </td> </tr>`	Table tags, including column headings
`<%`	Start ASP
`while (! (rs.EOF)){`	`While` loop: iterate through all players.
`    Response.Write("<tr> <td>");`	Output table tags
`    Response.Write(String(rs.fields.item("name")));`	Output player's name, extracted from recordset
`    Response.Write("</td><td>");`	Output table tags
`    Response.Write(String(rs.fields.item("score")));`	Output player's score, extracted from recordset

(continues)

TABLE 15.15 The ASP/JavaScript Script for Displaying Scores *(continued)*

`Response.Write("</td></tr>");`	Output table tags
`rs.move(1);`	Advance to next record in recordset
`}`	Close while
`Response.Write("</table>");`	Output close of table
`%>`	Close ASP
` `	Line break
`<a href="choosecategory.asp">Choose category for new question </a>`	An a tag to choose a category for a new question
`</body></html>`	Closing HTML

REFLECTION

The quiz show application can be the basis of a game or an educational application. It makes use of many features of middleware and databases, including temporary tables and LEFT JOINs.

When you master the examples in this text, you will be in a position to build many different types of applications.

EXERCISES, QUESTIONS, AND PROJECTS

1. Enhance the *inputquestions* scripts by validating the input. Specifically, check that the value is a number. Do research and implement a way to validate the answer pattern for a question as being a valid regular expression. It would also be appropriate to add functions (`addslashes` and `stripslashes` for PHP, and escape and unescape for ASP/JavaScript) to handle special characters.
2. Modify the system by adding a categories table. A possible design is for the fields to be `category_id`, `category_name`, and `category_description`. Questions must refer to one of the given categories.
3. Design and add a script or scripts to edit one or more of the fields in the questions table. You can then remove the listing of all the questions from the inputquestions scripts.
4. Enhance the *showscores* scripts to show when each player last played the game. This field is not used in the present implementation.
5. The questions in the database each have a field for points. This field could be any number. Modify this field to be a level, say from 1 to 5, indicating easiest, easy, moderate, difficult, most difficult, or the words indicating level. You can investigate MySQL and Access for support of a datatype

called *enumerated types*. Modify the inputquestions scripts to offer a radio box instead of a field for the level. Then, modify choosecategory to accept a level indication.

6. A name submitted by a person generally is not considered distinctive enough. Develop a system in which the player name is checked against existing names, and the player asked to confirm if he or she was the player who last played on a given date and had a given score. Alternatively, design and develop an ID and password system.

16

SCALING UP
YOUR APPLICATION

The goal of this chapter is to identify certain issues that you must address when building a robust application for your organization. The sample code demonstrates a way to implement a system of user IDs and passwords, and makes use of sessions.

BACKGROUND

Building and maintaining an application for real-world use is a substantial undertaking. The basis is the understanding of Web technologies and database technologies that you have gained from studying this text, implementing the examples, and working on the exercises. However, most applications will require attention to additional matters. In this section, we will provide a brief introduction to several issues that can be critical to the operation of applications.

The first sentence of this section contained hints of important, but frequently overlooked, aspects of application development. You must not only build an application, you need to maintain it. Furthermore, you are building the application for use in the real world. The context of operation is important. You need to pay attention to how this application relates to everything else going on in your own organization, and how it fits within the life of the users. This involves keeping track of the actual usage and making modifications as required. You might encounter problems of success: your site might have more business than you anticipated. This can cause changes in the storage space allotted on the server for the application. It also could mean that you need to focus on controlling concurrent access to the database by multiple users. You also must provide for problems such as electrical outages and attacks by hackers. Particular instances of such problems might be beyond your control, but it is your responsibility to build a system for detection and recovery. One unpleasant thing to consider is how to guard against mis-use of the information by insiders of your organization.

Facilities exist both in the database management systems (DBMSs) products and in more elaborate coding of PHP and ASP that support the building and maintaining of robust applications. Plug-ins are available for a fee, and open-source developers continue to provide new offerings. Web Services, described briefly in the next chapter, will emerge as an important category of tools. You need to consider and continually monitor the specific circumstances of your situation to determine what is required.

CONCEPTUAL EXPLANATION

This section presents general concepts to help you in the process of refining your application for implementation.

Context

Your database Web application exists in the context of your entire organization. One formal definition of a computer information system is that it consists of hardware, software, people, and procedures built to provide a function for a specific group of users. It is easy to forget the "people and procedures" while you are struggling with programming. You need to identify the ways in which users come to the first script of your application. What are their expectations? Are they prepared to fill out the form or forms that your scripts present?

If everything goes well, you might need to determine what follow-up action is required. This is sometimes called "the back office" operation. A problem with early e-commerce businesses was inadequate back-office capability. You can implement some of the back office application using middleware scripts. However, if your business contains the shipping of tangible goods, you will need ways to initiate acts such as collecting goods from warehouses and shipping them to your customers. A slang way of describing this is going from moving bits to moving atoms.

When you build a Web application, you probably need to include ways for your user (client, customer) to contact you. This might be a link to send e-mail or an e-mail address, a telephone number, or an address. You need to make sure someone knowledgeable is in place to receive these messages or calls.

Offensive and Defensive Interface Design

Many of the sample applications presented in this text involved someone filling out a form, or clicking on hyperlinks that had the effect of filling out a form. You need to design these interfaces for your clientele to minimize the chances of erroneous information coming into the system. You need what can be called *offensive* and *defensive measures*. An offensive measure would involve a design that does not give the user a chance to make a mistake. Examples of this are the use of radio buttons or drop-down lists as opposed to text boxes. Text boxes allow the user to enter anything. Buttons and lists minimize the choices. Radio buttons prevent more than one choice from being selected. The use of default values might be appropriate, but require careful planning. You also need to consider the possibility that the default value will be overlooked and remain unchanged even when your user intended to change it.

Defensive measures include checking the input and displaying the values to be confirmed by the user. You can use regular expressions to check values input by users if the input must conform to a known pattern. You can do online searches to find regular expressions for many common situations.

If your database product allows you to specify relationships and other conditions on fields, then the DBMS will signal an error if a query, such as an INSERT, has any problems. You need to do what is termed "trap" or "catch" the error to prevent your user from seeing it. Your PHP or ASP code then would take the appropriate action.

An additional technique is to present the user with the values for confirmation. This can try the user's patience. However, it is an accepted practice by many online organizations, and if the transaction is important enough—for example, if it involves a significant amount of money—users will accept the burden of making one more click.

Scaling Up

When building an application, you need to analyze the situation in order to do a sizing of the requirements. The tables shown in applications in the text were quite small. You need to estimate how big the tables will become once the system is in operation. If the application already exists, you will have historical data to support your estimates. Your server administration probably will request sizing information. The estimates will help determine how long certain operations take that require searching whole tables.

Most DBMS products have facilities for improving the performance of queries. You can, for example, specify that certain fields are to be stored as indexes (note: this spelling often is used in technical publications). This requires extra space, but speeds up queries involving these fields. Another facility is called "stored procedures." This speeds up the performance of an SQL statement at what generally is a modest cost in space.

You might choose to change the design of certain pages as the size of tables increases. The origami store displayed all the products in one page. You might choose to display a fixed number at a time. This is termed *paging*. You can do this directly using the LIMIT clause in the SQL statements, or you can use facilities present in the database product. Another alternative is to incorporate additional fields to specify categories.

Backup and Recovery

An unfortunate fact is that computers and networks do go down, perhaps because of programming errors, but also because of hardware failures, electrical problems, or other catastrophes. It is a good practice to establish a procedure of scheduled backing up of all the data. You can also incorporate keeping a record of all modifications to the database in what is called a *log file*. This is another area in which the database products promise and, indeed, do provide facilities.

Transactions

The concept of transaction refers to the set or sequence of steps required for a single operation. For example, the quiz show application modified the players table and the history table after determining whether the player's answer to a question was correct or incorrect. For a banking operation, a transaction could involve checking that the customer's account contained enough money to cover a withdrawal, making the withdrawal by signaling to the ATM machine to dispense the money, writing out a record to a history file, and updating the account to reflect the new total. You want the entire transaction or none of it to occur.

When you are building an application for widespread use, you need to consider the possibility that more than one person might be using your system at any one time. The DBMS driver that executes the SQL statement passed from the middleware script will make sure that an update to a single table is completed before another update is started. However, what if the transactions involved multiple tables? You do not want two people with access to the same account to make changes at the same time, because that might prevent accurate operations. Generally, you do not want to lock out other access during a time period when your customers or clients are staring at the computer screen, because this could be an unlimited period of time. Instead, a technique is to check the data a second time just before the update to make sure that it still meets the condition for making the change.

Transactions also are important in designing systems that are robust with respect to system failures. If the system failed—say, due to an electrical outage—in the middle of a transaction, you want a method for what is termed *rolling back* the system to the state before the transaction began.

The solution to these problems making use of the concept of transaction depends on the features of the DBMS. Some have features that allow you to define transactions explicitly. Others provide simpler mechanisms such as locking tables to prevent other access. Incorrect use of locking can cause problems, such as what is called "deadly embrace" when each of two or more processes is waiting for the other(s) to complete. This can cause an entire system to stop operation.

Security

The security of the information of your application—that is, decreasing the possibility of someone other than your customer or client viewing information and even changing it—is a complex issue. Tools and techniques such as encryption, passwords, and log files exist to decrease the chances of inappropriate viewing or changing information, although no one would claim that any system is absolutely safe. In most cases, you and your clients need to make tradeoffs of security versus convenience and other costs.

Opportunities for security incursions exist at different places or stages of the application. The techniques to improve security vary. Let us follow the path of information from your users from when they enter it into forms at their computer to the server and then to the database.

The term *authentication* refers to methods for ensuring that someone such as your users, customers, and clients can be confirmed to be who they claim to be. This is normally done with some type of identification and password system. In most cases, the customers or clients are given the opportunity to select their own IDs and passwords. If the ID has already been used, the system tells the person to try again. Frequently, the system sets a minimal size for IDs and/or passwords. This is the approach demonstrated in the *Examples* section. However, you should keep in mind that user-created passwords often are easy to guess. If your application demands a heightened level of security, consider using tools such as the md5 function used in the *Examples* section to generate randomly constructed combinations of letters and numbers for passwords. In addition, consider establishing a schedule for changing passwords periodically.

You can provide what we can call "over-the-shoulder" security by using the input type of password for certain fields of forms and by specifying the method of a form to be POST and not GET. Someone standing behind your client and "looking over his or her shoulder" would not see any information entered into form fields that were designated password as they were being typed. If the method was GET, no one would see information passed in query strings. The latter means that if you did use GET during the debugging of your application, you will have to make changes in the code. If you passed along information in a query string, possibly as part of a hyperlink, consider whether the information would be considered private. People are accustomed to typing in a password without the feedback of seeing the characters. For the other information, most people need to see what they type, even if they consider the information sensitive. You need to depend on your clients to maintain their own privacy.

For both PHP and ASP, we have demonstrated use of shortcuts for form input. Since someone could find out the purpose of a script and trick it by using a link with a query string, you might consider only using the long forms.

Before virtually leaving the client computer, you need to consider that information entered into the forms of your application might be left on that computer after the person has left. This could happen because of cookies you implemented, cached pages, or the actions of the operating system that asks the users if they want to save information entered into a form. You really cannot protect your clients from themselves, but you might consider issuing a warning to erase cached pages and provide an option to not create a cookie if the person is on a public computer. The mini-application in the *Examples* section contains a script that ends the session, thus destroying the authentication setting that allowed access to the application pages.

The next stage for data is to travel over the communications links to the server. The topic is beyond the scope of this text, but you can arrange for a secure connection and a secure server. This will mean that form data and the request for the page itself will be encrypted and then decrypted. The information, whether it is passed via the query string or the HTTP headers, will be hidden from prying eyes.

You might choose to reconfirm the authenticity of the user on each script of your application. This would be appropriate if different scripts required different levels of rights. In addition, checking on each page would prevent malicious action from someone navigating directly to a particular script through special knowledge of the application.

The next stage of security concerns the database itself. The issue is very delicate, because the main category of trespasses are members of your own organization. What you must rely on here are facilities of the database products and your own code and procedures. One technique to consider for passwords is to store them in an encrypted form. Programs (md5 and crypt) exist for so-called one-way encryption. The "one-way" refers to the fact that there does not exist an easy way to get the original plain text back from the encrypted text. You might now ask how you make use of this. The answer is that you store the original password in the encrypted format and compare only encrypted versions. This will be shown in the *Examples* section.

EXAMPLES

ON THE CD

The scripts in this section will demonstrate the use of PHP and MySQL for authentication of users. You will find the code for the authentication project on the CD-ROM in the folder named chapter16code. The mini-application consists of six scripts:

- *createpasswordtable.php* creates a stand-alone table with fields for user ID and for the password encrypted using the md5 program. The md5 program uses standard encryption techniques to produce a 32-character string.
- *register.php* is a form and a form handler for accepting new IDs and passwords. If the ID already exists in the database, the user is prompted to try again.
- *signin.php* is a form and a form handler for accepting an ID and a password. If the ID and password pair exist in the database, a session variable is set and the user can continue to a page of the application.
- *page.php* essentially is a place holder for a real application. If users navigate to this page without signing in, they will see a message with a link telling them to go sign in. If they are signed in, as indicated by the presence of a session variable, they see a message indicating this and a link to sign out.
- *endsession.php* says goodbye to the user and destroys the session.
- *showids.php* would not be part of a regular application, but is produced here for you to use to examine the encrypted passwords.

Although the reasoning in this exposition was to produce a stand-alone system for you to study, it still would make sense when building an entire application to define a distinct table for IDs and passwords. You might detect that this table is part of the shopping cart application database. Notice that this code, shown in Table 16.1, resembles other code for creating MySQL tables. The records in the table have two fields.

TABLE 16.1   PHP Code to Create Tables for Passwords

`<?php`	Start PHP
`function createtable($tname,$fields) {`	Header for function
`global $DBname, $link;`	Use global values for database and link. Assumes connection has been made
`$query="CREATE TABLE ".$tname." (".$fields.")";`	Define query
`if (mysql_db_query($DBname,$query, $link)) {`	Invoke query and test if it worked
`    print ("The table, $tname, was created successfully. \n");}`	Print positive message
`else {`	Else
`    print ("The table, $tname, was not created.  \n");}`	Print negative message: table was not created
`}`	Ends function definition
`?>`	End PHP
`<html><head><title>Creating password table </title> </head><body>`	HTML starting tags
`<?php`	Start PHP
`require("opendbo.php");`	Connecting to database
`$tname = "ptable";`	Set name of table
`$fields="uid char(10) NOT NULL PRIMARY KEY, pass char(32)";`	Define fields
`createtable($tname, $fields);`	Invoke function to create table
`mysql_close($link);`	Close link
`?>`	End PHP
`</body></html>`	Closing HTML tags

The *register.php* script, shown in Table 16.2, is invoked to establish a new user. Anyone can register as long as he or she choose a unique ID. The password is encrypted for storage in the database. Figure 16.1 shows how the screen looks after filling out the form.

TABLE 16.2   PHP Code for Registration

`<html><head><title>Registering</title> </head><body>`	Starting HTML tags
`<?php`	Start PHP
`require("opendbo.php");`	Connecting code

TABLE 16.2   (*continued*)

`$tname = "ptable";`	Set name of table
`if (@($submitted)) {`	If test to see if form has been submitted
`$pword1 = trim($pword1);`	Trims the input (removing white space)
`$pword2 = trim($pword2);`	Trims the input
`$uid = trim($uid);`	Trims the input
`$oksofar = true;`	Sets the oksofar variable, which might be set to false if there are any problems
`$pattern="^[a-z0-9]{4,10}$";`	Sets up a pattern specifying between 4 to 10 alphanumeric characters
`if (!eregi($pattern,$uid)){`	Does a case-insensitive test on the user ID
`print ("Please make your id a combination ");`	If the test fails, prints instructions…
`print ("of at least 4 and not more than 10 alphanumeric characters. ");`	… continues with instructions
`print ("Use the BACK function on your browser to return to the form.");`	More instructions
`$oksofar = false;`	Sets the oksofar variable to false.
`}`	End of clause for first test
`if (!eregi($pattern,$pword1)){`	Checks the first password for its format
`print ("Please make your password a combination ");`	If the test fails, prints instructions…
`print ("of at least 4 and not more than 10 alphanumeric characters.   ");`	…continues with instructions
`print ("Use the BACK function on your browser to return to the form.");`	More instructions
`$oksofar = false;`	Sets the oksofar variable to false
`}`	End of clause for test
`if (StrCmp($pword1,$pword2)!=0) {`	Test to see if the user entered two identical copies of the password. This requires the use of the StrCmp function for comparison of strings
`print ("The two passwords did not match. Please try again. ");`	If test fails, prints out message
`print ("Use the BACK function on your browser to return to the form.");`	Prints out instructions

(*continues*)

TABLE 16.2   PHP Code for Registration (*continued*)

`$oksofar = false;`	Sets the oksofar variable to false
`}`	End of clause for test
`$query = "Select * from ptable where uid='$uid'";`	Define query to check if the user ID is already in the table
`$result=mysql_db_query($DBname, $query, $link);`	Invoke query
`if (mysql_num_rows($result)!=0) {`	If this query produced a recordset with more than zero rows—that is, there was an entry with that ID
`print ("The id is already taken. Please try again. ");`	Print out message to try again.
`print ("Use the BACK function on your browser to return to the form.");`	More instructions
`$oksofar = false;`	Set oksofar variable to false
`}`	End of clause for test
`if ($oksofar) {`	If there have been no problems
`$pw1 = md5($pword1);`	Encrypt the password.
`$query = "INSERT INTO $tname values ('$uid','$pw1')";`	Define a query to insert a new record in the table
`$result = mysql_db_query($DBname, $query, $link);`	Invoke the query
`if ($result) {`	Check on result
`print("Registration successful. \n");`	Print positive message
`}`	End of clause
`else {`	Else
`print ("Registration not successful.  \n");`	Print negative message
`}`	End of clause
`}`	End of if no problems
`$submitted = FALSE;`	Reset submitted variable
`mysql_close($link);`	Close link
`}`	ends if submitted
`else {`	Else (present form)
`print ("<h1>Register \n </h1> ");`	Print out heading
`print ("Create a user id and a password. Make each a combination ");`	Print out instructions

TABLE 16.2   *(continued)*

print ("of at least 4 and not more than 10 alphanumeric characters. ");	....continue with instructions
print ("<form action=\"register. php\" method=post>\n");	Print out form tag
print ("User name: <input type=text name=\"uid\" size=10> \n");	Print out username tag (that is, user ID)
print ("Password: <input type=password name=\"pword1\" size=10> \n");	Print out input tag for password as a password tag so typing is not revealed
print ("Enter password again: <input type=password name=\"pword2\" size=10> \n");	Print out second input tag
print ("<input type=hidden name=\"submitted\" value=\"True\"> \n");	Print out hidden tag to hold submitted value
print ("<input type=submit name=\"submit\" value=\"Sign up!\"> \n");	Print out Submit button
print ("</form> \n");	Print out form end tag
}	End of clause for form not submitted
?>	Close PHP
</body> </html>	Closing HTML

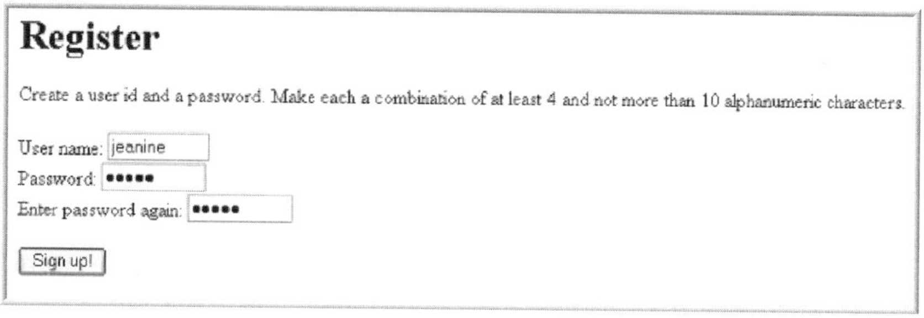

FIGURE 16.1   Form for creating user ID and password.

The script presents and handles the form. Note that several tests are done on the input.

The signin PHP script, shown in Table 16.3, is for a registered user to sign in, giving ID and password. Figure 16.2 shows the screen.

TABLE 16.3   PHP Code for Signing In

`<?php`	Start PHP
`if (@($submitted)) {`	Check if form has been submitted
`    $pword1 = trim($pword1);`	Trim the password
`    $uid = trim($uid);`	Trim the user id
`    $oksofar = true;`	Set oksofar to true
`    $pw1= md5($pword1);`	Encrypt the submitted password
`    require("opendbo.php");`	Connecting to the database
`    $query = "Select * from ptable where uid='$uid' and pass='$pw1'";`	Define the query
`    $result=mysql_db_query($DBname, $query, $link);`	Invoke the query
`    if (mysql_num_rows($result)==0) {`	If test: checks for a match
`      print ("No match for id and password. ");`	If test fails, that is, there is no match, prints a message
`      print ("Use the BACK function on your browser to return to the form.");`	Prints instructions
`      $oksofar = false;`	Set oksofar variable to false
`    }`	Ends clause for test
`    if ($oksofar) {`	If there was a match, indicated by oksofar still being true
`      session_register("user");`	Register user as a variable
`      $user=$uid;`	Set user to the value $uid
`      print("Sign in okay as $user. <a href='page.php'>Continue. </a>");`	Print out message and give option to continue
`    }`	End clause
`    $submitted = FALSE;`	Set submitted variable to false
`    mysql_close($link);`	Close link
`}`	ends if submitted
`else {`	Else clause (to present a form)
`?>`	Ends PHP
`<html><head><title>Sign in</title></head><body>`	Regular HTML tags
`<h1>Sign in </h1>`	Heading
`<form action="signin.php" method=post>`	Form with action indicated as this script
`User name: <input type=text name="uid" size=10> `	User field

TABLE 16.3   *(continued)*

`Password:  <input type=password` `name="pword1" size=10> `	Password field
`<input type=hidden name="submitted"` `value="True"> `	Hidden tag (submitted flag)
`<input type=submit name="submit"` `value="Sign up!"> `	Submit button
`</form> `	End of form
`<?`	Start PHP
`}`	End the clause for form to be displayed
`?>`	End PHP
`</body> </html>`	Closing HTML tags

FIGURE 16.2   Form for signing in.

This script both handles and presents a form. Notice that the typical HTML starting tags are not placed at the start of the script. This is required since the code to set the session variable must precede any output.

The *page.php script*, shown in Table 16.4, is a placeholder for the first page of an application. Note that it starts the session explicitly using the `session_start` function. This really means start or resume a session. It was not necessary in the *signin.php* script because the `session_register` function started the session.

TABLE 16.4   Code to Check for Valid User

`<?php`	Start PHP
`session_start();`	Resume or start the session
`if (!session_is_registered("user")) {`	Check if user exists as a session variable
`?>`	End PHP

(continues)

TABLE 16.4   Code to Check for Valid User *(continued)*

`You need to <a href="signin.php">SIGN IN.</a>`	Print message and link for the visitor to sign in
`<?`	Restart PHP
`}`	End clause for there *not* being a registered user
`else {`	Else clause
`print("<html><head><title>First page </title></head><body>");`	Print out starting HTML tags
`print ("You are signed in. User id is $user");`	Print out message to user
`print (" <a href=\"endsession.php\ ">Sign out and end session </a>");`	Print out option to sign out
`}`	End clause for there being a user
`?>`	End PHP
`</body></html>`	HTML closing tags

Figure 16.3 shows what *page.php* produces when the user has signed in.

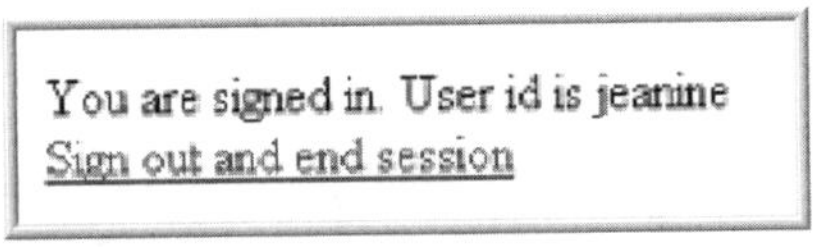

You are signed in. User id is jeanine
Sign out and end session

FIGURE 16.3   Screen showing successful sign in.

The *endsession.php* script, shown in Table 16.5, signs the user out by printing a goodbye message and destroying the session. In a real application, you should insert similar code either in a script by itself or as part of other scripts. This protects any user who does not exit the browser after completing his or her business. Figure 16.4 shows what *endsession.php* produces.

TABLE 16.5   PHP Code for Signing User Out

`<?php`	Start PHP
`session_start();`	Start or resume session
`print("Good-bye, $user.");`	Print out message, making use of the session variable $user
`session_destroy();`	Destroy session
`?>`	End PHP
`</body></html>`	Closing HTML tags

Goodbye, jeanine.

FIGURE 16.4 Screen showing goodbye message.

The *showids.php* script, shown in Table 16.6, is to show you the state of the password table.

TABLE 16.6   PHP Script to Show Contents of Password Table

`<html><head><title>Show ids and passwords</title> </head><body>`	Starting HTML tags
`<h1>Id and encrypted passwords</h1> <p>`	Heading
`<?php`	Start PHP
`require ("opendbo.php");`	Connecting to database
`?>`	End PHP
`<table border=1>`	Table tag
`<?php`	Start PHP
`$query="Select * from ptable";`	Define query to get the entire table
`$result=mysql_db_query($DBname, $query, $link);`	Invoke query
`while ($row=mysql_fetch_array ($result)) {`	While loop: iterates over the entire recordset, fetching a row at a time
`  print ("<tr><td>");`	Print out table tags
`  print($row['uid']);`	Print out the uid field
`  print("</td>");`	Print out table datum close tag
`  print("<td>");`	Print out table datum start tag
`  print($row['pass']);`	Print out the pass field
`  print("</td></tr>");`	Print out the table tags closing the row
`}`	Ends while loop
`print ("</table>");`	Print out table closing tag
`mysql_close($link);`	Close link
`?>`	End PHP
`</body> </html>`	Closing HTML tags

Figure 16.5 shows the display of the password table. Can you guess either of the passwords?

Id and encrypted passwords

| jeanine | ef3758d0804d0b29338a6b163858cb7b |
| jmeyer | 4c4a865afb338a3fe49e168ca40f5264 |

Figure 16.5   Display of IDs and encrypted passwords.

REFLECTION

You can replicate almost, but not quite all the functionality of the example application using the ASP and Access you have learned. You will need to find a version of md5 or its equivalent in order to store encrypted as opposed to plaintext versions of the passwords. Note also that ASP sessions do require the client computer to accept cookies.

The concepts introduced in this chapter will become clearer to you when you confront them in the course of building a real application. Keep in mind that there are many facilities, including DBMSs and auxiliary products and services, that compete on the basis of how well they address the challenges of building robust, industrial-strength applications. The good news is that your work will be based on the understanding and skills you have developed in writing HTML, middleware (PHP and ASP/JavaScript), and SQL queries.

EXERCISES, QUESTIONS, AND PROJECTS

1. Add a password feature for customers to the origami store application.
2. Add a password to the quiz show application for adding (and editing, if you have added that feature) questions. This is a situation in which different scripts in an application would require different types or levels of authentication.
3. Go on the Web and do research on PHP's alternative formats for form data. (Hint: you can look up `$HTTP_POST_VARS` and `$HTTP_GET_VARS`.) Similarly, do research on ASP's `Request` versus `Request.Querystring` versus `Request.Form` collections.
4. Go on the Web and do research on transaction support for MySQL, Access, SQL Server, Oracle, or other DBMSs.

EMERGING TRENDS

The goal of this chapter is to introduce briefly certain products and technologies that might gain increasing importance in building Web applications.

BACKGROUND

It is difficult to predict the future, but a safe prediction is that new products and technologies as well as new combinations and packaging of products and technologies will emerge. The Web has evolved from a medium in which scientists could share information, to a channel for complex interactions involving the use of databases. As the applications become more complex, the application developers will look for improved tools, and software developers will attempt to invent new solutions.

This chapter will describe a collection of products and issues. A principle one is eXtensible Markup Language (XML), which is a component of other technologies cited here, including Web Services, Wireless Markup Language, and VoiceXML. The *Examples* section will show you a use of XML with PHP. The *Reflection* section will guide you in the use of the *Exercises* section to do your own research on these issues.

CONCEPTUAL EXPLANATION

This section will provide background on XML and introduce other technologies that are emerging as significant in computing.

Communications

An important consideration underlying Web development will be the penetration of high capacity, so-called broadband communication, replacing dial-up or no access at all. At the present time, you cannot predict the bandwidth and the reliability of the communications link used by the visitors to your site. Costs and local availability can prevent people and organizations getting high performance connections. Early predictions that everyone would move immediately to high-speed access were premature. It is safe to assume that access and reliability of connections will improve. However, the variability of connections continues to make the design of sites a challenge.

XML

XML is a format for presenting information for use between computer applications that also can be created and read by people. XML resembles HTML. Both are variants of Standard Generalized Markup Language (SGML). An XML document has one element, called the *root* or *document* element, which contains other elements. Elements can contain attributes, child elements, and text. An example of XML is the following:

```
<?xml version="1.0"?>
<country name="USA">
<state capital="Juneau">Alaska</state>
<state capital="Cheyenne">Wyoming</state>
</country>
```

This example starts with the XML declaration. The document element for this example is the country element. It contains an attribute by the name of "name," with value "USA." The document element contains two child elements, each of type state. Each state element contains an attribute named "capital." The content of each state element is a text string: Alaska in one case, and Wyoming in another. An XML document can be viewed as a tree of nodes. Each node can potentially have any number of child nodes as well as attribute values. Another way to view XML is as a form of HTML in which you specify the tags. An XML document cannot be as loosely defined as an HTML document. It must be what is called well formatted. The nesting must be proper: no closing of an outer tag before closing all contained tags. All attribute values must be enclosed in quotation marks (single or double). Singleton tags must contain an internal closing slash:

```
<image src="bird.gif" />
```

One of the original motivations for XML was as a way to express content independent of formatting. Someone would define the content of an application in XML. Various tools could be used to produce HTML or text or anything else from the XML content. The eXtensible Stylesheet Language Transform (XSLT) is a way of specifying transformations of XML into something else. An XSLT document is itself an XML document, which can be both confusing and helpful. The language for wireless applications, Wireless Markup Language, and the language for voice applications, VoiceXML, are each an XML language. JavaScript, ASP, and PHP each have facilities for manipulating XML documents. Yet another approach is to create ASP and PHP scripts to produce XML documents instead of HTML documents. These XML documents would include the content of the application. The documents could contain a reference to an XSL document that specifies the formatting.

The DBMS products are adding features for generating and interpreting XML. For example, SQL Server has a new form of the select statement:

```
SELECT * FROM [tablename] FOR XML AUTO
```

You now can consider the relationship of XML and databases. Does the advent of XML mean that we will no longer use databases? The answer to that question is "no." Some information is well suited to databases as they currently exist with tables and relationships between tables, and some information is well suited to the tree structure of XML. An XML document is, underneath, linear text. The various DBMS products handle large amounts of data much more efficiently than any of the tools handle text. However, for small(er) amounts of data, especially information for which the tree structure fits, XML will be the way to go. It is likely that you will build an application that incorporates use of a database and XML. An emerging technology is so-called Native XML Databases that will hold the XML data in a format for efficient processing.

The XML format has been adopted as a model for handling data for many areas, including several of the technologies described next.

Macromedia Flash™

This text has focused on the middleware systems of PHP and ASP with JavaScript in which the result of the middleware was an HTML file. It also is possible to use Macromedia Flash with PHP or ASP. Since Macromedia Flash has emerged as one of the main tools for producing dynamic Web content, it would make sense to combine its use with server-side programming. Macromedia Flash also can be used with ColdFusion, the first of the new style middleware products, and now also a product of Macromedia. Consider it as a way to produce customized Web sites, featuring data-driven animations. ActionScript, the programming language for Macromedia Flash, has facilities for passing data back and forth from Macromedia Flash to middleware scripts, such as the ones we have discussed using PHP and ASP. Macromedia Flash also has facilities for reading XML documents.

Web Services

The term *Web Services*, with uppercase "W" and capital "S," refers to systematic ways to integrate services or what is also called functionality in your application. For example, a vendor could offer as a service the function of verifying or billing credit card companies. You would create the rest of your application, using PHP or ASP as described here. Your code would incorporate the features of your particular organization. When it came to constructing the code to invoke the vendor's service, you would use Web Services to make the product work for you. The integration of your application and the vendor's product might require you to pay attention to multiple layers of communication and multiple, and sometimes competing families of standards. The Simple Object Access Protocol (SOAP) defines one of these levels. The open-source world, IBM, Sun, Microsoft, and other companies are all presenting possibilities. At the moment, IBM, Sun, and others are pushing open-source standards, with Linux and Java J2EE as critical components. The Microsoft Corporation is pushing .net. Some of the families of solutions specify XML as the format for conveying content.

The area of Web Services appears to be even more acronym intensive than is the general rule in technologies. Be on guard against conflicting definitions. The acronym ASP might stand for active server pages or application service providers. The acronym WML might stand for wireless markup language or Website meta language.

Wireless

Wireless devices, including cell phones and personal digital assistants, are emerging as an important class of access to the Web. These devices might not replace the desktop computer, but might be the class of choice for current and new types of applications. These applications might require server-side programming accessing databases and files.

The underlying design constraints for wireless devices is a small(er) screen size and bandwidth more limited than that with desktops. One language for wireless is Wireless Markup Language (WML). This is an XML language. A WML script can refer to a WMLS file that has a version of JavaScript.

Speech Recognition and Speech Synthesis Using the Telephone

Advances in speech recognition and speech synthesis have created opportunities for an ordinary telephone to serve as an interface for computer applications. A standard called *VoiceXML* can be used to prompt callers and detect responses as long as the responses can be characterized as fitting a grammar or menu of choices. One action of the code could be to invoke a program, written in PHP or ASP, which accesses a database.

EXAMPLES

As is the case with other matters, you will need to check with your server administration to find out the ways in which the PHP installation accesses XML, because there is more than one way. The approach shown here requires you to define functions for handling different categories of tags. The categories are starting tags, ending tags, and character data tags. The action of the functions is to output to the browser fragments of HTML. This is not unlike what you did with PHP and ASP in previous chapters. However, the requirements of handling XML mean the tasks are divided differently. You need to think about what action is to be triggered by the start of an element, the contents of an element, and then close of an element.

The assumption is that the XML documents contain tags of the following structure:

```
<contact>
<name>John Doe </name>
<email>john.doe@xxx.yyy</email>
</contact>
```

The XML file could contain other tags, but these are the only ones recognized by this PHP script. The PHP script, shown in Table 17.1, will produce an HTML table, with a new row for each contact.

TABLE 17.1   PHP Code Handling XML Data

`<html><head><title>PHP xml SAX test </title>`	HTML starting tags
`<style type="text/css">`	Style section
`td {font-family: Arial; font-size: smaller}`	Style for table elements
`h2 {font-family: Comic Sans MS}`	Style for type h2 heading
`</style>`	End of style section
`</head>`	End of head section
`<body>`	Start of body
`<h2>Address book </h2><p>`	Heading
`<table border="1">  <tr><td>Name</td> <td>E-mail</td></tr>`	Start of table
`<?`	Start of PHP
`$file="D:\inetpub\wwwroot\jeanine\ xmlstuff\contactsnoref.xml";`	Address for xml file
`$currenttag="";`	Variable holding current tag
`function startElement($parser,$name, $attrs) {`	Function definition. This function will be cited later
`  global $currenttag;`	Will use the global variable
`  $currenttag=$name;`	Sets `$currenttag` to be the `$name` passed as argument for call of function
`  switch($name) {`	Switch statement
`    case "CONTACT":`	For the contact case...
`      print("<tr>");`	Start a new row
`      break;`	Break out of the `switch` statement
`    case "NAME":`	For the name case...
`      print("<td>");`	Start a new table datum (new column)
`      break;`	Break out of the `switch` statement
`    case "EMAIL":`	For the e-mail case
`      print("<td>");`	Start a new table datum
`      break;`	Break out of the `switch` statement

TABLE 17.1   *(continued)*

`default:`	All other cases… (this line and the next could be omitted, but is a placeholder in case you need to add something later)
`break;`	Break out of `switch`
`}`	End of `switch`
`}`	End of function
`function endElement($parser,$name) {`	Start of function. This function will be cited later
`global $currenttag;`	Will use global variable
`switch ($name) {`	`Switch` statement
`case "CONTACT":`	For contact case
`print("</tr>");`	End row of table
`break;`	Break out of switch
`case "NAME":`	For name case
`print ("</td>");`	End table datum
`break;`	Break out of `switch`
`case "EMAIL":`	For e-mail case
`print("</td>");`	End table datum
`break;`	Break out of `switch`
`default:`	Default case
`break;`	Break out of `switch`
`}`	End of `switch`
`$currenttag="";`	Reset variable to empty
`}`	End of function definition
`function characterData($parser,$data){`	Definition of function. This function is cited later
`global $currenttag;`	Will use global variable
`switch($currenttag){`	The global variable `$currenttag` is what guides the cases
`case "NAME":`	For name case
`print("<b>" . $data . "</b>");`	Output character data; namely, the contents of the tag in bold
`break;`	Break out of `switch`
`case "EMAIL":`	For the e-mail case
`print($data);`	Output the contents of the tag

(continues)

TABLE 17.1   PHP Code Handling XML Data *(continued)*

`break;`	Break out of `switch`
`default:`	Default case
`break;`	Break out of `switch`
`}`	End of `switch`
`}`	End of function
`$xml_parser=xml_parser_create();`	Calls one of the built-in PHP functions for handling XML to define a parser object
`xml_set_element_handler($xml_parser, "startElement","endElement");`	Calls another of the built-in PHP functions to specify how starting and ending elements are to be handling by citing the functions just defined
`xml_set_character_data_handler ($xml_parser,"characterData");`	Calls yet another of the built-in PHP functions to specify how character data is to be handled
`if (!($fp=fopen($file,"r"))) {`	Error handling: if the XML file cannot be located
`die("Cannot locate XML data file: $file");`	The `die` command ends the PHP script
`}`	Ends `if` clause
`while ($data=fread($fp,4096))`	Starts a `while` statement that reads the file. The parameter specifies a maximum number of characters
`{ if (!xml_parse($xml_parser,$data, feof($fp))) {`	If the XML contents end prematurely
`die(sprintf("XML error: %s at %d", scriptxml_error_string(xml_get_error_code ($xml_parser)),`	Signal error and close PHP
`xml_get_current_line_number ($xml_parser)));    }`	Continuation with output of line with error
`}`	
`xml_parser_free($xml_parser);`	Release the object created for doing the parsing
`?>`	End PHP
`</table>    </body> </html>`	Closing HTML tags

The code contains `switch` statements. These are the PHP versions of case conditional statements. In the PHP version, it is necessary to use a break command to exit the `switch` statement at the end of the particular case when you do not want to drop in to the following case. Notice that the `$currenttag` variable is set in one function and used in another.

REFLECTION

This chapter is intended to give you a brief introduction to certain emerging trends. In addition to the technologies mentioned, ASP and PHP will continue to evolve, as will DBMSs such as Access and MySQL.

Talking about emerging trends is risky. It could be that the technologies mentioned here will not achieve the presence predicted, but be replaced by something very different. In any case, you can continue your education by investigating the online sources given in the next section and ones you find on your own. When visiting a Web, be sure to keep in mind whether it is a strictly commercial site or the site of an organization attempting to establish an open standard. This is not to imply that the commercial sites are suspect and the organizational sites are not, but the distinction is one factor to keep in mind. You also should investigate the acceptance of the standard. Technology and business considerations cannot be separated in the area of Web development.

EXERCISES, QUESTIONS, AND PROJECTS

1. After checking what XML support is available for your PHP connection, implement the example described in this chapter. Then, modify the PHP script to output something different. For example, use the e-mail address to create a clickable link.
2. Do the research to implement an ASP script accessing an XML file.
3. If you are a Micromedia Flash developer, go to *www.macromedia.com* to learn about how you can use ActionScript to invoke server-side programs written in PHP or ASP.
4. Investigate the following organizational sites for information on trends: *www.w3c.org*, *www.uddi.org*, *www.opensource.org*, *www.php.net*, *www.apache.org*, *www.wapforum.org*, and *www.voicexml.org*. This list is not complete. Identify other organizations.
5. Investigate the following company sites for information on trends: Microsoft: *www.microsoft.com*, IBM: *www.ibm.com*, Sun: *www.sun.com*, and SAP: *www.mysap.com*. These appear to be the principle players, but others might emerge as important, such as Oracle or the communications companies.
6. Go to Google (or another search engine) and identify developer forums/ user groups for PHP, ASP, Web Services, XML, and so forth, independent of companies or organizations.
7. Visit the MySQL site (*www.mysql.com*) to investigate tools such as MySQLCC, a tool for database administration.

8. If you plan to study the use of wireless markup language in cell phones or personal digital assistants, the Nokia company (*www.nokia.com*) and others provide tools to download to simulate the workings of a WAP-enabled phone. Visit this site and, after studying the examples, create a WML script that displays a list of people and telephone numbers.

9. If you plan to study the use of the telephone as an interface for online applications, the Tellme company provides services for developers at *studio.tellme.com*. Visit this site to take their VoiceXML tutorial, sign up as a developer, and try some experiments. Create an online application in which you recognize the names of three different friends, and give each a personalized greeting.

A

RUNNING ASP AND PHP SCRIPTS ON YOUR OWN COMPUTER

You might find it advantageous during development to test ASP and PHP scripts on your own computer. To do so, you need to turn your computer into a server using software such as Internet Information Server (IIS), which includes support for ASP. You also need to install PHP and MySQL. The product Personal Web Server is available for older versions of Windows. These notes assume you are using Windows XP Professional (tested on version 5.1) and have Microsoft Access already installed.

INSTALLING IIS

1. You can install IIS in the original installation of Windows XP Pro or add it to your system. Put the Windows SP Professional CD-ROM in the CD-ROM drive.
2. Open the Control Panel. Click on Add/Remove Programs, and then click on Add/Remove Windows Components.
3. A window will appear with boxes next to the various components for Windows XP Professional. Click on the box next to Internet Information Server. Click Next. When the installation is complete, a window will be displayed. Click Finish.
4. Click on Start > Control Panel (choose Classic view). Click on Administrative Tools and then Internet Information Services. Expand by clicking on the plus sign next to the name of your computer (local computer). You should see Web sites. Expand this to see Default Web site. Left-click on this and click on Properties. You will be using these

panels several times again. Click on Home Directory. Click on the box next to Directory Browsing. The browser will list the files and folders in a folder when you omit the name of a file (unless there is a file named *index.htm* or *html*).

RUNNING ASP SCRIPTS, INCLUDING USING ACCESS

1. Scripts must be in the folder Inetpub/wwwroot or a subfolder of this folder. Assume that you make a subfolder called aspstuff.
2. Save ASP scripts in Inetpub/wwwroot/aspstuff. Copy into this folder the *miniquizask.asp* and *miniquizcheck.asp* files described in the text.
3. Invoke Internet Explorer and enter in the address: *http://localhost/aspstuff/ miniquizask.asp* This will invoke the *miniquizask.asp* script.
4. You can name your computer (and might have already done so). To see the name or to change it, click the right button on the My Computer icon. Click on Properties. Select the Computer Name tab. You should see a name. If you want to change the name, click on Change and then enter a new name. Once you have done this, you can use that name in place of localhost. For example: *http://jmeyer/aspstuff/miniquizask.asp*
5. To invoke a script using a database, you can use the DSN or DSN-less method. This information is generally in a script that is included in each script accessing the database. Let us assume that you have such a script. The critical thing you need to do is set the permissions for reading and writing to the file. The default permission will probably be read-only.
6. Click on the Start button and then select Control Panel. Change to Classic View. Click on Folder Options. Click on View. Scroll down to the end and clear (click to remove the x) Simple file sharing (recommended). Note: this is an extra step required for Windows XP.
7. To set permissions, right-click on the Start button and click Explore on the pop-up menu. Right-click on the folder containing the database. Click on the Security tab. Click on Advanced and then clear (click to remove the x) Inherit from parents the permissions.... Click OK. Click Add. The Select Users or Groups window will appear. Click on Advanced and then Find Now. Scroll down the list to locate IUSR_computername. For our computer, this will be IUSR_JMEYER. Select this entry. Click Add, and then click OK. The Security Tab panel reappears with the new entry. Select this entry and add Read and Write permissions.
8. Repeat this step, except for the clearing of the Inherit from the parents..., for the database.

INSTALLING MYSQL

1. You need to download MySQL. Go to *www.mysql.com* and follow the instructions. Read the terms and conditions for downloading the software. You might want to create a Downloads folder (version tested was 3.23.55).
2. You will need to extract the files using WinZip. If you need this program, it can be downloaded from *www.winzip.com*. You might want to create a new folder for the MySQL files as well. This is not the folder to which you will install MySQL.
3. Double-click to run the file setup.exe. You will be presented with a sequence of windows. You will be asked to confirm or enter a new name for the destination folder for MySQL. The default name is C:\mysql. You also will be asked to choose Typical, Compact, or Custom types of Setup. Choose Typical. Click Next, and then click Finish.
4. The extracted files contain a Windows program to configure MySQL: winmysqladmin.exe. You can find it in the bin subfolder of the MySQL folder. Double-click on the icon. You will see a panel titled WinMySqladmin Quick Setup and textboxes to enter a username and a password. The default user name is root. Since, presumably, this is your home computer, you can use a simple password such as 12345— this choice is up to you. Click OK. This creates a my.ini file. You can examine and change the settings for this as you learn more advanced MySQL.

 If you made a mistake or forget the password, you can force WinMySqladmin to show you the Quick Setup window again by finding the my.ini file and renaming it.

5. To test MySQL, click on Start, select Run, and type in a command. You will see the command prompt screen. Change the directory to mysql\bin by entering cd .. twice, and then cd mysql, followed by cd bin.
6. You can now start MySQL by typing in mysql. You will get a greeting, starting with Welcome to MySql monitor... Refer to Chapter 8, "Database Management Systems: MySQL and Access," for sample commands to create databases, create tables, insert records, and so on. Keep in mind that the practice in the text was to create MySQL databases in command mode and then use PHP scripts to create the tables. You can create the tables in stand-alone mode as well.

INSTALLING PHP

1. You need to download PHP. Go to *www.php.net*, click on downloads, and then choose the zipped binaries (version tested was php-4.3.0-Win32.zip). Note: this is not the "installer."
2. Go to the directory named Inetpub\wwwroot and create a subfolder named php. Create another folder named phpstuff. Invoke WinZip and extract the files to the php folder.

3. Copy the file named *php.ini-dist* into Windows and rename it *php.ini*. To use the short style for form input as is done in the examples in this text, you need to make a change to the *php.ini* file. Open the file in Notepad, search for registers_global, and change the line to `registers_global = on`. Be sure to remove any semicolon in front of the line. A semicolon marks the line as a comment. You also might want to change the designation for the include_path. This path indicates two possible places where "include/require" files go. One of the default options is the same folder as the calling file, which would work for all the examples in the text. Keep in mind that if you change the ini file, you need to shut down and restart the computer for the changes to take effect.

4. Copy the file named php4ts.dll into the Windows/system32 folder.

5. Click on Start and then Control Panel (Classic view). Click on Administrative Tools and then Internet Information Services. Click on the plus sign next to your computer (local computer), and then click on the plus sign next to Web Sites. Left-click, and then click on Properties. You will see a panel with several tabs. You will be using three of these tabs. Click on the tab labeled ISAPI Filters. Click Add. Enter php as the Filter name and then use the Browse feature to enter Inetpub\wwwroot\php\php4isapi.dll as the Executable. Click OK.

6. (Still under Properties for the Default Web site): Click on the Home Directory tab. Click on Configuration. Click Add. Under Application Mappings, click Browse to find Inetpub\wwwroot\php\sapi\php4isapi.dll. You might need to change the type of file being searched from exe to dll. Enter .php as the Extension (be sure to include the dot). Click to select All Verbs, Script Engine and Check that File Exists.

7. (Still under Properties for the Default Web site): Click on the Documents tab. Add the default document *"index.php."*

8. Shut down and restart your computer.

9. Open Notepad and create the following to test your installation:

```
<html><head><title>PHP info </title> </head>
<body>
<?php phpinfo();?>
</body>
</html>
```

10. Save it as *phpinfo.php* (change type of file to All files from Text) in the php-stuff folder. Invoke a browser, type in the address *http://localhost/phpstuff/phpinfo.php.*

You should see several screens of information on your PHP installation.

RUNNING PHP AND MYSQL

1. To run an application involving a database, create the database in command-line mode using MySQL. Click on Start > Run. Make sure the word *command* is in the box. Enter `cd..` twice and then `cd mysql`, followed by `cd bin`. This will take you to the mysql\bin folder. Enter `mysql`. This starts MySQL. Assuming *quiz* is the name you want for your database, type:

```
create database quiz;
quit;
```

2. Close the command prompt window. Click End Now.
3. In Notepad, write the following and save it as *opendbq.php*.

```
<?php
global $DBname, $link;
$host="localhost";
$user="root";
$password="12345";
$DBname="quiz";
$link=mysql_connect($host,$user,$password);
mysql_select_db($DBname,$link);
?>
```

4. Use `include` or `require` as appropriate to include *opendbq.php* in all your files requiring access to this database.
5. Note: files can be in any descendant folder of *wwwroot*. For example, you can create a subfolder of phpstuff called *quizphp* and place all the quiz scripts in it. You would start the game by entering:

```
http://localhost/phpstuff/quizphp/choosecategory.php
```

APPENDIX

B

ABOUT THE CD-ROM

CONTENTS

The companion CD-ROM contains the code for the major applications described in the text.

The code is contained folders for each chapter that contains code. The major projects are noted in parentheses.

chapter1code (sample asp and php)
chapter2code (HTML basics)
chapter3code (rollover, slide show)
chapter4code (state capital quiz)
chapter9code (favorite shows)
chapter10code (favorite shows)
chapter11code (regular expression, LIKE)
chapter12code (files)
chapter13code (cookies)
chapter14code (shopping cart)
chapter15code (quiz show)
chapter16code (user validation)

The CD-ROM also contains a folder named figures that contains folders for each of the chapters containing figures:

chapter1figures
chapter2figures
chapter3figures
chapter4figures
chapter5figures
chapter6figures

397

chapter8figures
chapter9figures
chapter10figures
chapter11figures
chapter12figures
chapter13figures
chapter14figures
chapter15figures
chapter16figures

When required, the chapters also contain image files (heart.gif, frog.gif, crane.gif, and bird.gif), the scores.txt file, and Access databases.   You will need to follow the instructions in the text to upload the Access databases and to create the MySql databases.Overall System Requirements

The PHP and ASP files can be created using any ASCII/TEXT editor, such as NotePad on any Windows system. To create an Access database, you need Microsoft Access. The files must be run on a computer that has a Web server such as IIS. Appendix A shows you how to set up IIS, MySql and PHP on a Windows XP Professional system. The files have been tested in the following three environments:

- A remote server running Windows NT, Apache, MySQL, and PHP
- A local computer running Windows 98, Personal Web Server, MySQL, and PHP
- A local computer running Windows XP Professional, IIS, MySQL, and PHP (see Appendix A, "Running ASP and PHP Scripts on Your Own Computer," for instructions on how to install the software on XP Professional)

You can use any browser to access the files; for example, Internet Explorer, Netscape, or Opera.

CONNECTING TO THE DATABASES

For each application, there is a file (for example, opendbq.php) that makes the connection to the database and is included (using the `require` command in the case of PHP, or the `include` instruction in the case of ASP). These files each need to be changed to work on the reader's local computer (set up to be the server) or on the remote server. This includes the use of passwords. See Appendix A for an example. The ASP applications assume that an Access database is created and uploaded to the server. The PHP files include code to create tables in a MySQL database already created by the server administration, or by using MySQL in command-line mode on the local computer.

BIBLIOGRAPHY

Buczek, Greg. *ASP Developer's Guide*. McGraw Hill, ISBN 0-07-212294-3, 1999.

Lovejoy, Elijah. *Essential ASP for Web Professionals*. Prentice Hall, ISBN 0-13-030499-9, 2001

Luce, Thom. *Developing Web Applications with Active Server Pages*. Scott/Jones, ISBN 1-57676-061-8, 2001.

Mellor, Robert. *ASP Learning by Example*. Franklin, Beedle & Associates, ISBN 1-887902-68-6, 2002.

Ullman, Chris, David Buser, et al. *Beginning Active Server Pages 3.0*. WROX Press, ISBN 1-861003-38-2, 2000.

Ullman, Larry. *PHP for the World Wide Web*. Peachpit Press, ISBN 0-201-72787-0, 2001.

Welling, Luke and Laura Thomson. *PHP and MySQL Web Development*. SAMS, ISBN 0-672-31784-2, 2001.

Yank, Kevin. *Build Your Own Database Driven Website Using PHP and MySQL*. SitePoint.Com, ISBN 0-9579218-0-2, 2001.

Many Web sites provide information for using ASP and PHP. In particular, consult the official sites:

Microsoft Corporation: *www.microsoft.com*
PHP: *www.php.net*
MySQL: *www.mysql.com*
World Wide Web Consortium: *www.w3.org*

Many other sites provide information and can be reached using search engines such as Google at *www.google.com*. Many people contribute and maintain sites for the community of developers. Be warned that sometimes the information is not fully reliable. One site that we did find helpful for guidance on installing server support was Denis Bourdon's *denbourdon.free.fr/development/php4iis5/php4iis5_en.htm*, updated and viewed on February 8, 2003.

INDEX

A

Access
- and ASP, 175–176
- concatenated primary keys, 83, 85, 87, 190
- connection scripts, 318–319
- database, creating, 140–151
- as DBMS, 7, 78
- features of, 127
- like operator, 248
- primary keys, specifying, 143
- queries, specifying, 148–151
- records, updating, 319–322
- regexp operator, 250
- relationships in, 207, 208, 209, 210
- stand-alone system, 190–191
- tables, creating, 140–151, 206–211
- warning records, inserting, 190–191

Active Server Pages. *See* ASP

addslashes function in PHP, 183

addup function, JavaScript, 39

ADOVBS constants, ASP, 163

agents defined, 93

airline flights database, creating, 120–122

alter query, SQL, 186–187

alter statement, SQL, 105, 113

Andreesen, Marc, 16

Apache, 5

applications, planning, 5–6

arrays
- associative, 169, 302–303
- defined, 46
- indexing of, PHP, 66

askquestion.asp script, 355–359

askquestion.php script, 343–347

ASP
- Access and, 175–176
- adding warning, script, 220–223
- ADOVBS constants in, 163
- catalog of favorite TV shows, project
  - delete specific titles, script for, 195
  - displaying categories, 225
  - displaying favorites with counts of warnings, 223–225
  - displaying favorites with warnings in specified category, script, 226–227
  - display titles, script for, 193–194
  - find warnings with specified term, 248–250
  - inputting new data, 178–180
  - script for, 176–177
  - showing favorites for adding warning, script, 219–220
- defined, 2, 101
- delimiters for, 8, 54–55, 66
- escape/unescape functions, 181–183
- field size, altering, 192–193
- files and records, 254–255
- form data, obtaining, 55–57, 71
- getVarDate() method in, 278
- include command, 161
- mail order business
  - collecting customer information, script for, 327–331
  - displaying shopping cart, script for, 324–327
  - inputting quantities, script for, 322–323
- math functions in, 58–59
- open method of the recordset in, 162
- problem input, 180–183
- programming in, 57–61
- pseudo-random functions in, 58–59
- purpose of, 126
- queries, making, 162–164
- query string in, 74